CW01548057

# STRONG BY NIGHT

'Fortis Nocte'

History and Memories of
No.149 (East India) Squadron
1918/19 – 1937/56

by John Johnston and Nick Carter

AN AIR-BRITAIN PUBLICATION

Copyright © 2002
John Johnston and Nick Carter
and Air-Britain (Historians) Ltd.

Published in the United Kingdom by:

Air-Britain (Historians) Ltd.,
12 Lonsdale Gardens,
Tunbridge Wells, Kent TN1 1PA

Sales Dept:
41 Penshurst Road, Leigh,
Tonbridge, Kent TN11 8HL

Correspondence to the Editor:
J. J. Halley, 5 Walnut Tree Road, Shepperton,
Middlesex TW17 0RW
*and not to the Tunbridge Wells address.*

All rights reserved. No part of this publication may be reproduced, stored in a retrieval system or transmitted, in any form or by any means, electronic, mechanical, photocopying, recording or otherwise, without the prior permission of the author and Air-Britain (Historians) Ltd.

ISBN 0 85130 313 7

Printed in the United Kingdom by:
The Cromwell Press Ltd,
Aintree Avenue,
White Horse Business Park,
Trowbridge, Wiltshire BA14 0XB

Origination by Howard Marks, Hastings

*Cover picture:*
*Short Stirling Mk.1 W7639 Q-Queenie minelaying*
*by Keith Aspinall*

# CONTENTS

| | | |
|---|---|---|
| Foreword | | 4 |
| Acknowledgments / Abbreviations | | 5 |
| Chapter 1: | The Beginning | 7 |
| Chapter 2: | An F.E.2b Pilot's Story | 13 |
| Chapter 3: | Build up to the Second World War | 15 |
| Chapter 4: | Second World War Begins – Wellington Days | 21 |
| Chapter 5: | 1941 – and still Wellingtons | 33 |
| Chapter 6: | Mildenhall Stories | 43 |
| Chapter 7: | No.149 Squadron's Stirling Story | 49 |
| Chapter 8: | Still Stirlings | 59 |
| Chapter 9: | Methwold, D-Day and, finally, Lancasters | 71 |
| Chapter 10: | Lakenheath and Stirling Stories | 77 |
| Chapter 11: | Lancasters! | 83 |
| Chapter 12: | Methwold Stories | 95 |
| Chapter 13: | No.149 Squadron Post-War | 99 |
| Appendix I: | Roll of Honour | 105 |
| Appendix II: | Individual Aircraft Histories | 118 |
| Appendix III: | No.149 Squadron Aircraft Losses | 129 |
| Appendix IV: | Operational Statistics | 135 |
| Appendix V: | Signals, Codes and Frequencies | 136 |
| Appendix VI: | Bombs, Mines and Incendiaries dropped by No.149 Squadron | 137 |
| Appendix VII: | 'G-H' and No.149 Squadron | 138 |
| Appendix VIII: | Bomber Command Minelaying Area Codes 1940-45 | 139 |
| Appendix IX: | Operations 'Manna' and 'Exodus' Statistics | 139 |
| Appendix X: | Extracts from The United Services Review, 21st October 1937 | 140 |
| Appendix XI: | Stations and Movements | 141 |
| Bibliography | | 142 |
| Index | | 144 |

# FOREWORD

A bomber squadron comes into its own in time of war, and this is the story of just one squadron in two world wars, told by those involved, and in particular during 1939-1945 when Bomber Command contributed so much to ultimate victory, but at a terrible cost of young men's lives.

No.149 Squadron was one of only two squadrons to serve continuously in Bomber Command from 1939 to the end of the war and, in assembling so many personal stories, the two authors have produced a fascinating tale. When I joined the squadron in April 1941, the senior officers were all experienced pre-war regulars and the C.O., 'Speedy' Powell, told us: "149 is the finest in Bomber Command – keep it that way." He also made it clear that other squadrons might fly above 10,000 feet, but 149 stayed well below, where you had a chance of seeing what you were flying over. My first trip did not exactly encourage either Speedy or our redoubtable Navigation Leader, Lofty Watkins. That it was a navigational disaster was not surprising – it was only the third time that I had been up in a Wellington in the dark!

Dependent on astro-navigation and map-reading at night, few navigators could find an inland target with any certainty, as was proved with the arrival of night cameras and their flash bombs. We chose our own courses, etc., and things were pretty casual.

For the aircrew officers off-duty life was not bad. Due to enemy attacks, we were billeted in a requisitioned country house a few miles from the airfield, which was good for parties, and I still remember my 21st birthday party!

And then things changed with the conversion to Stirlings and the move to Lakenheath just as Sir Arthur Harris became C-in-C and changed the whole Command attitude to war. Crews were now briefed on which track to follow, their time over target, height and course, and it shows in their stories as they battled against ever-improving defences in their determination to achieve success and survive.

Although by transferring to the new Canadian Wellington squadron at Mildenhall I did not go to Lakenheath, but still kept in touch with friends for some months, so this book revives a host of memories, especially that in March 1942 of watching Charles Pilkington trying to land his damaged Stirling and then crashing at Holywell Row with that awful glow in the sky.

It has been said that flying in Bomber Command was an experience which could be shared only with others who also flew. Perhaps this story will help others to understand.

Continuously operational, No.149 Squadron lost over 130 aircraft during the war and, while this represented the lowest loss rate in the Command, it was still a fearful loss of life, so it is only right to end this foreword with the reminder that the 149 Squadron Roll of Honour is preserved for all to see in the Church at Methwold, and that the words above it read:

*'Flying from the airfields of Mildenhall, Lakenheath and Methwold, these young men, many under the age of 21, fought for their country and died. They are remembered here'.*

**Lord Sandhurst**
**(Observer 149 Squadron)**
**December 2000**

# ACKNOWLEDGMENTS

Rev. Roy Abbott, Albert Adams, Leslie Belton, Jim Berry, Frederick Biggs, Hal Birch, B. B. Bradley, Kate Brethell, Jim Brigden, Jeff Brown, Stan Burnett, Frank Campbell, P. Carter, Alf Cassidy, Jim Chisholme, E. E. Chrisford, Ron Colledge, T. H. Collett, Jim Coman, Frank Cork, Jack Cornelius, Les Douglas, George G. Downing, Les Feakiss, Hugh Frazer, John Freeman, Gerry Gerrard, Gerry Grant, Greg Gregory, David Giacomelli, John Gow, Keith Hagward, Trevor Hansen, Charles Hedges, Leslie Hinken, Marcel Hore, Len Hurdle, Martyn Ford Jones, Lawrence Kearns, Doug Kebbell, Des Lampard, Colin M. Laverick, Charles Lofthouse, Cecil Loughlin, Al Lovatt, J. L. MacDonald, Frank Mann, Don Mayston, David Mitchel, Alex More, Roy Morgan, Bernard North, Ken Oakes, Dave Oddy, Dennis Outhwaite, Andy Padbury, John Philp, Alex Robb, John Rootes, Peter Rowland, Sid Rusher, Huia Russell, Peter Russell, Lord Sandhurst, Gordon Smith, Claire Strachan, Michael Strutt, Spud Taylor, Geoff Thompson, Deryck Thurman, Robert Todd, Douglas Trigg, R. Vann, Peter Wilson, Mick Worsfold.

Also with thanks to all other ex No.149 Squadron members of family contributors who may have been accidentally overlooked.

Thanks are also due to those who loaned photographs to illustrate No.149 Squadron's aircraft: Philip Jarrett, Stuart Leslie, Ray Sturtivant, Andy Thomas.

# ABBREVIATIONS

**Ranks**

| | |
|---|---|
| AC | Aircraftman |
| AOC | Air Officer Commanding |
| AOC in C | Air Officer Commanding-in-Chief |
| CO | Commanding Officer |
| Flg Offr | Flying Officer |
| Flt Lt | Flight Lieutenant |
| Flt Sgt | Flight Sergeant |
| Grp Capt | Group Captain |
| LAC | Leading Aircraftman |
| NCO | Non-commissioned Officer |
| Plt Off | Pilot Officer |
| Sqn Ldr | Squadron Leader |
| Sgt | Sergeant |
| SWO | Station Warrant Officer |
| Wg Cdr | Wing Commander |
| WO | Warrant Officer |
| AG | Air gunner |
| W/Op | Wireless Operator |

**Units**

| | |
|---|---|
| AGS | Air Gunners School |
| B&GS | Bombing & Gunnery School |
| CU | Conversion Unit |
| EFTS | Elementary Flying Training School |
| HCU | Heavy Conversion Unit |
| ITW | Initial Training Wing |
| LFS | Lancaster Finishing School |
| MU | Maintenance Unit |
| (O)AFU | Observers Advanced Flying Unit |
| OTU | Operational Training Unit |
| PFF | Path Finder Force |
| PNB | Pilot-Navigator Bomb Aimer Training Scheme |
| SHQ | Station headquarters |
| AAF | Auxiliary Air Force |
| RAF | Royal Air Force |
| RAAF | Royal Australian Air Force |
| RCAF | Royal Canadian Air Force |
| RNZAF | Royal New Zealand Air Force |
| USAAF | United States Army Air Force |
| WAAF | Women's Auxiliary Air Force |

**Armament**

| | |
|---|---|
| ammo | Ammunition |
| AP | Armour piercing |
| HC | High capacity (bombs) |
| HE | High explosive (bombs) |
| MC | Medium capacity (bombs) |
| SABS | Stabilised automatic bomb sight |
| SAP | Semi armour-piercing (bombs) |
| SBC | Small bomb container (usually for incendiaries) |
| TI | Target indicator (pyrotechnics) |

**Electronics**

| | |
|---|---|
| AI | Airborne Interception (Radar, Fighter Command) |
| D/F | Direction finding (radio) |
| GCI | Ground controlled interception (Ground radar) |
| 'Gee' | Navigation aid (Radar, all Commands) |
| G-H | Navigation/bombing aid (Radar, 3 Group, Bomber Command, and USAAF 8th Air Force) |
| "H2S" | Navigation/bombing aid (radar, plan position indicator, Bomber Command) |
| IFF | Identification Friend or Foe (Radar, all Commands) |
| Monica | Tail warning Radar identifying the presence of another aircraft in the area (Bomber Command) |
| RDF | Radio Direction Finding, the original cover name used for radar |
| R/T | Radio telephone |
| SBA | Standard Beam Approach (radio) |
| VHF | Very high frequency |
| Window | Strips of aluminium foil to jam and confuse enemy radar |
| W/T | Wireless Telephone |

**Miscellaneous**

| | |
|---|---|
| acc | Accumulator |
| API | Air position indicator |
| auw | All-up weight |
| DI | Daily inspection |
| DR | Dead reckoning |
| DZ | Dropping zone |
| EA | Enemy aircraft |
| ETA | Estimated time of arrival |
| FTR | Failed to return |
| F700 | Form 700, maintenance log book for each aircraft |
| IAS | Indicated air speed |
| I/C | In charge |
| Kcs | Kilocycles |
| KRs | King's Regulations (The book of law and conduct for the RAF) |
| Met | Meteorology or meteorological |
| MT | Motor transport |
| 'M' Gear | Medium supercharger gear |
| POW | Prisoner-of-war |
| psi | Pounds per square inch |
| revs | Revolutions |
| rpm | Revolutions per minute |
| RSJ | Rolled steel joint |
| SOC | Struck off charge |
| 'S' Gear | Full supercharger gear |
| TAS | True air speed |
| u/c | Undercarriage |
| u/s | Unserviceable |
| u/t | Under training |
| 2 x 4 | Linen-like cloth used for cleaning rifles |

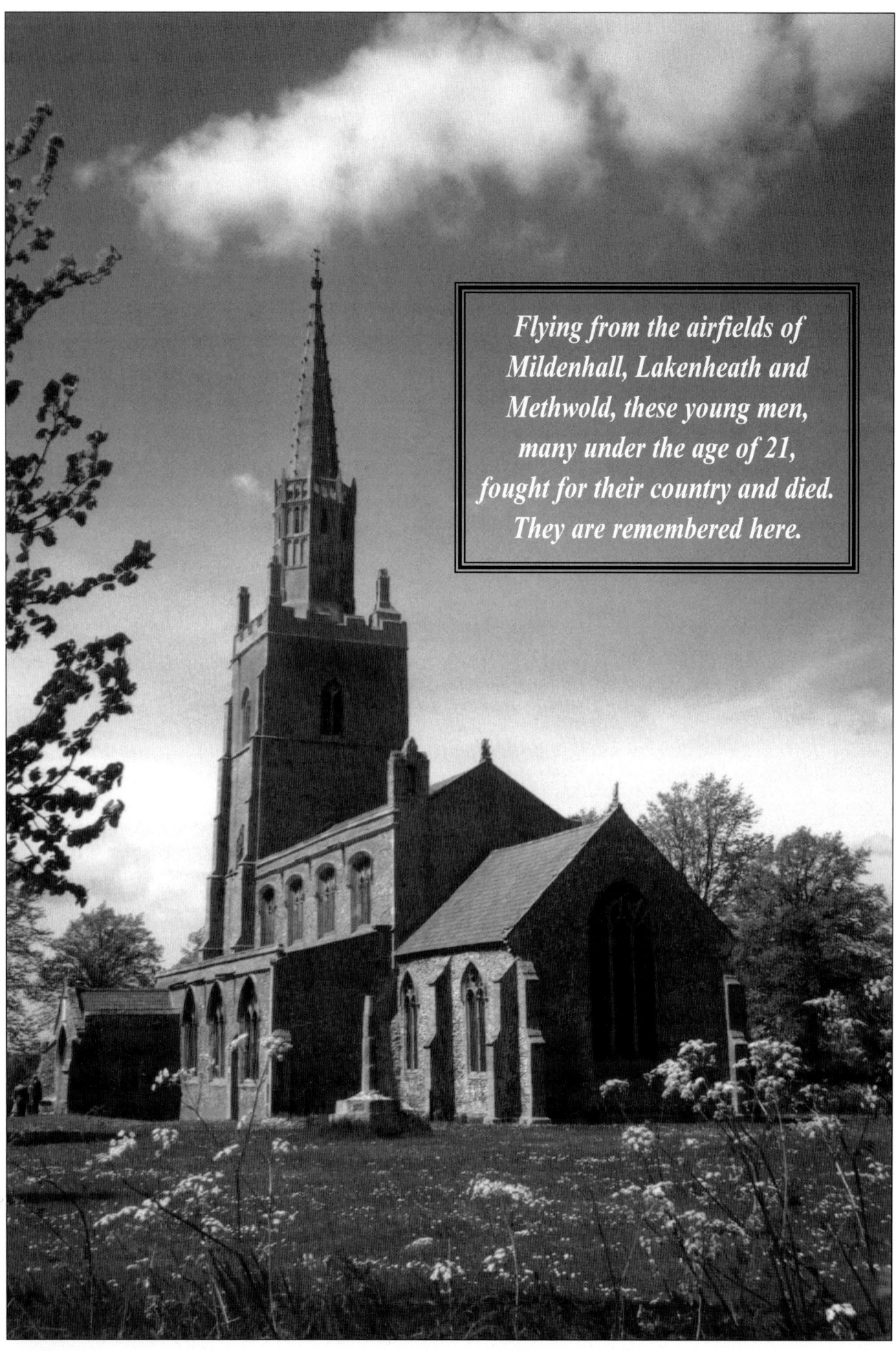

*Flying from the airfields of Mildenhall, Lakenheath and Methwold, these young men, many under the age of 21, fought for their country and died. They are remembered here.*

St. George's Church, Methwold, shown above, whose very tall spire could be seen for miles, holds the No.149 Squadron Roll of Honour. [Peter Rowland]

*No.149's pilots and observers gather for a group photograph in front of one of the squadron's F.E.2bs.* [IWM C12086]

# Chapter 1: The Beginning

The history of British military aviation can be seen to have started on the 28th February 1911, when a special order was promulgated to establish an Air Battalion, to be formed by the Royal Engineers in April 1911, the capabilities of the early aircraft having finally being realised.

In February 1912, at the request of Lord Asquith, the Committee of Imperial Defence was requested to consider the future development of aerial navigation for naval and military purposes. Their recommendation was for the formation of a unified aeronautical service to be called The Royal Flying Corps, which would include both a naval and military wing, as well as a Central Flying School at Upavon, Wiltshire to train pilots for both services. On 13th April 1912, a Royal Warrant was issued for the formation of The Royal Flying Corps, and a month later, on the 13th May, it came into being, its first commander being Captain Frederick Sykes, who in January 1914 was given the temporary rank of Lieutenant Colonel.

In the event of a major conflict, the army had already drawn up provisional plans to send a British Expeditionary Force to Europe, comprising seven Infantry Divisions with the intent to augment this by the addition of seven companies, later renamed Squadrons, with a total of 131 aircraft, and with a further company of balloons. Each Squadron would consist of three flights of four aircraft while a balloon Squadron would consist of two airships and two flights of redundant aircraft.

With the formation of the RFC the previous Army Air Battalion became obsolete, to be used to make good any casualties. In the winter of 1911-1912 the question of reform was already being discussed, and any further development of the Air Battalion was suspended. By the date of the RFC formation, the Military Wing had eleven aircraft in active service, a further eight being held at the Headquarters Workshops at Farnborough, Hampshire, either being repaired or adapted.

The early planes were still very basic, with no altimeters, and a maximum speed of about 60 mph. The search for better machines saw trials taking place on August 1912, on Salisbury Plain.

The first full-scale military exercise, involving the Military Wing, was conducted in September 1912. Seven aircraft and one airship were attached to each of the 'forces' participating. The importance of aircraft was realised when one of the 'forces' was both detected as being deployed 'en masse', and the direction of their planned attack established by an aircraft of the opposing force. The ethos of the Adjutant of the Military Wings, Lt. B H Barrington-Kennett, was that 'the Corps should combine the smartness of the Guards with the efficiency of the Sappers'. This was achieved by the Military Wing demanding high standards of education and achievement for its recruits.

Major Hugh Trenchard, who in April 1913 was second in command at the Central Flying School, instituted firm discipline

*No.149 Squadron's mascot, a night owl, who also appears in the squadron photograph (top of page).* [IWM Q12094]

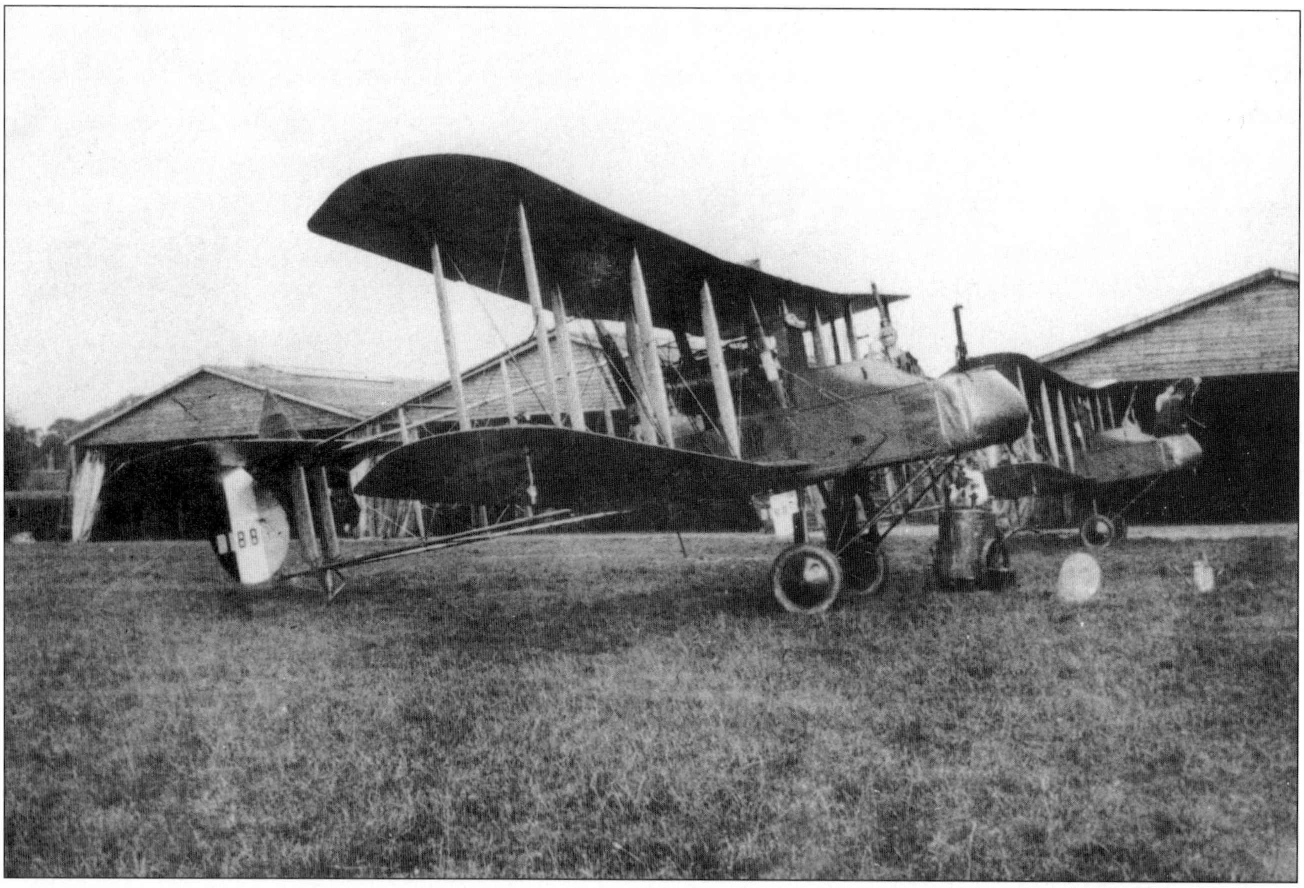

*Rearward firing was difficult in a pusher. This F.E.2b shows the observer's two Lewis guns, one of which could be fired over the top wing.*
*[Philip Jarrett collection]*

*No.149's armoury at St. Omer in 1918. Two aircrew and a sergeant armourer inspect a couple of Lewis guns. As the aircrew are suited up, they appear to be heading out on operations. Note how young the boy at the bench appears to be.*
*[IWM Q12087]*

and stressed the need for an academic grasp of the science of aeronautics. The men who were recruited into the rank and file were also of the highest standard, and needed to be reliable and intelligent. Due to the construction of early aircraft, experienced tradesmen were required, carpenters, mechanics, smiths, riggers and wheelwrights. The public fascination with flying and the associated glamour meant that it was an honour to be a member of The Royal Flying Corps.

In June 1914, the whole of the Military Wing moved to the new aerodrome at Netheravon, near Larkhill, Wiltshire. It was just two years after its formation and it had progressed considerably towards the aim of providing the British Expeditionary Force with its air power. The original plan of attaching one Squadron to each of the army divisions could not as yet be fully realised. Nos.2, 3, 4 and 5 Squadrons were operational but No.1 Squadron was still converting from dirigibles to aircraft. Nos.6 and 7 Squadrons, although formed early in 1914, were still undergoing training.

The plans for the deployment of the BEF were already some ten years old by the time the events of 1914 began to unfold, and new developments like the RFC had been incorporated. Almost all of the serviceable aircraft that were originally kept at Farnborough had already been sent abroad as reserves for the front line Squadrons. As new Squadrons formed, and the task of training new pilots and observers increased, the RFC inevitably grew accordingly.

When the RFC departed for France it consisted of a Headquarters, four complete Squadrons and an aircraft park based at Amiens, which acted as a mobile supply and repair unit for the front line Squadrons. Nos.2, 3, 4 and 5 Squadrons with a total of 63 aircraft flew from their peace-time stations for Dover, and from there they would fly to Maubeuge, in France, on the River Sambre, near the Belgian border, the logistical support following by sea. By the start of mobilisation 2 and 4 Squadrons had been equipped with the B.E.2 as standard, the remaining two Squadrons having a mixture of aircraft, which included Farmans, Bleriots, B.E.8s, Sopwith Tabloids and Avro 504s.

Mobilisation and embarkation began on the 12th August 1914. The first Squadron to arrive at Amiens on 13th August was No.2 Squadron. When mobilisation was complete the four Squadrons totalled 105 Officers and 755 other ranks. They launched their first reconnaissance flights from Maubeuge on 19th August, their first casualties being sustained on 22nd August, when observer, Sergeant-Major David Jillings, No.2 Squadron, was shot through the thigh and an Avro 504 was shot down over enemy lines. However, the importance of the early reconnaissance flights, and the intelligence gathered was 'lost' on some of the senior officers in the BEF who refused to accept and recognise the potential of the new weapon they had been given.

The first contact with the RFC's counterpart, the *Luftstreitkrafte* (Imperial German Army Air Service), occurred on 23rd August over the Marne/Mons battlefield, before the retreat from Mons had begun. With the German Army's rapid advance, on the 23rd August the RFC withdrew to Le Cateau. More moves followed to St.Quentin, La Fère, Compiègne, Senlis, Jilly, Serris, Pezarches and Mélun. Eventually, from 6th to 11th of September at the Marne, the Allied forces stopped the German advance, the latter withdrawing between the 13th to the 25th of September to the River Aisne.

By the time the BEF had moved to Belgium the RFC had lost forty aircraft. It was only after the first battle of Ypres that more satisfactory airfields were found. The early aircraft were extremely difficult to land, and the fabric coverings were susceptible to the weather.

The first incident of 'friendly fire' occurred on 26th October 1914 when a B.E., flown by Captains Hoskins and Crean, was shot down by British troops, who mistook the aircraft as German. Up until then the British roundel had not been applied to aircraft, unlike the *Luftstreitkrafte*, who applied a black cross on a white background, the British carrying a Union Jack painted on the side of the fuselage. However, in late 1914, after much experimentation the roundel was applied to the wings and fuselage of all aircraft of the RFC.

Although the primary role of the RFC was reconnaissance, opportunities for strikes against targets on the ground led to the initiation of and experimentation in bombing methods, which was both dangerous and lethal.

Bombing, especially of large German troop formations, had become a favourite activity of RFC pilots. Initially 'bombs' were hand grenades simply thrown from the cockpit. Later an improvised petrol bomb, which contained two gallons of petrol and a Very cartridge in the nose, was slung beneath the undercarriage of certain aircraft. These 'initiatives' were not officially encouraged, but they did much to enhance the image of the RFC.

By the end of November 1914 the two armies found themselves in stalemate. The RFC continued to expand rapidly, under the Lord Kitchener recruiting campaign, 'Your Country Needs You'. Brigadier General Henderson had been appointed to command the RFC in the field, and Major, now Colonel, Trenchard continued to increase the RFC manpower against competition from the army. The whole spectrum of trades was required, and not just pilots and observers. Civilian pilots were signed up and commissioned as officers.

To cope with the influx of new recruits, new training establishments were formed. To this end, the airfield complex at Brooklands was purchased by the Government outright, including the local public house!

The problem of suitable aircraft for new pilots to fly was a continual problem, as no provision had been made for the unexpected rapid expansion of the RFC. British aircraft manufacturers, being accustomed to dealing with small volume private individuals and not to these new needs, were unable to meet the demand for the large number of aircraft being demanded. Aircraft engine supply was also a problem, as most pre-war aircraft engines were imported from France.

In December 1914, Kitchener, who had revised the size of the RFC, saw that one Squadron could be attached to each headquarters of the Corps within the BEF. His original estimate of fifty Squadrons was doubled to one hundred, with the B.E.2c chosen as the standard aircraft.

The RFC was re-organised and Squadrons were formed into wings. In France two wings were formed, eventually followed on March 1915 by a third wing, and over the winter of 1914/15 the RFC developed its tactical role.

The battle of Neuve Chapelle, between the 10th and 12th of March 1915, saw the intended British advance lose momentum, but the importance of the RFC in its reconnaissance role was recognised. Aircraft were able to identify the small changes taking place in the German trench lines, and behind the German front lines they were able to identify any unusual build-up of troop movements.

Bombing was developed further, and by this time the RFC was never short of targets beyond the German lines. Techniques for dropping bombs had advanced from the previous haphazard method of throwing grenades from the cockpit, and simple bomb racks had been developed, although still primitive. Bombs occasionally exploded prematurely on the ground with the inevitable disastrous results amongst ground crews and pilots alike. Bombing was no longer a casual affair and raids were planned against specific targets.

On 22nd April the Germans launched a major offensive north of Ypres, involving the use of gas. Nos.7 and 8 Squadrons of the newly arrived Third Wing were directed to attack German transport bringing in troop reinforcements but they were not successful. The following day, on 23rd April, four aircraft of No.2 Squadron, each carrying one 112-lb bomb, bombed German communications, without much success, the inadequacy of the bomb and the limited number of aircraft involved being the overriding factor. The potential of the RFC as an offensive weapon was being recognised, identified by the tasks being assigned to it, but as yet the equipment could not fully rise to the occasion. In August, Trenchard was appointed to command the RFC in the field, with the rank of Brigadier General.

The Battle of Loos began on 25th September, preceded by the first use of gas by the British, to bolster inadequate artillery fire. The First Wing RFC was assigned to support Allied troops of the First Army, directing artillery, observing and photographing the results. During the battle, concentrated bombing raids were carried out on targets beyond the German front lines, but again the results were disappointing.

Emphasis was now centred on the development of a more efficient bomb sight. A series of experiments led to the development of the CFS (Central Flying School) bomb sight by Lt. Robert Bourdillon and 2nd Lt. G. M. B. Dobson. On 21st September, the Third Wing, using the new bomb sight, attacked trains from 500 feet, with notable success. Between the 25th to the 28th of September 5½ tons of bombs were dropped, and at least five trains were put out of action. The most impressive was the attack on the engine sheds at Valenciennes when a direct hit on an ammunition train caused severe damage, although very little disruption was caused to the German reinforcements being sent to the front line. The problem again was the lack of the right kind of aircraft and ineffective bombs.

By July 1916, the strength of the RFC on the Western Front was twenty-seven Squadrons, an expansion of fifteen Squadrons over the previous September. Trenchard, now Major General, saw just how subordinate the RFC was to the Army. No casualties or risks were too great in the tasks of reconnaissance, artillery observation or bombing raids. Little emphasis had been placed on preventing the Germans from carrying out operations in the air. A balance needed to be struck between offensive and reconnaissance roles. The French experience at Verdun had shown that if 'scout' aircraft were employed on reconnaissance and artillery observation, then the 'working' machines could be employed in attending to the German aircraft. As a consequence all offensive aircraft were organised into 'Army wings' and the remaining aircraft into 'Corps wings'.

In January 1916, No.20 Squadron arrived with the first Royal Aircraft Establishment's F.E.2bs on the Western front as a fighter-reconnaissance aircraft. The F.E.2b was a tandem twin-seat single-engined pusher biplane, and was powered by a 120 hp Beardmore engine producing a speed of 72 mph at 700 feet, reaching its service ceiling of 9,000 feet in forty-two minutes. It soon earned for itself the affectionate nickname of the 'Fee' plane, or the 'Flying Piano', by the several Squadrons in the Royal Flying Corps in World War I who serviced and flew in her. Although slow and lumbering, in formation the F.E.2b could generate considerable group firepower. The tactic, on being attacked, was that the aircraft would form a circle, in which each aircraft covered the tail of the one in front. Any Fokker attacking the F.E.2s did so at their peril, and most decided against it. Although the F.E.2s were less manoeuvrable and slower than the Fokker, the Fokker pilots developed a great respect for the combined firepower. It was an F.E 2b that accounted for the demise of air ace Lieutenant Max Immelman, and the 'Red Baron', Manfred von Richthofen, was shot down by one, from which he never fully recovered.

As the war progressed, with the development of aviation technology and tactics, and with Trenchard's leadership, the Royal Flying Corps was becoming less and less of an observation handmaiden for the British Army and was developing more and more into a striking force in its own right. As its value as a striking arm became more apparent, the continued need for the expansion of the Royal Flying Corps grew, with more specialised Squadrons being added to the strength. By the Spring of 1917, the RFC strength was five brigades each of two wings, usually of four squadrons per wing. In addition there were five aircraft parks and five balloon wings. Wars bring with them a geometric progression of technology and tactics, and by that time the 'Fee' plane was already totally outclassed as a fighter. However its usefulness as a fighting machine was far from over. So while the F.E.2b had outlived its service life as a fighter, its possibilities as a night bomber were considered, beginning with No.18 Squadron making night bombing attacks with its F.E.2bs in November of 1916. No.100 Squadron was then formed in February 1916, specifically to investigate that opportunity.

*Changing an engine on an F.E.2b was difficult, but a special sling was developed so that it could be extracted from the web of struts.*

*[J M Bruce/S Leslie collection]*

*The pilot and observer look on while the armourer fuses a bomb slung under one of No.149's Fees at Alquines on 18th July 1918. The objects slung under each wing are flares.* [IWM Q12091]

The bomber version of the F.E.2b was fitted with fluorescent-coated key instruments for visibility while night flying, bomb racks for 20-lb bombs under each wing and a rack for a single large bomb under the fuselage giving it a possible bomb load of up to 350 lbs, with one free moving 0.303-in Lewis machine gun in the front cockpit. The Beardmore engine had been stepped up from the original 120 hp to 160 hp, giving it a maximum speed of 80 mph at 6,500 feet. Signal pistols were carried and fired on the way home with colour codes to be given if it was clear to land. If the crew were lost they would fire red lights, and the aerodromes would send up different coloured rockets in reply. This simple method worked well, until the Germans broke the 'code'. They too would fire off red lights, the aerodromes would respond, and then were promptly bombed!

No.100 Squadron quickly proved the viability of the F.E.2b night bomber, starting with a night attack on von Richthofen's Flying Circus' airfield at Douai on the night of April 5th/6th 1917, two more raids putting the 'Circus' airfield out of business. The night bombing raids continued on through 1917 with their now all-black night bombers, convincing the powers-that-be that an F.E.2b night bomber force should be raised, eventually resulting in 395 F.E.2bs seeing service as night bombers.

Returning to their base in the dark with totally inadequate navigation aids resulted in 'Lighthouses' being set up on night bomber bases, to guide the returning aircraft back safely to their own base. The concept of 'lighthouses on wheels' was still in use through World War II. The night bomber force began with the formation in mid-1917 of No.101 and 102 Squadrons with F.E.2bs, then Nos.58 and 83 Squadrons converting to F.E.2bs in December, and finally two more new Squadrons were raised, No.148 Squadron at Andover in February which was moved over to Ford, also known as Yapton, in Sussex within three weeks, and then No.149 Squadron, which was split off from No.148 Squadron and formed as an independent squadron, also at Ford, on 3rd March 1918. It is to the history of No.149 Squadron that this book is dedicated.

Within three months, and with a strength of 18 aircraft and now part of the Royal Air Force, newly formed on April 1st, the Squadron was sent over the Channel on 2nd June to St. Omer, in France, to join the fray as part of the Air Echelon of the British Expeditionary Force, in support the British Second Army. One key role of the night bombers would be to disrupt German reinforcements coming to the front line. A British squadron during this period could expect 30% casualties, which meant a turnover of a squadron's flying personnel in just four days. No.149 Squadron's first operation was on the night of the 23rd/24th June from St. Omer, and from then on from various satellite airfields as the Allied troops advanced, including Marquise, Alquines, Quelmes and Abeele, and finally from their new base in October at Clairmarais with St.Marguerite as satellite to remain close to the retreating German front line, the Squadron attacked enemy communications, supplies, ammunition dumps, airfields and similar targets in Belgium and Northern France, fulfilling the role of a reconnaissance squadron as the need arose. During this time tactical bombing, with increased bomb loads, and effectiveness, were carried out continuously against key targets. The F.E.2b, although obsolete for daylight operations, provided good service as a bomber.

Operations, for a Squadron, usually began with the posting of orders on the Squadron notice board, approximately an hour before sunset. Pilots would be briefed by the mapping officer. This would be followed by plotting a course from the airfield to the target.

Pilots would go to the mapping room, with a map and a course and direction indicator. Telegrams from the Met Office gave wind direction and speeds at differing heights. The pilot, with the information, would plot a course allowing for drift due to wind, and decide on an altitude. Bombing was usually carried out from 2,000 feet, carrying a 112-lb bomb.

On 8th August 1918 the Allies' fight-back began at the Battle of Amiens with the necessary air support. Finally in October 1918, No.149 (Night Bomber) Squadron moved to Clairmarais with St.Marguerite as a satellite airfield, attacking targets in Belgium and Northern France. Notable attacks were two very successful heavy tactical raids to support the Allied advance at the end of October, followed by bombing raids on the roads to Ypres in the driving rain and a 1,000-foot ceiling, dropping twelve tons of bombs in two nights and strafing every enemy light with their forward-firing Lewis guns, some crews flying as many as nine sorties per night. From then on, it was back to strategic bombing. One unusual task assigned the night bombers was to create enough noise in the air over the enemy trenches to mask the sound of the tanks that were being brought up to the front lines under cover of darkness. In the final offensive, No.149 Squadron supported cavalry operations, the first such support seen on the Western Front since 1914, which accounts for the horseshoe which centres the Squadron badge.

Night bombing always remained a difficult task, and ground targets were always difficult to identify, occasionally the crews losing their way in the dark, as shown by the Casualty Report issued by Major B P Greenwood, who was then the Commanding Officer of No.149 Squadron, on 4th November, 1918. This indicated that F.E.2b No.9903 with Lieutenant Frank H Marsh as pilot and Lieutenant Cuffe as Observer had failed to return from a bombing mission to the railway sidings at Renaix. The bomb load was one 112-lb bomb and eight 20-lb bombs. They turned up after 24 hours, having been lost in the mist, and force-landing behind Allied lines.

The flame from an engine exhaust gives a very clear indication of the location of a night bomber. No.149 Squadron was always an innovative Squadron, and so it was not surprising that Captain C E S Russell of No.149 developed a device which fitted over the Beardmore engine exhaust, known as a flame reducer, to obscure this. This was so effective that it became a standard fitting with other night bomber squadrons and the concept continued as a standard fitting for night bombers throughout World War II. A further No.149 innovation, the creative thinking of Chief Mechanic Latham, was the installation of racks which could accept either bombs or Michelin flares, to adapt to the role as a bomber or reconnaissance Squadron, as the operation called for, without the need for equipment change.

At the war's end on November 11th 1918, No.149 was still operating seven of the original eighteen aircraft, with the loss of only two air crew, having dropped 80 tons of bombs, and having made 161 reconnaissance flights, their last operational mission being on 10th/11th of November.

On 26th November it was another move for the Squadron, this time to Fort de Cognelée just to the north of Namur in central Belgium, which brought them much closer to the borders of Germany, and well over the other side of the 'Armistice Line' drawn up only two weeks before. Perhaps this was in preparation for their next move, for on 24th December, No.149 was selected to become part of the Army of Occupation in Germany, being based at Bichenbach airfield in Bickendorf, the only F.E.2b squadron so chosen. There they remained until 26th March 1919, when they returned to England, but then moved to Tallaght in Ireland, before being disbanded on the 1st of August the same year.

*An F.E.2b of No.149 Squadron undergoing maintenance. Photographs confirmed as being No.149 Squadron aircraft are very rare.*
*[J M Bruce/S Leslie collection]*

*Believed to have been taken at No.149 Squadron, this photograph shows the underwing bomb rack.* [J M Bruce/S Leslie collection]

## Chapter 2: An F.E.2b Pilot's Story

The following story is of the life and times of a Pilot with No.149 Squadron, and is typical of so many others in the forefront of the new technology and tactics that were being developed.

Edward Frank Wilson was born on 12th August 1889 in Birmingham and received his education and Officer training at King Edward's High School in the City. He joined the RFC on 14th March 1917 and after initial basic training, reported to No.7 (Training) Squadron at Netheravon on 22nd June to begin tuition as a pilot.

On 23rd June 1917, Wilson had his first dual instruction on Maurice Farman B1953 and then Farman B1985. More flights followed during the next three weeks, Wilson making his first solo flight on 12th July with Shorthorn A7054.

In August, there was a transfer to No.76 (Home Defence) Squadron whose headquarters were at Ripon, Yorkshire, with detached flights at Copmanthorpe, Helperby and Catterick. Frank Wilson had both day and night flights on B.E.s including A8627 and B4012 before another move followed, this time to Turnberry for Aerial Gunnery instruction.

With the course completed by October, Wilson reported to No.38 (Home Defence) Squadron on the 27th where he was introduced to his operational aircraft, the F.E.2b/d used for night bombing.

No.38 (HD) Squadron had its headquarters at Melton Mowbray, with detached flights at Buckminster, Leadenham and Stamford, all equipped with F.E.2bs, some fitted with dual controls. Stationed at Stamford, Wilson had numerous training flights building up eighteen hours of night flying on 'Fees' A5616, A5690, A6422 and several others. A number of these flights were acting as 'enemy' aircraft to test the reactions of the Home Defence anti-aircraft guns and searchlights around London in readiness for Gotha and Zeppelin raids.

It was while on one of these night flights that Frank Wilson was shot down by anti-aircraft fire. Aloft on 4th January 1918 for a one-hundred-mile reconnaissance flight, he strayed too near the London air defences, and having forgotten the pre-arranged flare signals for British night flying machines, was promptly fired upon. Despite evasive action the F.E., A5698, was held by searchlights and hit, forcing Wilson to crash-land near an anti-aircraft battery. The 'Fee' was a write-off, hitting a tree and spinning around, the nacelle ending up in a ditch from which he crawled uninjured.

Still in flying kit, Wilson was hurriedly ordered to London to see Major T C Higgins, the commander of the London Air Defences, not to find out his condition or to be reprimanded, but for Wilson's first-hand account of the anti-aircraft and searchlights action against him! Presumably, no German aircrew had been captured alive for their opinion!

With his training completed, and having logged 119 hours flying time, Frank Wilson reported to an operational unit. This time the newly-formed No.149 Squadron under command of Major B P Greenwood which had been created at Yapton on 3rd March 1918 and was equipped with black-painted F.E.2b/ds for night bombing.

The Squadron was located at Ford Junction near Littlehampton when Wilson joined them and his first flight with the unit was on 3rd April 1918 in F.E.2b A6549. He also flew 'Fees' B469 and D9089 before the Squadron moved to Lympne and then flew over the Channel to St.Omer. This was on 2nd June, with Wilson piloting his regular F.E., D9089, to the unit's destination, Marquise. Hard work was required from all Squadron members before an adequate airfield was established.

After local flights around the area to get his bearings, Wilson's first operational mission was on 4th July 1918. Taking off at 22.50 hrs with his regular observer Lt. Sturgies, the targets were at Merville and Armentières where eight 20-lb bombs were dropped. Five days later, a night reconnaissance over Armentières and Bailleul was carried out with six Cooper bombs also being dropped. On the 18th another mission was flown over Merville, Armentières, Lille and Ypres, four 25-lb Coopers falling on selected targets.

With the opening of the Allies major offensive in August 1918, No.149 Squadron had a busy period, short-distance targets often being attacked by the F.E. crews three or four times during a single night. Frank Wilson logged missions on the 6th, 11th, 13th and 24th, the 6th August target being Courtrai railway station. On 11th August and 13th raid, the 112-lb bomb was used on Lille and Bac St.Mair, but on 24th August Wilson was forced to return safely with a dud engine.

In September, Wilson had a startling experience during a bombing mission over Lille. With Lt. Cuffe in the observer's seat, the F.E.'s engine suddenly cut out over the city, but in the dive towards enemy territory the engine restarted and they were able to get home safely.

On 25th September Wilson dropped one 112-lb bomb and eight 25-lb Coopers on targets in Roulers. Then, three days later, No.149 dropped forty-two 112-lb bombs and 326 25-lb Coopers (over five-and-a-half tons) on Menin, Courtrai and Lille, eight 'Fees' making four trips each during the night whilst Lt. Haldiman and 2/Lt Jones made five trips starting at 19.50hrs and finishing at 04.50hrs.

On 4th October, Frank Wilson completed his last operational sortie with a raid on Menin. He was due to fly another on 13th October, but on taking off the F.E. lost a wheel and bad weather forced an early return to the airfield. They were about to land when the observer noticed the missing wheel, so the bomb load was jettisoned over enemy territory before Wilson landed safely with only minor damage to the 'Fee'.

Going on leave immediately afterwards, Frank Wilson returned to the Squadron at Clairmarais on Armistice night. The festivities were followed by a move to Namur in December 1918 where all of No.149 Squadron's 'Fees' were kept in the giant Zeppelin hangar. A further move was made to Cologne, Germany, where No.149 stayed as the only F.E.-equipped squadron until March 1919, when they returned to the UK and were stationed at Tallaght, Ireland. Although the Squadron was not disbanded until August 1919, Frank Wilson did not remain until the end, being demobbed from the RAF on 15th April 1919.

*A collection of 112-lb bombs equivalent to those dropped in one night in July 1918 by No.149's aircraft.*
[IWM Q12088]

*An F.E.2b built by Boulton & Paul of Norwich in the snow.*
[Philip Jarrett collection]

*The distinctive shape of the Handley Page Heyford made it unmistakable. The bombs were carried in the lower wing centre section between the wheel spats. Defensive armament consisted of nose and dorsal guns with a third gun in a retractable dustbin turret below the fuselage.* [Ray Sturtivant collection]

# Chapter 3: Build-up to the Second World War

With the impending threat of war in the late 1930s following the rise of the Nazi party in Germany, the rapid expansion of Britain's armed services was imperative, and so the disbanded squadrons of World War I were re-formed. No.3 Group of Bomber Command was formed and headquartered at Mildenhall in January of 1937, with No.149 Squadron being re-activated as a heavy bomber squadron and part of this new No.3 Group, and also stationed at Mildenhall in Suffolk on 12th April 1937, by the conversion of B Flight of No.99 Squadron. Officers transferred from No.99 Squadron included Flight Lieutenant A T H White, Flying Officer F Holman and Pilot Officers D A Kerr, A G Duguid, J B Stewart and F W Turner, remaining under the temporary command of No.99 Squadron's Commanding Officer, Squadron Leader A D Rogers, AFC. The new equipment consisted of six 'Nivo' (green)-coloured Handley Page Heyford Mark IIIs, the Squadron activities being concentrated on practice bombing, air gunnery and various military exercises.

These six Heyfords were soon handed back to No.99 Squadron, being replaced by five Mark IAs from No.10 Squadron. On 17th May, Squadron Leader G R Ashton was posted to No.149, followed by Squadron Leader E H Richardson on the 31st. Things were now in place for No.149 to cut the umbilical cord with No.99 Squadron, forming its own headquarters on 8th June with Squadron Leader Richardson becoming the first Commanding Officer. From August to September four more Heyfords were transferred from No.99 Squadron. Charles Hedges, a flight mechanic (engines) with No.149 Squadron who, as an LAC, was also assigned air gunner duties flying with Heyford K4039, remembers the Heyfords flying in to enable two flights to be formed, and ground crew arriving directly from training units, with some ex-apprentices from Halton, to provide the needed support. Squadron Leader Richardson was promoted to Wing Commander on 1st October, Squadron Leader V D E Moreshead being given command of 'B' Flight.

On 19th October 1937, a top-level German military mission visited England, and this included General Erhard Milch, the mastermind behind the *Luftwaffe*. They were given a tour of inspection of Royal Air Force aircraft at Mildenhall, and this included the Heyfords of Nos.149 and 99 Squadrons, followed by a fly-past. Then it was lunch in the Officers' Mess followed by a flight to Cranwell to stay there overnight. While the aircrews were briefed to give the German visitors misleading information, much can be learned by the trained eye, and there is no question that valuable information on the readiness and capabilities of the RAF must have been taken back to Germany.

Nos.99 and 149 Squadrons also received a tour of inspection from the Under-Secretary of State for Air at Mildenhall on 12th November 1937. Just one day later, during a Squadron night exercise on 13th December, No.149 had its first Heyford tragedy. LAC Charles Hedges was lucky that night. Having been considered to have had more than his fair share of flying, he was given 'crash party' duty by his Flight Commander, instead of his usual position as gunner on board K4039, and his friend LAC Sillence took his place. Seeing the crew and aircraft off, and with crew's positions open to the elements, Charles' parting words to his friend were "Rather you than me on a night like this!" Two hours after take-off, the worsening weather caused the exercise to be cancelled and the aircraft were recalled, none of them making it back to Mildenhall and landing at other airfields. Too late for Heyford K4039 on that rainy night. It flew into the ground at Stopham, near Pulborough, Sussex, killing the four crew, Pilot Officer Aitken, the pilot, the navigator, Sergeant Ross, the wireless operator Corporal Roberts, and the gunner, LAC Sillence.

On 21st December 1937, Air Chief Marshal Sir Arthur Ludlow-Hewitt, the AOC-in-C of the RAF visited Mildenhall to present the newly-authorised badge to No.99 Squadron. Two months later, in February 1938, No.149 Squadron was awarded its own Squadron badge, a horseshoe interlaced by a bolt of lightning, with the Squadron motto 'Fortis Nocte', 'Strong by Night', both linking No.149 Squadron with its First World War cavalry support, and indicating the Squadron's primary role as a night bomber Squadron. With the situation in Europe deteriorating, No.149 Squadron's training programme was accelerated, attending No.8 Armament Training Camp at Evanton from 15th February 1938 for an annual armament training exercise.

Aircraft major inspection programs were a time-consuming job, partly because of the limited equipment being tied up at a

*Bombs being prepared for loading on Heyfords using a loading trolley.*

*[Philip Jarrett collection]*

*Above: A Squadron Heyford coded 'H' (K4877) at Mildenhall in 1938.*
*[Mildenhall Museum]*

*Right: The local newspaper showed Heyfords lined up for inspection at Mildenhall in May 1937 by King Edward VIII.*

*Heyford K4037 after hitting a hedge in a forced landing due to engine failure at Shotton Farm, near Sedgefield, Co. Durham, on 15th February 1938.*
*[Philip Jarrett collection]*

given aircraft while needed at another, extending a major inspection to as long as three months. To accelerate this process, Nos.99 and 149 Squadrons pooled their equipment and formed a joint maintenance flight. Working together, a major inspection was reduced to three weeks.

Adolf Hitler's plans for the domination of Europe by Germany was only too clear in 1938, first with his invasion and annexation of Austria in March, then with his demand that the Sudetenland, an area of Czechoslovakia along the German border, should be annexed as part of Germany. To prevent the outbreak of war, Britain, France, Italy and Germany met at a joint conference in Munich, these few days being known as the Munich Crisis. During this period, the Heyfords of No.149 Squadron were fuelled, bombed up and armed, ready to take off at a moment's notice should war be declared. Knowing the then-existing fighter equipment of the *Luftwaffe* it could well have been a slaughter. France and Britain, believing they were not yet in a position to oppose Germany militarily, eventually acceded to Hitler's demands, the four countries signing a joint agreement to that effect, but without the participation of Czechoslovakia.

The Sudetenland was Czechoslovakia's protective barrier between that country and Germany, recognised and awarded to Czechoslovakia at Versailles in 1919 to provide the needed buffer. Now the barrier was gone and Czechoslovakia was open to attack. Britain had been brought to the brink of war, and its military weakness was all too obvious, calling for an intensive increase in armament, an improvement in equipment and heightened military training. RAF squadrons were now assigned squadron codes, and at the end of September, the 149 Squadron ground crews worked overtime painting the new three-foot-high Squadron code 'LY' on their aircraft. The work on airfield defences at Mildenhall, begun earlier in 1938, was accelerated and completed, rehearsals for war were stepped up, and families living in married quarters on the base were alerted that they would need to be ready to leave their homes at short notice. Not one family left voluntarily.

Training flights inevitably brought with them accidents, both flying and on the ground, and No.149 Squadron had its share throughout 1938. On 15th February, after three weeks at the practice camp at Evanton in the Highlands of Scotland, both engines of Heyford K4037 seized while returning back to Mildenhall. The two Heyfords accompanying K4037 on the return journey saw streams of smoke from both engines shortly after take-off, which stopped soon after, but this was unnoticed by the crew. The pilot was the Squadron Commanding Officer, Wing Commander Richardson, with A Flight Commander, Squadron Leader Ashton as co-pilot; they force-landed the aircraft in a field at Shotton Farm, in Durham. Unfortunately it hit a hedge, causing the Heyford to tip on its nose. The damage was such that three days later it was struck off charge. On 1st March, K4032, code 'D', while at the same practice camp at Evanton, taxied into a wall. It was repaired on site, but on 8th September it overshot the flare path at Mildenhall and hit a fence, damaging it beyond repair. On 30th April, K4021, a Mk IIA that had been converted to a Mk III, ran out of fuel, being wrecked on landing at Mildenhall in bad visibility. On 17th August, K4870 'bounced' on landing at Mildenhall and tipped on its nose. It was struck off charge on the 29th, twelve days later.

Then on 2nd December the brakes of K4866 failed, and it ran into a hangar door at Mildenhall, the aircraft being struck off charge. Finally, on 16th January 1939, K4865 gave a repeat performance, also hitting a hangar following brake failure, and was also struck off charge. This was the last Heyford loss for No.149 Squadron, coinciding with their replacement with Vickers Wellingtons four days later.

The conversion of No.3 Group to an all Vickers Wellington group began on 10th October 1938, and on 20th January 1939, No.149 Squadron began to receive the new Vickers Wellington heavy bombers at Mildenhall, to replace their outdated Heyfords.

**First Wellington Is to No.149**
| | |
|---|---|
| 20th January | L4252, L4253, L4254 |
| 24th January | L4255*, L4256, L4257, L4258 |
| 6th February | L4249, L4259 |
| 7th February | L4263, L4264 |
| 10th February | L4265, L4266 |
| 17th February | L4271, L4272 |
| 9th March | L4270 |
| Total: | 16 – Even numbers to 'A' Flight; Odd numbers to 'B' Flight. |

Two days later the Squadron moved temporarily to Feltwell to a camp erected on the south-east corner of the airfield for a tactical exercise, returning to Mildenhall two days later. On 26th June, ten Wellingtons of No.149 moved over to Tangmere in Sussex, to take part in practice bombing attacks on HMS *Centurion*, a radio-controlled target ship, in the English Channel the following day, then returning to Mildenhall. The last Heyford on Squadron strength, K3495, was delivered to No.5 Maintenance Unit at Kemble on 10th July, although Des Lampard, a rigger with No.149, remembers seeing a Heyford parked at Mildenhall as late as October 1939.

By 9th March a full complement of sixteen Wellington Mark Is had been received, with the even-numbered aircraft assigned to A Flight and the odd numbers to 'B' Flight. Some of the Heyfords would eventually be transferred to Training Command, and would continue for the training and conversion of bomber crews until 1940. As a note of interest, the fourth Wellington L4255* received by No.149 on 24th January, was later transferred to the Air Transport Auxiliary, White Waltham, to be one of the very first Wellingtons used in the transport role. It was converted into a flying ambulance and saw service until 19th November 1944, when it was struck off charge.

Now the crews needed to become totally familiar with their new aircraft, this calling for formation flying and long distance flying, including flying over France, to determine the operational range of the new Wellingtons, as well as the usual bombing practice, air gunnery and so on. The public had an opportunity to see the new 'modernised' Royal Air Force, including No.149 Squadron, on Empire Air Day, May 20th, when Mildenhall was one of 63 RAF bases to be opened to the public. On 14th July, No.149 Squadron Wellingtons flew into France to be part of the *La Fête de l'Air* at Villacoublay, which included having the honour of leading a formation of 52 aircraft from twelve RAF squadrons over Paris, including Hawker Hurricanes and Supermarine Spitfires, as part of France's Bastille Day celebrations that same day. However it may perhaps have been a show of strength to Germany that the Heyfords had gone, and any confrontation would not be as easy as it appeared in 1937. The aircrew took every advantage of the opportunity to visit Paris, in that it became a 'Champagne delivery flight' home and a celebration on French grapes that night lasting until later the following morning. On 18th July, all serviceable aircraft of No.3 Group were detailed for a further flight over Europe, but the flight was cancelled due to bad weather and the aircraft redirected to fly over the south coast of England. The weather worsened and a wireless signal was issued that all aircraft should return to base. There was no R/T at that time and, in the confusion, aircraft wound up flying towards one another, which almost resulted in a major disaster.

The Commanding Officer of No.3 Group, Air Commodore A A B Thompson, MC., AFC, was based at Mildenhall. In the summer of 1939 he flew from Marham to Boscombe Down to take part in the testing of a new bomb. The bomb release mechanism failed, and the aircraft landed so that they could see what was wrong. As the plane came to a stop, the bomb fell to the ground and, with the real possibility that the bomb might explode, the Air Commodore hurried from the aircraft, to be hit by the still-rotating propeller blades. He died in the arms of his air photographer, Corporal E J Bullock.

The possibility of a continuation of gas warfare was very real, and all military personnel and every civilian in Britain prior to the outbreak of war had been issued with a gas mask, to be kept with them wherever they went. To check the effectiveness of the gas decontamination ability of Nos.149 and 99 Squadrons, aircraft of No.2 Group carried out a mock gas attack on Mildenhall using tear gas as their weapon. It was found that it was possible to fully decontaminate an aircraft within fifteen minutes.

War seemed inevitable and so on 1st August, 1939, partial mobilisation was ordered, with full mobilisation of the Auxiliary Air Force and Volunteer Reserve on the 27th, to begin to bring the Squadron up to full strength, and word was given to assume a state of readiness for war. Reservists of all ages joined the ranks, some of World War I vintage, not the least of their problems being to unlearn their style of marching in fours to the new threes. Training took on a frenzied pace with repeated simulated bombing and gas attacks on Mildenhall, and a total black-out was imposed. The base fuel tanks were topped up, food stocks were brought up to war strength, identity discs were issued and a field dressing tucked into an appropriate pocket became part of every airman's uniform. On Bomber Command's 'Scatter Plan', aircraft were dispersed to minimise the effect of an enemy air attack, No.149's Wellingtons being scattered around the airfield perimeter and under the trees, while No.99 Squadron aircraft were sent to Newmarket Heath for dispersal. The Squadron codes were all changed, No.149's becoming 'OJ', which it kept for the duration of the war, and afterwards. Newmarket Heath became the take-off point on other occasions for No.149, when the longer runway there would allow a take-off with a heavier all-up load.

One of the missions seen for Bomber Command aircraft at that time was in support of the Royal Navy, seeking out the location of enemy shipping in the English Channel and North Sea, attacking where possible, but informing the Navy of the enemy's location, so that the fleet could go in pursuit. Therefore part of the flying training schedule called for long distance flying training over the North Sea. This resulted in two losses in August, both due to bad visibility and low cloud.

After taking off from Mildenhall at 21.58 hours, with pilot F/O T A Darling, co-pilot P/O F E Board, Sgt A Linkley, AC1 R C B Robbins and AC1 J W Sadler, L4258 crashed somewhere in the North Sea on the 9th with all crew lost, their last radio transmission being received at 01.12 hours on the 9th. Then L4257, 'OJ-P', piloted by Sergeant Pitt, was seen by a skipper of a trawler to dive into the North Sea, all of the crew being lost. As a result of a forced landing of Wellington L4214, near Brandon, the observer, acting Sergeant A F Freeman was injured, later dying of his injuries at sick quarters in Mildenhall.

On 10th August, the Squadron underwent a mobilisation exercise, the Squadron being placed on the establishment of Bomber Command with effect from 1st August 1939. Squadron Leader Harris, who had been posted from No.214 Squadron, assumed command of B Flight, replacing Squadron Leader Bellairs who was posted to Middle East Headquarters for staff duties on 25th August.

At that time, the Air Officer Commanding No.3 Group was Air Vice Marshal J E A Baldwin. The location of the Squadrons of No.3 Group were as follows:

| | |
|---|---|
| Honington | Nos.9 and 215 Squadrons |
| Feltwell | Nos.37 and 214 Squadrons |
| Marham | Nos.38 and 115 Squadrons |
| Stradishall | Nos.75 and 148 Squadrons |
| Mildenhall | No.149 with No.99 at Newmarket, but still under Mildenhall control. |

Nos.75 and 148 Squadrons were then moved to the 'Group Pool' at Harwell, as training squadrons, with No.214 to Methwold and No.215 to Bramcote as reserve Squadrons for No.3 Group. Finally No.215 Squadron was moved to Bassingbourn and then to No.6 Group (Training) on 27th October 1939, becoming No.11 Operational Training Unit on 8th April 1940.

Bomber Command now consisted of 23 home-based front-line squadrons, with the six Wellington squadrons of No.3 Group, six Bristol Blenheim Mk IV light bomber squadrons, and the rest Whitleys and Hampdens, in contrast to the Spanish Civil War battle-hardened *Luftwaffe*.

September 1st brought with it a ban on all civil flying over the Eastern half of Britain, followed quickly by a total ban on all civil flying except those authorised as National Air Communications flights, and this included all Empire air mail flights. On the same day, No.149 Squadron received its first Wellington Mark IAs, N2866, N2867, N2868 and N2869, with Frazer-Nash nose and tail turrets and a ventral gun position, to replace the inadequately armed Mark Is. Also on 1st September 1939, Germany began its unprovoked 'Blitzkrieg' attack on Poland. Britain immediately put its 'War Plan' into effect, all Royal Air Force front-line aircraft being armed and brought to a full state of readiness. Those military buildings and aircraft that had not yet received their coats of camouflage paint were brought in line, and windows were taped to restrict shattering. On the home front, the children were moved from the cities to be scattered across the countryside in small towns and villages that had no military value and so were considered 'safe'.

On 2nd September all of No.149 Squadron's aircraft were moved to Rowley Mile racecourse on Newmarket Heath, the Squadron strength standing at 24 officers and 194 airmen, with 20 Wellington Mk Is, two due for disposal, and three Mk IAs. The pilots needed to be very aware of Devil's Dyke, 20 feet high, along one boundary and on the south side by Mons Wood. At 11.00 am on 3rd September, Prime Minister Neville Chamberlain announced that, since Germany had ignored Britain and France's appeal for its withdrawal from Poland, the country was now at war.

*Wellington L4268 arrives with No.149 Squadron in February 1939. After the Munich Crisis, squadron codes were applied, in this case 'LY', soon to be changed to 'OJ' on the outbreak of war.* [Ray Sturtivant collection]

*Wellingtons of No.149 Squadron during one of their formation training flights shortly before the outbreak of the Second World War.*

[Ray Sturtivant collection]

*Crew board an early Wellington of No.149 Squadron. The nose position carries a single gun, but the Mk.IC was fitted with a twin-gun nose turret.*
*[Philip Jarrett collection]*

# Chapter 4: Second World War begins – Wellington Days

The war in the air began very differently for No.149 Squadron and for RAF Bomber Command than it would end. The most capable bomber of its day was No.3 Group's Vickers Wellington, but the Mark IA was woefully inadequate for the tasks that would be assigned to it. With fuel tanks that were not yet self-sealing and no defensive side armament, the Mark IA Wellington was fair game for any current German fighter. Added to this was a stockpile of old bombs, many of which would never explode on impact and these were 250-lb and 500-lb general-purpose bombs. These were virtually useless against the heavily armoured decks of the German fleet. It was this same fleet, and German merchant shipping, that were initially the only targets available and assigned to Bomber Command following an agreement with the US President, Franklin D Roosevelt that Britain would meet his request that bombing be limited so as not to damage German private property or take civilian lives. With bombing being so inaccurate, this also implied that German shipping could only be attacked when at sea.

This also linked Bomber Command as the Royal Navy's handmaiden, one of the primary initial tasks of Bomber Command being to sweep the seas on reconnaissance missions, seeking out German shipping movements, and reporting any sightings immediately to the Navy who would respond appropriately. The aircraft were given a suitable bomb load on such missions, to give them the ability to attack whatever shipping provided targets of opportunity, and so the missions were described as armed reconnaissance missions. The radios of the day were also woefully inadequate and many sightings were often not reported until the aircraft returned to base. With such a long delay, events had usually changed dramatically before any response from the Royal Navy could be forthcoming.

So it was that on the evening of 3rd September, the first day of the war for Britain, a signal was received at Mildenhall at 17.00 hrs to attack German warships leaving Wilhelmshaven. Three bombed-up Wellingtons of No.149 Squadron, with their new wartime Squadron codes 'OJ', took off at 18.30 hrs, led by Sqn Ldr Dabinett, to be joined by six Wellingtons from No.37 Squadron and 18 Hampdens of No.5 Group, going out over the North Sea on the first armed reconnaissance mission of the war, seeking out the reported enemy shipping in the Schillig Roads area. Nothing was found, and with the weather turning for the worse, the aircraft were recalled, most of the bombs being jettisoned in the North Sea. No.149's Wellingtons returned at 22.00 hrs.

4th September brought the first air action but only highlighted the inadequacy of the day. The German fleet had been reported by a lone Blenheim Mark IV as entering the Kaiser Wilhelm Canal, with the battle-cruisers *Scharnhorst* and *Gneisenau* at the entrance to the Kiel Canal, these warships being the primary targets. A raid on the warships was immediately put into action and 14 Wellingtons, consisting of two flights of three aircraft from No.149 Squadron, led by Squadron Leader Paul Harris, and a further eight Wellingtons from No.9 Squadron, took off shortly before 15.00 hrs with the *Scharnhorst* and *Gneisenau* as their targets, together with 15 Blenheim Mk IVs of Nos.107 and 110 Squadrons, who would seek out the *Admiral Scheer*.

On his way to the target, Sqn Ldr Harris ordered his gunners to test fire their Browning machine guns. Not one of them was working, but he decided to continue to the target nevertheless. Bad weather forced five of the six No.149 Wellingtons to return to base, so Sqn Ldr Harris continued alone. Not finding the assigned target he decided to seek out a target of opportunity that complied with the Roosevelt

*As war approached, Mildenhall's hangars acquired camouflage paint. Taken on 8th March 1940, this photograph shows no Wellingtons as aircraft were now parked at dispersal points around the airfield and not on the tarmac close to the hangars.*

agreement. In doing so his aircraft received a direct hit by anti-aircraft fire over Tonning on the German coast and his fuel tank was holed. He dropped his bombs on a bridge over the Eder then headed home, just making the 300-mile journey back, with a final emergency landing at Honington, Suffolk. Total time in the air, six-and-a-half hours.

The No.9 Squadron Wellingtons reached the target area, but there were no hits on the primary targets. It was to be a sad portent of many future raids over the next year or two. One of the aircraft mistook the Eder for the Kiel Canal, while another dropped their bombs near Esbjerg in Denmark, which was a full 110 miles north of Brunsbüttel on the Kiel Canal, killing two civilians. Two of the No.9 Squadron Wellingtons fell prey to German Messerschmitt Bf 109 fighters and were shot down, both crews being killed. The Blenheims fared worse, five of them being shot down. One of the Blenheims of No.107 Squadron, piloted by Flying Officer H L Emden, crashed on the deck of the cruiser *Emden*, killing nine crew and wounding others, doing more damage than any of the bombing.

Already, with the first true combat sortie of the war, important weaknesses had been shown which were the inability of the aircrews to find the target and generally poor navigation skills. Also the vulnerability of the bomber in daylight attacks. Bombs that hit the target did not explode, indicating that the time delay set on the fuses at 11 seconds, was far too long. Added to this was the fact that the bombs in use were from old stocks, resulting in a high chance that they would never explode. Britain was fighting a WW II war with WW I leaders and WW I tactics. It would be some time before the military would wake up to the need for change.

Casualties came not only from training exercises, nor the war. On 4th September AC2 Thompson and AC2 Hoey were involved in a motorcycle accident near Newmarket. AC2 Thompson died of the injuries received and AC2 Hoey, who was seriously injured, was taken to Newmarket hospital.

Des Lampard, a rigger, remembers arriving on Station: "I had passed out as LAC at Locking, Somerset, just after war broke out, and within a few weeks I was on my way to Mildenhall and No.149 Squadron. Within a couple of days, as my personal records had not arrived, there was much doubt expressed to my claim to be an LAC and I was promptly wheeled up in front of the Flight Commander,

Flt Lt Kerr, a very nice young gentleman, who asked me in front of the W.O, who had done the wheeling, why I was not wearing my propellers. I quietly told him that there were none in the stores, which a quick phone call by him confirmed. So I was dismissed but still under suspicion until my papers came through. The lack of LAC badges was a good indication of the promotion prospects for the 'erks'. However, I managed to get a set when I next went on leave, from a shop near King's Cross Station.

"The second day after arrival, I was taken over to dispersal and given this beautiful aircraft, Wellington IA, 'OJ-H', (N2984), and told to look after it, ably tutored by Corporal George Lee. I kept with the same letter aircraft, as was the custom, until I was posted to a Fitters Conversion Course, about June 1940".

Wing Commander Russell called all flight commanders and captains together on 5th September at 19.15 hours to personally inform them of the absolute necessity of only bombing the targets allocated or the alternative targets. If they were unable to identify either the main or secondary targets bombs were to be dropped into the sea.

Retaliatory attacks by the *Luftwaffe* on Britain's bomber airfields were expected, and so on the 6th No.149 Squadron's aircraft were moved temporarily from Mildenhall to Netheravon in Wiltshire, but with no response from the *Luftwaffe*. This did not affect training, and on the 8th the Squadron was ordered to carry out air-to-ground firing practice at Berners Heath range; four aircraft participated. They returned a month later on 5th October. It was about this time that the Ministry of Information made a propaganda film about the Royal Air Force to boost public morale, titled 'The Lion has Wings' and No.149 Squadron was chosen to take part. The majority of the Squadron was given a special viewing of the film at the Comet theatre, Mildenhall on the afternoon of 14th November. A number of shots of aeroplanes and personnel of the Squadron were included in the film, the majority of shots being taken between 1st and 4th September 1939.

More training followed on 19th September with stick bombing practices carried out at Berners Heath, using manual bomb distributors recently fitted to the Squadron's aircraft. On the same day six crews were detailed to 'stand-by' and be available at two hours' notice. The following day the Squadron was detailed to 'stand-by' at two hours' notice again, as Group Duty Squadron.

The No.149 crews now needed to be fully conversant with the new Mark IA Wellingtons and so conversion trials began on 19th September. With the 1,500-lb bomb load together with 720 imperial gallons of petrol on board, the Mark IA needed 3,240 feet of runway to get airborne, leaving no room for error at Mildenhall. So raids calling for maximum all-up weight would begin with the aircraft at Rowley Mile, Newmarket, which at that time had the longest runway in Britain. The next day six aircraft dispersed to Newmarket Heath. There would be other occasions when Newmarket would also be the take-off point on operations, using the straight section of the race track, when rain turned the Mildenhall field to mud, making take-offs with a full bomb load impossible.

The 20th again saw the Squadron undertake stick-bombing practice at Berners Heath. One aircraft, L4252, was damaged whilst Sergeants Wey and McLeod were carrying out night flying practice.

Leica cameras entered into trials with the Squadron for photographic purposes on the 22nd. Between 24th and 30th September, the Squadron carried out air firing practice at Carew Cheriton in Pembrokeshire, South Wales, and 'stood-by' at two hours' notice as Group Duty Squadron with further bombing practice at Berners Heath.

Over the next three months, No.149 Squadron took part in occasional sweeps as armed reconnaissance missions over the North Sea and the Friesian Islands, seeking out German shipping.

These sweeps were hampered by bad weather, and so most of the activity was concentrated in training, bombing practice, formation flying, fighter affiliation, air-to-air gunnery exercises, naval co-operation, navigation exercises, and so on. During this time Mildenhall was honoured by His Majesty King George VI, on 2nd November, who paid a courtesy visit to Mildenhall. It was snowing, so after touring the base, the inspection of the Squadron and presentation of medals was held in one of the hangars. During the proceedings a Dornier bomber flew overhead but was engaged by the airfield defences and no bombs were dropped. After inspection of the Squadron, several of the officers were met in the Officers Mess, including Pilot Officer Ron Landau, a Polish Officer in the RAFVR on detachment to No.149. Previous visits were by Air Commodore, The Marquis of Londonderry, KG, MVO, on 18th October and Marshal of the Royal Air Force, The Viscount Trenchard, GCB, GCVO, DSO, DCL, LLD, on 29th October, who inspected a Wellington Mk.Ia and a Fraser-Nash instructional turret.

On 6th November, on the posting of Wing Commander G H Russell, DFC, to No.6 School of Technical Training at Hednesford, Wing Cdr R Kellett assumed command of the Squadron. In 1938, then as Squadron Leader Kellett, he led three Vickers Wellesleys on their long-distance record-breaking flight from Ismailia, Egypt, to Darwin, Australia.

The 3rd of December brought No.149 Squadron back into action when 24 Wellingtons of No.3 Group, consisting of a total of twelve aircraft from Nos 38 and 115 Squadrons from Marham, and twelve aircraft from No.149 Squadron, bombed up with 500-lb semi-armour-piercing bombs and with 620 gallons of fuel, were sent out on a high altitude mission to attack German warships reported to be off Heligoland. The raid was planned for 2nd December but bad weather postponed it for one day. Wing Commander Richard Kellett, the Commanding Officer of No.149 Squadron, led the formation.

The formation was in four blocks; each consisting of two 'Vees' of three, the leading 'Vee' being headed by Wing Commander Kellett. Sqn Ldr Harris headed the following 'Vee'. Behind and to the right, a young Canadian, Flight Lieutenant J B Stewart headed the leading 'Vee'. Behind him were the three aircraft headed by Flight Lieutenant Duguid. Aircraft from Nos.38 and 115 Squadrons occupied the six slots to the left of the formation, and the six trailing slots.

Two cruisers were spotted at anchor in the roads between the two tiny rock outcrops that are Heligoland in the German Bight. Kellett prepared to attack from out of the sun. There was heavy flak over the target and as a result of the early losses, the bombing altitude had been raised to 7,000 feet, which was considered then to be high level. Although radar had warned the German gunners of the impending raid, the thick cloud at their bombing altitude had fortunately hidden the Wellingtons from them. Four Messerschmitt Bf 109s climbed and intercepted the bombers but their aim was spoiled by cloudy conditions. One RAF gunner LAC Copely of No.38 Squadron did manage to destroy one of the Messerschmitts with a well-aimed burst from the rear turret.

Sqn Ldr Harris claimed hits on one of the cruisers and Flight Lieutenant Stewart attacked a large merchantman anchored outside the harbour but cloud obscured the targets and results were unconfirmed. Again the bombs were to fail miserably, although an enemy minesweeper was sunk when one of the bombs passed, unexploded, completely through the ship's hull. Back at the British bases hopes ran high now that the RAF had penetrated enemy air space, had duelled with the *Luftwaffe* and had escaped unscathed. Their hopes were to be short-lived.

The winter of 1939/1940 brought with it more dangers, this time not from enemy aircraft. Des Lampard recalls:

"The dreadful winter of 1939/40, very heavy snow made life extra difficult, at work, bomb trolleys had to be towed by half-tracked tractors, new to the drivers. Aircraft warming up, before taxying for take-off had to be given a wide berth, one which was so doing when the chock slid forward, the aircraft half spun round and hitting the 'erk' on duty as dispersal point guard, killing him instantly and causing the aircraft to miss the sortie due to the prop being damaged."

Gordon Smith was a pilot on one of the first operational raids on Germany, albeit not on the mainland, December 3rd 1939. He recalls:

"Daylight raid on Heligoland: this was my crew's first operational flight. Aircraft from Mildenhall, Feltwell, Marham and no doubt Stradishall were all involved. Fighters and flak engaged us – the first time many of us had seen either. I can remember sticking like glue to the leader of our flight since the safety of all of us depended, to a large degree, on being able to concentrate the firepower of all aircraft in the flight, on an attacking fighter. I'm not sure that the raid was quite as successful as the newspaper clipping makes out, and all of the No.149 aircraft suffered some damage though I believe all returned safely to base."

From 4th September to 13th December, all ten aircraft losses in No.3 Group were from training exercises. Then on 14th December things changed rapidly. Twelve Wellingtons were sent out from No.3 Group on shipping searches. While they were fortunate enough to locate an enemy convoy off Wilhelmshaven, poor visibility prevented an immediate attack. While waiting in the area for a half-hour in the hope that the weather would clear, they were themselves attacked by German Messerschmitt Bf 109 and Bf 110 fighters and five of the No.99 Squadron Wellingtons were lost, three being shot down and a further two colliding in mid-air while attempting to evade the fighters. One more crashed on return, landing in a field next to the Newmarket racecourse. The shooting down of one German fighter by one of the Wellingtons was on the credit side. The administration would still not believe that the Wellington was so vulnerable to enemy fighters in a daylight attack, and so put the losses down to anti-aircraft fire.

On the evening of 17th December, Wing Commander Kellett and Sqn Ldr Harris were summoned to Group Headquarters at Mildenhall, along with the Commanders of Nos.9 and 37 Squadrons, for another briefing for a daylight raid on the Schillig Roads and Wilhelmshaven to take place the following morning, the target being 'any German warships'. The bomb load would be three general-purpose 500-lb bombs per aircraft. In order to avoid anti-aircraft fire, orders were given not to attack below 10,000 feet. Unfortunately, there would be little cloud cover over the target. On the 18th Sqn Ldr Harris was informed that Flight Lieutenant Peter Grant of No.9 Squadron would be flying with him, leading the three of No.9 Squadron's aircraft. This was the first time that they had flown together and, as they strolled away from the briefing, Paul Harris put his hand on Peter Grant's shoulder and said: "Stay close to me whatever happens". Peter Grant followed his instructions to the letter, and in doing so he probably saved both their lives.

The 18th December raid would again be led by Wing Commander Kellett, and would consist of nine aircraft from No.149 Squadron, nine aircraft from No.9 Squadron and six from No.37 Squadron, making a total of 24 Wellingtons. The Group was led by two 'Vees' of No.149 aircraft with Wing Commander Kellett leading. Following and to the right would be Sqn Ldr Harris of No.149 Squadron with three No.149 Wellingtons. Behind him, the second 'Vee' would be three No.9 Squadron aircraft led by Flight Lieutenant Peter Grant. To the left would be a matching six Wellingtons in two 'Vees', from No.9 Squadron. Trailing in the rear were the three staggered pairs of aircraft from No.37 Squadron. Both Nos.149 and 9 Squadrons favoured 'Vee' formations of three aircraft while No.37 Squadron preferred staggered pairs.

The No.9 Squadron aircraft were airborne from Honington at 09.00hrs, joined over King's Lynn by No.149 Squadron's aircraft, which left Newmarket Heath at 10.00hrs. No.37 Squadron's aircraft from Feltwell joined them and tagged at the end of the formation out over the North Sea. Not too much later, Flight Lieutenant Duguid's Wellington of No.149 Squadron, leading the second 'Vee' behind Kellett, had engine trouble, losing speed and dropping back, so he signalled by Aldis lamp to the two other Wellingtons in his formation to close up on Kellett's group. His No.3, Flying Officer Riddlesworth, obeyed, but Flight Sergeant Kelly, to his left, either failed to pick up the message or it was mis-read, in that he also dropped out and accompanied Duguid back to Mildenhall.

It was absolutely clear skies and Kellett sighted Sylt 50 miles ahead at 12.30 hrs, taking this route to avoid the flak ships located among the Friesian Islands. Petts with No.9 Squadron reports:

"We left Sylt to port and shortly afterwards turned left towards the Schillig Roads where we had been told at briefing there were likely to be warship targets. We saw none but continued on a south-westerly course and I remember wondering how far we were going in search of battleships and cruisers."

However, unknown to Britain, Germany was equipped with defence radar, and a 'Freya' radar set on the island of Wangerooge had picked up the formation when they were still 50 miles from their target. Around 50 fighters, both Messerschmitt 109s and 110s, were sent up to intercept, which included Wolfgang Falck, who would eventually head the *Luftwaffe* night fighter force, and Macky Steinhoff, who would later become one of the *Luftwaffe's* outstanding air aces, and would eventually head Germany's post-war *Luftwaffe*.

Petts continues: "My rear gunner called 'There's a fighter attacking behind – they've got him!' Then to starboard I saw a Me 109, with smoke pouring from it, change from level flight to near-vertical dive so abruptly that the pilot could hardly have been alive and conscious after that change of direction. I remember that at this stage I thought, rather prematurely, that encounters with German fighters were 'easy'."

The Wellingtons flew on past Bremerhaven then made a wide turn to starboard to take the formation over Jade Bay to Wilhelmshaven. Petts, at outside left of the whole formation, found it increasingly difficult to maintain position.

"Repeated calls to my Section Leader to ask him to slow down brought no reply and in spite of opening up to full boost and increasing propeller revs to maximum, I still could not keep up. Over Wilhelmshaven we flew into intense land-based ack-ack fire, joined by the anti-aircraft guns mounted on the battle-cruisers *Scharnhorst* and *Gneisenau*, and in trying to work out whether evasive manoeuvres were any use against the black puffs bursting all around I was for a while less pre-occupied with the problem of staying in formation. Quite suddenly the black puffs stopped and there in front were the fighters, and still in spite of full throttle and full revs, I was lagging behind".

Kellett led the formation through the flak-stained sky over Wilhelmshaven and each bomb aimer prepared to drop his three bombs. Suddenly, Kellett gave the order not to bomb. All the battleships and cruisers were berthed alongside the quayside; his orders were precise; he was not to risk German civilian casualties. No bombs fell.

Moored in the middle of the harbour were four large ships that appeared to be merchantmen. Heavy anti-aircraft fire was coming from them. It was all the encouragement Paul Harris needed. They appeared to be fleet auxiliaries so he dropped his bomb load on them. Another Wellington in his section did the same but the results were obscured by cloud.

Kellett's formation had now become strung out and disjointed. No.9 Squadron on the left of the 'Big Diamond' and No.37 Squadron, bringing up the rear, had become detached and had fanned out in the face of heavy flak.

*A trio of Wellington ICs formate over Thetford Forest in June 1940 carrying their wartime squadron codes, 'OJ'. They are OJ-M (R3206), OJ-W (P9245) and OJ-N (P9273).* [Vickers-Armstrong 5892-7]

The Wellingtons were easy pickings for the fighter pilots of the *Luftwaffe*. The RAF gunners were unable to give return fire as they made beam attacks from above. Previously, attacks had been made from the rear but now the German pilots tore into the bombers, safe in the knowledge that the front and rear turrets could not traverse sufficiently to draw a 'bead' on them and the non-self-sealing wing fuel tanks made ideal targets. Further, the German cannons outdistanced the British 0.303-inch machine guns.

Petts jettisoned his bombs, hoping it would gain him a little speed:

"About this time Balch on the front guns got his first fighter. A Me 109 away to port was turning in a wide sweep, possibly to attack the sections in front. I saw tracer in Balch's first burst hit in the cockpit area and the canopy, or part of it, fly off; the second burst also hit and the 109 immediately went into a catastrophic dive, with white smoke pouring from it.

"At this period I decided that in spite of my full throttle and full revs I should never keep up. Ginger Heathcote pointed out to the 37 Squadron six forming the rear of the formation, and suggested that I drop back to them. It was as well that I did not. 37 Squadron were flying in their own formation of three pairs stepped in line astern. As the attacks developed, one of the six, Flying Officer 'Cheese' Lemon went to dump his bombs. To open the bomb doors he first selected master hydraulic cock 'on', not realising that he had flaps selected down. The result was sudden lowering of full flap leading to a sudden gain of considerable extra height. Enemy fighters left this aircraft alone but shot down the other five of 37 Squadron.

"Having decided that I could not catch up with my Section Leader, I turned about 40 degrees to starboard, put my nose hard down and with the dustbin turret still lowered, screamed down to sea level. All the way down from 15,000 feet and then for some time just above the water I kept full throttle and full revs except when I reduced power for short periods in an evasive manoeuvre as fighters lined up to attack.

"During the dive I was too pre-occupied with what was going on outside to pay much attention to my instruments. I did, however, notice that my ASI reaching the 1 o'clock position, second time round. It was not until we returned to the aircraft next morning that I looked to see what that meant in terms of indicated airspeed - it was 300 mph! This was about twice the normal cruising IAS and I could not help wondering how much faster I could have gone before something broke.

"I cannot remember just how many fighters there were, the first came before I left cruising altitude, there were more on the way down with Me 110s passing us as they broke away, and finally we were chased along the water by three Me 110s. Robertson, the rear guns, kept me informed as each attack developed and there were commentaries from the other two gunners.

"We met each stern attack with a drill that we had agreed as a result of experience gained in fighter co-operation exercises. The usual sequence ran 'There's one coming in, he's coming in, Get ready, get ready. Back, back'. Throttles slammed shut and pitch levers to full coarse. Bursts from the guns and enemy tracer passed the 'windows. 'OK, he's gone'. Open up again to full throttle and full revs.

"Mostly tracer was on the starboard side and it was not until some weeks later when we started taking aircraft back to Brooklands to have armour plate fitted behind the port wing tanks that I realised that previously we had enjoyed this protection only on the starboard side.

"Altogether that day my gunners claimed three 110s and two 109s. I saw Balch's first 109 before we left formation and a 110 which also was his and I have a clear recollection of Robertson's jubilant shout as he got the last 110. For the other two I could not offer much in confirmation even later the same day and there may have been some duplication of claims from other crews over hits before we started the descent.

"Balch's Bf 110 deserves a mention. The attack developed in the same way as the others but immediately the tracer ceased there as a shout from Robertson, the 110 came past close to our starboard wing, next there was a burst from my front guns and the 110 was gone. This was a fine example of the effectiveness of sudden throttling back at the right moment in causing a fighter to close more quickly than he intended to. Robertson said that he had fired without apparent effect on this 110 as it closed and then as it overshot and passed beyond his reach the enemy rear gunner put his fingers to his nose at Robertson before opening fire. At that moment Robertson saw Balch's tracer and that was that.

"I believe the first of the three 110s, which followed us down was hit by both Robertson and Kemp. The drill had proceeded as before but Robertson's, 'Get ready, get ready, back' was followed by a jubilant 'I've got him; he's gone in'. The 110 had, of course, been obliged to get down to our level just above the water for his stern attack and there was no height in which to recover any loss of control. Robertson's next comment was, 'The other one's going home; he's had enough!'

"There had already been calls from Kemp and Balch that they had been hit and Heathcote had gone back to Kemp. Whilst I started checking at my end he helped Kemp (who was losing a lot of blood from a thigh wound) out of the 'dustbin' and into the rest bunk. Kemp in full kit was a tight fit in the dustbin and this move must have called for quite an effort from both. Heathcote next let Balch out of the front turret and went aft again. Balch had been hit in the sole of one foot but he was not in urgent need of attention.

"Robertson reported that he had emptied his guns into the last 110 and Kemp had called that the centre guns were out of action. Heathcote reported that there appeared to be no major damage to the aircraft, although it was a bit draughty as there were plenty of holes!

"For my part I eased back to normal cruising throttle and propeller settings and checking around was shaken to find the starboard oil pressure gauge reading zero. The propellers on Wellington IAs did not feather so I had to be content with pulling the starboard engine right back as with that setting it would give less drag than if switched off and if it did not seize it might be of some use if I wanted it. I opened up the port engine to 'climb power' and found that I was able to climb gently to a further 1,000 feet or so. During this time I had turned onto a course of 270 degrees. When Heathcote came forward again he agreed that 270 degrees was as good as any because we did not know where we were and steering due west ought to hit England somewhere."

For almost half an hour 44 *Luftwaffe* fighters had torn into the Wellingtons. Fighter attacks continued until the bombers were only eighty miles from home. In the lead, Wing Commander Kellet remembered Paul Harris' suggestion after the 3rd December raid and 'flew a little slower' to allow the stragglers to keep up. Off to his right Flight Lieutenant Peter Grant obediently stuck rigidly to Squadron Leader Harris' Wellington. This tightly-knit formation of ten aircraft fought their way through with only one casualty. 'OJ-B', piloted by Flying Officer J H C Spiers, was shot down with all of the crew being killed, during a beam attack by a Bf 110. There were no survivors.

Of the remaining seven Wellingtons of No.149 Squadron, badly shot-up 'OJ-P', flown by Flying Officer M E Briden almost made it back home, but with a holed fuel tank they ran out of fuel, ditching in the North Sea near Cromer Knoll. Sqn Ldr Harris circled the scene of the crash and attempted to drop a dinghy to the stricken crew but its attached rope snagged the tail of the Wellington and Harris was forced to land on the fighter airfield at Coltishall, near Norwich, which was still under construction. All of Briden's crew perished. This brought No.149 Squadron's losses to two. Wing Commander Kellett crashed on return to base, listed as Category 2 damage.

Of the nine No.9 Squadron aircraft, four were shot down with no survivors while one ditched 100 miles from The Wash, with four survivors. Five of the six No.37 Squadron aircraft were lost with only four survivors. The one remaining aircraft from No.37 Squadron, piloted by Flying Officer Lemon, returned to Feltwell. This totalled ten aircraft shot down and two crashing on return. Only two of the attacking German aircraft were shot down although others had been damaged including Falck's Bf 110, who force-landed. Earlier that day Germany had lost their pocket battleship, the *Admiral Graf Spee*, which, following a losing naval engagement, had been scuttled by its skipper, Captain Hans Langsdorff, in the estuary to the River Plate outside Montevideo Harbour. They badly needed a morale booster and the Battle of Heligoland Bight provided one, Germany claiming that they had shot down 38 of the attacking 22 aircraft.

Some time later, when the war-weary Wellington N2980, 'OJ-R', Sqn Ldr Harris's aircraft, had passed successively through No.37 Squadron to No.20 Operational Training Unit in Lossiemouth, Scotland, it would be force-landed and ditched in the dark on Loch Ness, to lie at the bottom of the Loch for over forty years, eventually to become the famous 'Loch Ness Wellington'. It would be recovered and rebuilt for public display at Brooklands, the only surviving World War II Wellington.

The year closed for No.149 Squadron with two more armed reconnaissance flights, with shipping attacked but with unknown results. The RAF post-mortem into the raid on Wilhelmshaven concluded that its Wellingtons and Hampdens could no longer cross German territory in daylight and expect to survive against *Luftwaffe* opposition. From thenceforth Blenheims, whose losses had been lower, were despatched singly or in pairs, to overfly the German North Sea bases. Yet despite the clear message given by the Wilhelmshaven raid as to the futility of daylight raids, the RAF High Command still continued with occasional daylight missions until mid-1940.

This included 2nd January 1940, when three Wellingtons of No.149 Squadron were sent back to the Schillig Roads on an armed day reconnaissance. There they were attacked by twelve enemy fighters, two of the Wellingtons being shot down near Sylt, one of them, N2943, being piloted by Flying Officer H L Bulloch, who was one of the survivors of the December 18th raid, the other, N2946, by Sergeant J Morrice. Both crews were killed.

Early operations against German shipping were becoming costly, and the Wellingtons were unable to carry out daylight bombing without a fighter escort. The War Cabinet was shaken. And so from the 4th to the 19th of January, 25 Bomber Command aircraft, nine of them Wellingtons, were sent over Germany on leaflet raids, these being the Squadron's first night operations of the war. These were nicknamed 'Nickel' raids or 'Bumphlet' raids, the only purpose, as described by 'Bomber' Harris later, being to supply Germany with toilet paper. The first leaflet raid for No.149 Squadron was on the 11th, when two Wellingtons dropped leaflets over Hamburg and Bremen. Also 18 Wellingtons were sent out on 11th January; then again on the 12th, twelve Wellingtons, all from No.3 Group, were sent out on reconnaissance sweeps over the North Sea, no enemy shipping being found. The bad weather following, until later in February eliminated the possibility of any night missions during this period, with no day missions in February covering this same period. The night leaflet raids had served one useful purpose, which was to give the bomber crews valuable night flying experience. They had also shown how difficult it was both to navigate accurately in the dark, and to find the target.

It was not until March 1940 that the so called 'pleasantries' of the bombing war ended, and Bomber Command was permitted to bomb land targets for the first time. The 2nd of March claimed another No.149 aircraft and crew when Wellington N2984, piloted by Flying Officer L R Field, suffered first one engine failure then the second engine cut, just after take-off for a leaflet raid on Bremen. The aircraft crashed and burnt at Burnt Fen in Norfolk, killing the crew.

When the weather cleared on 17th February, the night leaflet raids began again, and from then until 8th April there were 102 such sorties by Wellingtons of No.3 Group. The reconnaissance missions over the North Sea continued, and on 20th February, twenty Wellingtons were sent on a night raid to find and bomb any German warships at Heligoland. However a sudden change in weather conditions resulting in fog led to their being recalled. One

Wellington from No.38 Squadron was lost over the sea while another was abandoned over England, and a third, this one from No.99 Squadron, crashed on return.

It was in March that the headquarters of No.3 Group moved to Harraton House at Exning, near Newmarket, with subsequent changes at Mildenhall. On 3rd March the first Wellington 1Cs were issued first to No.149 Squadron, then to No.99 Squadron. The Mk.1C had redesigned hydraulics and a 24-volt electrical system, which permitted the use of the new directional radio compass. Crews, ever mindful of the beam attacks made by the *Luftwaffe*, soon installed hand-held Vickers machine guns in the long narrow 'windows'. Mark 1Cs were first used on 20th March during a sweep over the North Sea.

'Friendly fire' is one of those contradictions in terms, as no one shooting at you can be considered friendly, and such 'friendly fire' accounted for the deaths of 33 Wellington crew in WW II, another seven being seriously injured. Such 'friendly fire' occurred on 23rd March, when Wellington IA P9225 of No.149 Squadron piloted by Sergeant S A Williams, was hit by French anti-aircraft fire near Dunkerque while returning from a reconnaissance raid over the Weser and Elbe rivers and the Mitteland Canal. The pilot turned the aircraft inland, so that they would be over terra firma rather than over the Channel. The crew then baled out near Hondesschoote near the France/Belgium border, returning to England by boat train on 26th March.

Being forced to bale out was always good for a yarn over a pint or in the Mess. One can remember a crew being forced to bale out over France whilst engaged in leaflet dropping, and returning to the Squadron a week later. Also the amusement caused by the rear gunner, recounting with indignation that, after making his way to a farm, he was met by a French farmer who threatened him with a shotgun.

Another accident befell No.149 on 4th April when Wellington P9267, 'OJ-F', piloted by Flight Lieutenant J M Griffiths-Jones crashed on approach to Mildenhall airfield following a training exercise. The pilot was injured and five of the seven on board were killed.

On 9th April, Germany invaded and occupied Norway and Denmark and, as the invasion of Norway was by sea, an attempt was made to slow down the German troop movements by attacking them at sea when they were most vulnerable. This resulted in the biggest Bomber Command activity to date, which took place on 12th April when 83 aircraft, including 36 Wellingtons, were sent out on a daylight anti-shipping sweep. This included six Wellingtons from No.38 Squadron at Marham, trailed by six Wellingtons from No.149 Squadron with the mission to search for and attack any German shipping off the Norwegian coast near Stavanger.

They were intercepted by Messerschmitt 110s and three of the Wellingtons were shot down, two of the Wellingtons, P9246 piloted by Sergeant H J Wheller and P9266 piloted by Sergeant G E Good being from No.149 Squadron. Both crews were killed. Corporal J H Langridge, one of the crew of P9266, was the first New Zealander to be killed on active duty with Bomber Command. The invasion of Denmark did not go totally without response and on the 17th, 21st and 23rd April the hangars and runways of Aalborg airfield, now occupied by the *Luftwaffe*, were bombed. Anti-aircraft fire was heavy and poor weather hampered the raids. Sola airfield at Stavanger was also attacked on the 21st. The raids were not without price and, on the 21st, P9218, 'OJ-O', piloted by Flying Officer F T Knight was shot down while attacking Aalborg, the aircraft crash-landing in the surf near the airfield, the crew being taken prisoners of war.

On 25th April, six Wellingtons of No.149 Squadron took off late at night in another attempt to bomb Stavanger. It proved abortive. Thereafter, the Wellingtons were employed on North Sea sweeps and night reconnaissance operations over the Island of Sylt to prevent mine-laying operations.

Beginning on 10th May, the German 'blitzkrieg' was now fully under way, the German army sweeping over Europe to occupy the

*Wellington OJ-O (P9218) lies in the surf close to the beach near Aalborg airfield after being shot down by flak on 21st April 1940. This happened while Flg Off F T Knight and his crew were on a bombing raid on the hangars and airfield following the German invasion and occupation of Denmark. All the crew were taken prisoner.*

Netherlands, Belgium, Luxembourg and France. By good fortune it coincided with Winston Churchill taking over as Prime Minister of the British Government. Bomber Command operations were now swung around in support of the Allied troops attempting to stem the advance, by attacking railways, roads in France and Northern Belgium, troop and supply concentrations. Knowing that German aircraft, notably Heinkel He 115s would be mine-laying in the various river estuaries leading to ports and other British shipping channels, it was decided to attack their operations at the source and so security patrols were begun, No.149 Squadron aircraft patrolling the area around the islands of Sylt and Bochum. However, with the German invasion of the Netherlands and Belgium calling for retaliatory action, Bomber Command aircraft were needed elsewhere and the security patrols were called off. The attacks on German airfields in occupied countries continued, Waalhaven airfield receiving a successful attack by No.149 Squadron aircraft on 10th May, while attacks in support of the troops in Europe were maintained until the British army and remnants of the French and other allied armies reached the beaches at Dunkerque.

The German violation of Dutch and Belgian neutrality had opened up a path for British bombers to fly directly from England to the Ruhr, where sixty percent of Germany's industrial strength was concentrated. However, political in-fighting between the French and British commands delayed matters. The French, with German troops already sweeping across their soil despite their attempts to hold them back, were alarmed at the possible repercussions of such an action. So, with its sixteen squadrons of Wellingtons, Whitleys and Hampdens, Bomber Command was prevented from carrying out this action and had to content itself with fringe targets in Germany. On the night of 14/15th May Wellingtons of No.149 Squadron bombed Aachen and on the following day the War Cabinet authorised Bomber Command to attack east of the Rhine.

During this time, No.149 lost a further Wellington, P9270 'OJ-G', piloted by Flight Lieutenant I D Grant-Crawford who, returning from the battle area in France, crashed near Barton Mills in Suffolk, while attempting to land at Mildenhall, three of the crew including the pilot being killed. 'Operation Dynamo', the recovery of the British Army across the Channel, from 26th May until 4th June was supported by No.149 Squadron attacking the German advancing front to prevent their reaching the Dunkerque area before all of the troops had been recovered. 338,226 British and French soldiers were landed safely on British soil.

Corporal Crisford, a Fitter IIA, remembers Mildenhall well:

"I was stationed at Mildenhall, on detachment from 54 MU (Cambridge) to repair shot-up aircraft with a party of civilian fitters from Vickers-Armstrongs. The Squadron was No.149. Mildenhall was known in those days as 'Happydrome'. It contained some famous names, including Harry Wragg, the Newmarket trainer, who in those days was Gunner H Wragg RA, one of the Bofors gun crews, and LAC 'Denny Dennis' a 'Pop Singer' who made his name with 'Mexicali Rose'.

"I remember one night in the NAAFI, I was watching a local 'Rep' Company playing 'The Housemaster' by Ian Hay, and at the climax of the play the tannoy announced that an enemy aircraft was overhead with evil intent and there was a fire in 'A' Flight hangar and all personnel should take cover. I still don't know how the play ended.

"The 'Bird In Hand', next to the airfield, and on the outskirts of the small village of Beck Row, with George Ashley as landlord, was our local. Still fairly new, it had been built by Hall, Hutlack and Harlock, the brewers at Ely, and was noted for its lovely barmaids. One of the regulars had lost part of his left arm in WW 1, but was by reputation one of the finest shots with a 12-bore for miles around.

"The SWO was W/O Cooke, who claimed to have the deepest voice in the RAF; if you fell foul of him you were not left in any doubt.

"Mildenhall had its share of heroes, like a rear gunner who put out a fire in the rear of the aircraft by smothering it with his parachute. The hole in the fuselage was as big as an escape hatch. I believe he was decorated.

"The unsung heroes of 1941 were the Armourers who sweated through that long hot summer loading bombs, only to be told at the shortest possible notice 'change that load to incendiaries' and then back again to H.E. How those lads worked.

"I remember one incident; a certain LAC was employed as a 'runner' for the Flight Sergeant Discipline at SHQ. One of his duties was to take the 295s to the Guardroom on Friday nights for the troops to draw on Saturdays. This particular Friday his own pass was amongst the pile, which he carefully extracted and went home 24 hours early.

"That night his complete set of bedding disappeared from the barrack room and re-appeared next morning completely made up on the front steps of SHQ. The sheets neatly turned back and on the pillow was a note that said, 'This is LAC Robinson's bed, where is he?' You can gather from this he was not too popular, although he slept three beds from me, I never heard a thing. The culprits were never traced."

In order to counter the *Luftwaffe* raids, the Mildenhall airfield perimeter was equipped with Bofors guns and fitted with a system known as P.A.C. or Parachute Attached Cables. As reported by Peter Russell, an airframe fitter with No.149 Squadron at that time, should the airfield be under attack, rockets would be fired from vertical tubes, taking several hundred feet of wire cable with them, connected to a parachute, the idea being that a low-flying enemy aircraft would fly into the wire which would then become entangled around the propeller. As can be imagined accidental operation caused havoc, as when it was struck by lightning in the summer of 1941. Corporal A A Crisford, a fitter, continues: "it festooned the base with steel cables, resulting in the idea being abandoned."

The French army was still putting up a gallant resistance to the German advance, and in support of them, beginning on 5th June, Bomber Command, including No.149 Squadron, attacked German troops, roads, rail and bridges along what was known as the Weygand line. On one of these raids, to Soissons, Wellington L7800 of No.149 Squadron, pilot Flying Officer J S Douglas-Cooper was shot down and believed crashed into the sea off the Belgian coast with the loss of the crew.

Now that it looked to the Italians as if Germany was about to win the war, on 10th June Italy had joined the Axis side. Mussolini's intentions had already been anticipated and it was agreed that as soon as Italy joined the war her heavy industry in the north of the country would be added to Bomber Command's possible targets. The range from bomber bases in Britain to Italy was excessive and so it was decided to set up a small bomber force known as 'Haddock Force' based at Salon, in the Provence area in France, under the command of Air Marshal Arthur Barratt. This would consist of twelve Wellingtons, six from No.99 Squadron, which were sent out on 11th June, to be joined by six from 'A' Flight of No.149 Squadron. Salon would be a refuelling, re-arming and jumping-off platform to bomb industrial targets in Northern Italy, notably the Caproni aircraft factory in Milan and the aluminium manufacturing plant in Genoa.

On 15th June six Wellingtons from No.149 Squadron, together with two Wellingtons from No.99 Squadron of the Salon detachment were sent to attack the aluminium factory at Genoa. Violent thunderstorms arose, and only P9268 of No.149 Squadron claimed to have bombed the target. France capitulated on 17th June, and, fearing reprisals by the German army, French trucks were driven onto the runway at Salon and in front of the Wellingtons to prevent their taking off, making future missions impossible. Evacuation was ordered and No.149's entire air and ground crews were flown back to Mildenhall on 18th June.

The collapse of France and the fall of Belgium, The Netherlands, Norway and Denmark gave Bomber Command an additional mission, that of depriving Germany of its imports, and of its Navy which supported its merchant shipping. Ports and harbours, its warships and merchant shipping, were high priority targets. Added to which was the mission to knock out its industries. So, on nine nights from the middle to the end of June No.149 Squadron targets included the aircraft factories at Bremen, the refining plants in Hamburg, the railway marshalling yards at Hamm and the towns and cities of the Ruhr. It was on one of these raids, to the Naval installations at Bremen, on 11th July, that Wellington L7805, with Pilot Officer J S Torgalson was shot down, killing the crew.

Ports along the coast of Europe now became assembly points for the next step by the German army, the invasion of Britain, barges, troops and supplies being amassed. Beginning on 15th July, these ports now became prime targets for Bomber Command. Recognising that a sea-borne invasion of Britain could be imminent, aircraft of Bomber Command were placed on perpetual standby, to attack any such attempt while the invasion fleet was still crossing the Channel. Three Wellingtons of No.149 Squadron were assigned this standby duty, these being known as the 'Invasion Aircraft'. On 17th July these aircraft were temporarily stood down.

Accidents continued and on 11th August, while returning from a raid on Gelsenkirchen, Pilot Officer J G Miller, flying Wellington P9244 'OJ-E', while attempting a landing at Mildenhall, was misaligned with the runway, resulting in a collision with the radio mast, killing the crew.

The 15th of August brought with it 'Eagle Day' and the onset of the Battle of Britain, with 'Operation Sea Lion', the planned invasion of Britain by German forces, to follow. The following day, Sqn Ldr E H T Thwaites, flying No.149 Wellington R3174 'OJ-A', was shot down while on a raid to the dockyard facilities at Koleda. Three of the crew were killed, the rest being taken prisoners of war.

Mastery of the air for Germany was essential before any invasion could take place, and this meant destroying RAF Fighter Command, both in the air and on the ground. The German attacks on the British fighter airfields were such that Fighter Command was hard pressed to make up the losses and it looked as if the *Luftwaffe* would win the battle of attrition. Then, by plan or by good fortune, on 25th August, Bomber Command, with 103 aircraft, attacked various targets in Germany, approximately half of its bombers, including aircraft of No.149 Squadron, attacking targets on the outskirts of Berlin. This was No.149 Squadron's first attack on Berlin. This attack so enraged Adolf Hitler that he redirected his bombers to attack British cities, especially London, giving Fighter Command the necessary time to recover sufficient fighter strength to defeat the *Luftwaffe* in the skies over the Southeast coast of Britain. 'Operation Sea Lion' was cancelled.

The raids on German ports and harbours continued, with Wellington P9272 'OJ-A', with Flight Lieutenant P F K Vallant being shot down while on a raid to Kiel, the crew being taken prisoners of war. A reflection of the desperate times is shown in the desperate measures taken. In September it was decided to try and destroy the German crops while still in the fields, and also to attack German armament hidden beneath the trees, by dropping a myriad of small phosphorus devices, usually as a sandwich between cellophane. These devices were nick-named 'Razzles', and had been tried out on the night of 11th August by aircraft of No.149 Squadron, each aircraft carrying 50 biscuit tins with up to 500 'Razzles' in each, immersed in water. These were poured down the flare chute. Unfortunately, as reported by Leslie Hinken, an armourer, the phosphorus would brush against the aircraft fabric on exit and, after drying out on landing, would set the aircraft on fire. While no aircraft was lost, at least two Wellingtons caught fire, causing quite a lot of work, both in hosing down the aircraft and in repairing the damage. The 'Razzle' technique was later proven to be ineffective and abandoned. It was on such a 'Razzle' raid to the Schwarzwald (Black Forest) area on 4th September, in an attack on the heavy armaments that was being amassed there, that Flying Officer H Burton and his crew in Wellington R3163 'OJ-G', was shot down, all being taken prisoners of war. It is worth noting that Flying Officer Burton escaped from his prison camp in May of the following year.

Flt Sgt Collett in charge of 'B' Flight remembers a conversation with a certain member of aircrew during these months:

"In my office one morning the Rt Hon Bruce Grimston was discussing the previous night's raid with another young pilot. The young pilot said, ' I don't understand it Bruce; I was over the target the same time as you. I did what you said you did and yet you got wonderful pictures and I got nothing – how do you explain it?' Bruce turned to the young pilot and answered 'Just luck old boy. Just luck'.

"Shortly after moving to Lakenheath I was sitting next to Flt Sgt Middleton in the mess, during our evening meal. He was telling us how cannibalism was still practised in some of the islands off Australia. As he got up to leave he got hold of my arm, pretended to bite it and said, 'Very tasty – very sweet'. Two weeks later he was dead."

In the first two weeks of September, the Battle of Britain was still very much a reality, and so attacks on the various invasion ports along the coast of Europe, from Delfzijl in Holland to Bordeaux in France, together with attacks on the German supply dumps and troop concentrations, were the order of the day, No.149 Squadron making it a routine operation when weather permitted. It was on such a raid to Boulogne on 8th September that No.149 Squadron lost two aircraft. Wellington P9245 'OJ-W', piloted by Squadron Leader L V Andrews was hit by anti-aircraft fire over Boulogne. Then, to compound the problems, they were caught in a severe electrical storm coupled with turbulence, which iced up the aircraft including the windscreen. Then the port engine failed and caught fire. The compass was out but they could see the coast of England for a short while by the searchlights, but they were soon turned off. Then the starboard engine failed. Flying parallel to and several miles away from the English coast, the crew baled out. In full flying gear minus flying boots, the second pilot, Flying Officer Parish, swam for several hours, using the North Star and the searchlights to guide him, until he made the seven miles to the English coast. He was the only survivor and he was soon back on duty; within two-and-a-half weeks he was on a raid to Berlin but sadly, was lost on operations two-and-a-half years later, as a bomber pilot. It was his 54th mission.

R3175 'OJ-V', piloted by Pilot Officer J L Leeds was also lost that night, being shot down by a night fighter. This was from *Luftwaffe* night fighter unit 1/NJG1, the first night fighter squadron formed by the *Luftwaffe* and was supposedly the first bomber shot down by a German night fighter, a dubious honour. The aircraft crashed into the sea and all of the crew were lost. A further Wellington was lost in attacking the Channel ports, this one on 18th September, being R3160 'OJ-B', piloted by Pilot Officer J S Pay, on a raid to Le Havre. Again all of the crew were killed.

With the threat of an invasion greatly diminished, attention was once again turned to targets in Germany, and with it came the inevitable casualties. On a raid to Hanau on 28th September, R3164 'OJ-B', piloted by Pilot Officer H R Bjelke-Peterson was shot down, one of the crew being killed, while the rest were taken prisoners of war. Then on 9th October P9273 'OJ-V', piloted by Pilot Officer R G Furness was shot down on a raid to Herringen, all of the crew being lost.

No.149 Squadron again became a victim of 'friendly fire' when a British anti-aircraft battery opened fire on T2740 'OJ-E', piloted by Flying Officer D W Donaldson on 23rd October while they were returning from a raid on Emden. With a damaged aircraft, the pilot needed to make an emergency landing and the nearest landing ground was St Osyth, near Clacton, in Essex. To compound the problem, someone opened fire on the aircraft as it approached the field, sending a bullet through the cockpit. This certainly took the pilot's attention away from concentrating on the landing approach, resulting in him hitting an obstruction, and the aircraft crashed. However, the crew survived.

The RAF bombing raids, while rarely hitting the target, were of sufficient concern for the *Luftwaffe* to set up a major retaliatory attack on various airfields throughout East Anglia, Yorkshire and Lancashire on 27th October. Mildenhall and Newmarket were on the list of targets, receiving the attention of both Dornier Do 17s and Heinkel He 111s. Twelve high explosive bombs were dropped, hitting the cookhouse, sick quarters, a hangar and a barrack block, killing two airmen and injuring a further ten. One unexploded bomb by the water tower needed to be disarmed.

November brought with it the usual replacement aircraft but one was to be immortalised. Wellington P2517 was received, which was later to become the 'star' aircraft, 'OJ-F' F-for- Freddie, in a forthcoming Ministry of Information film 'Target for Tonight'.

November and December kept the pressure on the attacks on German industry, and No.149 Squadron's targets included Cologne, Kiel, Gelsenkirchen, Wilhelmshaven, Munich, Leipzig, and Hamm, plus six attacks on Berlin. It was during the 19th November attack on Berlin as a secondary target that N2774 'OJ-A', with Pilot Officer K J Hide at the controls, was shot down, with the loss of all of the crew. The primary target was the Skoda works at Pilsen in Czechoslovakia, but most aircraft attacked a secondary target that night. Potential targets in Italy didn't go unnoticed, and these included the Fiat factory at Turin, the docks at Genoa and various industrial targets in Milan, and the first direct bombing from England to Italy took place with an attack on the Fiat aircraft engine factory in Turin on 4th December, in which No.149 Squadron took part.

The 16th of December brought two losses, both at Mildenhall. Sergeant R S W Lloyd had taken R1294 for an air test and to his crew were added trainee pilots, giving a total complement of seven. During the air test the fabric stripped from the starboard wing. With undercarriage down and preparing to land, the aircraft stalled and crashed during a low altitude turn, killing all on board. Then, on returning from a raid on Mannheim, Sergeant J S Marr, piloting P9268 'OJ-A', overshot the runway and crashed into the bomb dump. Luckily all survived.

While the next year or two would still be very hard for Bomber Command, as it was still low on the learning curve, the 'heavies' were arriving to replace the obsolescent existing bombers, and by the end of 1940, the Short Stirling, the Handley Page Halifax and the Avro Manchester, while still in small numbers, were already in service. What was needed were navigation and bombing aids, and the right kind of bombs. Airborne radar was still in the development stage, and the 4,000-lb bomb not yet a reality, but the crews, both air and ground, were ready. They were always ready. All they needed were the right tools.

Leslie Hinken, an armourer with No.149, remembers the day he arrived at Mildenhall:

"I was posted to No.149 Squadron on passing out as an Armourer at Armament School, RAF Manby, in August 1940. The Squadron was then based at RAF Mildenhall and flying Wellington (Wimpey) aircraft. Mildenhall had been built in the early 1930s and before being handed over to the RAF had been used as an airfield for the England – Australia air race during which every previous record for the flight had been broken. Amongst the pilots taking part in that particular race were Amy Johnson and Jim Mollison, who had previously broken the UK to India record, where they were forced to land with mechanical problems, and forced to retire.

"A new hotel had been built by Hall, Cutlack and Harlock, the brewers of Ely, just in time for the air race, and was named 'The Bird in Hand'. This, of course became the 'local' for No.149 Squadron. RAF Mildenhall was, in fact, on the outskirts of the small village of Beck Row, and was possibly named after the nearest place of any size, being Mildenhall village.

"After the usual paperwork I reported to the No.149 Squadron armoury and saw the NCO i/c, at that time a Sgt Whelans. A grand chap. Straight away he made me feel at home and within a short time I had got to know the other NCOs and airmen.

"I was first of all sent with another Armourer to do the daily inspections and with a crew 'bombing up'. After a week or two I was allocated my 'own' aircraft and given an armourer's assistant.

"All work except for major inspections was carried out on the dispersal points, as it was considered the hangars presented too much of a target for the *Luftwaffe*. The aircraft were equipped, front and rear turrets, with two 0.303 Browning machine guns. An armourer's job was to maintain these turrets and guns, hydraulic systems and bomb gear. Every morning an inspection was carried out after which one would sign the obligatory form.

"The afternoon would be spent 'bombing up', if there were 'Ops' on. Often during the 'bombing up' the load would be

*'F for Freddie', OJ-F (P2517) was used as the 'star' aircraft in the Ministry of Information film 'Target for Tonight', piloted by then Squadron Leader 'Percy' Pickard. It served with No.149 Squadron from November 1940 to September 1941, but never saw actual combat operations.*

*A Fordson tractor gets ready to tow Wellington OJ-N to a new location on the field at Mildenhall in 1941.* [IWM HU-44865]

changed, sometimes as many as three times. You can imagine some very choice words were said about this. This would also apply to the refuelling crews who had to change petrol loads.

"Various checks were made and the aircraft was left to the night crews, who saw to the taking off and return. We all took turns on night crew after which we would be excused duties for the following morning, perhaps all day if no 'Ops' were on, and no major aircraft inspections were on.

"The comradeship amongst the Armourers was fantastic. It had to be seen to be believed. In the evenings (funds permitting) we would adjourn to the 'Bird in Hand', and a good time was had by all.

"Those on night shift had quite a hectic time when the aircraft returned. They checked the Very pistol was unloaded, also the main guns. Bomb bays were checked for 'hang ups'. Incendiary bombs by virtue of their shape did sometimes 'hang up' in the small bomb containers but as each bomb weighed only four lbs they were easily removed; even if they dropped out they would not ignite. This did not apply to Stirlings. Of course, not all aircraft returned and one used to hope that they had landed somewhere else, especially if it was one's own aircraft, as ground and air crews grew very close.

"The bombs carried in my early time with the Squadron were mainly 250 and 500 lbs with, of course, 4-lb incendiaries, which were carried in small bomb containers containing initially 60 but later increasing to 90 per container. The containers, of course, remained in the aircraft after the incendiaries had been dropped for re-use.

"A lot of leaflets were also dropped. First of all these were pushed out of the flame float chute but after a time these were also carried in a small bomb container. I remember cans of liquid being carried in aircraft these contained phosphorus leaves, the idea being these ignited on drying out. Unfortunately, these also brushed against aircraft, and when the aircraft dried out after landing, being fabric, they 'went up' in flames! I don't think we lost any aircraft this way but two certainly were damaged, causing quite a repair job.

"I did see these used out of Stirlings but carried in small bomb containers. I don't think the idea was very successful, as it was soon discontinued.

"I remember well the first 1,000-lb bomb we loaded. This seemed huge to us, as we were used to dealing with 250 and 500-lb bombs and incendiaries. This bomb was to be dropped on Munich and we hoped it would be dropped on the 'Beer Kellar' (*sic*). Later three Wellingtons equipped with Rolls-Royce engines arrived. These aircraft could carry the new 4,000-lb bombs, and were equipped with special bomb gear and the bomb doors had been removed.

"Mildenhall had no concrete runways, so during very bad weather we operated from Newmarket racecourse. At Mildenhall we were bombed on several occasions, the first being on a Sunday evening in 1941. Several people were killed and the cookhouse put out of action, so for a few days we had cold food, though the cooks always managed to get us hot drinks.

"Armourers were excused all parades, as we were very short handed at this time. We were called 'The Plumbers', as we always seemed to be carrying pipes, oil etc., about to top up the hydraulic systems.

"Squadron Headquarters' Staff (SHQ) did not like us, as they believed that we got everything our own way. We in turn looked down on them with their smart uniform and polished shoes.

"During our stay at Mildenhall we took part in two thousand-bomber raids. Every available aircraft was called into service and this meant we worked around the clock. A German night fighter once got over the airfield and into the stream of aircraft returning from a raid. He had it all his own way, as it was the practice for A/G's to vacate the turrets before landing. He shot down two or three aircraft over the airfield, one crashing on a house in Beck Row (OJ-M) killing all the crew. Two other aircraft were also lost trying to land without a flare path, as all the lights had been put out, when it was realised what was happening."

*During a raid on Duisburg on the night of 18th August 1941, Wellington OJ-X (X9746) was attacked by a Junkers Ju 88 night fighter; cannon shells hitting the rear of the aircraft and setting the tail section on fire. The rear gunner, Sergeant Billington, fought the fire for fifteen minutes using his hands and parachute, while the pilot, PO Gregory, kept the Wellington under control, then brought it back to base, even though the elevators had ceased to respond. This resulted in immediate awards of the DFC and DFM to Gregory and Billington respectively.* [L G Gregory]

*King George V and Queen Elizabeth looking at a flash photo taken from OJ-O during a raid on Porto Marghera.* [Ron Priest]

# Chapter 5: 1941 – and still Wellingtons

The New Year opened with an attack on Bremen on 2nd January. Many large fires were reported. Further raids on German targets, then a raid to the Porto Marghera oil refinery and storage facility in Venice, Northern Italy, on 12th January 1941, led by the Squadron Commander, Wing Commander 'Speedy' Powell, during which he earned the DFC. Various targets in Northern Italy were chosen by Bomber Command this night. One aircraft was lost, that of Sergeant R A Hodgson, Wellington T2807, which was shot down by an armed naval patrol ship in the lagoon. The crew were picked up and made prisoners of war.

Sgt John Rootes remembers the raid on Venice, and the considerable discomfort felt by him in the rear turret. The aircraft was T2897, 'O' Olive (OJ-O), the Captain being The Honourable Bruce Grimston.

"When the aircrews of No.149 assembled in the afternoon of 12th January 1941 to be briefed for the night's bombing raid, all eyes went, as usual, to the big map of the British Isles and Europe. The red ribbon on it was pinned at one end to the home base, Mildenhall, Suffolk; but it was the other end, which caused the whistles and astonishment. This stretched right across Europe, over the Alps and down through Northern Italy to the target, Venice Porto Marghera. A round trip of 1,500 miles, most of it to be done by dead reckoning (pencil and ruler), as there was very little navigational help available.

"The Squadron had flown two previous raids on Northern Italy: to Turin on 4th December 1940 and Genoa on 18th December 1940, but this was the longest raid yet. During the briefing it transpired that six aircraft would make the raid, led by Wing Commander 'Speedy' Powell and that one aircraft – 'O' Olive – captained by The Honourable Bruce Grimston, would carry a new flash bomb camera in the bomb bay to record where the bombs landed.

"The bomb load would consist of only three 500-lb bombs instead of eight, as the rest of the load was fuel, contained in overload tanks. These were used first and then jettisoned. It seemed a long way to go just to drop three bombs. However, from later reports it was obvious that damage to the morale of the civil population was indeed severe. Later evidence of the panic caused in Northern Italy by the raids was overwhelming.

"Take-off was scheduled for six in the evening, but at that time the whole airfield was blanketed in fog and the raid was in danger of being cancelled. The Met Forecast was that the fog extended to 300 feet, and that the weather was clear above that height. At 7.30 pm, the fog having thinned slightly, Wing Commander Powell decided on a somewhat risky take-off and led the way in great style, followed by the other five Wellingtons. The forecast was correct and the aircraft popped out of the blanket into a bright clear sky, although the moon was not yet up. Over France, the ground below was seen to be covered in snow. At 14,000 feet the temperature had fallen to minus 30 degrees.

"Over Lake Geneva the engines of Wellington 'O' Olive coughed and stuttered and five voices shouted over the intercom to the second pilot, who was resting on the bed, to switch over the overload tank. A sleepy voice eventually answered; the switch was hurriedly made and the engines picked up.

"Although Switzerland was neutral, Bomber Command used to overfly it to save fuel. The Swiss, to assert their neutrality, used to fire a small gun to 5,000 feet. As the aircraft approached the foothills of the Alps at 15,000 feet the moon had risen, revealing the cruel peaks reaching up like giant fingers seeking to claw them down. Mont Blanc on the right appeared to be higher than the height of the aircraft. The temperature had dropped to minus 50 degrees.

"The rear gunner, me, without any turret heating, who had long since lost all feeling from the waist down, was picking icicles from his chin as his breath froze.

"It was an awesome and unfriendly place to be and when the Wellington had cleared the mountains and began to descend, the crew were much relieved. The navigator finally, after much searching, found Venice and could see its towers and palaces seemingly floating upon the lagoon, like one of its own once-famous fleet of galleys.

"The Wellington turned and bombed the oil refinery at Porto Marghera obtaining a direct hit in the middle of the oil tanks. The flash bomb went off at the same time with a brilliant white light and the camera took the photo. The Wellington then dived on the aerodrome at Padua and machine-gunned it from 500 feet, giving the front and rear gunners some practice.

"Then we turned for home, climbing back up to 15,000 feet. Half way across the Alps a frost came down, covering the Wellington in a white mantle from end to end. The temperature plummeted even further and it was deathly cold inside. Shortly afterwards the aircraft flew into thick cloud, the crew seeing nothing for some three hours. At 04.00 hrs the navigator predicted Calais underneath and the Wellington started to descend 10,000 feet – 5,000 – 1,000 – and still thick cloud. Then at 400 feet, with the cloud almost touching the sea and pouring with rain, the Wellington broke out into the Channel. Ahead was the North Foreland light and I was five miles from home. The navigator had completed his task magnificently without a single pinpoint to help him.

"The Wellington turned to starboard and flew up the Thames Estuary, avoiding the Harwich balloon barrage and let down into RAF Mildenhall some ten hours ten minutes after leaving.

"One Wellington did not return. A flare caught fire on the chute and the aircraft crash-landed in the Venice lagoon. The crew were all safe and were rowed ashore by Italian police to spend four years in captivity.

"The crew of Wellington T2897 went to bed after debriefing, but were not to have their usual complement of sleep because at mid-morning they were woken up and told to 'smarten up'.

"Their Majesties King George VI and Queen Elizabeth had arrived at Mildenhall on a visit to Bomber Command. They were shown the flash photograph of the bombs falling on Porto Marghera the previous night and asked to see the crew who had taken it. The sleepy crew of 'O' Olive, were paraded in the photographic section before the Royal visitors. All tiredness fell away as the Queen questioned them about the raid. She showed an amazing knowledge of navigation, wireless and gunnery and soon the straight line was a circle with her in the middle.

"Outside it was snowing; overhead the Spitfire escort flew round the aerodrome, guarding the Royal visitors.

"The crew of Wellington T2897 went back to bed."

Once again, King George VI accompanied by Queen Elizabeth visited Mildenhall and inspected the Squadron, this time on 18th January, and while there, invested Wing Commander Powell with his DSC.

Sid Rusher also recalls those days as an Airframe Mechanic:

"I arrived at Mildenhall in January 1941, from Technical Training School, Hednesford, as a flight mechanic (airframes), and was seconded to 'U' Uncle on 'B' Flight. I remembered at the time that there were three Wellington Mk IAs used for blind approach training. Also, one of the hangars was occupied by another Squadron, No.99, who operated from Newmarket Racecourse. 'U' Uncle's pilot, named Milstead, was the first I had met. After a daily inspection, all trades involved had to sign the Form 700. Then the crew would take off on a flight test. On one occasion this pilot 'shot up' the drome and climbed up high, and went into a half roll. It took nearly all the rest of the day to clean up the mess – the 'Elsan Closet' was empty!

"During my time at Mildenhall, I saw only two fatalities. At the time there were no proper runways; if the wind was North/Northeast, take-off was from the shortest run. The Wellington concerned took off with another crew, hit the trees at Beck Row and crashed. I believe there were no survivors.

"The second – at about 4.00 a.m. when I was on duty at dispersal, a German night fighter followed 'M' Mother in and shot it down on the run-in; I think they all perished. There was quite a stink at the time, apparently the rear AG had left his turret before arriving at dispersal. Of course, I cannot confirm this.

"In the winter of '42, the Squadron was visited by the King and Queen, and we were stood down for three days. An investiture was held in one of the hangars. I can remember it snowing at the time, and the Spitfire that was circling round had to come in and land.

"Another thing has come to mind: - an aircraft was diverted on returning from a raid for several reasons. The radio may have been damaged or a shortage of fuel, maybe enemy raiders were around. Ground crews were sent out to see if the aircraft was airworthy; if not, the controls had to be locked and engines had to be 'pickled'."

*Luftwaffe* raids on Mildenhall continued throughout February, with considerable damage both to aircraft and to buildings on 1st February, and again on the 2nd. One enemy aircraft received a direct hit by airfield defences on the 18th. On that night enemy bombing broke communication between Mildenhall and Newmarket for a while.

The British weather always played havoc with flying and the weather on 12th February did far more damage than any enemy action. A total of 78 aircraft, including No.149 Squadron, had been sent to attack Bremen. With no losses due to enemy action, the aircraft returned to an England that was shrouded in fog. With the inability to see the airfields in order to land, eleven Wellingtons, together with seven Whitleys and four Hampdens crashed in England, most of them after their crews had bailed out. Five crewmen were killed. No.149 Squadron lost two aircraft. Wellington P9247, 'OJ-M' piloted by Sergeant R Warren flew into the ground near Digby airfield in Lincolnshire while trying to get below the cloud cover, one crew member being killed, while the crew of L7811, 'OJ-C' with Sergeant Turner as pilot, abandoned the aircraft and baled out over Congresbury.

No.149 was back at Wilhelmshaven on 22nd February, on one of many such trips, losing Wellington R1045, piloted by Flying Officer I S Henderson, all of the crew being killed. German warships, including a *Hipper*-class cruiser, were reported to be docked at Brest and so 57 bombers, including those of No.149 Squadron, attacked the dock area on 24th February. This was the first raid in which the Avro Manchester, from No.207 Squadron, took part, one of them crashing on return.

The month closed with another attack by the *Luftwaffe* on Mildenhall, this being by a single bomber, identified as a Dornier Do 215 but more probably a Do 17Z, which made three runs over the field, dropping eleven bombs on its third run but only causing crater damage. There was a simultaneous attack on the 'K'-site for Mildenhall at Cavenham, which was a dummy airfield, hopefully to draw away possible attackers; in this case, it did just that.

March started well with a raid to Cologne on the 1st totalling 131 aircraft including No.149's Wellingtons. Considerable damage was done and two steamers were sunk. Again, fog covered the airfields on return and while only one Wellington was lost due to enemy action, a further fourteen aircraft were abandoned over

*Wellington IC P9245 was coded OJ-W in 1941.* [R C Sturtivant collection]

England, resulting in twelve air crew being killed, five injured, and two missing.

Frank Cork, alias Sgt Catt, recalls a raid on Cologne. He had just got married and was returning to Mildenhall, filled with the concerns of being newly married, and how long he and his crew would be able to survive. It no doubt reflects the concerns of many service personnel throughout this period:

"Sgt Catt looked through the 'window' of the train at the flat Suffolk fields rushing past. He decided that he didn't feel any different now that he was a married man. He recalled how a grateful Government, in the form of his Squadron Commander, had given him 48 hours to get married. A kindly vicar had opened up his church in Margate, one of the most desolate, bomb-spattered towns in 'Hellfire Corner', only yesterday. He looked at his new wife sitting opposite him in the carriage. She was clutching her bridal spray and looking very young. He wondered if they had been wise; statistically, the life of a rear gunner in Bomber Command, at the moment, was only three months. However, they had talked it over and had faith in their future.

"Squealing brakes brought his mind back suddenly. The train stopped at Shippea Hill, the nearest station to Mildenhall, eight miles away. The two jumped out, straight onto the track, which could only have been taken from an Arizonian film set. The one and only ancient taxi bore them off to their rented bungalow, near the airfield.

"The Sergeant knew he was on Ops that night, and when he arrived at the 5 pm briefing his crew found the usual confusion of sound, smoke and forced gaiety. This night raid on Cologne would be his 28th operation, a good score for these days, and he knew that 'sprog' Wellington crews took heart from his own crew's apparent longevity. After receiving some jocular remarks about his newly-acquired marital status, Catt tried to concentrate his mind on the briefing. The Intelligence Officer was remarking that the Germans were now grouping searchlights in cones of 50-100, instead of using them singly as before.

"Take-off had been at 19:15 hours and as they crossed the coast at Orfordness, Sergeant Catt sat comfortably in his rear turret sucking his barley sugar sweet issue. He thought about his wife. Was she coping in the bungalow? Had she heard them take-off? This being a short trip, about five hours, he could be back with her soon after midnight, with a bit of luck.

"Catt was keeping a good lookout, swinging his turret from side to side. They must be about 100 miles inside enemy territory by now. Noticing a cone of searchlights flickering towards them he called up the captain.

"'Keep your eyes open for fighters!' came the terse reply. Almost immediately, the lights were upon them, illuminating the inside of the Sergeant's turret with intense brilliance. Others came and trapped them until they were held in about 60 beams. Something like 10 million candlepower, thought Sgt Catt, as he sat terrified yet enthralled as the flak began to shoot up like colourful showers of fireworks, 'bock-bocking' when some distance away and roaring like thunder when close to the aircraft.

"Suddenly the flak stopped. 'Fighter astern' came a shout from the second pilot, up in the astrodome. Sergeant Catt, almost blinded by the light was just in time to see twin tails of an Me 110 flash past and green blobs of 20mm cannon fire coming at him. A second Messerschmitt attacked and came in so close astern that Catt, who was firing his Brownings like crazy, wondered how it was that neither of them had been hit at this point blank range. He, in fact, wasn't even using his gunsights! A third Me started to come in, and as Sergeant Catt became aware of even more green blobs flashing past like express trains, suddenly everything went blank, and thankfully realised that they had been saved by the bell. Or rather the pilot, who having tried everything for twenty minutes to escape the lancing beams, had finally dived out of the area just in time.

"As usual after a crisis, the intercom was quiet and the crew were very shaken. All, that is, but the captain it seemed, for they heard his exaggerated Cambridge drawl calmly saying, 'Navigator, give me a course for Cologne, please'. Sergeant Catt knew where he wanted to go; and it wasn't Cologne.

"Wellington T2897 and its weary crew finally let down at Mildenhall at 15 minutes past midnight after a successful raid. After debriefing, the Squadron Commander, having heard the details, came over to them and smilingly said, 'A funny way to start your married life, Catt'. Sergeant Catt could only agree.

"Back at the bungalow all was quiet. Catt shrugged himself out of his flying clothing and climbed into a warm bed, exhausted. What a honeymoon!

"In the newspapers the following day, the headlines read: 'Shoots down plane at twenty yards'. They were credited with one aircraft probably destroyed! So that's the way it was?"

On 13th March, No.149 Squadron received two of the six Mark II Wellingtons assigned to No.3 Group, two each also going to Nos.9 and 99 Squadrons. The Mark II Wellington had in-line Rolls Royce Merlin engines and a single bomb bay, rather than the triple bomb bay of the Mark I varieties. It could also fly a little higher and a little faster. The 4,000-lb bomb had reached the development stage where it was about to be dropped over enemy territory and the bomb bay of the conventional Wellington couldn't accept it, but the Mark II Wellington could. This was not the 'blockbuster' or 'cookie' which was to become the standard 4,000-lb bomb used by Bomber Command, one of which was carried by the Lancaster on almost every raid towards the end of the war, this one being dropped by parachute, much like the German and British sea mines. For the next two and more weeks, crews would be on familiarisation training in preparation for the eventful day.

The next day, on the 14th, No.149 Squadron was part of a 101-aircraft force, which attacked the Gelsenkirchen oil plants, one of No.149's Wellingtons, L7858, 'OJ-A' piloted by Sergeant L R Hawley, being shot down by a night fighter near Sevunum in Holland, the crew being killed. The greatest damage to Gelsenkirchen was due to their own anti-aircraft shells, which did not explode in the air but exploded on returning to the ground. Three days later, on the 18th, another No.149 Wellington was shot down, but this one was much nearer home. Seven Wellingtons of No.149 Squadron were part of 158 aircraft scheduled to attack Bremen.

'M-Mother' had returned safely from the raid on Bremen, and with wheels down and flaps down, Sergeant R. Warren was bringing his Wellington, R1474 'OJ-M', in for a landing at Mildenhall. But it was 'jumped' by a Junkers Ju 88C intruder flown by Leutnant Rolf Pfeiffer of 1 Staffel, NJG 2, which had followed the bomber stream back to base, and was shot down, the Wellington crashing into a bungalow at Beck Row near Mildenhall. All of the crew were killed. The occupants of the house, an insurance agent named Titmarsh and his wife, escaped unhurt as they had taken refuge under their bed when they heard machine gun fire.

Another case of bad visibility causing an aircraft loss occurred on 20th March, when R1159, 'OJ-N', piloted by Sergeant W Hall, returning from a raid on Cologne, came down through a thick haze trying to locate the airfield, being guided by searchlights, a technique known as 'Darkie' which was a regular inter-services act of co-operation. He hit a tree at Peaseland Green in Suffolk, and then force-landed in a field. Luckily there were no casualties.

For one month covering the last two weeks in March and the first two weeks in April, No.149 Squadron's aircraft and crews were used as background for the Ministry of Information film "Target for Tonight" with P C (Charles) Pickard seconded from No.311 (Czech) Squadron to play the part of the pilot of No.149 Squadron's Wellington P2517, 'OJ-F' for Freddie' around which the story was written, the film being made at Blackheath Studios in London with Harry Watt as director. The man in the flare-path caravan shown in the film was No.149 Squadron's Commanding Officer, Wing Commander 'Speedy' Powell. Pickard later rose to Group Captain, but was killed while leading a Mosquito attack on the Amiens prison on 18th February 1944.

Merchant shipping losses in the Atlantic were almost at breaking point, Winston Churchill giving a direct order in March that that Battle of the Atlantic was to take top priority. So Bomber Command was ordered to attack German warships whenever and wherever it was possible. On 30th March eight Wellingtons of No.149 Squadron, together with 101 other bombers, attacked the battle-cruisers *Scharnhorst* and *Gneisenau* in Brest harbour. It was known that it would be on this mission that one of No.149 Squadron's aircraft would drop the bomb which would bring the total tonnage of bombs dropped by No.149 Squadron to 1,000 tons. So it was decided to hold a lottery as to who the crew would be, using the reported time of bomb drop of each aircraft as guide. The bomb load was to be 500-lb bombs. Naturally two crews, in order to win the lottery money, flew over the target several times, dropping one bomb at a time.

Leslie Hinken recalls how the problem was resolved as to which crew dropped the bomb that made the 1,000 tons:

"No.149 Squadron were proud of the fact that they were the first Squadron to drop 100 tons of bombs in the last war. A sweepstake was run on the first crew to drop the bomb to make the 1,000 tons, dropped in this war.

"On checking it was found that two crews dropped their bombs at the same time. The tie was resolved by awarding it to the crew who were flying lower when the bomb was dropped!"

Meanwhile, practice at dropping the new 4,000-lb bomb from the Mark II Wellington was under way, using a dummy bomb with inert filling. The bomb doors were removed and, while much attention had been paid to the bomb, little attention had been paid to the bomb rack to carry it. On the first trial run over the bomb range, the bomb refused to drop, and so it was a return to base and a little creative modification of the bomb rack. On the second trial, the bomb still refused to drop over the bomb range, but it did drop as the Wellington was on its approach to land, covering a large area of a neighbouring farmer's field with inert filling, much to his annoyance. This was on 31st March and the mission was planned for that night. So a further jury-rig was made with the bomb rack. This time it was fitted with a wedge, and the bomb aimer was equipped with a hammer. On the call 'Bomb gone!" from the navigator the bomb aimer would hit the wedge with the hammer and release the bomb.

The two Wellington Mark IIs were bombed up with two further Wellingtons as escorts, and a similar arrangement was set up at No.9 Squadron. As it turned out, each Squadron managed to put only one of their Mark II Wellingtons in the air. W5399, 'OJ-Q', with the nose art 'The Wizard of Oz' failed to get airborne, sliding into the neighbouring field of barley. 'Oz' was the nickname for Australia, so perhaps the pilot was Australian, as quite a few Commonwealth crews flew with No.149 Squadron. The target was marked by Wellington R5413 from No.9 Squadron piloted by Squadron Leader K M M Wasse. With Pilot Officer Franks at the controls and Alex More as navigator, No.149's W5439 'OJ-X' dropped the first 4,000-lb High Capacity bomb over Emden. The bomb fell on the quay at the extreme south of the estuary, with a huge yellowish explosion, covering a large area, and throwing huge quantities of debris into the air. It was followed by a further 4,000-lb bomb dropped by No.9 Squadron.

Greg Gregory was second 'Dickie' on one of the new Wellington Mk.IIs which was being piloted by Johnny Franks, who in Greg's words was a 'first rate chap who was killed on his second tour'. Greg remembers the day when No.149 Squadron made history in the majority of national newspapers but not for the reason they wanted. Poland had been bombed by the RAF! Greg goes on:

"The story was that the Squadron had just received two Wellington Mk IIs, with Merlin engines and modified bomb bays to take the early 4,000-lb bombs. The Mk. II was a fine aircraft, the Merlins enabling us to fly at about 18,000 feet, both faster and higher than the Mk.ICs. The navigator somehow missed these rather important details, so we flew ever onwards towards the East. After some hours he spotted a large town on a river, and reckoned that it was Frankfurt-on-Oder, some 200 miles east of Berlin. The skipper said, "Let's drop the bloody thing and go home". We turned west and flew over Hamburg in early daylight and very short of fuel. It was a nail-biting time but Franks put it down at the first airfield we saw, Watton, practically out of fuel. After breakfast and sleep, the *Daily Express* featured an article that the RAF were now bombing Poland! It was in fact Poznan, another couple of hundred miles east of Frankfurt.

"The navigator was closely questioned and sacked. Sandy knew him and did meet up with him later on when he was Group Navigator."

Wellington R1229 'OJ-H', with Sergeant G J P Morhen at the controls, was one of the escort Wellingtons to the Mark II Wellington. On returning to Mildenhall, the aircraft landed heavily, bounced, stalled, and then caught fire. One of the crew, Sergeant P E Butler, died from his injuries. With such a calamity, the airfield was closed to traffic and 'OJ-X', the Mark II Wellington, landed away, at Feltwell.

Following Winston Churchill's directive, April was devoted to continued attacks on the *Scharnhorst* and *Gneisenau*, on the French and German ports and anti-shipping sweeps, but also the occasional raid on German industries. Another non-combat loss occurred on 4th April, when Wellington P9267 with Flight Lieutenant J M Griffiths-Jones as pilot, stalled while attempting an overshoot of the runway at Mildenhall during a training exercise, killing the crew.

At this time the *Luftwaffe* fighters were also heavily engaged in the Balkans, mainly the Greece and Yugoslavia area. It was decided that, if enough stress could be created by Bomber Command, perhaps the *Luftwaffe* would draw fighter units away from the Balkans to defend their homeland and ease the situation in the Balkans. So a 229-bomber raid to Kiel on 7th April initiated the plan. This raid included twelve Wellingtons from No.149 Squadron and resulted in considerable damage. Another raid to Kiel was carried out on the 8th and on this raid X3167, 'OJ-H' piloted by Sergeant J B C Jago was shot down. Another raid on the *Gneisenau* in Brest Harbour on the 10th, and in taking off for this raid, R1181 OJ-W, piloted by Pilot Officer J H Fisher lost height, crashing into the trees and a cottage at Holmsey Green in Suffolk, killing two of the crew and the lady living in the cottage. Four of the bombs dropped hit the *Gneisenau*.

In a letter to his wife on 12th April 1941 AC Bradley, a Fitter/Armourer, which he wrote from Room 6, 'K' Block, gave his first impressions of his first week at an operational Bomber Command airfield:

"This my first week on a real operational Squadron has been extremely interesting and enlightened me on numerous details of this war in the air. This camp is very comfortable having all one-storey brick buildings, all conveniences; a cinema every night with three programmes a week and a show now and again. Food is still good even getting for breakfast yesterday, egg, bacon and sausage, also coffee, rather exceptional but eggs seem plentiful. Food can always be obtained as so many chaps finish at different times, having to leave the planes 'Wellingtons' in perfect order. I have been getting rather greasy, more like a garage hand today, having

an oily job removing a gun turret for repairs. Most of my work will be on guns, which is very much more interesting than bombs. We start around 8.30 each morning, 12.30 until 1.45 for dinner and tea at 4.30, though often we are still working after 5 o'clock, especially when operations are on for the night. 'Ops' as we call them. So far it does not seem that this camp could be better, the only point is that as on all these types of Squadrons, one works seven days a week, so one day is the same as the next. We do not have to salute or very rarely do so, and call our NCOs by their nicknames, everything is free and easy."

Enemy airfields remained on the target list, Merignac airfield near Bordeaux being attacked by No.149 on 13th April, resulting in T2897 'OH-O', piloted by Sergeant R R Morrison being shot down near St.Sever-Calvados in France, five of the crew being killed, one being taken prisoner.

A further raid to Kiel by No.149 on 15th April resulted in only slight damage to the target, but with the loss of R1439 'OJ-W', piloted by Sergeant P R B Meynell, which was shot down by anti-aircraft fire, all of the crew being killed. The 17th brought a raid to Cologne and a further loss, this being P9248 'OJ-G', piloted by Sergeant J Peel, which was lost without a trace, one of three Wellingtons lost on the raid.

The next two or three weeks brought raids to major cities in Germany, including Berlin, Mannheim, Bremen, Hamburg and Cologne, not forgetting Kiel once again, and also repeated attacks on the warships *Scharnhorst* and *Gneisenau* holed up at Brest.

It was at Hamburg on 8th May that No.149 suffered its next loss, R1506 'OJ-D', with Flight Sergeant C R Burch at the controls being shot down into the sea off Heligoland by a German fighter while returning from the raid. Four of the crew were killed, the other two being taken prisoners. Immediately following, again on a raid to Hamburg on 11th May, R1512 'OJ-H', piloted by Sergeant J G Keymer was shot down, killing the crew.

May brought a new four-engined bomber to Bomber Command, the American-built Boeing B-17 Flying Fortress I, equipping No.90 Squadron. It was a disappointment, Bomber Command's survivors eventually being handed over to Coastal Command for reconnaissance patrols. However, valuable lessons had been learned which were handed over to America, these being incorporated into the redesign of the new Flying Fortress, the strong right arm of the US Army Air Force bomber force when it entered the war.

The next No.149 Wellington loss was a mid-air collision on 17th May by 'OJ-M', R1587, piloted by Squadron Leader A W J Clark which collided with Hurricane V7225 of No.1401 Meteorological Flight, near Ely in Cambridgeshire, the subsequent crash killing the crew. The next loss did not occur until almost four weeks later, on 12th June, and was to be one of No.149's two Mark II Wellingtons, when W5439 'OJ-X', 'The Wizard of Oz', piloted by Sergeant W Harrison was shot down by anti-aircraft fire while on a raid to Düsseldorf, crashing near Bergharen in Holland. Fortunately the crew survived and were taken prisoner.

Enemy warships at Brest were again a target on 1st July, and this time it was the heavy cruiser *Prinz Eugen*, with 52 Wellingtons of No.3 Group being sent on the raid. Two Wellingtons, both from No.149 Squadron, were shot down, but in this act more damage was done than the other bombing. R1408 'OJ-J' with Pilot officer J E Horsefield at the controls, was shot down at Plouzane with the loss of all of the crew. The other aircraft, piloted by Pilot Officer S L Vincent-Welch RAAF, R1343 'OJ-B', was shot down over the target. The aircraft crashed alongside the *Prinz Eugen*, and it is believed that a bomb from this crashing aircraft struck the *Prinz Eugen*, exploding inside the ship, causing serious damage and killing the executive officer and 60 of the crew.

*The Duke of Kent, as Group Captain, paid an official visit to Mildenhall on 25th June 1941. He is seen here inspecting a mix of both air and ground crew. Pilot Officer, the Hon. Michael Strutt, who served as an air gunner with No.149 at this time, later became Personal Equerry to the Duke. They died together in the tragic crash of the Duke's Sunderland in Scotland.* [RAF Museum]

Attacks on the major German cities intensified with the ports being high on the list. On 14th July the target was Bremen, with 47 Wellingtons, including those of No.149, assigned. With thick fog and icing conditions only a third of the aircraft were able to bomb the target. Sergeant Tony Gee, flying R1593 'OJ-N', was caught in the searchlights over the target, and so dived to 2,000 feet to avoid the intense accurate flak. T2737 'OJ-A', piloted by Pilot Officer P L Dixon RAAF, was not so lucky and was shot down, all of the crew being taken prisoner. Meanwhile, badly damaged and radio out of action, Sergeant Gee made it back to Mildenhall. On inspection, his Wellington was categorised as 'not repairable' and was shipped to No.1483 Flight, No.3 Group's Gunnery Flight. On interrogation, crews reported that 'the whole town was ablaze'.

The 15th of July brought with it one of the more memorable moments in No.149's history, during a raid on Duisburg, when the Wellington flown by Pilot Officer 'Greg' Gregory was attacked by a Junkers Ju 88, told in Pilot Officer Gregory's own words:

"Most of our luck ran out on the 18th August when a night fighter got a couple of cannon shells into us, still with the bomb load aboard! Luckily, I was not hit, the second pilot standing on watch in the astrodome got the worst of it but the rear gunner and navigator were both injured, not fortunately all that badly. The rear gunner was dealing with a fire round and above his turret. The aircraft was manageable after I jettisoned the bombs and I turned south-westerly to get out of trouble. The engines were overheating and the tail trim was heavy but I thought we could cope for a bit. I had no wish to bale out over Germany!

"I told the front gunner to exit his turret and do what he could for Harold Reed, the second pilot. He piled flying suits on to him and gave him doses of Morphia. (Sergeant) Billington, the rear gunner, got the fire under control, using his parachute to blanket the flames! We seemed to have stabilised matters a bit so I turned northerly to home. We raised a little flak on the French coast but we made landfall on UK, and I decided to ease us back to Mildenhall. I made radio contact as we got close and called for an ambulance. It was broad daylight by then, as I was about two hours behind the other crews. In the circuit I checked the undercarriage and to my surprise they locked down. I did my usual smooth landing! But we then swung hard left. No damage but the bugger had put a shot through the port tyre".

The rear of the aircraft had been severely damaged, and the fire had burned off huge areas of fabric from the fin, tailplane and fuselage and put the tailplane out of action. For Pilot Officer Gregory's action, showing superb airmanship in bringing the aircraft back to base, he was awarded an immediate Distinguished Flying Cross. Sergeant Billington for his part was awarded an immediate Distinguished Flying Medal. The co-pilot, Harold Reed, recovered well after many operations and still carries bits of the shell inside him. Sergeant Billington was later killed on another tour. Harold Reed, seriously injured on his first operation, spent the next few years in RAF Hospital, Ely.

The 17th and a raid to Cologne brought another loss to No.149, but not by enemy action. While Sergeant D C Stewart's Wellington, N2853, was hit by flak he made it back only to be blinded by searchlights as he tried to bring in his damaged Wellington to land. The aircraft hit the trees at Cockfield in Suffolk and crashed, killing one of the crew and injuring others.

August brought with it a visit to the Squadron by a Mr. Bayliss, an American who, until recently, had been attached to the

American Embassy in Berlin. He gave the Squadron a talk on the British bombing of Germany, speaking from personal experience.

The 5th of August saw two No.149 Wellingtons being shot down on the same raid to Mannheim, R1524 'OJ-P', piloted by Sergeant F D Fowler crashing at St Martens Voeren near Liège, while X9633 'OJ-R', with Sergeant J T Farmer at the controls, crashed near Wavre in Belgium. Both crews were killed. The raid was very successful, with 'serious damage' being reported by Mannheim's administration.

A similar twin aircraft loss occurred less than a week later, on the 12th, when 65 Wellingtons were sent on a raid to Hannover, R1024 'OJ-V', piloted by Pilot Officer F H Beemer RCAF, crashing into the sea off Sylt, with the loss of all of the crew. T2716, 'OJ-W' piloted by Pilot Officer Fox, after being hit by both anti-aircraft fire and a night fighter, made it back to Elvedon in Suffolk where he made a forced landing. One of the crew died of injuries sustained in the action. On this particular raid, two aircraft of No.115 Squadron from Marham were carrying the new radar navigation aid, 'Gee', on a trial flight. One of the 'Gee'-fitted aircraft was shot down, giving grave concern that the new equipment had been compromised in that as yet there were insufficient sets to fit out even a reasonable number of aircraft. This would take about six months, and the expected working life of any new airborne radar equipment was about six months before the Germans could learn its operation, then take countermeasures, including jamming.

A highly effective programme of misinformation was set up by Dr R V Jones, head of Air Intelligence, calling the new equipment 'J' and purporting it to be a homing device much like the 'Lorenz' Beam equipment, allowing the 'Gee' transmitters to remain operational. The trays pre-installed in new aircraft to accept the 'Gee' receiver and indicator were marked 'J' and air crew were falsely briefed, should they become prisoners of war and were questioned as to the intent of this new 'J' equipment. While the crashed No.115 Squadron aircraft gave no premature clue to 'Gee', the misinformation worked, German Intelligence reporting the function of the equipment as Dr Jones had wanted them to believe, buying enough time for 'Gee' to be installed throughout Bomber Command.

An attack on the Duisburg railway yards by 41 Wellingtons of No.3 Group from a clear sky gave good bombing results, but at the loss of another No.149 Wellington, X7904 'OJ-B', piloted by Pilot Officer J C Lynn, which crashed near Roermond in Holland, killing two of the crew. The other four were taken prisoners-of-war.

Corporal Bradley wrote to his wife again on 6th September, about conditions at a nearby airfield:

"Wednesday I was given the half day off so made the most of it and cycled to Newmarket. My chief interest lay in the local Squadron, as I had a chum who has been posted there. Having entered the drome I was taken out by a van to him. From my short stay and from what he told me, Mildenhall is a king to that station, which bears out most accounts of this drome. He hardly ever has a half-day and often is working until after 6 o'clock, all this is due to it being a Group Training Centre for Air Crews, which means many flying hours and gun practices so give me Mildenhall every time."

Raids to Berlin always brought with them great risk, as the capital was always very strongly defended both by massive anti-aircraft fire and by fighters. It was on 7th September on a raid to Berlin that X9705 'OJ-J', with Sergeant G W Fenton as pilot, was shot down, with the loss of the crew. The raid itself was reported to

*A posed photograph shows crews watching the return of three of No.149 Squadron's Wellingtons.* [Don Clarke]

*Wellington OJ-N (R1953) with peculiar nose art being bombed up at dispersal at Mildenhall. 'N' was the aircraft of PO Sandy Mansfield.* [Don Clarke]

have been effective. Only four days later, X9879 'OJ-V', with Sergeant D W Bennett RCAF, was shot down during the Squadron's raid on Kiel, with the loss of all of the crew.

Jim Coman, W/Op on a Wellington IC, X9823 'OJ-R', remembers the visit to Berlin, the 'Big City':

"We were airborne at 2020 hours, from our Mildenhall base, and we climbed slowly turning onto our first heading. All went well, with the gunners testing their guns over the North Sea, until the target was reached. Being slightly north, our bombing run was made north to south, there being a great deal of flak and numerous searchlights. Bomb doors were opened and our observer took control with the normal left – left – steady – right – steady – bombs gone. At that moment we were coned by searchlights and started taking numerous hits. Mike Evans, pilot, tried everything he knew to get clear of the lights but to no avail, as at 9,000 feet they had really boxed in, so he dived the aircraft. Pulling out at roof-top level, being peppered with light flak and machine gun fire all the time. We were now so low we could see parts of buildings being destroyed by their own gunfire, in their endeavour to shoot us down.

"We soon passed over a stretch of water and 'Happy' Hanson, rear gunner, shouted "get up a bit Mike, my feet are getting wet" Almost immediately we were flashed a green light and saw we were approaching an airfield, obviously being mistaken for a friendly aircraft. They soon realised their error and started firing at us, but our gunners soon quietened them. Being unsure of our position we turned onto a westerly heading climbing to about 5,000 feet, where I broke radio silence to get a navigational fix from the Hull RDF. Eventually we arrived at the Dutch coast and Mike informed us all the main tanks were near enough empty and that he was switching to the engines nacelle tanks, giving us approximately twenty minutes flying time. Just then 'Happy'

warned us of enemy aircraft, a Ju 88, making an attack. We took one hit in the wing, but our gunners drove him off and he was last seen diving through the clouds with his engines trailing smoke. As we were so short of fuel I contacted Hull on SOS, so that our position would be pin-pointed across the North Sea, in case we had to ditch. We reached our coast and received permission for an immediate landing at Martlesham Heath, that being the nearest airfield to the coast. With our tanks showing empty we touched down; turning off the flarepath, our engines cut out. From the control tower, we informed base, then went to the Mess for breakfast. On our return to the aircraft, it was being refuelled and one airman was on the port wing and decided to drop off the leading edge, but whilst hanging by his hands, prior to dropping, one hand slipped sideways into the cable cutter, where he lost two fingers. He was quickly taken away to sick bay in severe shock, as being a fighter station he had no idea that cable cutters were fitted to bombers.

"We took off again, landing at Mildenhall, where back on the 'pan' the ground crew counted over 150 holes and noted that we had taken a hit in the main spar, which had cracked across, and it was surprising the aircraft had stayed in one piece."

September was to herald the dawn of a new era for No.149 Squadron, with the delivery of their first Mark I Short Stirling, N6095, on the 24th, followed by W7451 on the 25th, No.149 becoming the third squadron in Bomber Command to convert to Stirlings. Two more were delivered on 12th October, N6093 and W7448, and by the end of the month, with eight Stirlings on strength, crew conversion began in earnest. This was part of the over-all program to upgrade most of Bomber Command to four-engined bombers. The Halifax and Lancaster were still to come. Wellingtons would be gradually moved out of No.149 as Stirlings came in to replace them, most of the Wellingtons winding up at Heavy Conversion Units or Maintenance Units.

Meanwhile, No.149 operations using Wellingtons nevertheless continued throughout, the Wellingtons flying further afield with attacks on major German and Italian cities. As navigator Terence 'Sandy' Mansfield recalls:

"On 26th September, while en route to Genoa, we had been recalled over France due to forecast bad weather at base. Three days later the Wellingtons went all the way. We had a lovely view of the Alps but Genoa was mostly covered by cloud so bombing was on estimated position using the coast. After leaving Genoa our wireless blew up and cloud developed solidly below 10,000 feet so navigation was solely on astro fixes. Fortunately, we hit Mildenhall Lorenz beam almost on ETA. Duggie Fox, my pilot, turned on to it and descended in the low cloud. Honington had been alerted and they fired a massive assortment of pyrotechnics as we approached and we crawled in under a cloud base of, at most 200 feet."

On 30th September the Wellingtons carried a new weapon, as Terence Mansfield recalls:

"We carried a new 65-lb incendiary for marking purposes. This horrid weapon was very light case, rather like a large oblong tin, the contents of which were spontaneously combustible on contact with air. The resulting fire was very visible but it was a menace, as a leak brought fire".

*Right: Nose art 'Maximum Effort' on one of No.149 Squadron's Wellington, The Ozard of Whiz.*
*[Don Clarke]*

*Below: 'OJ-E' (N6103) carries the presentation marking 'East India I'.   [R C Sturtivant collection]*

On 10th October, Corporal Bradley wrote:

"The weather today has been brighter, but of late wet, which has cancelled Ops for the last ten days, so are pleased that we have some going over to bomb Jerry tonight.

"I had to collect my hockey kit from the PTI store. The afternoon was a 'Stand Down' for the Squadron – weather must be atrocious over Europe – so our team, as picked, all played against a Civvy team from Bury St Edmunds, we winning 4-1, and a fast game it was. The ground was rather too soft and the grass needed cutting, which made the ball very tricky.

"On 12th October we again carried 65-lb incendiaries to Nuremberg. We had orders to drop only on visual. It was totally dark and although we flew around the area for forty minutes, we could see no ground detail. The bombing started but it was not Nuremberg. Anyhow, we went over to investigate at just over 4,000 feet and I was confident that I could make out a small town. Since the fires were well established, we added to them and sent a signal back that we had bombed the secondary target. Further astro fixes on the return trip confirmed my calculated positions. On landing, we were told that we were the only crew not to find the target but our photograph proved that we were right and that almost the entire attack had been against the wrong place. We got our haloes back!"

With the arrival of the Stirling aircraft, there was an increase in personnel and Corporal Bradley again wrote to his wife on the 5th November:

"You may have read that there has not been so many 'Ops' as previously due to the bad weather but this sort of thing makes work very slack. The four-engine Stirling bombers are arriving on the drome making a 'C' Flight, already having 'A' and 'B', which means increased personnel in the camp and long queues at meal times."

Back to Mansfield:

"On 7th November, my last (trip) with Duggie Fox and No.149, we carried the 65-lb incendiary again. All the outward route was appalling, with high cloud, very bad icing, turbulence and rattling hail. Using the occasional breaks in the tops, I managed to get a series of astro fixes, so that at least we thought we were almost on track. Total cloud cover at the target meant that we could not drop our bombs and we brought them all the way back! That we crossed the Suffolk coast almost on track and only five minutes late on ETA proved the value of my sextant. We saw no signs of any defensive action and felt sure that high losses, 21 of 170, were due solely to the weather."

It was on a 156-aircraft attack on the shipyards at Bremen on 21st October that Z8795, 'OJ-C' piloted by Pilot Officer A C L Hodge, was shot down, killing the crew, the aircraft crashing into the River Schelde. As dangerous a target as the highly-defended Berlin was to attack, it still remained high on the list, and on 7th November it received the attention of 169 bombers, 101 of which were Wellingtons. 21 aircraft were lost, including ten Wellingtons, one of which was X9878, 'OJ-A' of No.149, piloted by Sergeant S W Dane, which was shot down with only one survivor, Sergeant F Jenkinson, who was taken prisoner. The last Wellington lost in combat by No.149 was on 16th November on a raid to Emden, and this was R1627, piloted by Sergeant R Bramhall, with the loss of the crew.

November brought with it a new commanding officer for No.149 Squadron, Wing Commander G J Spence. The grass runways at Mildenhall proved unsuitable for the heavy Stirlings and so a detachment of Stirlings were sent over to neighbouring Lakenheath with its concrete runways, which would soon to be No.149's new home. As described by Peter Russell, airframe fitter, compared to Mildenhall, Lakenheath was spartan. A few scattered buildings and no hangars, with the cookhouse a mile from the airfield. The ground crews, being exposed and in the open, soon learned to survive. Whatever materials they could get their hands on was collected together and soon makeshift huts were erected out on the dispersal to protect them from the wind, the cold and the rain, and eyeshields were dug out from their anti-gas equipment to protect them from the perpetually wind-blown stinging sand.

Pheasants were everywhere at Lakenheath, as Leslie Hinken, armourer recalls. However as weeks progressed the pheasant population decreased, until a notice appeared in the Daily Routine Orders putting the woods out of bounds, the owners of the shooting rights also complaining that the number of pheasant eggs in the woods had decidedly reduced. The local public house, The George, became a favourite hang-out, and Flight Sergeant T H Collett recalls the generosity of the publican, Mr Cole, who would provide hot soup to the ground crew to eat out at the dispersal site.

Eventually a T-type hangar was built at Lakenheath, as Peter Russell, an airframe fitter, recalls, which became the home of the R & I (Repair and Inspection) Unit, later renamed No.149 Servicing Echelon. However should an aircraft land away because of battle damage or some other major problem, a repair team was sent out to carry out on the spot repairs and enable the aircraft to return to base. Lakenheath was also the home of the idea of what was eventually to become 'FIDO', the fog dispersal system. Here narrow gauge railroad tracks were laid on either side of the runway. Coalmine metal wagons filled with coke, soaked in petrol and ignited were dragged along either side of the runway to disperse the fog. The wagon concept was replaced by pipes feeding fuel into troughs along either side of the runway. The fuel was ignited and 'FIDO' was born.

Compared to a Wellington, manoeuvring the Stirling on the ground by ground crew was no easy task, hauling the front of the Stirling around by means of cables attached to the undercarriage, while the back was swung around by means of an arm attached to the rear wheels. Moving a Stirling around the perimeter track with some poor 'erk' steering the rear end from the rear wheels could be back-breaking. However, they soon learned to stand on the steering arm and steer with the feet, while hanging on to the guns in the rear turret.

It was on 22nd November that No.149 would lose its first Stirling, but to a training accident. A starboard engine of Pilot Officer C Lofthouse's Stirling, W7456, caught fire while he was taking off for a training mission, causing him to belly-land at Boxworth in Cambridgeshire. Pilot Officer Lofthouse was then assigned N6103, which was received the next day, this becoming 'OJ-E', and in the traditions of No.149 Squadron, the 'East India' Squadron, this aircraft carried the honour of being named 'East India I'.

The first Stirling raid by No.149 Squadron took place cautiously with one aircraft, N6099 'OJ-C' being sent to Ostend, then again Stirling N6099, this time accompanied by five No.149 Wellingtons, was part of the raid on Bremerhaven on 30th November.

On 9th December the last Wellington was moved out of Mildenhall and No.149 Squadron, and transferred to a Maintenance Unit. Stirling N6122 was received to become East India II and training with Stirlings was intensified until the end of the year. On the 16th, a new tactic was tried by Bomber Command, code name 'Abigail Rachel', that of a general attack on a German city, initially in response to the German bombing campaign on British cities. The city chosen was Mannheim, with initial target marking by eight experienced Wellington crews using incendiaries, followed by the bomber force, which totalled 126 aircraft, 53 of them Wellingtons, the most aircraft to attack any single target to this point in the war. While not rated too successful the tactic would be one that would become commonplace throughout the rest of the war. Meanwhile, over at No.44 Squadron in Waddington, a new aircraft had arrived. The fault-plagued twin-engined Manchester had given birth to the four-engined Avro Lancaster, which would gradually become the standard equipment for most of the squadrons throughout Bomber Command. The bomber war had reached another key turning point.

*Ground crew of No.149, each at their respective duties, prepare one of the Squadron's Wellingtons for operations.*

# Chapter 6: Mildenhall Stories

What it was like to be a pilot with No.149 Squadron and in Wellingtons in 1941 is described by then Flying Officer Trevor A 'Happy' Hampton, who became a Squadron member in February of that year, and who found himself flying to Cologne with his Flight Commander on a shake-down flight, together with 125 other aircraft on the 26th of that same month:

"We had been assigned a brand-new Wellington 1C (R1474), which should have made me a little suspicious and my ground crew painted on it our Squadron letters 'OJ' our identification letter 'M-Mother'. Secretly, I was delighted. I had a good mother and she would look after me - it was an omen.

"After a few days in the Officers' Mess I seemed to detect a subtle sort of deference being bestowed upon me by other junior officers. Nothing was said, but everyone was so 'very nice'. At first I thought it might be that I had arrived as a fully-fledged Flying Officer, with 600 hours in my logbook, rather than the more humble Pilot Officer straight from training school. For a day or two I basked in my fool's paradise.

"I began to notice that my crew, also, were being treated with a touching courtesy quite alien to the wartime RAF. I mentioned it to my rear gunner, George 'Junior' Gray, who had previously been a commissioned pilot but was accident-prone. Junior looked at me incredulously. 'Don't you know Skipper? There have been eleven 'M-Mothers' since Christmas!'

"I was a bit shaken but I soon consoled myself - I still had faith in mother. Out of our Squadron of eighteen aircraft, they must have been losing one 'M-Mother' every week.

"The first trip was, more or less, a 'blitz' on Cologne. The Germans had had a go at Coventry in November 1940, which I had seen burning from our own aircraft, so I didn't feel too badly about it. My Flight Commander, Squadron Leader Sawry Cookson, accompanied us just to show us the ropes and let me see how 'easy' (his words) it was. He naturally assumed command and we left my second pilot behind.

"With an inferno below we steamed over the city at 140 knots, at 18,000 feet, the ceiling for a Wellington, with a bomb load. Having done two runs over the target area, we were chased off by ground fire and searchlights, diving into the protective cloak of darkness clear of the city and levelling out at 2,000 feet. Cooky let me take over and he went aft for a word with the crew. When he returned to the cockpit I was climbing but he stopped me - 2,000 feet would be OK.

"We cruised along quietly and eventually came across an enemy airfield, all lit up for night flying. 'Go down and stir them up a bit' said Cooky, so down we went. Once round the circuit and they realised there was a cat amongst the pigeons and let us have some flak and light tracer fire. I looked at Cooky and he nodded towards home. I set course and started to climb but again he told me to stay at 2,000 feet. It didn't seem right to me - but he should know.

"We stooged along for some time and I was beginning to feel confident. I noticed intermittent flickering lights immediately beneath the aircraft. So much for blackout precautions - I was looking straight down chimneys of a large city, probably Rotterdam, but I didn't get the chance to confirm with the Navigator, Sergeant Cymbalist.

"At that moment there was a blinding flash and 'M-Mother' was on the instant the focal point of countless searchlights and we seemed to be trapped in a cage of golden rods. I was petrified into immobility but it did slowly dawn on me that the air was composed of vicious tracer shells and bullets. The crack of exploding shells could be heard above the noise of our engines - that meant they were close, and then a much louder one rocked the aircraft. The starboard wing went down, followed by the nose.

"I had the stick right back and the wheel hard over to port but 'M-Mother' was diving out of the sky and I was quite helpless. The altimeter was unwinding like a mad thing, I watched it go past five hundred feet in numb despair and I knew we were 'going in' - this was it and on our first trip - Oh, Mother!

"Under such circumstances imminent death brings with it no acute agony of mind, as one would expect, but a hopeless numb realisation of the end. I knew it was no good struggling any more and I was just about to let go of the controls and cover my face for the final blinding crash when Cooky's voice came over the intercom. 'Come on, hold it!' We might have been on a training exercise. I hung on, with Cooky leaning across me, helping to take some of the weight and we eventually levelled off at 200 feet, the searchlights and flak losing us as we dived earthwards.

"Our speed was down to 85 knots and we were flying in a semi-stalled condition, tail down, nose up. Our engines were at full boost but we couldn't gain speed or height and I dared not let our nose or wing go down the slightest degree. We staggered home across the North Sea, every moment expecting the aircraft to drop a wing and spin in but as we burnt up our fuel, inch by inch we made a little height and crossed the English coast at 500 feet. Cooky could see that I was exhausted and he managed to slide underneath me into the pilot's seat.

"Cooky saved 'M-Mother' that night. He was a remarkable person who just did not acknowledge danger and was quite fearless. I felt I had the edge on him as a 'safe' pilot, but who wanted 'safe' pilots in 1941? I expected Cooky to make a full power approach and do a wheel landing but too late I realised he was holding off to do a 'three pointer'. The starboard wing naturally stalled first, a great chunk of it was missing and down we came into Mildenhall, a shaken crew.

"At dawn the ground crew pushed off for breakfast, having written us off as one more 'M-Mother'. However, they were soon out on 'M-site' again, and seemed genuinely pleased to see us back, although it meant the fitting of a new wing.

"I was rather looking forward to the interrogation by our Intelligence Officer, one John Cobb, of water and land speed record fame. 'Everything OK?' asks John. 'Yes, bombs on target', says Cooky. 'Come on, let's get some breakfast'. I was learning fast.

"After some sleep, to my surprise, I found that the night's experience had improved my morale and my faith in 'M-Mother' had been justified. My crew were not convinced and Junior privately expressed the hope that he would be re-commissioned before he got the 'chop'.

"A new wing was fitted and I carried out an air test. On reporting the aircraft serviceable again Cooky informed me that he was lending my 'M-Mother' to 'A' Flight for the coming night's operation. I could stand down with all my crew except for my second pilot, Sergeant E R Cook, who they wanted to borrow.

"During the afternoon of 17th March a Sergeant Pilot, the captain of the unserviceable 'A' Flight aircraft, sought me out in the 'B' Flight crew room. He was in a dreadful state and made little effort to hide it. 'I'm told I have to take your aircraft tonight, Sir - and its 'M-Mother'. I said, 'Yes, look after her; she's flying nicely with the new wing'.

"The poor boy was nearly speechless but in a rambling disjointed manner he told me he had done 28 operations without incident, had only two more to do of his present tour and now fate had dealt him 'M-Mother'. In No.149 Squadron she really was the 'end'. I felt a little piqued. I didn't like to think of my aircraft as a leper. In truth, there was little expressed sympathy wasted in the wartime RAF and none expected. This expression of fear to an officer he hadn't even spoken to before was unprecedented in my experience. It was more than just a premonition to the boy. He had

*Loading ammunition to the rear turret of OJ-D at Mildenhall.*

made up his mind they were for the 'chop'. Instead of trying to laugh him out of it, I found myself comforting him and my last words were, 'I guarantee 'M-Mother' will bring you back.

"I lived off the camp and the following morning, 18th March, driving along the road from Barton Mills to the airfield, I saw the tail end of a Wellington bomber sticking up out of the roof of a house. Just clear of the slates I read 'M-OJ'.

"'M-Mother' had returned safely from the (18th March) raid on Bremen, but had been 'jumped' by a Ju 88C intruder flown by Leutnant Rolf Pfeiffer of 1 Staffel, NJG2, as it was coming into land near Beck Row, Sergeant R Warren, the pilot, and the other five crew were killed in the attack. The occupants of the house, an insurance agent named Titchmarsh and his wife, escaped unhurt as they had taken refuge under their bed when they heard machine gun fire.

"A new Wellington (R1587) was towed out to 'M' site and yet another 'M-Mother' was prepared for operations. In this one we completed a few operations and to everyone's surprise, returned intact. One night, intent on blasting Hitler's three warships lying in Brest harbour, we were being shaken up by the combined defensive fire of the three ships and all the Brest Peninsula flak. The Navigator was chanting over his bombsight for my benefit... 'Left. Left. Steady. Right. Steady', when I heard Junior shout something about a fighter. Without any conscious intention on my part I had 'M-Mother' in a vertical diving turn to starboard. The Navigator shouted, 'Bombs gone!' But added that he didn't know where, and from the rear turret Junior led, 'Hell, Skipper. What are you doing?' 'You frightened the daylights out of the Jerry fighter'. 'You turned right across his bows'. It wasn't only the Jerry who was shaken.

"Back at base Junior got me on one side; he had been delegated by the others. 'Skip, you really must see Doc about your ears'. I did, and was grounded for further examination. To my surprise the news caused consternation in the crew. Squadron Leader Anthony W J Clark, just posted to the Squadron, took over 'B' Flight from Cooky, who was promoted, to Squadron Commander. Clark also took over 'M-Mother' and my crew for the time being and decided on a daylight training flight to get to know the aircraft and the boys. He had only been on the camp a few hours and could not have known 'M-Mother's' reputation. Being a senior officer and on such short acquaintance, my crew wouldn't have presumed to mention such a subject and I didn't say anything; what good could it have done?

"I watched 'M-Mother' climb away with mixed feelings on 17 May. It is not nice being grounded, even temporarily, and I had a guilty sense of having let my crew down. I wandered into the crew room, wondering what I should do until their return but hearing the commotion of the fire engine and the ambulance getting underway, I went outside to see what was up. Someone shouted across to me. 'Your aircraft has gone in. A Hurricane flew smack through her.' I jumped into my car and headed for the distant column of black oily smoke that marked the end of 'M-Mother'.

"Clark had been leading a box of four Wellingtons, and a Hurricane I of the Meteorological Flight (also based at Mildenhall) flown by Flying Officer I R MacDiarmid, DFC, had been carrying out fighter affiliation tactics when the incident occurred. MacDiarmid 'attacked' the leading Wellington, and severed the tail. The Hurricane lost its port wingtip and both aircraft fell near Soham. Although some parachutes were seen to leave the Wellington late, all seven men in the two aircraft were killed.

"'Happy' Hampton arrived on the scene: In the middle of the potato field I stumbled amongst the still smouldering remains of my aeroplane and friends until the station doctor walked me away. 'You shouldn't be here. You can't do any good.' It was, of course, bad for morale; my morale.

"One of the fire crew came up and told me that the tail and rear gun turret were in the next field, unburnt. My unspoken question was answered before I dare ask it. 'The rear gunner didn't have time to get out. They were only at 2,000 feet'. I walked over to a stretcher on, which was the only body they had recovered. From beneath army blankets protruded two beautifully polished boots. It was the last I was to see of Junior, the 'tail end captain' of 'M-Mother'. To the others around it might have seemed that I was staring morbidly at my dead friend but they didn't know I was trying to get the final message through to him and the intercom was worse than usual. 'You very nearly made it Junior - your commission has been approved'.

"I had a talk with Cooky, who laughed at me at first but once he realised I was dead serious he agreed to drop 'M-Mother' from the Squadron aircraft board and replace it with 'P-Peter'. I was posted away for training as a test pilot and lost touch with Bomber Command friends but I hope the trick worked. However, 'M-Mother' had looked after me. I felt she would - I had a good mother."

On the night of 14th July Sergeant Tony Gee brought 'N-Nuts' home to Mildenhall after being coned by searchlights at 8,000 feet over Bremen and fired on by accurate flak. Gee finally escaped but he was down to 2,000 feet. His Navigator/Bomb Aimer, The Right Honourable Terence Mansfield, who was flying his 11th operation, recalls: "No-one was wounded but as daylight came we found lots of it coming in everywhere. Our wireless was not working so we could not tell base that, although we were a long way behind schedule, we were still coming. By the time we got back to Mildenhall we were classified as overdue. Someone classified the damage to R1593 as not replaceable and 'N-Nuts' was taken away."

Charles Lofthouse DFC continues with his story:

"First, an explanation. Each year in May, those who served with Nos.149, 15 and 622 Squadrons at RAF Mildenhall during WW2, whether air or ground crew, gather at their old station, now an American Air Base, for the Annual General Meeting of the "Mildenhall Register". They attend a semi-formal dinner, and enjoy a general mingle with old friends.

"I last attended in 1995. In conversation with an ex-Air Gunner on Wellingtons in 1941, I mentioned that my Rear Gunner at the time was one Michael Strutt. This brought the reaction: 'Oh! He didn't do any flying, did he? He was never there, was he?'

"I remonstrated vigorously, and offered the view that anyone who had harboured such calumny over a period of 54 years without attempting to justify its validity should not be present at that particular gathering.

"It came to me that perhaps others were of similar thinking. Who, in fact, other than two French Canadians and myself would know of Michael's flying record in Bomber Command, 1941/42? Flying Log Books provide bald detail, but the official information is available in Squadron Records at the Public Record Office in London. I could add a personal touch, being present at the time. Michael spoke often of his baby son Joe, back in America. Joe would now be in his mid-fifties. Would he have any idea as to the nature of Michael's wartime effort? Should I attempt to trace him and acquaint him of his father's operational record?

"June 1941. Respective aircrew categories had completed training. Pilots, Navigators, Wireless Operators/Air Gunners, gathered at No.20 Operational Training Unit, Lossiemouth, to be introduced to the Wellington aircraft, and eventually to meet each other, following "crewing-up". I was to join with "Crew No.2", made up of Sgt Alan Austin, RAFVR, 2nd Pilot; Sgt Georges Langlais, RAAF, Navigator; Sgt Leo Langlois, RCAF, Front Gunner; and Sgt Michael Strutt, RCAF, Rear Gunner. We first flew together as a crew on 30th June, "Low level bombing exercise, photography and air firing". By 10th July, we had completed our conversion, proceeded on seven days leave and were posted, as a complete crew, to No.149 Squadron, at RAF Mildenhall, with effect from 17th July.

*Wellington navigator, Sgt Geoff Ising, RAAF.*

"Local flying and exercises followed, until on 2nd August, 1941, four of us, self, Alan Austin, Leo Langlois and Michael Strutt, were each crewed with an experienced crew, when the Squadron went to Hamburg. This was part of the "makee-learnee" process, and involved all "raw" new arrivals. The extracts from No.149 Squadron's Forms 540 and 541, included in this presentation, show every operation undertaken by Michael Strutt, from August 1941 to 8th June 1942 whilst with the Squadron.

"On 12th August 1941, we set off, as a crew, in 'H' Harry, to bomb Essen, in the Ruhr. An operational tour was recognised as thirty operations.

"I have some vivid recollections of incidents which are not recorded in Flying Log Books. An entry such as 'Operations Duisburg' (6th August 1941) does not properly do justice to being heavily coned in searchlights, taking violent evasive action, the air speed indicator unserviceable all the way home due to flak damage, and the hydraulics also found to be u/s on return. Karlsruhe, 16th September, when crossing the English coast on return, a two-letter flashing beacon reading passed to Geoff Ising, our Navigator, who deciphered it as Manston, when in fact, it was later established as Tangmere, and we ended up entreating the aid of "Darkie" (now "Mayday"), talked to Hullavington, or was it Lyneham, and landed at Colerne!

"The 28th September saw us detailed to attack Genoa. Over Southern France, beyond Dijon, we jettisoned one bomb, to assist obtaining height. As we did so, a general recall was received and we turned back for home (the original recall had been sent two hours before!). We were the last aircraft aloft. Fog and an official visibility of 60 yards was all over East Anglia. We were given diversion instructions, but I chose to overfly Marham, a large grass airfield where I was informed of the direction of landing, was able to line up on a compass heading over the Chance Light shining through the fog, completed a circuit of timed turns, and landed, much to everybody's surprise when they located us! Michael's first fag after the nearly seven-hour flight was the best he'd ever had, he said. An officer from HQ 3 Group visited me the following day to enquire if the Standard Blind Approach System performed satisfactorily. I told him I hadn't used it.

"I recount such tales as they served to cement the bonds of friendship and trust which builds up in crews. Michael Strutt was part of all this.

"On 30th September we set off for Hamburg. Coastlines and the Elbe normally gave adequate pinpointing, but cloud obscured and we dropped on a "DR" position, and turned for home. North of the Friesians, the starboard engine gave up the ghost, suddenly, when seizure was indicated by fire and sparks from the propeller hub. We shut down the engine but fireworks continued until, and I can still see it, the yellow disc outlined by the painted propeller tips flew forwards and gently drifted, still spinning, out to starboard, down and away. 7,000 ft with some height to play with, but ditching was a certainty, the Wellington not being renowned for its one-engine performance. The weather was clear. An SOS call, collecting together all the in flight rations, chocolate, Ovaltine tablets, biscuits, all prepared for the worst, but quietly confident. But we kept on flying, crossing the Norfolk coast some hour and a half later, at 1,500 ft, heading for Base, where we landed safely. It was suggested that had we not lost the propeller completely, we would have been forced to resort to the Dinghy! A feathered or spinning prop provided too much drag to guarantee prolonged flight.

"At this stage, almost half way through the tour, and with Mike Evans and his crew, similarly placed, we were detached to RAF Waterbeach, to convert to the four-engined Stirling aircraft. During this break, Michael went on a Gunnery Leaders' course, for which he had been recommended. It was December 11th before we operated again, but P/O Michael Strutt was on leave following his commissioning, effective 13th December 1941. He entered the Station Hospital on 2nd February 1942, until the 8th, and was not available for operations again until 3rd March".

In a letter home, on the 5th March Corporal Bradley, wrote to his wife recounting his journey back to camp, and gave news of the activities that the Squadron had been involved in:

"I arrived into my billet at 9.45 last night after a wet ride as you must have imagined, though the worst hardship was the driving snow and the weather becoming colder. The roads were not slippery as the snow melted. The motorbike ran very well, no trouble at all though the battery holding out even after having to use the main headlamp bulb all the way from Chelmsford, it being so dark. I know the road quite well now; I suppose I should for the number of trips I have made to Mildenhall. The snow settled during the night and the ground has been covered all day, about $^1\!/_2$ inch thick.

"The Squadron here dropped 60 tons of bombs on the Renault and other factories during Tuesday night all found their target and have been congratulated on putting up a good show. The change in the weather might delay us again for a time."

Pilot 'Greg' Gregory relates:

"I joined the Squadron in April 1941 from OTU at Lossiemouth, with a full crew, and having a total of 205 flying hours. At that time a crew from the Squadron were involved in making the film 'Target for Tonight'. The only member of the crew not from No.149, during the making of the film, was Wg.Cdr Percy Pickard (subsequently killed on the Mosquito raid on the prison at Amiens, France).

"The Station commander, at the time, was Gp.Capt. 'Joe' Fogarty, subsequently Air Chief Marshal, C in C Far East Air Force at the end of the war. Joe was married on the Station that summer.

"We had quite a bit of 'blue blood' in the Squadron, Sandy Mansfield, now The Lord Sandhurst, Honourable Bruce Grimston, and the Honourable Michael Strutt. Bruce was later lost in the war; Michael finished his tour, as a rear gunner, and was posted as ADC to the Duke of Kent. Regrettably, he was killed when the Duke and he crashed somewhere in Scotland, on a communications trip. 'Sandy', Lord Sandhurst is still flourishing in Jersey on the proceeds of his family's old-established wine merchants business (Hatch, Mansfield). When we first met some 50 years after the war we found that he had done two 'trips', with me after my own Navigator was wounded.

"My own crew were a first-rate bunch. I once had to clamp down on them over the Ruhr, one night, because they broke into song at midnight, to acknowledge my 21st birthday! It was also many years later that I found that my rear gunner, Sgt Becket by name, had made his fame as Kent Walton, the ITV all-in-one wrestling commentator!

"The tour covered targets at Brest, the Ruhr, Hamburg, Kiel and Berlin, as well as numerous others. Incidents are too numerous to mention, until most of our luck ran out on the 18th August when a night fighter got a couple of cannon shells into us, still with the bomb load aboard! Luckily, I was not hit, the second pilot standing on watch in the astrodome got the worst of it but the rear gunner and navigator were both injured, not fortunately all that badly. The rear gunner was dealing with a fire round and above his turret. The aircraft was manageable after I jettisoned the bombs and I turned south-westerly to get out of trouble. The engines were overheating and the trim tail was heavy but I thought we could cope for a bit. I had no wish to bale out over Germany! I told the front gunner to exit his turret and do what he could for Harold Reed the second pilot. He piled flying suits on to him and gave him doses of morphia. Billington, the rear gunner, got the fire under control, using his parachute to blanket the flames! We seemed to have stabilised matters a bit so; I turned northerly to home. We raised a little flak on the French coast but we made landfall on UK, and I decided to ease us back to Mildenhall. I made radio contact as we got close and called for an ambulance. It was broad daylight by then, as I was about two hours behind the other crews. In the circuit I checked the undercarriage and to my surprise they locked down. I did my usual smooth landing! But, we then swung hard left. No damage but the bugger has put a shot through the port tyre.

"Harold Reed recovered well after many operations and still carries bits of the shell inside him. Billington was later killed on another tour but I have not succeeded in locating any of the other crew. I completed 32 trips in all, flying with new crews to give them a bit of experience of the fireworks!

"I was posted to Central Flying School, the instructor's academy, and later in '43' to a Mosquito Squadron for another tour of 'Ops'. By the way, I received a DFC, immediate and Billington a DFM for the 'hairy' episode.

"Michael Strutt, my rear gunner's service record shows that he was first moved to the No.149 Squadron Conversion Flight, (10th July 1942), and on to RAF Hixon (20th July 1942), and on to 30 OTU, Hixon, as Gunnery Leader (30th July 1942). On 10th August 1942, he was moved to the Staff of the Inspector General, to take up the post of Personal Equerry to the Duke of Kent.

"Michael Strutt was a lovely chap, as all those who came to know him would avow. There was no side with the Honourable Michael Strutt. I am proud to have known him and to have been close. I do not take lightly this opportunity to enlarge on his operational involvement, conscious of the fact that I am perhaps the only person who can apply himself to such a task.

"He was buried at St. Winifred's Parish Church, Kingston on Soar, Nottinghamshire. The Strutt family had purchased the Kingston Estate in May 1796, and from 1845, they lived in Kingston Hall. Members of the family have continued the support of the Church since those times, as a number of memorials in the Church show. Ronald Strutt, 4th Baron Belper, and Michael's' elder brother, has also been involved.

"Michael enlisted in the RCAF on 13th May 1940, in Toronto, and underwent Initial Training as aircrew from 27th May. Then to No.3 Elementary Flying Training, London, Ontario, from 21st June, but eventually to No.1 Bombing and Gunnery School, Jarvis, from October to 21st December 1940, when he was awarded his Air Gunner's Badge. On 26th February 1941, he arrived at the Embarkation depot and 'Embarked-Dep-Elsewhere' on 8th April, arriving 'UK from Canada' on 2nd May.

"He rose from Aircraftman 2nd Class, 10th May 1940, through Leading Aircraftman to Temporary Sergeant (Paid) 21st December 1940, to Temporary Flight Sergeant, 1st November 1941, and to commission Rank, Pilot Officer, from 18th November 1941. It is likely that he carried increased acting rank from the date of his appointment as Personal Equerry to The Duke of Kent, but time factor precluded promulgation.

"Off duty, Michael ran a Ford 8 car whilst at Mildenhall and Lakenheath. He drove me to Kingsbury, London, NW9, on several occasions, on his way to London Town. He met all my family, including my most impressionable sister, Marion, all of 15 years of age at the time. On one occasion he was invited to leave his personal laundry, being hawked around in his car waiting for a convenient moment in his life. He went out to the car, pulled out a full pillowcase, and emptied it through our sitting room 'window' on the floor, and apologised for the mess. All silk!

"The 'blue blood' in No.149 Squadron's ranks, including 'Sandy' Mansfield, now the Lord Sandhurst, the Right Honourable Bruce Grimston, lost in action later, and the Honourable Michael Strutt could raise a few eyebrows when it came to the addresses given on leave passes, and give the impression that they were trying to take the 'mickey' out of the Squadron's administrative staff.

" 'Plum' Warner, our Squadron Adjutant, tackled me one day.

" 'What's with this Rear Gunner of yours? He puts Arundel Castle as his weekend leave address. Is this on?' I said, 'Of course. His sister is the Duchess of Norfolk, and lives there!'

"One weekend he invited me to accompany him to Manchester where he was to meet up with his mother, Lady Rosebery. We were to call, en route, at the Newmarket Stables of Jack Jarvis, trainer of Lord Rosebery's horses. It was here I was introduced to my first roast pigeon (two). We drove to Manchester, that evening, Jack Jarvis accompanying. Some dozen or more people sat down to dinner, at the Majestic Hotel (?), with Lady Rosebery presiding. I was partnered by a Lady Pamela, I seem to recall. The conversation throughout centred on horses, by horses, out of horses, and I was not equipped to participate. Brother Ronald, resplendent in the uniform of the Coldstream Guards, arrived later. I wasn't up in time to accompany the morning gallops party, but I moved around with others at the afternoon race meeting, placing modest bets and losing my money like most others. I walked some 50 yards with Lord Rosebery, having been introduced.

" 'So, you fly with young Michael, do you?' he enquired. 'Yes, Sir', I said. 'Hhrrummpphh', he said, with some conviction.

"I have a sneaking feeling that No 2 crew's posting from Lossiemouth to RAF Mildenhall was engineered by Michael and his contacts. If I'm wrong, please forgive. If I'm right, I thank my lucky stars."

Frank Cork, DFC, rear gunner, writing of his experiences with No.149 under the pseudonym Sgt Catt, recalls the discomfort and dangers facing crews who relaxed too early before touching down at base:

"It was the 17th of March 1941. Sergeant Catt was very tired and very cold. He was seated in the rear turret of a Wellington bomber, which was returning from a raid on Bremen. Dawn was just breaking, and as he looked out he could see that they were crossing the Yarmouth sands.

"About a mile to starboard was another Wellington returning and dead astern yet another. The Sergeant wondered whether these two aircraft had had the same target as his crew. His mind began to indulge his lonely pastime of thinking about his crew up front. He knew that the 2nd pilot would be flying the aircraft; all 4 feet 11 inches of him, and he would have some difficulty in handling the heavy plane. Sitting next to him would be the captain, all 6 feet 8 inches of him, a product of the aristocracy; Marshals and Cambridge. Sergeant Catt smiled to himself as he hummed the lewd words of a song, 'The young, the short and the tall, bless 'em all'.

"Not only was Sergeant Catt very tired, he was also very foolish. In anticipation of a quick getaway from the aircraft on landing approximately ten minutes time, he had put the guns on 'safe', switched off the reflector sight and locked his turret. His motto, 'first into debriefing, first out and first into breakfast'.

"Sergeant Catt collected his thoughts and looked outside. The sky was much lighter now. The Wellington on his left was still about the same distance away, but what was this? The one dead astern was nearer, much nearer.

"Alarm bells began to ring in his mind as he realised that it wasn't really like a Wellington at all. His recognition of the Junkers 88, and the stream of tracer bullets that shot past his head into the port tail plane was almost simultaneous.

"His pilot, seeing the tracer going past his ear shouted 'Shit' and put the nose hard down towards the sands. Sergeant Catt, with feet in the air was frantically trying to put his guns to 'fire', put on the sight and unlock the turret all at the same time. When he finally achieved this he found that the Junkers 88 had also made a mistake and, over confident, had followed them down to within a hundred yards. Sergeant Catt, thankful for a second chance, opened fire with a straight non-deflection shot and saw his bullets strike the Junkers which continued its dive and crash into the sands, killing its crew of four.

"On attempting to land back at base, they found a Wellington burning fiercely in the middle of the runway. Returning from the same Bremen raid, with flaps and undercarriage down for a normal landing, it had been shot out of the sky by the same Junkers 88 intruder and the all-Sergeant crew killed.

"The Junkers had very nearly notched up two – but not quite! The Wellington was diverted to Honington. As Sergeant Catt sat drinking his debriefing rum, he wondered just how long his luck would last.

"He also knew that never again would he . . . !"

*An example of the Combat Report Pro-Forma, utilised throughout the Second World War for 'Attacks' and 'Combats' reports by crews.*

*Stirling I 'OJ-B' was W7455 which served with No.149 Squadron from November 1941 to February 1942, when it was transferred to No.149 Conversion Flight until June 1942. This photograph was taken at Lakenheath in February 1942.* [Philip Jarrett collection]

# Chapter 7: No.149 Squadron's Stirling Story

For those who are new to the Stirling, one pilot once said that the best way to get used to the height of its cockpit above ground was to ride on the front seat on top of a double-decker bus. Towering as it did some 22 ft 9 ins above the tarmac, the view from the cockpit coupe was very different to that of a 'Wimpey' or a Hampden, and its ground-handling characteristics were equally unique. Viewed from the ground, perched on its tall undercarriage, the Stirlings great height was probably its most striking feature.

Of the eight heavy bomber types in service with the main combatant nations during the Second World War, the RAF's Stirling was unique in a number of vital aspects: it was the tallest at 22 ft 9 ins, the longest at 87 ft 3½ ins, and the slowest at a maximum speed of 260 mph; at 99 ft 1 ins it had the shortest wingspan, at 44,000 lbs the greatest empty weight, and the shortest range with a maximum payload, at 740 miles. Of the three British 'heavies' it was the only one to be designed from the outset to take four engines and the only one to have full dual control.

The Stirling was introduced into RAF squadron service in August 1940 and a total of 2,371 were eventually built and flown by the RAF. With the arrival of the Halifax and Lancaster in 1941-42 the Stirling quickly became the poor relation of the trio of heavies, principally for its lack-lustre performance. Lack-lustre it may have been in the eyes of the Halifax and Lancaster crews but, as the saying goes, 'Beauty is in the eye of the beholder', and to the majority of Stirling aircrews their machine was undisputedly the best.

Although 'officially' it was hard pushed to reach more than 13,000 feet with a full load, there are fully-documented instances of individual Stirlings bombing the target from heights of 18-19,000 feet with a 7,000-lb bomb-load; others are recorded as reaching more than 21,000 feet on unloaded test-climbs. Thanks to its solid construction the Stirling was able to absorb an amazing amount of damage and still make it home. Following a night fighter attack one badly damaged Special Duties Stirling, on fire and flying on one engine, made it home across the North Sea with wounded crew on board; at 13,000 feet over Berlin a Main Force Stirling was attacked by a Junkers Ju 88 and went into an uncontrollable power dive after its pilot was critically injured and slumped forward across the controls. It took the combined strength of the wireless operator and navigator to level the aircraft out at 1,500 feet, without it suffering any structural damage. With testimonials like these it comes as little surprise when former crews argue that with the Stirling it was a classic case of 'give a dog a bad name'.

At the zenith of the Stirling's operational career with Bomber Command in 1943, just twelve squadrons were equipped with Short Brothers' mighty bomber before unacceptably high losses forced its relegation to second-line duties. In its modified guise as a Mk IV, the Stirling fulfilled an important role as a paratroop transport and glider tug with No.38 Group until the War's end. At the close of its RAF flying career in July 1946, 641 Stirlings of all marks had been lost through a combination of enemy action and accidents, representing more than a quarter of the total Stirling production.

An inside view. The Stirling was a big aircraft from the outside but a very different story on the inside. There were two ways of entering the aircraft: a crew door at the back on the port side forward of the tail unit, and a hatch under the nose up at the front. The latter was rarely used because it required a very long ladder. With an aircrew man clutching his parachute, flying rations and flight bag or a flight engineer's toolbox, this combined weight made the ladder very unsteady and increased its tendency of sliding along the ground at the bottom. For the ground crew, however, it was a useful and convenient means of access to the aircraft when topping up different services onboard by pipeline, or for loading ammunition belts. The rear door, which opened inwards and to the right, required a small three-runged ladder in order to gain access, but it too was unstable if not a little springy.

With help from the ground crew, aircrew would arrive inside the fuselage standing on a small step just inside the door. Down the fuselage to the right was the Elsan chemical toilet and another short ladder giving access, by way of a short tunnel, to the rear turret. Climbing a short distance down from the step you landed on a narrow aluminium walkway about 4 ft wide. Turning to the left you continued for some 12 ft up the length of the fuselage where you were confronted by a 4-foot-high platform upon which flying kit could be deposited before scrambling up. This was actually the roof of the bomb bay, which continued for another 42 ft 7 ins forward.

Three strides further on and you came across a small fixed three-rung ladder in the centre of the fuselage, which gave access up into the mid-upper gun turret. After wriggling sideways-on around the turret mechanism and ladder - with full flying kit there was very little room to spare - you arrived in the space beneath the cabin roof escape hatch, also the home for ammunition storage boxes for the mid-upper turret. Passing through a small sliding door in the rear fuselage bulkhead you were confronted with the main gear.

Pushing your gear ahead of you, you clambered over the spar and into the centre section where the crew rest bed was located. The name 'rest bed' was something of a misnomer since nobody had the time to take a rest during the course of an operation! Its true purpose was to act as a bed for any crew member who was wounded and it took up a fair amount of space. The mattress itself was covered with a plastic-like material to prevent blood from soaking through and soiling it. Overhead were two racks of oxygen bottles, which were the main supply for the crew when flying above 10,000 feet. Fitted in the roof on either side were seven levers for turning on and off the petrol supply to the fourteen fuel tanks. For the aircrew who needed to operate these levers in an emergency if their flight engineer was incapacitated, many later remarked that it was a good thing the tank numbers were marked on the levers.

Opposite the bed was the position from where the main undercarriage could be raised or lowered manually in the event of an electrical failure. The shaft came through the fuselage at this point and the handle and other pieces needed for this operation were strapped beside it. Most flight engineers also kept their toolboxes tied securely to the floor in this area. The credit for access to this manual operation can be given to Sergeant Vesey, ground staff with No.149 Squadron, who fortuitously was on board a Stirling when the electrical drive shaft to one of the undercarriages sheared in flight. Taking the fire axe, he chopped through the fuselage leading to the wing area, and then manually lowered the undercarriage, calling for several hundred turns of the drive shaft. This resulted in a Mentioned in Despatches award for Sergeant Vesey, the fuselages of all Stirlings being marked in red as to where emergency entry could be made and, later, proper manual fittings installed.

Climbing over the front spar, you proceeded down a narrow gangway on the right hand side of the fuselage, passing the wireless operator's curtained-off cubby hole on the left and the flight engineer's seat and panel further on the right, just inside the heavy armour-plated doorway of the forward fuselage bulkhead. In the cockpit area that lay beyond - and where you could finally stand upright - could be found the navigator's seat and chart table on the left, curtained off as before.

At the very front were the two pilot's seats, positioned side-by-side on a raised platform, with a control column, wheel and rudder bar each. Between them was the throttle quadrant with throttle and constant speed controls, mixture levers, undercarriage selector, landing lamp adjuster, brake lever and a comprehensive instrument panel before them. The first pilot's seat on the left-hand side was fitted with a huge piece of downward-hinging armour plate to protect his head and back. In the roof of the cockpit canopy were the main petrol cocks, slow-running cut-offs, tail trimming and rudder trimming cranks. In the vee of the windscreen were the flap operation switch and indicator.

A hinged step in the centre-floor behind and below the pilot's platform gave access down two steps and forward into the bomb-aimer's compartment, where he lay prone on his stomach when sighting the target through the Perspex clear vision panel in the floor of the nose. Access could also be gained from here into the front gun turret situated in the extremity of the nose, above the bomb-aimer's position.

As with all RAF aircraft, modifications to the airframe were continually being issued and Peter Russell, airframe fitter, recalls having to do these as well as regular maintenance and repair work. One worth mentioning was to blank off the three small circular Perspex 'windows' which enabled one to look into the bomb bay from inside the aircraft. Later, on a visit to the Austin factory at Longbridge, Peter saw Stirlings being manufactured, which included the Perspex 'windows' he was blanking off in Squadron service. Communication between the services and industry was obviously slow.

Manually winching bombs from the mainplane of a Stirling, as John Freeman, an armourer (guns) reports, was done 22 feet from the ground and was a hard job, on occasions the bomb load being changed up to three times before the actual take-off. Whether you were 'guns' or 'bombs' all armourers had to take a hand when it came time to bomb up. The shortage of armourers, as reported by Bomber Harris himself, also the shortage of radar mechanics, plagued Bomber Command throughout the war.

It seemed fairly clear that the War Cabinet weren't too happy with Air Marshal Sir Richard Pierse's leadership of Bomber Command in that on 8th January, he was posted to India. A new more aggressive leader was needed. However, until then, Air Vice Marshal J E A Baldwin, Air Officer Commanding No.3 Group, was put in charge.

1942 began for No.149 Squadron by being ordered to raise a Conversion Flight at Lakenheath, under Squadron Leader Speare, consisting of two Stirlings and two reserves for crew training, reducing the Squadron strength to 14 aircraft. The main preoccupation for Bomber Command, which naturally included No.149 Squadron at this time, was preparation for the planned bomber offensive. However operations still continued throughout the preparation period for No.149, with a detachment of Stirlings operating from Lakenheath.

When it was understood that the *Scharnhorst* and *Gneisenau* could be leaving Brest and heading for the Atlantic, 'Operation Fuller' was put into action on 6th January, when 154 aircraft, No.149 Squadron included, were sent to attack both the warships and the docks at Brest. The raid was scheduled for dusk, but the aircraft didn't become airborne until 11.00 pm. Two crews from No.149 Squadron reported that they saw no enemy shipping. A heavy smoke screen was put up, and so the results of the bombing were unknown, calling for further raids on Brest for the following four nights, damage being received by the *Gneisenau* on the 6th. Four Stirlings of No.149 Squadron accompanied the raid to Brest on the 9th/10th, leaving at 4.15 am. Two were hit by flak, one returning to base with a holed, empty fuel tank, while another, with a seriously wounded rear gunner, landed away at Weston Zoyland in Somerset.

Raids to Brest continued, as described by Sergeant Jim Coman, the Wireless Operator with Flying Officer Evans' crew, in Stirling OJ-F, N3862:

"11th January 1942. Air tested aircraft at 1145 hours. Everything OK. Briefing at 1400 hours. Weather could be foggy on return. Took off at 1700 hours in misty conditions, en route to Brest, climbing to 17,000 feet. Approaching the target area we noted the normal pyrotechnic display of low and high flak, with plenty of 'flaming onions'. Bombing run was made at 17,000 feet. Some bursts were seen on target although the visibility was poor due to cloud cover and smoke. A photographic run was made and we turned for home having received quite a few minor flak holes. On one of the half-hourly transmissions from base, the Squadron was diverted to Boscombe Down, and we landed after 3+ hours flying time. We returned to base the following afternoon. On our return we were told we were on 24-hour standby as one of our photographs showed the bows of the *Prinz Eugen* crossing the head of one of the piers in the harbour. Our Observer (Sergeant Felstead) had noted in his logbook that he had thought it to be the *Scharnhorst* tied to the jetty. Apparently it was thought that the movement of the warships out of Brest was imminent. During the period until 12th February 1942.... two more trips to Brest, one on 31st January and the other on 6th February. In each case no movements were observed."

The first Stirling loss in 1942 was on 16th January, when W7461, 'OJ-N' piloted by Flying Officer W G Barnes suffered engine failure following battle damage during a raid on Hamburg. On returning to England, the pilot gave orders to the crew to bale out, and then force-landed the aircraft at Toderick Bar, one mile south-west of Anston, in Yorkshire. Despite the Conversion Flight's Stirlings being assigned to the training role, the aircraft were still used on operations, and this state of affairs continued until October. One of them, however, quickly came to an untimely end, highlighting the major weakness of the Stirling, which was its undercarriage. Tall and gangly, to give the wings the necessary angle of incidence for take-off, accident after accident occurred when the undercarriage buckled and collapsed. So it was with Stirling W7458, with Flight Lieutenant M R Evans at the controls, the sun reflecting on the wet runway resulting in a heavy landing following a training mission, when the undercarriage collapsed, the first of many such losses for No.149.

Word had been received that the German battleship *Tirpitz* was moored at Aasfjord, near Trondheim in Norway. This, coupled with major activity observed at Brest seemed to indicate that the *Tirpitz* was about to sail, putting into operation Bomber Command's planned attack on the *Tirpitz* known as 'Operation Oiled'. This called for eight Stirlings of No.15 Squadron and four Stirlings from No.149 Squadron, the No.149 Squadron Stirlings being accompanied by two Harrow transports from Doncaster carrying the necessary ground crew with their equipment. Ten Halifaxes joined Nos.15 and No.149 at Lossiemouth, and from there they would attack the *Tirpitz* on the first suitable night, using 2,000-lb armour-piercing bombs together with 500-pounders.

On 29th January seven Stirlings and nine Halifaxes took off in search of the *Tirpitz*. The visibility was very poor and the battleship was well camouflaged, resulting in none of the aircraft finding the target. Two of the aircraft attacked enemy shipping seen in the area as targets of opportunity. On return, Stirling W6462 'OJ-T', pilot Flight Lieutenant R W A Turtle skidded on the ice on the Lossiemouth runway, overshooting and landing in a ditch.

Eventually, the No.149 Stirlings together with their Harrow support returned to Suffolk, but instead of the aircraft landing at Mildenhall, they landed instead at the neighbouring Lakenheath airfield, which up till now had been the location only of No.149 Squadron's detachment to be told this would soon be the Squadron's new home.

Another of the Conversion Flight's Stirlings was lost in February in the same manner as the first in January. On 11th February the starboard knee joint of W7457's undercarriage collapsed on landing from a training mission, the aircraft being written off.

The War in the Atlantic had already dictated that everything possible should be done to keep the German warships bottled up at harbour. On 12th February word was received that the German battle fleet, consisting of the *Scharnhorst*, *Gneisenau* and the *Prinz Eugen* with a strong destroyer escort and huge fighter cover, had sailed from Brest up the Channel to home ports in Germany, known as 'Operation Cerberus', a lone Spitfire having spotted them off Le Touquet late that morning. Aircraft of all Commands plus Fleet Air Arm aircraft were ordered to attack. Regrettably all of Bomber Command but No.5 Group had been 'stood down' and so bringing the Command up to readiness for an attack took several hours. The eventual attacking force of 252 aircraft of all types was the largest Bomber Command daylight operation to date and included two No.149 bombed-up Stirlings, all of whom attempted to find the

*Flg Officer Al Watts RCAF and his crew of 'H-Harry' (W7457), 6th December 1941.*

German fleet, but with the Channel covered in thick cloud with driving rain and with visibility less than 2,000 yards, most failed.

Sergeant Jim Coman, wireless operator, continues his story:

"12th February 1942. After breakfast we reported to the Flight Office at Lakenheath and air tested 'OJ-G', Stirling I, N6102. We landed and went straight to briefing where we were informed of the 'Channel Dash', and the loss of aircraft from the Fleet Air Arm. The aircraft was armed and bombed up with eighteen 500-lb AP bombs and we were put on standby, together with two other aircraft. After a few false alarms we took off at 1645 hours. Crossing the coast at about 9,000 feet, we headed for the target area, using 'Gee' navigational aid, still climbing to get above the cloud, which was 9/10ths. Reaching the area we searched for a break in the clouds, dropping to 8,000 feet, which was the lowest recommended height for bombing, to get maximum penetration. After searching for some time we couldn't get a sighting through the clouds and returned to base at 2020 hours; as we touched down, with the bombs still aboard, our port undercarriage collapsed, the wing hit the ground, spinning us round, and breaking across No.2 wing tank. A quick exit was made from the aircraft, as the port inner engine was sizzling in the spilt fuel. However, there was no resulting fire and we returned to the aircraft to recover our equipment. The three aircraft from No.149 Squadron and three from No.419 Squadron (Wellington Mk III) from Mildenhall went on this trip, but two Canadian Wellingtons were lost."

Those who bombed missed. The *Scharnhorst* and *Gneisenau* were however, slowed down by damage from mines laid by No.5 Group ahead of the fleet, in the Friesian Islands area, earlier. The German fleet made safe German ports by nightfall. Now that the capital ships were no longer holed up at Brest, Bomber Command could redirect its attentions elsewhere. Unknown to the Allies, both the *Scharnhorst* and the *Gneisenau* had been badly damaged by the bombing at Brest and were being moved by Germany for their own protection.

The Fleet Air Arm had proposed a strike on the *Prinz Eugen* from the carrier *Victorious*, the German vessel now being holed up in a Norwegian fjord near Trondheim following a torpedo strike from the submarine *Trident*. A diversionary raid was requested and obtained that Bomber Command would attack the *Luftwaffe* airfields in Norway. A mixed bag of fifteen aircraft, Halifaxes, Manchesters and Stirlings attacked for airfields, Jim Coman again picking up the story:

"On 21st February 1942 three Stirlings from the Squadron, our aircraft, Stirling OJ-D, R9296, being one of them, were briefed to attack the fighter airfield at Lister, Norway, where fighter cover was being given to the German flotilla. Take-off was 0400 hours in severe icing conditions. We climbed in cloud with ice breaking off the wings etc. and striking parts of the fuselage, making a lot of bangs. The gunners kept their turrets moving to stop them icing up. The bomb load was eighteen 500-lb AP bombs, as we were informed that our target, Lister, had one runway, which had been laid using a loose rock foundation and the AP's penetration would create the most damage. We eventually broke through the cloud at dawn, over the Norwegian coast, just north of the target. The navigation by 'Dead Reckoning' and using 'Gee', also radio beacons, was very good.

"Turning south we headed to the airfield at 18,000 feet and decided to drop the bombs in one 'stick' down the runway. The rear and mid-upper gunners saw the bursts right down the centre of the target and as it was a fighter drome the Skipper immediately turned onto a heading to bring us to The Wash, dropped the nose slightly and increased engine revs. We broke cloud over The Wash at 1,000 feet with, as usual, the 'IFF' (Identification, Friend or Foe) turned on. On landing back at Lakenheath, at 0945 hours, we were informed that we were the only aircraft that actually went, as one did not take off due to an engine malfunction and the other had turned back when all the turrets had iced up. As there had been strict radio silence we had not been told. During the debriefing, it was thought that although we could describe the target so well, it was impossible for a Stirling to have been to Norway and return in the time. Not until a Photographic Reconnaissance Unit Mosquito returned from Lister with the photographs of the target, showing the devastation caused to the runway, were we believed."

The 22nd of February brought with it a profound change for Bomber Command, that of the appointment of Air Marshal Arthur 'Butch' Harris as Air Officer Commanding-in-Chief of Bomber Command, who was recalled from his role as head of the RAF delegation to Washington to take up his new position. Prior to that he had been the Air Officer Commanding No.5 Group. His change in tactics in carrying the bombing war to the enemy would soon earn him the nickname throughout the Royal Air Force, and history, as 'Bomber' Harris.

March brought with it a further role for the aircraft of No.3 Group, that of minelaying. Minelaying was known as 'Gardening' and each of the dropping zones was given the code name of a 'vegetable' or 'flower'. Dropping sea mines called for both low-level flying and precise navigation in a limited area, to drop the mines at very specific locations. This often meant a possible descent through low cloud with the risk of crashing into the sea. Strategically placed flak ships were invariably in the area and the dropping zones were near enough to the enemy coast to invite *Luftwaffe* fighters, alerted to the presence of mine-laying aircraft by ground radar. Yet Bomber Command only awarded aircrew members one-third of a mission towards their tour on such risky endeavours, because 'it wasn't over enemy territory'. Much like the thinking of 'no parachutes for air crew' in World War I. Mines had been shipped to Oakington for distribution early in 1941, but minelaying by the heavy bombers had been delayed, concentrating their efforts instead on bombing the Reich. No.3 Group records at the time showed that it had acquired 'packets of seeds, implements, and a catalogue'. On 3rd March three crews from No.15 Squadron dropped the first 'sowing' for No.3 Group with two more crews repeating the process the following night. As sea mines fell under the province of the Royal Navy, it was now not uncommon to find sailors and petty officers working as part of the bomb armourer ground staff on many a Bomber Command airfield

On 3rd March, ten Stirlings of No.149 Squadron as part of a 235-bomber raid, including 29 Stirlings, attacking the Renault truck manufacturing works at Boulogne-Billancourt, just off from the centre of Paris. The gasometer exploded, and the tyre manufacturing plant, the truck assembly shops and power plant were hit, causing 40% destruction of the plant. This was the trial of a new 'saturation' technique, with a maximum concentration of aircraft over the target in the shortest possible time, dislocating the anti-aircraft defences and the fire and rescue organisations. Luckily there were no air-to-air collisions, which would occur with regularity in future saturation bombing operations. Congratulations were received by all of the squadrons on the operation from the AOC, Air Marshal Arthur Harris.

Once again, a training mission accounted for another loss for No.149 Squadron, this one on 9th March. When Stirling W7452 'OJ-A' titled 'East India IV' piloted by Sergeant A Austin landed at Ayr as part of its cross-country exercise, it was 'ground-looped' to avoid running through a fence, resulting in one undercarriage leg collapsing. On that same night, No.149 paid a No.3 Group bombing visit to Essen, the aircraft carrying bombs, while those accompanying aircraft of Nos.7 and 218 Squadrons carried incendiaries.

The following raid to Essen on 10th/11th March resulted in the loss of two of No.149's Stirlings, N6126, 'OJ-U' piloted by Pilot Officer L W Bailey of the RAAF, being shot down and crashing near Kleve, in Germany, with seven of the crew killed, one being taken prisoner. Stirling R9295, 'OJ-G East India III' with Flying Officer C L Pilkington at the controls was damaged by enemy action. Unable to lower the undercarriage due to battle damage, he was forced to make a belly-landing on return. Unfortunately he overshot and hit the trees at Hollywell Row in Mildenhall resulting in seven of the crew being killed and one injured. Two Lancasters took part in this raid, this being their first attack on a German target.

Undercarriage problems followed by belly-landings plagued any Stirling squadron, not only following operations, as reported by Colin Maverick, an Instrument Repairer, then LAC:

"One of my duties was to air test the auto-pilot on the Wellingtons and then the Stirlings of No.149 Squadron. On the last Sunday afternoon of March 1942, flying 'OJ-O' on a five-hour acceptance test flight with Flt Lt Evans as Captain, we were on landing approach at Mildenhall. It was found that the starboard undercarriage would not come down, despite the efforts of the Flight Engineer and a Sgt Fitter, using the emergency winding handle. Except for the Flight Engineer, Flt Lt Evans then offered the rest of us the chance to 'bale out', but we all refused. The Flight Engineer then 'jettisoned' 400 gallons! As we were about to 'touch down', Flt Lt Evans cut the two inner engines, and made a successful 'belly landing."

The 24th of March began No.149's mine-laying career, when three Stirlings laid mines off the French coast near Groix. It began with four mines per aircraft but as time passed the number of mines carried was increased. Minelaying would prove to be one of No.149 Squadron's outstanding achievements in World War II. The 28th/29th of March brought an attack on the port of Lübeck by No.149, with the submarine assembly shops as one target, this being in support of the 'Battle of the Atlantic', and the stockpile of stores intended for the German campaign on the Russian front being the other. Many fires were seen.

April brought with it a permanent official move by No.149 Squadron from Mildenhall to Lakenheath. It also brought the regular task of laying mines, chiefly around the Friesian Islands.

Essen was again the cause of the write-off of one of No.149's Stirlings on the night of 7th April when N3726 'OJ-G' was attacked and damaged by a Messerschmitt Bf 110 night fighter as they reached the coast of Europe on return. The second pilot on board, on his first operation, was the very popular Australian, Sergeant Rawdon 'Ron' Middleton. It is best described in Jim Conan, the Wireless operator's, own words:

"After the bombing run and turning for home, Canadian 'Happy' Hanson, the rear gunner, shouted to the pilot, Flight Lieutenant Mike Evans to take evasive action, 'Fighter under tail - go port. Corkscrews'. Evasion was immediately taken and both 'Happy' and Australian Aub Mace, in the mid-upper turret opened fire. We took a hit in the port wing near the inner engine, just as 'Happy' shouted, 'We got him, Aub!' Another Me 110 less. It wasn't claimed as a definite kill as we lost sight of it. It dived through the clouds trailing smoke. We were more concerned about our damage as we were losing lots of fuel. 'Smithy' our flight engineer closed cocks and opened others to minimise loss (400 gallons). The rest of the flight to base was uneventful but we weren't sure of any damage to our port undercarriage. We let down the undercarriage, and it locked OK. 'Smithy' and I examined it from the 'window' using torches but no damage could be seen. Still being unsure we made our approach and landing, port wing high, and all was well until we lost speed and the wing dropped, then the undercarriage disintegrated. The wing touched the ground and swung us round, everything was switched off and we evacuated the aircraft to examine the damage. Quite a start for Ron, but taken in his stride."

It is worthwhile continuing with Jim's narrative:

"The next operation was to Dortmund on the 14th of April in 'OJ-B', W7510. Besides being coned over the target and taking a bit of flak damage we didn't sustain anything serious. After landing, Ron (Middleton) commented to Eddie (Felstead) that if the two trips were a sample of what was normal, he didn't think he'd make his 30th."

Four more losses were to take place before the month's end, two being because of a collapsed undercarriage, R9307, with Pilot Officer A F Cheetam as pilot, swinging on take-off for a raid on Le Havre on the 22nd, and on the following day, N3719 'OJ-S', pilot Flight Sergeant G H R Woodhouse, swinging on rough ground after returning from a raid on Cologne. April was a busy month for No.149, with targets including Hamburg, Cologne, Rostock, Le Havre, Dortmund, Dunkirk and Kiel. The defences at Kiel were particularly heavy, one pilot reporting that it "made the Ruhr defence seem 'pansy' ". The other two losses by No.149 Squadron in April were by enemy action, N6068 'OJ-T', the pilot being Pilot Officer M L Field being shot down while on the raid to Dortmund on 16th April, crashing at Steene in Belgium with the loss of all of his crew. No.149 Squadron took part in three out of four of the consecutive raids to the Baltic port of Rostock, including the Heinkel aircraft factory there, from the 24th to the 27th. It was on 27th April raid that W7512 'OJ-A', with Pilot Officer J H Thomson RCAF as pilot, was shot down, crashing at Schönhagen in Germany, again with the loss of all of the crew.

In late April, Bomber Command sent representatives to each squadron in the Command to collect data on that squadron's readiness. The serviceability record reported for No.149 Squadron at that time was 50% serviceable, with 95% of the normal servicing personnel strength, added to which was the complaint of 'frequent personnel posting'. Other complaints were that the guards on the engine air intakes were breaking up and that the hydraulics on the turrets were 'troublesome', as were the undercarriage 'Up' locks. The fuel contents gauges on the Stirlings were inaccurate, added to which there were problems with the 'Extractor' throttle, flak damage repair was not readily available, engine ignition leads were burning out and there were primary pipe fractures. Enough to keep the engineers at 'Shorts' busy for some time correcting the shortcomings. On one Stirling, the turret refused to rotate during violent manoeuvres. Rumour-mongers highlighted this as being a general complaint and it even went as far as blaming it for the Lancaster losses on the Augsburg raid, claiming that the FN 20 turret was faulty.

Life at ground level for the ground crews was testing and the conditions under which they worked could be extreme. The hours were long, and the frustrations of keeping such a large and complex aircraft serviceable are recalled by one of the ground crew of No.149:

"In order to keep the aircraft fully serviceable and to enable the Squadron to mount a maximum effort raid if called upon to do so, there were a number of other crucial tasks that had to be performed by the ground crews. Some were messy and others uncomfortable, while a few were looked upon as being downright dangerous.

"An engine could often develop an oil leak and, assisted by the slipstream, the oil would spread over a very large area behind the engine. If during a raid the aircraft was caught in a searchlight beam it would shine like a mirror and this was not appreciated by the aircrew. It was an unpleasant job having to wash the oil from under the wing, which meant lying on your back on a trestle with a bucket full of petrol and plenty of rags. You can imagine how wet it became with the petrol running up your arms while 100-octane petrol itself would leave a white deposit on your skin and sting like fury. The aircrew would sometimes help by filling your buckets for you!

"During the winter when ice and snow were around, the unpleasant task of de-icing the wings would have to be carried out. This involved sitting on the wing with a rope tied around one's waist, wearing waterproof overalls (which did not remain waterproof for long). A de-icing fluid was sprayed on to the wing, which was only effective for about four hours and sometimes the aircraft would need to be sprayed twice before take-off. The leading edge was covered with a brown putty-like substance called 'Kilfrost' de-icing paste. Over a period of time it gradually became thin and it seemed that all one's spare time was needed to replace this paste.

*'OJ-O' (N3752) flew into the ground, believed due to a faulty altimeter setting, at Risegaards Mark, 30 miles north of Flensburg after laying mines off the Friesians on 16th May 1942.* [J Helme]

"The Stirling had seven petrol tanks in each wing, some of which were near to the trailing edge. To fill them one had to lie on the wing because it was too steep an angle to stand up. During the winter, with the frost and ice, one tied a rope round one's waist and anchored the other end to the undercarriage. This helped to stop you from falling down over the edge, a long way to drop!

"One did not always have to fill a tank right up since the amount required was measured by a gauge and a dipstick. However, a gauge could sometimes develop a fault but the dipstick never did. The individual amount of fuel was recorded on the aircraft's Form 700 - the aircraft's 'Bible'. Everything that was done to an aircraft was recorded and signed for in this book. The Stirling's fuel system was very good and all four engines could run from any tank in either wing. In the event of a tank being holed, the remaining petrol in the tank could be pumped into the others. The horizontal level would have been lost but this could be corrected by moving petrol from one tank to another.

"Lack of proper maintenance equipment often caused a lot of trouble with servicing. The oleo legs on the undercarriage needed daily attention and consisted of two metal sleeves, one contained within the other, filled with a mixture of very thin oil and air. Under pressure this caused a spring-like action which helped the undercarriage to soak up the bumps on landing. The rocking of the aircraft during the course of a day or night caused the legs to creep and sink so they needed to be topped up each day by the airframe fitter to bring them back to their normal height.

"Two cylinders were left on the ground at the edge of the dispersal pan. One filled with compressed air, the other with oxygen. The air was used for topping up the oleo legs on the undercarriage, the oxygen for replenishing the small mobile oxygen bottles at various positions in the aircraft, used by the crew when moving around inside in flight. Having no trolleys to move them they were pushed across the ground by your feet and before long they were covered in mud. In such conditions it was difficult to see what the colour-code bands were (compressed air-yellow, oxygen-white/blue) which identified the contents of the cylinder. The danger arose when, instead of compressed air, an oxygen cylinder was connected to an oleo leg to top it up: oil and oxygen together create a dangerous explosive mixture."

The Stirling losses in April were a portent of the future for No.149 with Stirlings, typically losing an average of well over one a week until the Squadron eventually converted to Lancasters in 1944. With lower speed and at low altitude the Stirling made a fine target for both fighter and anti-aircraft guns alike.

May brought with it a new Commanding Officer for No.149 Squadron, Wing Commander C Charlton-Jones. He was not to command very long, being lost in action only four months later. Minelaying activities continued, and extended to the Baltic Sea.

Back-to-back raids to Stuttgart accounted for one No.149 loss on each raid, N6124 'OJ-R' with Pilot Officer A F Cheetham as pilot was lost on 5th May, crashing at Agiulcourt, France, all of the crew being killed, while DJ792 'OJ-T' was attacked and damaged by a night fighter on 6th May. The pilot, Flying Officer M A Brogan, brought the aircraft back to base, but it swung on landing and the undercarriage collapsed.

The 18th of May was a disastrous day for No.149 Squadron. A major No.3 Group mining operation was planned for 18th May, involving 32 Stirlings and 28 Wellingtons, the dropping zones being off Heligoland and in the Friesian Islands. Points off Denmark known as the 'Daffodils' area had been chosen for No.149. Five Stirlings and two Wellingtons were lost, three of the Stirlings being from No.149. N3752 'OJ-O', with Sergeant J A Jerman as pilot was shot down off Copenhagen in the Baltic, crashing at Risegaard, near Aabenraa in Denmark, all of the crew being taken prisoner. Sergeant Lauriston in this crew exchanged identities while in prison camp with Private W Moffatt, of the Border Regiment, no doubt in the hope of future escape. R9320 'OJ-S', piloted by Flight Sergeant G H R Woodhouse, was shot down by anti-aircraft fire off Copenhagen, crashing in Femer Bælt, off Lolland, Denmark. Two of the crew were killed. A Danish fishing boat picked up the remainder, but reluctantly had to hand them over to the German authorities; they then became prisoners. The crew of R9310 'OJ-P', piloted by Pilot Officer A J Frost were not so fortunate. They were also shot down off Copenhagen, crashing in the Great Belt, near the Asnæs Peninsula in Denmark, all of the crew being killed.

While 'history' makes it appear that the decision for the saturation bombing of German cities was 'Bomber' Harris' idea, it was actually decided by the Air Ministry and with the Prime Minister's blessing, several days prior to Harris taking command. His directive from Sir Charles Portal, Chief of the Air Staff, was to carry out their orders and plan a strategy of night area bombing on German cities. Such bombing to the limit of the available technical capability at the time was not new. It had been the campaign of the German Condor Legion in the Spanish Civil War, it had been the Japanese strategy on cities in China and had World War I not ended when it did, Berlin was to be the target of Royal Air Force bombers. Indeed, it was the *Luftwaffe* who showed its power and effectiveness in bombing Warsaw in 1939, and in their bombing of Britain following. It was now Harris' task to determine the most effective way of achieving the objectives he had been set.

The 30th/31st of May was to be a landmark in Bomber Command history. While thundery conditions persisted over Germany, the weather over the Rhineland, and bomber airfields in Britain, looked good and would remain so throughout the night. This was the night that 'Bomber Harris' could begin his 'Operation Millennium', that of putting 1,000 bombers over a single target. Both by weather and by location, the city being easily identified from the air, Cologne was chosen as the target. The attack would be by 1,046 aircraft, 338 of them being heavy bombers, including the new Avro Manchester, and 80 Stirlings from the five Stirling squadrons. The remainder would be made up of Wellingtons, with a few Whitleys and Hampdens to make up the number. The attack would be in three waves, each 15 minutes apart, and the aiming point was to be the city centre. As aircraft from Nos.1 and 3 Groups were by this time fitted with the new navigation aid, 'Gee', they would be in the first wave, and act as target markers. The second wave would be aircraft from the Operational Training Units, with instructors at the controls and trainee crews, needed to make up Harris's magic number of 1,000 aircraft, while the third wave would be Nos.4 and 5 Groups. The mixed bomb loads included the new explosive incendiaries. The Stirling bomb loads would be two-thirds incendiary bombs. Eleven No.149 Stirlings accompanied the raid with no losses, although No.149's Stirlings were plagued by engine troubles, N6079 and N6080 being forced to return early for this reason. One of the No.149 Stirlings shot down a Messerschmitt

Bf 110 over Mönchen-Gladbach on the way. N6083 is known to have jettisoned its bombs near Tilburg, while R9296 went into a spiral dive following a climb and was forced to jettison its bombs to pull out of the dive. In all, 103,680 lbs of bombs were dropped, and the resulting damage to Cologne could only be described as 'devastating' with thousands of fires and many more thousands of buildings destroyed or damaged with considerable loss of life. Forty aircraft were lost, including two Stirlings, and 116 aircraft were damaged, twelve of which being so badly damaged that they had to be written off.

Mining continued as a key operation for No.149 Squadron for the following months, usually in the Baltic Sea, the intended targets being the ore-laden shipping plying from Norway to Germany and the entrances to the U-boat harbours. The shipping channels off the French and Dutch coasts were also part of the 'Gardening' operations. German industry and communications systems, particularly in the Ruhr area, would also be part of No.149's objectives, as would the German shipping, both warships and merchantmen, in the North German and Atlantic ports. Leaflets would be carried on the majority of operations over enemy territory.

Essen became the next target of choice in 'Operation Millennium', being attacked on 1st June by 956 aircraft, including fifteen from No.149 Squadron. One aircraft developed the prevalent engine trouble and had to return, but the other fourteen dropped incendiaries.

Essen received four more bombing attacks in June and it was the 5th/6th of June raid that proved to be just as disastrous as 18th May with again three of the eight No.149 Stirlings sent to Essen being lost on the same operation. Two of the aircraft were shot down by night fighters, R9321 'OJ-R' with pilot Squadron Leader R B Harris, crashing at Duisburg, Germany, all of the crew being killed, while W7508 'OJ-D' with Pilot Officer P L Clayton at the controls crashed in Brabant, Belgium. Six of the crew were killed, one was taken prisoner, while Sergeant Golsmith evaded capture.

The third aircraft, R9314 'OJ-T' was also brought down by an enemy fighter, but unconventionally. A Messerschmitt Bf 110 attacked the Stirling on its way home and collided with it, cutting off the rear turret and killing the rear gunner. The pilot, Flight Sergeant E W Whitney ditched the Stirling into the sea near the Belgian coast, where the crew were lucky enough to be picked up by an Air-Sea Rescue launch from Ramsgate.

Three days later, Essen claimed another of No.149's Stirlings when, on 8th/9th June, N6084 'OJ-C' with Flight Sergeant H L Davis as pilot was shot down, crashing at Gelsenkirchen-Hasel in Germany, killing all of the crew.

Perhaps No.149 Squadron was showing signs of needing a morale booster in that on 12th June, King George VI together with Queen Elizabeth once again visited the Squadron and talked to the crew and ground staff. The 17th of June brought another raid to Essen, N6080 'OJ-G' receiving battle damage and crashing on return. It was repaired and brought up to flying condition again, but perhaps not up to fighting standard in that it was sent on to No.1657 Heavy Conversion Unit.

The 18th of June brought a combined mining/bombing operation, two Stirlings being sent out with both mines and bombs. N6083, 'OJ-H' with Pilot Officer E P Wynn reported that he dropped the mines as ordered but brought the bombs back, while N9163, 'OJ-A' with Pilot Officer J M Forward at the controls reported that he was unable to recognise any specific island, so dropped his bombs on an island and brought his mines back. Only one Stirling was sent out that same night on the raid to Emden, with Flight Sergeant R Hockley as pilot. He reported that, because of poor visibility, he dropped his bombs by a 'TR' fix. Fires in the target area were seen. Then collapsing undercarriages claimed one more of No.149's Stirlings on 21st June when N6122, carrying the name 'East India II' from No.149 Squadron Conversion Flight, swung on landing.

*Returning from a raid on Mainz on the night of 12th/13th August 1942, Stirling 'OJ-A' (BF325), piloted by Sqn Ldr G A Watt, was attacked by a Messerschmitt Bf 110 while flying over the Ardennes. It crashed into a house in Rumfields Road, Broadstairs, Kent, on return. It was recovered, repaired and transferred to a Conversion Unit.*

Bremen and Emden were the other two key cities chosen for multiple attacks in June, each receiving four. It was on the 29th/30th June raid to Bremen that another triple loss was to befall No.149, two aircraft being shot down by night fighters, BF310 'OJ-H' with Pilot Officer C W Simmons RCAF and crew being shot down by a night fighter from II/NJG2, crashing into the IJsselmeer in Holland, all of the crew being killed, while N6082, 'OJ-Q' with Flight Lieutenant W Barnes DFC, as pilot, and Wing Commander Alexander as co-pilot, also crashed in the IJsselmeer, near Wons in Holland, seven of the crew being killed and the mid-upper gunner, Warrant Officer Len Collins, RAAF, being taken prisoner. While this was Wing Commander Alexander's first mission, it was the rest of the crew's 30th, apart from Len Collins, who had completed his tour, having already flown 32 missions, but volunteered to take the place of a sick air gunner. The third loss, R9330, 'OJ-O' with Flight Sergeant R Hockley as pilot had a failure in the starboard outer engine on take-off. The aircraft 'ground looped' followed by the inevitable undercarriage collapse.

The next intended '1,000-bomber raid' was scheduled for 25th June and the target was Bremen. Bomber Command was hard pressed to gather sufficient aircraft, eventually falling back on the lighter twin-engined bombers of No.2 Group, including the Mosquito and the Boston. Even so, only a maximum of 960 aircraft could be amassed and not Bomber Harris' goal of 1,000. Churchill stepped in and persuaded Coastal Command to add to the assembly, and they added a further 102 aircraft, while Army Co-operation Command submitted another five. This final 1,067 aircraft was an even greater armada than Cologne. The plan was to have the entire bomber force over the city in just over an hour, with a portion of the force having selected targets including the shipyards and Focke-Wulf factory while the rest would area-bomb the city. No.149 Squadron aircraft formed part of the armada with incendiaries as their bomb load. Stirling N6079, was attacked over the sea by a Messerschmitt Bf 110, resulting in serious damage to the port outer engine, the flaps and ailerons, compelling the crew to jettison their bomb load of 1,800 four-lb incendiaries. The fire in the port outer was extinguished, the pilot bringing the aircraft back to base. The results of this attack, while devastating, were not as intense as the raid on Cologne.

The Conversion Flight once more suffered a non-combat loss when, on 16th July, R9299 caught fire in the air. The aircraft spun in and crashed at Swaffham Bulbeck in Cambridgeshire. The four other Stirling losses in July were all combat losses over enemy territory. Operation 'Pandemonium' was a 16th of July raid on the U-boat manufacturers, 'Lübecker Funklundewerke AG', at Herrenwyk just outside Lübeck on the River Trave. Three Stirlings of No.149 Squadron were part of the Stirling force of 21, one of No.149's Stirlings BF312, 'OJ-A' with Pilot Officer J M P Forward as pilot, being hit by anti-aircraft fire, crash-landing at Steinfeld in Germany. Two of the crew were killed while the five others were taken prisoner. Then on 23rd July, W7580 'OJ-D', piloted by Flying Officer A J L Bowes, was shot down by a night fighter from I/NJG1 during a raid to Duisburg, crashing near Geffen, in Holland, with all of the crew being killed. The Saarbrücken raid on 30th July claimed two more; R9161, 'OJ-T' with Flight Lieutenant F G Neate, was shot down, crashing at Regniowez in France, the one survivor being taken prisoner, while BF320, 'OJ-H' with Pilot Officer T M F Hulse at the controls, was hit by anti-aircraft fire, crashing near the target with all of the crew being killed.

Mining operations claimed two more of No.149's Stirlings, a mission to the Kattegat on 11th August claiming R9162, 'OJ-Q' piloted by Flight Sergeant C W S Oliver, RAAF. which crashed in the sea in the mining area. Then on the 21st, R9329 'OJ-V' was damaged by anti-aircraft fire in the target area while mining off the French coast. The pilot, Sergeant G E Robertson managed to bring the aircraft back to England, crashing at Cornwood in Devon on return. In both cases all of the crew were killed.

W7589 'OJ-P' was attacked by a fighter on its return from the 18th August raid on Osnabrück, knocking out two of its engines.

The pilot, Sergeant D A Baker managed to bring the Stirling back to England, crashing near Sothery in Norfolk. The raid to Frankfurt on 24th/25th August resulted in the loss of two Stirlings, the first being N6083, 'OJ-N' with Pilot Officer E P Wynn, RCAF. Just after take-off for the raid an engine failed, followed by fire. The aircraft crashed just south of Lakenheath, killing all the crew. Then W7572 'OJ-R', with the same Sergeant D A Baker at the controls who had brought his crippled Stirling back from the Osnabrück raid six days before, was shot down by a night fighter on the raid, crashing at Thieulain in Belgium. Three of the crew were taken prisoner while the other four evaded capture. The final loss for August was N6081, 'OJ-H' with the Commanding Officer of No.149 Squadron, Wing Commander C Charlton-Jones, at the controls, which was shot down by a night fighter on a raid to Nuremberg, crashing at Airlenbach in Germany. Six of the crew were killed while the remaining two were taken prisoner.

August did herald a new stage in the bombing war. On the 17th, the Eighth Air Force, then part of the US Army Air Corps, joined the fray with a daylight attack on Rouen/Sotteville in France. It was a small beginning until they could learn what air combat over enemy territory in Europe was all about but soon they were hitting the Axis powers as hard during the day as the RAF had been doing at night.

With the loss of Wing Commander Charlton-Jones, a new Commanding Officer for No.149 Squadron arrived at Lakenheath in September, Wing Commander K M Wasse. A factory-new Stirling, BF372 was delivered to No.149 Squadron on 11th September. It would be this same Stirling that would carry a young Australian pilot who would become No.149's Victoria Cross holder only a few weeks later. On this same date, Flight Sergeant A F Potts' Stirling, R9170 'OJ-H', was shot down by night fighter during a raid to Düsseldorf, crashing near Oud Beyerland in Holland, the one survivor being taken prisoner. The Pathfinder Force had recently been formed on 15th August to mark targets on which the bomber force could accurately bomb, and this target had been marked successfully by them.

On 17th September, Stirling R9164, OJ-Q' piloted by Flight Sergeant M J Kynaston, was shot down by a night fighter on a raid to Essen, crashing at Tongrinne in Belgium with the loss of all the crew. This was the most successful attack on Essen to date, but the losses were high, over one in ten of the attacking aircraft being lost. One of the bombers shot down was loaded with incendiaries and crashed directly into the Krupps armament works, which also received fifteen of the bombs dropped.

Following the 19th/20th September raid to Munich, Stirling BF334 'OJ-R' from No.149 Conversion Flight was apparently badly damaged due to enemy action, suffering an engine failure on the return journey; then the aircraft broke into pieces. The pilot, Sergeant J Philp, ditched the aircraft in the sea off Ramsgate, Kent. Then he and Sergeant G K Reardon swam towards shore towing the injured Sergeant F H King, who regrettably died while they were doing so. They were picked up after four hours in the water by a fishing boat. Sergeant L V Fossleitner stayed with injured Sergeant I G Davies until they were rescued by an Air-Sea Rescue launch. The other two crewmembers were never found. Sergeants Philp, Fossleitner and Reardon were each awarded the British Empire Medal (Gazetted on 29th December 1942) but Reardon and Fossleitner were both killed in separate crashes before the announcement.

September closed with the news from Headquarters that No.3 Group had been identified as the most active group in Bomber Command, with No.149 Squadron highlighted as having the most sorties of the month. In six months the Group had carried out 7,096 sorties, 2,637 of those using Stirlings. The 6th of October brought with it the first Mk III Stirling to No.149 Squadron, BK597 'OJ-F'. As well as having a better mid-upper turret, No.149 would now have a Stirling which overcame at least some of the maintenance problems which plagued the Mark Is.

Mining operations during October accounted for three more of No.149's Stirlings, the first being on the first day of the month when BF328, 'OJ-D' piloted by Flight Sergeant S D Wells, RNZAF, crashed into the North Sea during mining operations off the Friesian Islands, the area having the code name 'Nectarines'. All of the crew died. Then on 10th October, BF348, 'OJ-P' with Flight Sergeant H J Hart as pilot, had technical problems on take-off for a planned mining operation in the Gironde area. On attempting an emergency landing at Watton the aircraft hit trees and crashed. Only one of the crew survived, he being injured. Finally on 17th October, BF392, 'OJ-D' piloted by Flight Sergeant J H Ekelund, RCAF, was lost on a mining operation, also in the Gironde estuary near Bordeaux, crashing at Ile de Yeu, with all of the crew being killed.

On 3rd October, R9167, 'OJ-N' piloted by Squadron Leader W R Greenslade, DFC, AFC, was shot down by a night fighter on a raid to Krefeld, crashing at Kronenburg in Holland, all of the crew being killed. Then on the 6th, N3755 'OJ-S' ran out of fuel on return from a raid on Aachen, crashing at Eastling, in Kent, the pilot, Pilot Officer R Lonsdale RNZAF, being killed. Flight Sergeant J C Brocket RNZAF, and all of his crew died when W7526 'OJ-V' was shot down on the 16th by a night fighter on a raid to Cologne, crashing near Tiel, in Holland.

In late October, Bomber Command once again redirected their attentions to Italy, which had for quite a while been by-passed in favour of targets in Germany and they resulted in the loss of W7628 'OJ-B' on the 24th. Piloted by Sergeant A A Siwak, RCAF, it ran out of fuel on return from the raid to Genoa, crashing at Cliffe, Kent, all of the crew being killed. To close the month, on the 27th BF389 'OJ-S' was written off when the pilot, Flight Sergeant J G Gow, RNZAF, overcorrected the characteristic swing on take-off at Lakenheath with resultant collapse of the undercarriage.

Once again a training flight accounted for the loss of one of No.149's Stirlings when, on 10th November, the starboard outer engine of W7582 'OJ-S', piloted by Squadron Leader W C Hutchings DFC, caught fire, the aircraft crashing in Mildenhall, Suffolk, killing all the crew. Mining claimed another when W7566,

*Returning from a raid on Aachen on 6th October 1942, Stirling OJ-S (N3755), flown by Pilot Officer Ralph Lonsdale, RNZAF (above), ran out of fuel on return to England. The pilot ordered the crew to bale out, staying at the controls until all had left the aircraft. He was unable to bale out in time himself, the aircraft crashing at Arnold's Oak Farm, Eastling, Kent.*

*[J Brigden]*

*Stirling III 'OJ-S' (BF309) lies broken into several pieces at Lakenheath after an undercarriage collapsed following a swing on take-off on 27th October 1942. The pilot was Flt Sgt John Gow RNZAF.*

'OJ-C' with pilot Sergeant T A West was lost on the 17th while mining off the coast of France. The aircraft crashed off Vielle-St-Girons, killing all of the crew.

Genoa and Milan in Italy having received Bomber Command's attention in October, in November it was the turn of Turin, and it was on the third raid to Turin in November, on the 28th/29th, that BF372 'OJ-H' piloted by an Australian, Flight Sergeant R A (Rawdon Hume) Middleton was lost. His standards were high in that he both reduced height to 2,000 feet over the target and made three passes to ensure that the target could be clearly and correctly identified. Continually under light anti-aircraft fire, his aircraft was hit with a shell exploding in the cockpit area seriously injuring the pilot, the co-pilot and the wireless operator. Initially Flight Sergeant Middleton was unconscious, the co-pilot, Flight Sergeant L A Hyder taking over the controls, the bomb aimer dropping the bombs. Middleton regained consciousness and once again took command despite his severe injuries. The Stirling was again hit over the target area and yet again over Boulogne in France on the return journey home. By now the fuel situation was critical so, on a course parallel to the English coastline, the pilot ordered the crew to bale out. Five did, but two of the crew insisted on remaining with the pilot until the last minute. Unfortunately they left it too late and were too low to bale out, so were killed together with the pilot when the aircraft crashed into the sea off Dymchurch in Kent. They were recovered immediately but Flight Sergeant Middleton's body was not recovered until two weeks later when it washed up on the Kent shore. He was awarded a posthumous Victoria Cross, the co-pilot, Flight Sergeant Hyder, being awarded the Distinguished Flying Medal, four other members of the crew also receiving awards. Unknown to Middleton, he had been promoted to Pilot Officer. He is buried in a simple grave at Beck Row, Mildenhall.

The month ended with the loss of R9202, 'OJ-K', on a second raid to Turin the following night, the 29th/30th, the aircraft crashing at Irasco-Finerola, Italy. All of the crew, including the pilot, Flight Sergeant V T Bowie RNZAF, were killed.

The 6th of December brought the loss of N3723 'OJ-E' when an anti-aircraft shell shrapnel severed the elevator control cables during raid on Mannheim. The pilot, Flight Sergeant F H J Ashley managed to bring the Stirling back to England then gave the order to abandon the aircraft over Ascot in Berkshire; it crashed near the Ascot racetrack. Then on 8th December, W7639 'OJ-Q' piloted by Pilot Officer J Philp BEM, returned early from a mining operation, crashing at Hockwold in Norfolk, killing the crew. The following day, two further Stirlings were lost, again relating to mining operations. The first one, at Warnemünde, was R9253, 'OJ-K' with Flying Officer L T Izzard RCAF as pilot, which was shot down, crashing on the mudflats at Westermarsche in Germany, again with the loss of all of the crew. Then BF391, 'OJ-T', was lost on a mining operation in the Fehmarn Channel, crashing at Dobersdorf in Germany, all of the crew, including the pilot Flying Officer M H Good, being killed.

The final loss for the year was on 19th December when R9265, 'OJ-N' piloted by Flying Officer E A R Hunt, was taken for a flight test. In pulling out from a dive during a height test with load, the wings came off, the aircraft crashing at Gransden in Bedfordshire, killing the crew.

*Left: Flt Sgt Rawdon Middleton VC.*
*[IWM CL 18165]*

*Below: The funeral of Flt Sgt Rawdon Middleton VC.*

*'OJ-H' tucked up for the night at dispersal with covers over turrets and cockpit.*  [L Hinkens]

# Chapter 8: Still Stirlings

There were no losses due to enemy action in January 1943, the only key activities of the month for No.149 Squadron and No.3 Group being minelaying operations and a series of raids on the French port of Lorient, which was being used as a U-boat base. However one loss did occur when Flight Sergeant J L Blair brought R9334 'OJ-G' back from bombing practice. On the first attempted landing he overshot the runway and so went around again to make a second attempt. His altimeter was faulty and he mis-judged his height in consequence, crashing in Lakenheath village. One crew member was killed and the rest injured. The story is best told in the excellent research of David Giacomelli, the son of the navigator, beginning with the formal write-up in the Squadron records.

3rd January 1943 - 'Training and maintenance carried out. 3 a/c detailed for night bombing practice. One a/c, R9334, R89695 Sgt Blair J.L, Captain, crashed. One member of crew, 657522 Sgt Whitelock killed. Aircraft was burnt out.'

David continues:

"The service number attributed to the pilot is in fact incorrect as it belonged to the navigator, (my father) 'Fritz' Giacomelli. The crew of R9334 was 'skippered' by PO Laurie Blair RNZAF and consisted of :

| | |
|---|---|
| Navigator | – F/Sgt Jake 'Fritz' Giacomelli RCAF |
| Bomb Aimer | – Sgt Tom Whitelock RAF |
| Flight Engineer | – Sgt Frank Johnson RAF |
| W/Op | – Sgt W H Clayton RAF |
| M/U Gunner | – Sgt Ronnie Zambra RAF |
| Rear Gunner | – Sgt Clark Barker RCAF |

"They were one of nineteen crews that had just completed the course on Stirlings at No.1657 Conversion Unit at Stradishall and were posted to No.149 Sqn effective 18th December 1942.

"At 1815 hours on 30th December 1942 the crew took up R9334 for a 3+ hour 'Bullseye'. On 3rd January 1943 they took the same aircraft up at 1750 hours for bombing practice at Rushford bombing range. Upon returning to base at 1910 hours the aircraft was instructed by Flying Control to land on runway 24. After reaching 400 feet of altitude on final approach, the pilot realised that the drift was too great for him to land. Accordingly, Laurie told Control that he was overshooting and would land on runway 02, which was more into the wind. Assisted by the bomb aimer, Tom Whitelock, Laurie commenced the overshoot procedure on the Stirling.

"A shallow ridge separated the village of Lakenheath from the aerodrome. Tom Burrows was on duty in the crash tender that night, parked next to Flying Control located on this ridge near the end of runway 24. They always parked there since it was possible to view the entire airfield, including the dispersals. Tom remembers hearing the engines open up as the pilot commenced the overshoot and seeing it pass by very close to them, barely clearing the ridge. It then vanished into the night followed by complete silence.

"At this point the Stirling gradually lost power on both inboard engines. Flaps were still partly extended and the undercarriage was still down, as they were operated from an auxiliary on one of the engines. The aircraft was in a squashing attitude and gradually sank with the pilot unable to do anything about it except keep it straight and level. As they flew beyond the runway toward the unsuspecting village of Lakenheath, the descending Stirling's main tyres were ripped off by high-tension lines along the village's High Street. This set the aircraft on fire and, as I always remember my father telling me, the wings knocked off the chimney pots from some council homes. The aircraft continued to descend until it ploughed into the far end of the Lakenheath playing field near Undley Road. Altogether, the whole incident was over in seconds from the time the pilot started to overshoot."

Stirling Aircraft Association member Harold Howarth remembered the crash very well, since at the time he was on his way into Lakenheath village. He heard the aircraft pass over and he hardly paid any attention to it until he heard the engines' note alter at a much lower height. Shortly afterwards he heard the unmistakable sounds of a crash landing. He made his way to the crash site quickly to offer assistance.

"Mr M G Rutterford was with his wife sitting by the fireside when suddenly they heard a tremendous rushing noise, almost like a tornado. Upon opening his front door, he saw an awful mass of flames. The thorn hedge 40 yards from their bungalow was blazing fiercely; 20 yards beyond lay the dying Stirling. At the same time many of his neighbours thought that the Stirling had crashed into his house. He ran across the road and into the field where the aircraft was fiercely burning.

"Mr B Flack was milking in the cow yard of his farmhouse next to the Rutterford bungalow. He later told his daughter, Mrs J Barker, who was present in the house at the time of the crash, that the Stirling looked like the devil coming out of the sky. He threw away his milking pail and lantern and ran to get his family into the ditch at the back of the house. He was afraid that the aircraft could have bombs on board. Mrs Barker told me that they never did find either the pail or the lantern afterwards. She remembers her father being particularly concerned that the family keep doors closed to observe the 'blackout' regulations - all this with a Stirling blazing almost in his front yard! Mrs Barker's aunt suffered a heart attack when she heard of the crash - she had thought it had hit her sister's house.

"Sheer luck determined that the Stirling came down in the Lakenheath playing field, as the pilot could not see anything in the darkness as the aircraft sunk towards the ground. With the main wheels ripped off and the aircraft alight, it was fortunate that it did not break up as it struck. Laurie Blair felt the squashing attitude of the aircraft contributed to the comparative safety of the crash landing. The stubs of the undercarriage ploughed into the field as she ground to a halt in front of Mr Rutterford's home.

"When the aircraft struck, the pilot was thrown forward in his seat and struck his head, but he remained conscious. My father was slumped unconscious over his navigation table. The bomb aimer who was in the second pilot's seat at the time of the crash was also thrown forward violently, as he was seen to be unconscious and draped over the control column. The armour-plated door which separated the Wireless/Operator and the Flight Engineer from the rest of the crewmembers slammed shut and buckled upon impact, effectively cutting off the forward crew. Ammunition was going off and the fire was beginning to take hold. Blair tried to open the armour-plated door but had no success. The Flight Engineer, Frank Johnson, described the crash as an 'unearthly experience'. He suffered a broken bone in his ankle but was able to evacuate the aircraft quickly through the rear of the aircraft. He and Clark Barker, the Rear Gunner, then realised that Ronnie Zambra, the Mid-Upper Gunner, was still inside. After helping him out, they all headed under a nearby tree. By this time the nose of the aircraft was burning fiercely and could not be approached.

"When Mr Rutterford arrived near the aircraft he met his long-time friend, Mr Frederick Sharpe-Bullen, whom he had told to be careful approaching the crash. Mr Rutterford returned to his house to get his protective tin hat and to put his lamp out in case of explosion. By the time he returned to the aircraft, Mr Bullen had already assisted two of the forward crew to safety. The citation for the British Empire Medal which he received for his actions states that 'The aircraft was burning fiercely, ammunition was exploding in all directions and there was a danger that the petrol tanks might explode. With difficulty he managed to open the escape hatch and assist a dazed and injured airman to safety (this was David 'Fritz' Giacomelli) He returned to the burning wreckage to help another airman to get away, who was dazed and in danger of being burnt (this was Laurie Blair). Mr Bullen sustained slight burns. His brave action, which led to the saving of life, is worthy of high praise'.

"Laurie Blair collapsed shortly after he cleared the aircraft and recovered consciousness in the cottage of Mr and Mrs Flack. Mrs Barker remembers clearly the chaos in her parents' house that night with it being full of RAF personnel. She also remembers the look on the face of one of the crew that suffered concussion. Wing Commander Michael Wasse, the Squadron Commander, was present and informed Laurie that my father, 'Fritz', was all right, but Tom Whitelock had been killed on impact. Mrs Barker's mother, Mrs Flack, subsequently received a letter of commendation from the RAF for her efforts in tending to the injured crew.

"The RAF crash tender had arrived within a few minutes and soon the fire, which was contained to the cockpit and nose of the aircraft, was out. Mr Bullen and Mr Rutterford then assisted the RAF personnel in removing the body of Tom Whitelock from the cockpit floor onto a stretcher. He was later buried in Manchester.

"As Harold Howarth made his way towards the sound of the crash, he could see a light glowing in the distance. After scrambling through the hedges he could see, through the trees, figures silhouetted against the flames. By the time he arrived the crew had escaped from the wreckage so he walked around the area just in case someone was lying injured on the ground. It was at this time he noticed quite a bit of parachute gear lying about in the grass although it was not easy to spot. For some reason, he stooped to pick up a few small, charred pieces of parachute silk and rigging lines. He was also dismayed by the actions of some of the local girls in that they were actively searching for parachutes so that they could no doubt use the silk in making items of clothing. Thanks to Harold, I now have in my possession some of the bits of the burnt parachute.

"Guards were quickly posted around the crash site and no unauthorised personnel were allowed near. The surviving crew-members were taken to hospital on the base, since all received various minor injuries. Laurie Blair did not return to the Squadron for a month since he received a gash on the head requiring 27 stitches. During this period, the Wireless Operator, Clayton, chose to crew up with F/Sgt F.A. Pearson. This was a fateful decision for him as he was killed in EF330 on 12/13th March 1943, when it was shot down by a night fighter at Bergh, Netherlands, during a raid on Essen. The remainder of the crew were also offered the opportunity to re-crew, but they chose to stick with their skipper, and all but Ronnie Zambra survived the war. He died in August 1944 while flying re-supply drops during the Warsaw Uprising with 31 Sqn SAAF, out of Foggia, Italy. As the rear gunner of a Liberator he was the only one to bale out when the aircraft was shot down by the Russians, but was too low for the chute to open. He was buried in Warsaw.

"Frank Johnson spent 14 days in the hospital recovering from a broken bone in his ankle. Apparently on the night before the crash, Frank went partying with another crew. In order to return to base they misrepresented themselves and used service transport. A WAAF turned them in and they were placed on a charge and recommended for Courts Martial. Frank continued flying due to a shortage of crews in the Squadron and was involved in the crash. While others were sentenced to 14 days detention Frank was permitted to serve his 14 days in hospital!"

A month later they flew as a crew again; Laurie Blair did four 'second dickey' trips and they commenced their operational tour on 27th February 1943 with a 'Gardening' Op to Bordeaux.

It was on 29th January that three Mosquitoes of No.105 Squadron were sent in on a low-level daylight attack on Berlin to disrupt Goering's planned and well-publicised 11.00am speech at an open air rally, putting him off the air for an hour and making him look like a jackass, followed by a similar disruption by three Mosquitoes of No.139 Squadron of Goebbel's 4.00pm speech at a similar rally, both squadrons being based together at Marham. While the damage by six Mosquitoes could only be considered as moderate compared to the heavy bomber raids, the propaganda value was enormous.

February was also a good month for No.149 helped somewhat by the winter weather, which always kept flying to a minimum, the Squadron losing only one Stirling in the month. The key raids were repeat visits to Lorient, Wilhelmshaven, and Cologne with a trip to Nuremberg, and one to Italy, to Turin. Stragglers were always very vulnerable to the *Himmelbett* defences, being easily picked up by a *Lichtenstein*-equipped night-fighter. It was on the 15th February trip to Cologne that W7638 'OJ-R' was shot down by a night fighter.

At 18.45 hrs on the evening of 14 February 1943, with Flight Sergeant J G Gow, RNZAF at the controls, the Stirling lifted off from Lakenheath for the crew's fifth operation. Loaded with eight

'OJ-N' showing signs of wear and tear. The long, narrow bomb bay is noticeable. [Philip Jarrett collection]

1,000-lb bombs and 2,000 lbs of incendiaries, they were part of the 243-strong force sent to bomb Cologne that night. There was a problem with one of the engines on the way over which slowed the Stirling down and John Gow could not get the aircraft any higher than 16,000 feet due to icing. Needless to say this made the crew late over the target. Canadian Flight Sergeant Cecil Loughlin was the Navigator/Air Bomber, in John Gow's crew. The story is best told in Cecil's own words:

"Two planes had been hit and were on fire a few miles ahead of us. It looked like night-fighters as there was no ack-ack. As we made our run in on the target the plane was shaking from the ack-ack explosions all around us. Two planes exploded to our right. We had to keep the plane straight and level as we made our run-in to bomb on the green marker flare, 'Bombs gone!'

"We made a left turn for home when we were boxed by ack-ack and searchlights. John threw the plane into a corkscrew dive at 300 mph (480 kph) diving and climbing all the time, turning for seventeen minutes. We could get out of the searchlights but the ack-ack was exploding all around us. We could feel the shrapnel hitting us and smell the explosive all through the plane. John was really breathing heavy as it was hard work weaving and diving for such a long time.

"All of a sudden it became quiet except for the roar of the four engines, so we set course for home, all the time taking evasive action. We started to check out the condition of the crew. The plane was operating beautifully so we had not been seriously hit.

"All of a sudden Jim Bridgen, mid-upper, yelled, 'You bastard!' We felt cannon shells hit our plane. A fighter had come up beneath and Jim didn't get a crack at him until he was breaking off and it was too late. All this time we had not heard from the rear gunner, Bill Summerson, and I believe he must have been a casualty of the ack-ack. We were on fire and the Skipper gave the order to bail out at about 22.00 hrs. I got my 'chute' and went down to open the escape hatch, which was in the front of the plane behind the front turret. I was just going to open the hatch when Val Tully, who had been sitting behind the pilot, hollered at me to wait until he got his 'chute' out of the front turret.

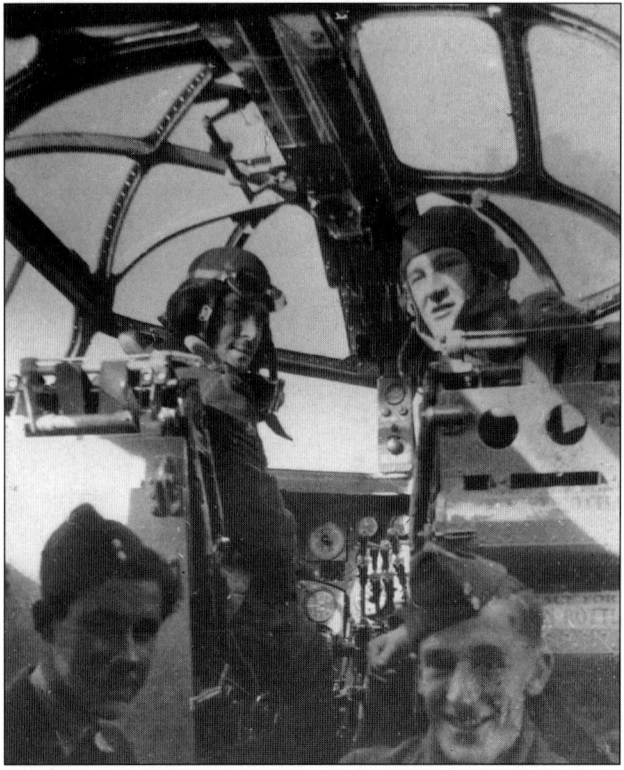

*The cockpit of 'R-for-Robert' while flying over Cambridge in 1943. Flt Sgt J Gow RNZAF and Sgt J Brigden RAF with two radio mechanics.*
[J C Brigden]

"Then I opened the hatch and baled out. Val was beside me and was ready to jump next. I tumbled out and pulled the rip chord and the 'chute' opened OK, and I started to float down. Our plane flew on straight and steady for three to four minutes, still burning, and then went into a long curving dive and into the lower clouds. I came through the cloud and saw a fire burning a few miles away which I took to be our plane. I landed in a field, buried my 'chute' and Mae West life vest and started walking west. It was the loneliest time of my life, in enemy territory, in the dark all alone and hearing the other planes above returning to England."

Stirling W7638 'OJ-R' was shot down at 21.30 hours by a Bf 110 of I/NJG1, probably flown by Oblt Martin Bauer, and crashed near Boxmeer, Holland, as one of nine aircraft lost from the Cologne force. At least six of the heavies fell victim to night-fighters of I and II/NJG1 manning *Himmelbett* boxes in the southern part of Holland and Belgium. Three crew-members of W7638 were found dead at the crash site next day, Skipper John Gow, Sergeant Paul Oldham, flight engineer, and Sergeant William Summerson, rear gunner. The four survivors were all rounded up, taken to the interrogation centre at Frankfurt then sent to Stalag Luft VIIIB at Lamsdorf, where they stayed until 1945.

The 2nd of March sent 300 aircraft, including those of No.149, to Germany's most heavily defended target, Berlin. On this raid, BK692, 'OJ-W' flown by Flight Lieutenant R E Richman DFM, was hit by a night fighter over the target area killing two of the crew including the pilot, the co-pilot taking over the controls. Then they were again hit by anti-aircraft fire crossing the French coast, the co-pilot giving the order to bale out. One of the crew was wounded and so he was dropped out of the escape hatch with his parachute already opened for him. Unfortunately he did not survive, bringing to total to three dead. The aircraft crashed at Gueutteville in France, the remaining five crew members being taken prisoner. This was the first Mark III Stirling to be lost by No.149 Squadron.

The 5th of March brought things back to reality with a thud, when Bomber Command began its 'Battle of the Ruhr', beginning with an attack by 442 bombers on Essen. 'Bomber' Harris decided that he now had sufficient strength and equipment under his command, including a considerable number of four-engined bombers with their longer range and bigger bomb load, to begin an all-out assault on Germany which would last over the next four months. Further, the targets would all be within the range of "Oboe", for target marking and so a high degree of accuracy should be possible. Bomber Command now had "Oboe", carried by the Pathfinders of Nos.105 and 109 Mosquito Squadrons and target marking was no longer the problem that it had been. To Harris, the shortest and most logical way to end the war would be to knock out the 'Industrial Ruhr' by concentrated bombing. Experience had shown that any attempt to accurately bomb and so totally put out of action any comparatively small industrial complex by night bombing was fruitless, and so Harris adopted the plan to destroy where the worker needed to live and sleep and to destroy his or her morale.

To prevent the *Luftwaffe* night fighter force concentrating their defence efforts on this same area, alternative targets would also be sought out which fell outside of the Ruhr. Escalation of the bombing war would certainly increase the casualty rate, but that casualty rate was to take place on both sides of the North Sea and the Bomber Command crews would pay a heavy price for their achievements.

The losses were not one-sided though, as was reported by David Giacomelli, son of Flight Sergeant Jake (Fritz) Giacomelli, navigator on Stirling EF343 'OJ-B', one of six No.149 Squadron Stirlings on the 9th of March raid to Munich, after interviewing the crew:

"The crew of EF343 was captained by P/O Laurie Blair RNZAF and consisted of a typical mix of Commonwealth nationalities, Navigator Flt Sgt Jake (Fitz) Giacomelli RCAF, Bomb Aimer P/O Don Maddocks RCAF, Flight Engineer Sgt Frank

Johnson RAF, Wireless Operator Flt Sgt Nanton Sunderland RCAF, Mid-Upper Gunner Sgt Ronnie Zambra RAF, and Rear Gunner Sgt Clark Barker RCAF.

"The Pilot recalls that they were very heavy that night, with an 'all up weight' of 70,000 lbs, including a bomb load of four 1,000-lb, four 500-lb long delay, and four canisters of incendiaries. There was no wind for take-off and every inch of the runway was used to get the aircraft into the air. Visibility was unlimited that night. The route was in from the south of Munich and the Swiss Alps were visible as they glistened in the moonlight. It was what was called a 'fighter's moon', but this night it would become a 'bomber's moon'.

"The Stirling was still heavy and weaving slightly at 12,000 feet, when at 00.15hrs the two gunners sighted a fighter flare dead astern at 200 yards range and at the same height as themselves. This was reported to the pilot and Barker opened fire at the flare. As he did so, tracer was seen coming from the port beam, a Ju 88 came in and, for some reason, flattened out and tried to follow Laurie's tight diving turn. It was at this stage that the 'boys' got him. Both gunners opened fire and the fighter was hit in the port engine. Fire was seen to break out immediately and the fighter was seen diving toward the ground out of control, where it exploded. All members of the crew, except my father, saw the aircraft destroyed. The wireless operator witnessed the action from the astrodome, but the pilot only got a glimpse as he was fully occupied with flying the aircraft. The Stirling suffered only one bullet hole to the port tailplane. The tail turret had fired a total of 350 rounds, the mid-upper 120.

"Meanwhile the Stirling had lost about 7,000 feet during the evasive action and Laurie pulled her out only with great difficulty. Since the target was still ahead of them, a great deal of fuel was consumed in getting the aircraft back to operational height to prepare for the bomb run. As a result, the pilot diverted the aircraft from its regular base, Lakenheath, and landed at West Malling.

"The excitement for the night was not yet over. After landing, the rear gunner was the first out of the aircraft, but hurried back inside and plugged into the intercom. 'Are you sure we're in England, Skipper? There's an FW 190 parked besides us!'. A few seconds later he came back on the line and stated that all was as it should be. The FW 190 was one of two supporting a hit-and-run raid on London, that had become confused in the concentrated British fighter defence and had landed at West Malling by mistake! The second one to land realised his error and tried to get back into the air. Ground defences, however, always on the alert, blew him to pieces. As Laurie Blair said, 'It was all go that night'. It doesn't take a great deal of thought to imagine the state of mind of the rest of the crew upon hearing that they had parked beside an FW 190!

"The Ju 88 was claimed as a kill at the debriefing. Since they were still considered a 'sprog' crew (it was only their third Op), they felt that Intelligence looked at them a little bit sideways, but it was a great day for all of them when two weeks later they were informed that their 'Ju 88' was confirmed destroyed near Amerzee."

The next two No.149 losses of common cause had the advantage that the aircraft did return to Britain and the crews survived. Returning from a raid on Nuremberg on 9th March, the starboard engines of EF328 'OJ-R' cut. The pilot, Pilot Officer G T P Southall RNZAF, crash-landed the aircraft at Sudbury. Then on 12th March once again engine failure, this time EF327, 'OJ-M' with Pilot Officer I T S Fulton, an American serving in the RAF, as pilot. When landing from a raid on Stuttgart, it swung on touch-down and the undercarriage collapsed.

A raid to Essen claimed EF330 'OJ-P' on 13th March, which was shot down by a night fighter, the aircraft crashing at Bergh in Holland, killing the pilot, Flight Sergeant F A Pearson, and his crew. Then on 30th March, BK708 'OJ-P', again with Pilot Officer I T S Fulton at the controls, was lost on a raid to Berlin, crashing at Lindenburg in Germany. Six of the crew were killed, the one survivor, Warrant Officer C L Blackford, being taken prisoner.

The month closed with the loss of BK715 'OJ-D' on 31st March. Flight Lieutenant L H Butler RNZAF had planned to take the aircraft up for an air test but the starboard outer engine caught fire while taking off, the pilot aborting the take-off. According to Peter Rowland, Flight Engineer, someone had left the cap of one of the wing fuel tanks off after refuelling, resulting in fuel pouring down the port wing on take-off leaving a trail of flame down the runway as it went. The pilot stopped the aircraft at the extreme edge of the airfield and the crew ran for it. The fire seemed to die down on return of the aircraft to the dispersal but then it re-ignited and the aircraft burnt out.

It was not continual 'Ops' and off-duty time was often spent in the Sergeants' Mess at Lakenheath relaxing over a pint of beer or two. After the beer had flowed freely there was usually a sing-song, and one song that echoed around the walls of the Mess in the Spring of 1943 was sung to the tune of 'That Old-fashioned Mother of Mine':

'Just an old-fashioned Stirling
With old-fashioned ways
A fuselage tattered and torn
Four Hercules engines keep chugging away
She's flying from midnight to dawn
Though she don't go so fast
No great height does she claim?
Sure there's something that makes her divine
When she flies there on high
She's the Queen of the sky
She's that old-fashioned Stirling of mine'

Such was the reverence of the crews who flew the Stirling . . .

R9327, 'OJ-M' piloted by Sergeant K A Way, was shot down on a raid to Kiel on 5th April, crashing at Obbekaer in Denmark. Then the raid to Stuttgart on 15th April claimed two more of No.149's Stirlings; BF500, 'OJ-M' flown by Pilot Officer D B White RCAF, was shot down, crashing near Tournes in France, while BK759, 'OJ-X' with T G Ogle as pilot, was shot down on the same raid, crashing at Studernheim in Germany. The raid to Rostock on 21st April claimed two more, BK698, 'OJ-O' piloted by Flight Lieutenant G I Ellis RNZAF, crashing into the North Sea. With all four aircraft from the beginning of April, all of the crew members were lost. Squadron Leader T L Howell, a long service pilot whose flying experience dated back to Wapitis, was on this same raid, flying BK714 'OJ-L'. Trying to avoid the heavy anti-aircraft fire, he flew the Stirling as low as possible. Unfortunately the altimeters in the Stirlings were never too accurate with the result that he literally flew into the ground at Broendum in Denmark. One of the crew was killed, while the other six were taken prisoner.

May was a black-letter month for No.149 Squadron, losing no less than nine aircraft during the month, eight of them being due to enemy action. Only one, on 11th May, was due to the traditional Stirling undercarriage collapse following an aircraft swing. This was BK812, flown by Pilot Officer K J Beetles, attempting to take the aircraft off in a high crosswind while transferring it to No.15 Squadron at Mildenhall.

A mining mission, this one to the southwest coast of France on 2nd May, claimed another of No.149's Stirlings when BK696, 'OJ-L' piloted by Pilot Officer P L Blair RNZAF, was hit by both anti-aircraft fire from a flak ship and by a night fighter. With the compass out and low on fuel, they hit an electrical storm. The crew baled out and the aircraft crashed at Havant in Hampshire.

Other than the 1,000-bomber raids, the attack on Dortmund on 4th/5th May was the biggest yet, with almost 600 aircraft, and the first major raid on Dortmund, causing considerable damage. EF343, 'OJ-B' with Flying Officer W E Davey as pilot, was shot

*No.149's armourers stop for a group photograph at Lakenheath in 1943.* [L Hinkens]

down by a night fighter on this raid, crashing near Smallebrugge in Holland, killing all of the crew. The 12th/13th of May attack on Duisburg was not too far behind in numbers of aircraft, 572 bombers making a very successful attack on the target. EF357, 'OJ-V' pilot Sergeant E G Bass, was shot down by a night fighter, crashing at Rotterdam in Holland, and killing the crew. Then the attack on Bochum on 13th/14th May took two more of No.149's Stirlings, both BF479, 'OJ-E' piloted by Flying Officer L C Martin, and BK726, 'OJ-Z' with Pilot Officer H E Forsyth RCAF, being shot down by night fighters, the former crashing at Kasterlee in Germany, the latter crashing at Immerath in Germany, all of the crew of 'OJ-Z' being killed.

There were two more losses on mining operations, the first being to the west of La Rochelle on 18th May. BK701, 'OJ-G' flown by Pilot Officer J E Hill crashed in the Loire estuary, sinking so rapidly that only three of the crew could escape to be taken prisoner, the remaining four crewmen drowning. Then on 21st/22nd May, in a major minelaying operation covering the Friesian Islands, the River Gironde and off La Pallice, involving 104 aircraft, BF510, 'OJ-P' with Sergeant C E Tomlin as pilot, was lost off the south-west coast of France, crashing in the Bay of Biscay, all of the crew being killed.

Despite the attack on Düsseldorf by over 750 aircraft on 25th/26th May, cloud cover and decoy sites resulted in very scattered bombing and this meant that some time in the near future another raid on the same target was in order. On this raid BK710, 'OJ-A' with pilot Sergeant J H Uden, was shot down by a night fighter, the aircraft crashing into the North Sea, all of the crew being lost. To end the month, BF507, 'OJ-S' flown by Pilot Officer A W Flack RNZAF, was shot down by a night fighter on the raid to Wuppertal on 30th May, crashing at Dormagen in Germany, all of the crew being killed.

One major highlight for Bomber Command in May was the attack on the dams by No.617 Squadron on the 16th/17th the leader and commanding officer, Wing Commander Guy Gibson, being awarded the Victoria Cross, with 34 more awards going to other crew members. Although eight of the nineteen specially-modified Lancasters on the raid were lost, the damage was extensive and it gave Britain a tremendous boost in morale. The bravado, daring and heroism of the crews on the raid made it one of the great moments in Royal Air Force history.

June brought two more collapsed undercarriage write-offs, the first being on 9th June when Sergeant T Nicholson in EH885 'OJ-V' swung on take-off for a wireless homing test, then again on 14th June when a tyre burst on BF531 'OJ-M' on landing, the aircraft swinging off the runway. Flying Officer A R Porter, the pilot, had been on a 'Bullseye' exercise with anti-aircraft searchlight batteries.

Over 700 bombers attacked Krefeld on 21st/22nd June, bombing on well-placed ground markers dropped by the Pathfinder 'Oboe' Mosquitoes, half the city being burnt out from the resulting fires. BK799, 'OJ-O' with Pilot Officer J Lowrie, was lost on the raid, crashing in the IJsselmeer in Holland, all of the crew being killed.

The month closed with a major raid on Cologne on 28th/29th June, involving over 600 aircraft, No.149 Squadron losing three Stirlings on the raid. BF483, 'OJ-C' with pilot Sergeant R K Scott, was shot down, all of the crew being killed. Then both EE880, 'OJ-O' with pilot Flying Officer A R Porter, and BK703, 'OJ-K' piloted by Flying Officer W R Booker were shot down by night fighters. 'OJ-O' crashed at Houwaart in Belgium, five of the crew being killed, one being taken prisoner, while one evaded capture. 'OJ-K' crashed at Netersel in Holland, all of the crew being killed.

The 'Oboe'-marked 3rd/4th of July raid on Cologne, with over 650 aircraft, was considered very successful. However it did account for two losses from No.149, one before it even got into the air. EF400 'OJ-C' had an engine failure while taking-off. When the pilot, Sergeant S W Rogers, brought the aircraft back down it swung on landing, with the inevitable undercarriage collapse. This was the last Mk I Stirling lost on operations by No.149 Squadron. Then BF530, with Pilot Officer G A Cozens DFM at the controls, was shot down by a night fighter, crashing at Geetbetz in Belgium. Six of the crew were killed; one was taken prisoner, while one evaded capture. This was the first night that the *Luftwaffe* night fighter command put a new technique into operation known as *Wilde Sau* (Wild Boar) using Focke-Wulf 190 single-engined fighters from *Jagdgeschwader* 300. Here the fighter was a free agent and sought out his own aircraft to attack from the bomber formation over the target area. The flak was limited in height to give the pilot free range over that height, the pilot using whatever source of lighting that was available from the ground to seek out his prey. As the bomber crews were not expecting both anti-aircraft fire and fighter attacks simultaneously they were taken completely by surprise, twelve aircraft falling to the fighters.

Targets in Germany, France and Italy were all candidates in July. However the most significant were the four attacks on Hamburg from 24th July to 3rd August, officially called 'Operation Gomorrah' but to be known later as the 'Battle of Hamburg'. Raids were by almost 800 aircraft each, on 24th, 27th and 29th July and 3rd August. On the first raid, "Window", myriads of strips of aluminium foil cut to the correct wavelength, were dropped for the first time, which would give so many false echoes on the German ground radar screens that they were completely jammed. While the first raid in itself was very concentrated and did untold damage, around 1,500 people being killed, it was the raid on the 27th/28th that would add a new word to the horrors of warfare. The bombing was very concentrated and it was on this raid that the many smaller fires became one single huge conflagration, giving rise to what became known as a firestorm. It was a warm dry night, ideal conditions, and that part of Hamburg was converted into a huge oven, consuming everything that was combustible for a full three hours, reaching the furnace temperature of 800 degrees Celsius. The air rushing in to feed the flames was at gale force of from 100 to 150 miles per hour, sufficient to lift people up and carry them into the flames as they attempted to escape. It was estimated that 40,000 people died, most of the remaining population of Hamburg fleeing the city. Not knowing just how truly effective the raid was, two more raids followed, the last being considerably diverted due to weather conditions.

What is not commonly known or recognised was that a number of the RAF night attacks on major cities were supported by co-ordinated attacks the following day by aircraft of the US 8th Air Force, Hamburg being an example. B-17 Flying Fortresses added their weight to the Hamburg attacks, a total of 252 aircraft carrying out daylight attacks on Hamburg on the 25th and 26th of July. These would be a similar co-ordinated night and daylight attack on Dresden following the 14th of February 1945, but most historians seem only to recall or emphasise the RAF involvement.

Another test flight, this one on 9th August, claimed a further No.149 Stirling and crew. BF512 undershot the runway on landing after a compass adjustment test flight, the pilot, Sergeant J W Cumming RCAF, then opening up one outboard engine in error as well as the two inboards. The aircraft swung and crashed near Lakenheath, killing all of the crew.

The 17th/18th of August brought 'Operation Hydra' to Bomber Command. It had been learned from photo reconnaissance and agents that Germany was carrying out secret rocket research, which would eventually lead to the V-1 flying bomb and the V-2 rocket, at a remote area on the Baltic known as Peenemünde. These weapons were such an advance over existing technology and were such a threat that the work simply had to be interrupted. So almost 600 aircraft were sent on the night of 17th August, with Wing Commander John Searby as Master Bomber, to 'interfere' with their research. A feint attack on Berlin by only eight Mosquitoes of No.139 Squadron, but using 'Window', known as 'Operation Whitebait', drew the fighters away from the bomber stream long enough for the first two of the three waves to bomb uninterrupted. Most losses were in the third wave. It is felt that the raid slowed down the development work by two months. Knowing the devastating effect of the V-2 in Germany's attacks on London and Antwerp later, and considering the demoralising effect of both weapons, a gain of two months by Germany would have effected the course of the war considerably.

Another raid to the 'Big City', Berlin, on 23rd/24th August involved 727 aircraft, with Mosquitoes marking the route like a road map. The loss was heavy, 56 aircraft, the greatest loss by Bomber Command to date, and it included two of No.149 Squadron's Stirlings. BK765 'OJ-P' with Squadron Leader J J E Mahoney as pilot was hit by anti-aircraft fire, all of the crew baling out but one, the aircraft crashing in the target area. The six survivors became prisoners. EE894, 'OJ-R' with pilot Flight Sergeant A E May was also shot down, crashing at Hannover in Germany. The one survivor was taken prisoner.

The raid can best be described by Observer 'Spud' Taylor from his diary:

"Berlin tonight. Over 800 'Kites' went, all four-engined. Visibility was good, so we could watch the attack as it developed. In six short minutes the place was glowing with fires and enormous flashes were lighting up the ground. Searchlights and flak, not very intense but bags of fighters about. Making our final 'run up' on to the marker we were suddenly attacked from very close range by a Dornier, which scored several hits on our 'kite'. Len and John (our two gunners) kept their heads and shot her down. Once in flames the Dornier was picked up by searchlights and finished off by flak. Bombed dead centre, on a marker, and got out like bats out of hell. Counted six of our 'kites' going down in flames in the short time we were over the target. On the way back we got considerably off course, crossing the Baltic and there were doubts of us reaching England. Also one engine packed up for a time. We threw out quite a lot of things including my guns and ammo, and just made Coltishall with 80 gallons left. Flying 8 hours 40 minutes, damned tired."

It must have seemed very strange to the inhabitants of Heilbronn when the leaders of the almost 700 aircraft in the bomber stream flying overhead on the night of 27th August would one after another drop a single bomb on them, instead of the expected salvo, while the following aircraft continued without response overhead. What was happening was that Heilbronn was being used to check the accuracy of the 'H2S' sets being carried by the Pathfinder aircraft, which would shortly be expected to accurately mark Nuremberg for that following bomber force, using 'H2S'. Even so, the marking was poor and most of the bombs fell on the suburbs and outside of the city. It was on this raid that EE877 'OJ-E' would be lost, crashing between Langel and Weiss in Germany, killing the pilot, Flight Sergeant G S Steer, and the rest of his crew.

A twin raid using almost as many aircraft took place three nights later on the 30th, this one to the neighbouring towns of Mönchen-Gladbach and Rheydt, the Master Bomber switching the attack from the first to the second during the raid when he thought it appropriate, the targets being marked by Oboe-carrying aircraft. It was on the first raid that EF438 'OJ-D' was lost, crashing in the target area. The pilot, Flight Sergeant E W Bower, and all of his crew were killed.

The attack on Berlin continued and with increasing earnest, with well over 600 aircraft on a raid on 31st August/1st September with seventeen of the 106 Stirlings sent being lost, including EE879, 'OJ-G' with Flight Sergeant H A More as pilot, which crashed at Sputendorf in Germany, killing all of the crew. The 5th/6th of September brought another 600-plus aircraft raid, this one a combined attack on Mannheim and Ludwigshaven. One of the problems in bombing missions was for the bomb aimers to drop their bombs on the first target markers seen, which caused the bombing to 'walk' backwards from the central aiming point. Here the target marking was excellent, and as Ludwigshaven fell on the approaching line to the markers at Mannheim, creep-back would have fallen on the second target. As it turned out, the creep-back on this raid was not excessive. Both targets received very severe damage, but not without loss, 34 aircraft being lost including three Stirlings from No.149 Squadron. BF477 with pilot Flying Officer C D Farmer suffered engine failure on the way to the target, crashing at Sorbon in France, killing two of the crew. Four were taken prisoner while one evaded capture. BK711, 'OJ-O' with Flight Lieutenant B Cottrell as pilot, was hit both by a night fighter and by anti-aircraft fire, crashing at Hockenheim in Germany. Four of the crew were killed, while the other three were taken prisoner. EE872, 'OJ-N' with pilot Flight Sergeant A A Brown, was shot down by a night fighter, crashing at Ludwigshaven in Germany. Six of the crew were killed while one was taken prisoner. This was the first mission for EE372.

Another raid of the same magnitude to Mannheim on 23rd/24th September, targeted the area of the city which had missed most of the previous bombing in the north, the mission achieving its objective with initial concentrated bombing, but with the usual creep-back. On this raid, EH883, 'OJ-A', Warrant Officer W J Leedham at the controls, was shot down, crashing at Herxheim in Germany, five of the crew being killed, one being taken prisoner, while the other evaded capture. The 27th/28th September's rather unsuccessful raid to Hannover with almost 700 aircraft accounted for one more of No.149's Stirlings, EF495, 'OJ-R', with pilot Flight Sergeant G S Hotchkis, RCAF, which crashed into the North Sea. Four of the crew were killed, while the other three were taken prisoner.

The threat of a gas attack by Germany, following World War I practice, perpetually hung over Britain like a spectre throughout the war, military personnel and civilians alike never being without their respirators wherever they travelled. No.149 Squadron had been one of those squadrons trained in gas warfare dating back to pre-war days, and gas exercises were still practised. It was on 4th October, following a gas exercise, that the undercarriage of Stirling EH987, 'OJ-P' with Pilot Officer B A Connor RAAF in command, failed to lock on landing, causing it to collapse.

October was kind to No.149, in that only one aircraft was lost on operations, this being on a mining operation to the Kattegat on the 8th, one of 79 aircraft on a mining mission. EJ106, 'OJ-O' with Flight Sergeant J G McInnes RCAF at the controls crashed into the North Sea, killing all of the crew, the only mining aircraft lost.

The Pathfinder Force, now No.8 Group, was well established as a strong right arm to aid Bomber Command in achieving its objectives. On 8th November, another Group would be added to this end, No.100 Group. It had become an electronic war, beginning with the ground radar stations on both sides of the North Sea, then airborne equipment for navigation, location and identification, bombing, and so on. As each side developed a new piece of equipment, the other would develop a countermeasure in a continuing game of scientific escalation. It had eventually reached a point where Britain had the technology to jam both enemy radar and communications signals. So No.100 Group became the Electronic Countermeasures arm of Bomber Command, to intersperse bombing aircraft with jamming capability throughout the bomber stream. No.199 Squadron's Stirlings, with 'Mandrel', would jam the 'Freya' early warning ground radar stations, while Lancasters from No.101 Squadron with 'ABC' in No.1 Group would jam their ground-to-air communications, or fed in false information through an eighth crew member who spoke fluent German. In addition, No.100 Group's Mosquito squadrons equipped with 'Serrate' radar would give a rearward signal making them appear like bombers but, with forward-looking fighter radar, would go in advance of the bomber stream and attempt to draw any *Luftwaffe* fighters who would otherwise be heading for the bomber formation and then engage them in prior combat.

Two more losses of No.149 Stirlings occurred on training flights in November, the first on the 13th, when EF412, 'OJ-F' with Pilot Officer G N Knowles as pilot, swung on take-off, one wheel hitting a sodium flare marking the runway and the undercarriage collapsing. Then on the 17th, MZ260 'OJ-C', with one engine out, overshot the runway and crashed, four of the crew, including the pilot, Pilot Officer G T Lowe, RNZAF, being killed.

On 18th November, the 'Battle of Berlin' began in earnest. While Berlin fell outside the range of "Oboe" for target marking, most bomber aircraft now carried 'H2S', which would be used as the primary target identification technique. There were two major disadvantages to this. The first was that Berlin was so large, no clear outline or shape was possible on an 'H2S' screen. The second was that the Germans were now capable of picking up the 'H2S' transmission and were able to track the bomber stream. Then the fighters, with suitable interrogation equipment known as *Lichtenstein*, or 'SN2', could home in on the individual bombers' 'H2S' transmission like a beacon, which it was. Further, the 'H2S' transmissions could be picked up the instant that the bombers were warming up at their dispersal points prior to take-off and an estimate could be determined of just how big each raid was to be.

From now until the end of February there would be fifteen major raids on the capital city. Being so heavily defended, the resulting losses to Bomber Command were inevitable, and the Stirlings, being lowest and slowest, would take the brunt. Woven between the attacks on Berlin were other major attacks on key German cities. It was on such a raid, to Mannheim, on 19th November, that EH903, 'OJ-L' with Flight Sergeant R L L Smith as pilot, was shot down in the target area, two of the crew being killed, the other five being taken prisoner.

Mining remained a major activity with No.149 Squadron, Stirling EF202, 'OJ-L' with pilot Sergeant K C Richardson, being shot down by a night fighter while on such an operation in the Gironde Estuary, crashing at St Etienne-de-Montluc. Two of the crew were taken prisoner while the other five evaded capture.

The year ended for No.149 with two aircraft losses in December, one of them being another accident while on a training mission. On the 16th EH904 'OJ-P' landed at Pembrey airfield in bad visibility. With an unforeseen obstruction on the runway, the pilot, Pilot Officer R N Johnstone, RNZAF, swung to avoid colliding with it, the undercarriage then collapsing. The aircraft was sent off as training airframe 4445M to No.1 Air Gunners School in December 1943. The evening of the 16th sent Stirlings of No.149 on their first attack on a flying bomb site in occupied France, this one being near Abbeville. There would be many more such raids during the coming year to knock out both the multitude of sites one by one, and also the stockpiles of supplies maintaining them. The last loss of the year was once again on a mining mission. On the 21st, BK798 'OJ-Q' was shot down by a night fighter while mining in the West Friesians, crashing into the North Sea, all of the crew, including the pilot, Flight Sergeant R J Ayers RAAF, were killed.

War on great cities, specifically German cities, continued unabated in 1944. The Lancaster had become the bomber of choice for Bomber Command, and more and more squadrons were rapidly converting to this superior bomber that could fly higher, faster, and with a much bigger bomb load. No.4 Group was now all Halifax Mk IIIs and the Canadian No.6 Group was equipped with a mix of Lancasters and Halifaxes. Nos.1 and 5 Groups were all-Lancaster, and it remained for No.3 Group to also convert to an all-Lancaster Group. The availability of Lancasters and Halifaxes throughout Bomber Command, together with the vulnerability of No.3 Group's Stirlings on such raids over Germany, could now excuse the one or two remaining Stirling squadrons from the bombing role, except when the target was close to home, in France and considered a 'safer' target. Nevertheless, until the Lancaster conversion took place, working parties from Shorts visited No.149 Squadron in January, paying a similar visit to Stirling-equipped No.199 Squadron, and installed 0.5 calibre machine guns behind a plastic shield in the ventral aft escape hatch to counter the upward-firing *Schrägemusik* cannon of the German night fighters, aimed at their previously-blind unprotected underbellies.

The threats of increased German U-boat activity in the Atlantic kept the pressure on No.149's mining operations and it was on another mining mission that Stirling EE969 was shot down on a mining mission to the Kattegat on 28th January.

With an easing of the Stirling's bomber role, January introduced an alternative role for the remaining No.3 Group Stirlings, including No.149, that of SOE or Special Operations Executive missions. These were lone trips into occupied Europe to drop supplies and arms to the Underground resistance movement, in France known as the 'Maquis', in their secret fight against their invader. This called for low flying to very specific drop zones, initially using 'Rebecca', a radar beacon system, flying in on a small 'Eureka' beacon worn on the chest, with a hand-held aerial and operated by one of the partisans. The final identity of the drop zone was usually by flashlights or hand torches, lit at the last possible moment. Nos.138 and 161 Squadrons had been used in SOE operations for some time, but now the invasion of Europe had moved from a possibility to a reality, actually well into the planning stage. Then much greater support was needed to those who would fight the war from within when the invasion came, calling for more support than the two SOE squadrons were able to offer alone.

Perhaps it was No.149's and other Stirlings' minelaying skill that made this new role a 'natural' for them, pin-point drops in the dark being their speciality. Routinely, arms, equipment and supplies would be dropped in containers from the bomb bays, while more delicate supplies, such as radios, would be dropped as well protected packages from the body of the aircraft. Later it would be secret agents that would be added to No.149's range of 'things dropped'. To get things rolling, a detachment of No.149's Stirlings was sent to Tempsford in January, where they stayed through February to support the SOE program. So it was that on 4th February, No.149 Squadron, and other No.3 Group Stirling squadrons followed No.214 Squadron's earlier six Stirling 'toe in the water' lead on 4th January, 27 of them taking part in SOE operations. Inevitably, on 5th February, Stirling EF187 of No.149 Squadron was lost on its second Special Operations mission involving 29 Stirlings, this one to Mont de Cras in France, with the loss of the pilot, Flight Lieutenant H J Colenutt and his crew, the aircraft crashing at Cussy-les-Forges, the Squadron's first such loss.

On 13th February, orders were issued to Bomber Command from the Combined Chief of Staff, "Intensify the bombing offensive against Germany" in order to put the pressure on. Perhaps Germany would be more willing to surrender and so save the countless lives that would be lost on both sides when the invasion of the European mainland did come. The German ability to resist was perpetually underestimated. So 20th February became the big week of attacks against Germany, with No.149 and its Stirlings on the sidelines.

No.149 now divided its function between mining and SOE missions, minelaying now involving as many aircraft as the earlier major raids, 50 Stirlings and 60 Halifaxes being sent on a mining operation in the Kiel Bay and the Kattegat on the night of 24th/25th February. Minelaying in the Kiel Bay area on the following evening was an even bigger operation, involving 131 aircraft. Once again, No.149 lost one of its Stirlings, EF308, piloted by Flight Lieutenant R N Johnstone, crashing into the sea with the loss of its crew.

Roy Abbott aboard EF 411 'OJ-K' relates the story of mining and the pressures put upon crews to deliver the 'Veg' in the correct position:

"Four days later and our name appeared on the 'Battle Order' once again. Operational meal was not until late, so we realised it would be a night sortie - and once again our thoughts ran wild as to what a night trip would be like.

"7.00pm briefing and we knew the target - it was Brest on the western tip of the Brittany peninsula, in France. There was a nice large patch of red around it on the wall map of Europe.

"We were to go "Gardening" (minelaying), and drop our "Veg" (mines) in Brest harbour. The weather would be clear, and we were to go in at 3,000 feet. Defences uncertain, but there may be flak ships in the harbour.

"With that we were sent out to our aircraft to do final run up one hour before take-off. It was a boiling hot evening - the sun was still up, and the run up was completed stripped to the waist. Still in daylight at 9.05 pm we took off on our second operation and set course for the Scilly Isles at 1,000 feet.

"Our route took us over Somerset, Devon and Cornwall with beautiful views of the Bristol and English Channels at the same time; and then came Land's End - and finally our last glimpse of England in the compact Scilly Isles.

"Here we turned due south, and went down low, just skimming the waves at a few feet - the other aircraft followed. By flying at zero feet we hoped to surprise the Hun. His radar equipment is less satisfactory at picking up low-flying planes, and so the dozen planes in the attack all headed south just above the waves.

"Slowly the sun sank below the horizon and no moon came up. It was a pitch black night, and then on instructions from the navigator we climbed to 3,000 feet, and before I realised it all hell was let loose - red and green tracer was coming up from all directions - it seemed to curl slowly through the air. Searchlights began to probe the darkness and the coastline and harbour were clearly visible below.

"We had been detailed to pin-point a headland, make a time run from there on a given course and then drop our mines at one-second intervals. We found the headland, flew immediately over it and on to our course. For fifteen seconds we flew dead straight at 3,000 feet - not the slightest deviation - through that flak. How it missed the plane still amazes me. Slow trails of coloured tracer curled in front of the nose missing us by yards, behind the tail missing us by feet, and above us it seemed to be missing us by inches. It was the longest fifteen seconds of my life. It seemed like hours - just 'stooging' on at a modest 160 mph, while all the guns in creation seem to be firing at you.

"12 - 13 - 14 – Drop', and the first of the mines went, but another four seconds had to be spent on course, as they were to go at one second intervals. Then as the last mine fell clear of the open bomb doors, a searchlight held us.

"We decided to dive for the waves. We could see other planes trying to weave through the flak, some climbing, some diving - one absolutely steady on its time run; but we were still held by the dazzling beam while concentrated light flak, and tracer was coming up in all directions. We counted three flak ships, several destroyers, as well as land batteries.

"The rear gunner had a burst at one flak ship on our way down, and seemed to silence one of the guns. After what seemed an interminable age we were skimming the waves - too low for their defences, searchlights or flak to touch us. What a relief to be out of that dazzling beam, and to see all the tracer curling slowly above us.

"Yet I wasn't really scared - it was too beautiful a sight to be frightened - just like November 5th at the Crystal Palace - a real fireworks night, and for nothing as well!

"One thing had shaken us a bit, though, on the way to the target - we had seen a plane burst into flames and plunge into the sea. Later it turned out to be Pilot Officer Adams' crew, No.149 Squadron.

"Anyway, our 1,820 gallons of petrol had taken us, our four 1,800-lb "Veg" and "Kitty" through the most heavily defended harbour in France, and after exactly five hours we landed at Chivenor (fog at base), and by 3.00 am we were all eating a hearty breakfast of egg and bacon.

"All that worried us, though, was that this counted as a major target, and provided we got the required number of "majors" in, our tour would be 30 Ops. If we did not get enough "majors" we would have to do 40 - which seemed a very long way off back on 6th August.

"The news next day simply stated: 'Mines were laid in enemy waters. One of our aircraft is missing'."

Perhaps as a 'reprieve' from the now-routine SOE and minelaying missions, an attack on the railway yards at Amiens in

France on 16th March involved 130 of those same Halifax and Stirling squadrons that had been minelaying together, and that included No.149 Squadron. It was on this raid that EJ124 was lost, crashing at Boves. Five railway yards, including Amiens, Laon, Aulnoye and Courtrai, were attacked by No.149 Stirlings in March.

Luckily for the Stirling crews, the almost 800 aircraft raid on Nuremberg, on 30th/31st March, did not include any Stirlings. While the raid itself was considered a failure, the loss to Bomber Command was to be the highest ever in World War II, 95 aircraft, or almost 12%. A good deal of the losses were due to the very heavy fighter cover that was put up proceeding to, and over, the target area. On that night, eight Stirlings from No.149 and 75 Squadrons laid 32 mines in the mouth of the Seine using 'Gee' for precise positioning, while seven Stirlings from Nos.149 and 199 Squadrons dropped supplies to the resistance fighters in France, mostly in the Haute Savoie area, between the River Rhône and the Swiss border. All aircraft returned safely. It is known that Flight Lieutenant C Danver, RAAF, with Flight Sergeant Miller, RNZAF, were on this drop, their drop zone being in the foothills of the Alps.

Preparation for the coming invasion of continental Europe continued, with supply drops to the resistance fighters in France being a continual role for No.149 Squadron, while minelaying to keep the German fleet and U-boats locked up in harbour while cutting Germany off from overseas goods and raw materials was the watchword of the day. Germany even resorted to using U-boats as cargo vessels, so desperate were they in need of key raw materials. There were now only three Stirling bomber squadrons remaining in Bomber Command, Nos.90, 149 and 218 Squadrons.

It was on a Special Operations mission on 10th April that Stirling LK382, piloted by Flight Lieutenant R V Sanders, was lost, crashing at Esmery-Hallon in France, with the loss of its crew. Then on the following night, EF502, with Pilot Officer D Bray as pilot, was shot down by anti-aircraft fire while on a similar mission, crashing at St Jean-le-Vieux, in France, one of four consecutive SOE missions. Only two of the crew survived.

Flt Lt Chappell and his crew completed forty sorties between September 1943 and September 1944; fifteen of these were Special Operations Executive (SOE) 'parachutages' trips to France in support of the French Resistance. Plt Off David Mitchell was the navigator in Bob's crew and relates something of their experiences on Special Operations:

"Our whole tour was fairly uneventful although we lost a lot of aircraft and friends on the Squadron. So we flew with a constant feeling of wondering when our turn would come, a strain which was often diluted by plenty of beer and mad singsong parties in the mess during stand-downs. But for the most part we had no trouble, apart from icing and some hair-raising moments flying round mountain peaks in the Alps looking for our dropping sites.

"Supplying the Resistance was all low-level work, flying at 500 feet across France, identifying our dropping site by a signal from a solitary figure in some remote field or plateau using a lamp or torch. Once codes were exchanged successfully three more lights would spring up in a line, which identified the wind direction. We would make the drop from 150-200 feet flying into the wind.

"We were fortunate enough to find all our reception parties and, having exchanged correct signals, to drop our canisters and make our way safely home. Except once. The fact that we did not have our own pilot that night has got nothing to do with the events that followed.

"It was the night of 10th April 1944. We had to fly with a substitute pilot, Flg Off Alan Bettles, and it had taken us a good four hours at 500 feet to reach the dropping zone most of the way across France. Arriving bang on ETA, sure enough as always the reception was there. The three lights were already on, indicating the wind direction, but on this occasion they were signalling the wrong letter(s). There was mild panic while I hurriedly checked my charts, the chosen pinpoint and 'DR' run. Sure enough, I confirmed to the pilot that this was for certain our dropping site. We made several circuits, which would have allowed us to make the drop.

"The frustration was heightened when once again I became the focus of attention. Pilot to navigator: 'Are you really certain this is our spot?'

"At this point I was beginning to doubt myself, especially since we noticed several dropping zones on the way. Many would give you a preliminary flash, hopefully. So I hurriedly rechecked everything once again. Navigator to Pilot: 'This is definitely our dropping point. Time is getting on. If they don't give us the correct letters we're getting out of here'. This was a terribly frustrating decision to take and so reluctantly we started to climb and make our way home.

"'They're doing it right now!' It was our rear gunner 'China' Town shouting into his mike – 'They're doing it right now, they're giving us the correct letters!' And he was right! So round we circled to make another approach. Bomb doors open. Wheels partly down and flaps partly down to reduce speed. We made our dropping approach. 200 feet…150 feet… Suddenly all hell let loose. Two searchlights opened up straight on to us. We seemed to be under a lot of fire from at least three guns on the ground, at point-blank range.

"The bomb-aimer, George Mackie, was in his niche beside the bombsight. The flight engineer, a young, canny, over-conscientious Scot named Ian Harvie, was a little concerned about the amount of time we had spent in the target area and was making a quick check of the fuel gauges. So there was no one in the second pilot's seat and the pilot was screaming his head off to this no one – 'For Christ's sake give me more boost, more revs!' he was weaving as much as he could with both hands on the stick.

"It was 'Taffy' Thomas, the W/Op, who obliged. He rushed forward from his table knocking everything flying and bruising himself black and blue on the way and pushed the throttle levers forward - as he described it, 'pushing everything through the gate'. The good old Hercules engines responded with a roar. For a moment we thought they had jumped the aircraft, like horses at the starting gate.

"During all this time 'China', the rear gunner, was taking care of the searchlights with a few accurate bursts from his guns. He said later he was reluctant to fire on the scurrying figures below who normally he knew to be our 'friendly' resistants.

"I'll say this for our pilot Bettles, he wasted no time. We were out of that danger zone like a flash. And so made our way home, the first time we had not delivered the goods. To relieve our disappointment and frustrations we shot-up two trains and some road transport on the way home, much to the flight engineer's horror. He was still checking those fuel gauges. The total flight took 8 hrs 40 mins, so we didn't have a lot of juice left. When we landed none of us was the least bit tired!"

At this time leaflets to the French civilian population also became part of the 'things dropped', explaining the need for the bombing of the French railway installations. A major minelaying operation took place on 19th/20th April when 158 aircraft laid mines in the Kiel Bay area, at Swinemünde and off the Danish coast, in an attempt to cut Germany's iron ore supply that was being brought across the Baltic. It was on this operation that Stirling LJ504, pilot Flight Sergeant E Jeal, was lost, crashing into the sea off Jutland with the loss of its crew.

The opportunity to perform once again as a bomber squadron with a target in France came on 22nd April, the mission being to Laon, with a total of 181 aircraft. EH943, flown by Pilot Officer H E Billens, was shot down, crashing at Cuissy-et-Gény in France, with no survivors. The following day, another minelaying mission, this one to the Kiel Canal, best described by Flight Lieutenant Robert Todd, RCAF, piloting 'OJ-Q', serial LJ511:

"We were baptised at last! Approaching the run-up area at 12,000 feet, the cloud top was 10/11,000 feet and 10/10 solid to the ground. Enemy Ju 88s dropped bright white flares above us and silhouetted us against the cloud tops. Then the battle started. Jim Newman, our navigator tried to record all the attacks, but they came so fast. I believe he only caught 10 or 12. When it started, I asked the mid-upper to take over as master gunner as he had a commanding view of the skies above where all the attacks would originate. Harry Churchward expended all his ammunition and left his turret to walk forward to the nose position and remove all the ammunition from that gunpoint and take it aft. Harry and Lou had me working the corkscrew circuit for 15 minutes straight during the encounters. One passed right across our nose and I could see the pilot's eyes in the bright light from the parachute flares. Oh, for a front gunner at that exact moment!

"After the drop, we did a steep descending turn in the cloud and reached for the 'bottom' heading in a northerly then westerly direction. I recall passing over Denmark so low that when we reached the North Sea, we were about 1,500 feet above the waves. Suddenly, a flashing light in the water! Our gunners were sure it was a dinghy. We circled, lowered our altitude and came abreast of them at 200/300 feet. Yes, it was some people in a dinghy, but how many and who, we could not be sure. Chances were they were a bomber crew who had to ditch. We kept circling for a few moments while the W/Op radioed and requested they fix our position for a rescue attempt and then we returned to a base leg. By this time, our petrol was becoming rare and the flight engineer, a Scottish lad named Ian Kennedy, was becoming concerned about making base. We radioed about three-quarters the way home for permission to land at Woodbridge, on the coast.

"For some reason, they could not accommodate us. We then requested the approval to land at the nearest aerodrome that was clear, fog having blanketed the whole of the area around our base in Norfolk. We were advised to come straight on in and 'FIDO' would be awaiting our arrival. This was our first experience with this emergency landing aid and it was most welcome. We landed and were interrogated. Don't ask about the petrol that was left. Only our ground crew would know and they didn't offer any sympathy about what was missing! We had a great ground crew unit and we were proud of the service they gave our kites. God Bless them all!"

Then on 24th April, LJ526 with Flight Lieutenant R J Freeman at the controls was lost together with its crew, as part of a 114-aircraft mining operation in the Baltic, LJ526's drop zone being in the Fehmarn Channel, the aircraft crashing at Oster Skerninge in Denmark. Then on 29th April, EF238 was hit by anti-aircraft fire while on a Special Operations mission but they completed their mission, making an emergency landing at Methwold on return due to a damaged undercarriage, the aircraft being a write-off.

What an SOE mission was like is well described, again by Bob Todd, on his trips on April 29th, May 1st and 4th:

"April 29th. LK397 'OJ-K', Special Operations, France. Successful drop. On way home ran across an enemy airfield at 600 feet that had shut down for the night and their 'ack-ack' opened up on us. We did a wide 360 and came in the second time with guns blazing to starboard beam. Then home where all good gardeners go after a bash.

"May 1st. LK388 'OJ-L', to south-eastern France on SOE mission, dropping supplies to French underground forces. Three white lights that formed an 'L' with the tail light giving the call letters for that night and forming the wind direction for the drop. Across France at 500 feet to landmark, map reading all the way on a moonlight night. Navigation by dead reckoning. Finding the last fix, we commence a run into a forest until we locate three white lights. Identify then circle 360 degrees and come in upwind at 600 feet, near stalling speed and if we hit the clearing first time the Bomb Aimer, Joe Cardall, lets go the three large parachute containers. Suddenly, little figures emerge from the trees, lorries drive into the clearing. Within two or three minutes, they are gone and all is silent. We, of course, drone away almost immediately so as not to alert Jerry's radar and protect ourselves from 'ack-ack' and night fighters. Watch those hills! That was close. Are there obstructions marked on the map we should look out for, Joe and Jim? Bomb Aimer and Navigator are in control of our destiny. Please get us home again. To get lost 300 miles deep in enemy territory is no joke. Please get us home again. Finally, Cherbourg off the port beam and away we go across the Channel. The south east coast of England looks mighty good as the dawn starts to awaken Germany.

"4th July. EF411 'OJ-K', and what a beauty to fly at low levels. We would take on our own fighters (playmates) during fighter affiliation practice and give them their money's worth, but at anywhere near service ceiling, close the office and go home! Tonight is France again, because it is a beautiful moonlit night. Special Operations drop to the Maquis, in the south, near Lyon. An Me 109 attacked us making one pass, then gave up, probably due to low altitude. Our gunners seemed to think they saw it shot down later by one of ours, but we could not confirm. For some reason, probably the enemy action, we lost our ground track on the way home and flew over the outskirts of Paris, and although it was dark and a complete black out, we saw many patriotic French citizens come out of their houses and small factories flashing lights, opening lit doorways and every conceivable manner to attract our attention. We waggled our wings and kept on for home."

More minelaying in May, one aircraft, BF570, 'OJ-J' laying six sea mines in the Friesian Islands and River Gironde, while on the following day five No.149 aircraft laid sea mines, also in the Friesian Island area, nearer to Borkum, EF410 'OJ-A' dropping to 500 feet to lay its five. BF570 'OJ-J', again on a minelaying mission, was hit by cannon fire from a Junkers Ju 88 on the return journey, returning to base with a large hole in the fuselage just ahead of the tailplane.

Jim Berry recalls his time at Lakenheath as a pilot, having joined 'B' Flight in November 1943, after completing training at the Heavy Conversion Unit, with just 36¾ hours to his and his crew's credit:

"I've thought many times since that it wasn't a lot! A good job that Stirlings had been taken off German targets due to heavy losses. As a result the Squadron was involved in minelaying, raids into Northern France on 'buzz-bomb' sites, long-range mining in Kiel Bay and the Kattegat, and in Jim's words both were 'ghastly'. In the spring of '44 they started supply drops to the Maquis, and then it was back to bombing the marshalling yards (Amiens, Laon, Courtrai) and minelaying again. In all they did 21 'Ops' from Lakenheath before, in April '44, the whole crew was posted to No.7 Squadron PFF at Oakington.

"Lakenheath in '43 really was out in the 'sticks', very sandy, rather like a desert and with about the same facilities! A bike was essential to get around and to get to the tiny village. I seem to recall a couple of pubs and a wooden hut run, I think, by the Women's Institute, or some such. You could get a 'cuppa' and a bun; not many seemed to use it, apart from the odd Land Girl, and the odd 'bod' from the camp. One of the pubs (The Bell?) had a plasticine type dartboard, with odd distorted wire in the doubles area, which suited a blossoming talent! My navigator and I rather fancied ourselves as a team playing either locals, or RAF, for half pints! Best of all we liked to beat the RAF Police.

"Sadly, my navigator is now in a home with advanced Alzheimer's Disease - what a sad end for a cracking 'nav' who kept us on the straight and narrow when it mattered.

"After No.149 moved to Methwold, the Americans took over and began a transformation to accommodate their Fortresses - or was it Super 'Forts'? Lots of rumours were around whilst we were there. I recall going past on the main road, a few years back, and seeing from the main gates a golf course inside the perimeter fence, tall watch towers, modern buildings - what a place! I didn't go into the village to see what had happened there. For some it would have changed out of all recognition!

"Back then it was a sleepy town and didn't stretch to the main road, although we did have a narrow lane running through the 'drome' at one side. Most odd! Strollers, from the village, used to walk along it to see what we were up to at the weekend. All very informal! It often gave rise to comments in the village as to the shape and size of our loads.

"When we began 'Moonlight' runs to the Maquis, in early February 1944, things were much, much tighter from a security aspect, no outgoing phone calls, mail liable to be censored etc. Whilst we were on 'Moonlights' the locals quickly 'twigged' that something different was happening. We were going off during the moon period, we were going off singly and returning singly then back to 'normal', when it was dark again. We just had to act dumb.

"There was a railway station in Lakenheath, more of a halt really, and when we had leave we had to get the 8 am(?) train to Ely, change at Peterborough and thence to wherever. The snag was that you usually 'worked' the night before and the SPs rarely gave you an early call, so often you had to stay awake from the time you got back. You started your week's leave 'all bloody knackered'! That, of course, is why my 'nav' and I loved to take the SPs to the cleaners at darts, to the extent that we gave all our 'winnings' to the locals!

"I seem to recall that there was a wood at the end of the main runway, plenty of clearance but I always wondered about an engine failure on take-off. I never felt the instructions were sufficiently explicit. Later on, at 'Pathfinders', they were.

"We had a fabulous chap, a Scot, I think, on Flying Control. He could really get us down quickly and encouraged prompt exit from the runway to the taxi track by the simple expedient of landing a Stirling fairly close behind you! You tended not to dally!

"Late January we got our own aircraft. No one else liked it! It was oddish but the engines ran cool. It just coped with a loaded climb and it was ours - EF411. It went on the achieve fame as the Stirling which did the 'mostest'. It was 'M' during our time. It was re-lettered 'K' and was eventually written off at a Conversion Unit, I believe. It was a gem. We had one weird incident. On going out to the aircraft one evening the Flt.Sgt i/c said there was a large 'mag' drop on each engine and after carrying out a complete check he couldn't find anything wrong. Did we want to take the spare aircraft? I opted to 'run up' and take a look for myself, and right enough there was an unacceptable drop on each magneto, on each engine. I asked if he (Flt Sgt) had checked everything - yes, he had, so I opted to take it. It was such a sweet runner. I think this was March 16th. We had no trouble at all and on reaching the dispersal point was greeted by 'Slim', the Flt Sgt and his team, who had waited up. Leave the engines running we want to check them! We did and went off to interrogation. Next day we cycled out to the dispersal to find out the latest on our beloved 'M'. Each engine had cut out dead on each 'mag'. So…on the 18th when we went to see 'Slim'; he said he still had the slightest of 'mag' drops - well within acceptable tolerance - and no way could we take it until it was perfect. So that night we had to take the spare. Fab aircraft, Fab ground crew."

*Flg Off R L Todd (second from right) with members of his air and ground crew at Lakenheath in May 1944. Left to right: Des Wheeler, Ian Kennedy, Jim Newman, Lou Lewis, Harry Churchward, Joe Cardall. The aircraft is Stirling EF411 'OJ-K', which flew 69 operational sorties before being passed to a Conversion Unit.*

*De-briefing a crew on return from an operational sortie took place immediately after landing.*

# Chapter 9: Methwold, D-Day and, finally, Lancasters

As the day for the invasion approached, drops to the Resistance were an almost nightly occurrence, being deterred only by weather conditions. On 11th May, Stirling LK500 swung on take-off for a Special Operations mission and hit a mound, the undercarriage collapsing. It was recovered, repaired, and re-serialled TS262, but then, with second thoughts, perhaps knowing that the day for the Stirling in Bomber Command was virtually over, or perhaps the rebuild just did not measure up to engineering standards, it was struck off charge. May brought with it another change for No.149, this one an administrative one, Wing Commander M E Pickford becoming the new Commanding Officer of the Squadron. This coincided with the move of the Squadron from Lakenheath to the dispersed airfield at Methwold in Norfolk, the Squadron being stood down for one week from Sunday 15th May to accommodate the move, the ground crews being flown over in the Stirlings. No.199 Squadron also moved out of Lakenheath and were re-established at North Creake. Following their move, Lakenheath runways were extended to provide for the newer types of aircraft that would be coming to the RAF.

Lawrence Kearns, an engine mechanic with No.149, quotes:

"There were the remains of a previous camp nearby, which had been used as pigeon cotes at one time. These huts were in a ruinous state and were infested by rats. We spent much time hunting them with a motley collection of dogs which followed us around. We cannibalised these buildings to make ourselves crew huts. At least here we were spared the dust storms that had plagued us at Lakenheath."

A new call sign for Methwold's flying control tower was issued…'High-heel'.

The last loss for No.149 prior to the invasion was on 1st June, when, on a mining operation to Knocke, Stirling LJ501 was shot down, the aircraft crashing at Zeebrugge in Belgium, three of the crew being killed. On that same night, seven of No.149's Stirlings were sent on SOE missions to the Mouterre, Peret and St Amand Montroud area in France, five of which made successful drops of 90 containers and five packages. Again, the following night, a further seven drops were scheduled, in the St Viatre, St Armand-les-Eaux, St Quentin and Péronne areas. One Stirling failed to take off, but 81 containers and four packages were dropped successfully by the others. Several bombing missions and SOE operations were pencilled in for No.149 in their June calendar but most never materialised. Mining operations remained the main focus, with five aircraft assigned to lay mines north of Ostend on 3rd/4th June, 27 mines being laid, Special Operations forming the second major group of operations. However the most remembered Special Operations mission for No.149 Squadron occurred on 'Operation Overlord', D-Day, the 6th of June, this Special Operations mission being known as 'Operation Titanic'.

This was a series of diversionary raids by Nos.90, 138, 149 and 161 Squadrons, the seven Stirlings of No.149 Squadron taking part

*The Squadron's radar section at Methwold.*

being led by the Squadron's Commanding Officer, Wing Commander M E Pickford. The operation involved dropping one-third scale dummy paratroops fitted with one-third scale parachutes. The dummies would carry pyrotechnics to simulate a real paratroop drop, giving simulated rifle, machine gun and mortar fire from the pyrotechnics when the dummies hit the ground. The dummies were made of canvas, filled with sand, the head being filled with straw. The aircraft dropped pintails simultaneously, which would hit the ground quickly and fire off Very flares as if someone on the ground were signalling the drop zone to the paratroops.

A 'window' curtain was also dropped to attract the attention of the German radar stations, to give them the impression that something big was happening. Drop zones were as follows:

'Titanic I', at Yvetôt, where 200 dummies were dropped.
'Titanic II', East of the River Dives, where 50 dummies were to be dropped but this segment was cancelled.
'Titanic III' south-west of Caen, where 50 dummies were dropped in support of the genuine drop of the 6th Airborne Division
'Titanic IV' at Marigny, where 200 dummies were dropped to support the 82nd and 101st US Airborne Division drops

SAS men were already in the Yvetôt and Marigny area to attack individual trucks or dispatch riders who should be in the area, but letting sufficient get away to warn others that something was happening. The drop was five to six hours before the troops hit the beaches.

At around 1.00 am on 6th June, the British Government Code and Cypher School picked up a German message that reported parachute drops in the Caen, Carentan and Le Havre area. The 915th Infantry Regiment of the 352nd German Infantry Division were withdrawn from the beaches to as far away as the Coutances/Isigny area, giving some relief to the landing of the Allied troops shortly afterwards on the Gold and Omaha beaches. Two of the No.149 Stirlings, 'OJ-C' and 'OJ-M', were shot down, LJ621 crashing at Marcelet in France, six of the crew being killed, while LK385 piloted by Squadron Leader C J K Hutchins, on the Titanic III mission crashed at Baudre in France, killing all on board. Meanwhile other No.149 Stirlings were laying mines, intensifying the minelaying already in the month, 48 in two days, mainly in the Ostend area, to protect the flanks of the invasion fleet from U-boats and light surface vessels, including E-boats. The night of 6th June sent eight more of No.149's Stirlings on Special Operations to the Bouresse, Chavigny and Pressigny areas, six of which were successful, 108 containers and six packages being dropped, and on the following night, two more drops in the Josselin area with 24 packages and one container. Six aircraft were assigned minelaying duties, four off the Brest peninsula, two assigned to the La Rochelle area. Of the four assigned to Brest, 'OJ-C' failed to take off while 'OJ-J' returned early with an unserviceable 'Gee' set, essential for accurate navigation and placement of the mines. The other two aircraft laid twelve mines under some anti-aircraft fire. Of the two La Rochelle aircraft, 'OJ-A' had burst a tail wheel and failed to take off. The other aircraft laid three mines, then made a crash-landing on return, with the flaps out of order and an unserviceable air speed indicator, caused by hitting some trees near Stroub when avoiding a group of B-17 Flying Fortresses who were flying below the low cloud.

The 15th of June marked the official transfer of No.149 Squadron to Methwold, this now becoming its permanent base. No.149 was back in action as a bomber squadron on the 15th, the target being the railway yards at Lens in France, a similar raid taking place at Valenciennes to deny the German army the use of the railroad to move troops and supplies. Six Stirlings of No.149

Squadron formed part of the 227-bomber force, accurately bombing on Pathfinder markers.

Mining operations were regular and distributed for the month of June, and included St. Nazaire, Lorient, St. Malo, Brest, Ostend, IJmuiden, Gravelines, Knocke and to the north of the Scheldt. It was a mining operation to Brest on 24th June that resulted in the loss of two of the four aircraft sent on the mission. EF188, with Pilot Officer E J Lincoln RAAF in command, was shot down, crashing at Plougonvelin, four of its mines blowing up on impact, while LK386 'OJ-O' was badly damaged by anti-aircraft fire. The pilot, Pilot Officer S E Lucas, made an emergency landing at Hartfordbridge (later known as Blackbushe) but overshot the runway due to failure of the brake pressure, the undercarriage collapsing. The Flight engineer was injured. Both of the other aircraft received flak damage, 'OJ-B' piloted by Reg Redman who landed at Methwold while Flight Sergeant Bemrose, RNZAF landed away. LK397, 'OJ-C' belly-landed at Methwold on the 23rd and was eventually written off, but the cause is unknown.

London and other places in the south-east of England were now under continual bombardment by V-1 flying bombs fired from various hidden launching sites in France, and No.149 Squadron was added to the list of squadrons sent to locate and destroy these sites or the supply dumps maintaining them. It was normal procedure to attack several sites on a given mission, one or more squadrons being assigned to one specific site. It was on such a raid to Ruisseauville on 25th June, with fourteen of No.149's Stirlings attacking the target with 335 500-lb bombs, that No.149 lost two aircraft, believed shot down by fighters, there being very little flak on this mission. EF140, 'OJ-A' with Flight Lieutenant J R B Roe as pilot, crashed into the sea off Boulogne, while LK394, 'OJ-D' with Flying Officer V F Wunsche, crashed at Lisbourg in France. The month closed with a mining operation by two Stirlings off the Brest Peninsula, and two further Stirlings off St. Malo. 'OJ-E's' starboard engine failed, the mines being jettisoned when the Stirling was down to 500 feet in order to recover the aircraft.

July was very much a 'Special Duties' month for No.149, with ten nights scheduled which would have equated to 83 drops, but six of these nights were cancelled. Added to this, No.149 aircraft would now drop agents into France by parachute, but these drops were shrouded in secrecy and so little is known about them. Ten drops were scheduled for the 4th/5th in the Le Mans, Prémery, Villefranche and Clamecy areas, six being successful, dropping 95 containers and six packages, with a further ten drops scheduled for 5th/6th July in the Péronne, Marle, Le Mans and to the east of Rouen areas. Two aircraft failed to receive any recognition, while LJ477, scheduled to drop at 'Gondolier 16', was hit by anti-aircraft fire, resulting in the load being jettisoned into the English Channel. The aircraft crashed at Thorney Island on return and caught fire. The navigator, Flight Sergeant F L A White was killed, while the others received burns. A total of 132 containers and seven packages were dropped successfully that night. A further ten SOE missions were scheduled for 7th/8th July, one of the ten aircraft taking off swinging and crashing but without injuries to any of the crew. Two aircraft were recalled while three failed to find their drop zones, the other four aircraft dropping 66 containers and four packages at Corbigny, Bellac and Prémery. Other drops were made on 4th/5th July at Le Mans, Prémery, Villefranche and Clamecy, and the 10th/11th of July at Clamecy, south of Orleans, south-east of Tours, Culan and east of Nevers - these two nights totalling 203 containers and 12 packages.

A heavy landing at Methwold following a return from a practice bombing exercise and the Stirling's totally inadequate undercarriage accounted for the loss of Stirling LK388 on 17th July. The starboard undercarriage collapsed, the aircraft overturned and caught fire. Two air gunners, Sergeants Jones and Davidson were thrown clear and killed. The bomb aimer, Flight Sergeant Cox, was seriously injured; the remainder of crew being slightly injured. Previously, on 9th July, LK392 'OJ-O' had overshot the runway on landing with the usual collapsed undercarriage, but the aircraft was repaired and returned to service.

More attacks on V-1 launching sites, known as 'Operation Ramrod' sent thirteen Stirlings of No.149 to Mont-Candon in

*'OJ-P' (LJ623) and air and ground crews. Note the yellow gas detection patch above and to the right of the door. On 17th July 1944, this aircraft collected three bombs through the port wing and put down at Woodbridge. Aircrew identified from left to right as Flg Off J Rugen RCAF, Flg Off A Davies, Pilot Off B Hislop, Pilot Off V Rees, Sqn Ldr Smart, Flt Sgt R Taylor, Pilot Off T Davies.* [P J Rowland]

*The crew of 'P-Peter' at Methwold in August 1944. Left to right: Alex Crisp (Navigator), Jack Chamberlain (Mid-upper Gunner), Scottie Scott (Wireless Operator), Jerry Tenduis (Skipper), Peter Rowland (Flight Engineer), Bob Graves (Rear Gunner), Luke Lukey (Bomb-aimer).* [P J Rowland]

*Squadron ground staff at Methwold. Left to right: Reg Taylor, Maurice Bunn, 'Smudgy' Smith, Reg Newman, 'Tubby' Baker, 'Yorky' Freeman.*

Northern France, known as 'Ramrod 1099', on 17th/18th July. One aircraft had three bombs dropped from an aircraft above go through the wing, and so landed away at the emergency runway at Woodbridge. The take-off for this raid had the Air Officer Commanding No.3 Group, Air Vice Marshal R Harrison and his guest, the British Ambassador to Peru, together with two RAF liaison officers, as witnesses. Then seventeen Stirlings attacked a site at Les Landes in Northern France on the 27th/28th, six to Wemar Cappeland, and seven to Fromentel on the 28th/29th and, to end the month, twelve to the Forêt de Nieppe on the 29th/30th, All of these were daylight attacks, the standard load being 500-lb bombs. The aircrews must have been pleased to return home on the 28th in that they set a record landing time of 1.27 minutes per aircraft.

Roy Abbott recalls one such raid on the V-1 sites:

"Our first operational flight. I think all of the crew had very much the same thoughts and that same empty sinking feeling. What would it be like? Where were we going? What would it be like flying through flak? Would there be any German fighters? Would we come back?

"None of us showed any signs of nervousness; but beneath it all, we were thrilled and at the same time rather dubious. For the first time in our lives our names appeared on the "Battle Order" - we were to go out and bomb the Hun. It all sounded rather thrilling. At last the moment we had been training for, for long months, had come.

"The morning dragged on all too slowly, and then at last came our operational dinner, and then briefing. The target was Mont-Candon - a flying bomb launching ramp in the north of France, just inland from Dieppe. We were to do a semi-circle around Dieppe, and just miss a large patch of red on the map - this red denotes a heavy flak area, and drop our bombs in a wood, in which the launching ramp was hidden. The route, even to us "sprogs", as we were then, looked easy enough.

"Briefing over, and out at the aircraft - Stirling EF411, "K" for Kitty, veteran of 67 missions, the armourers were just loading the last of the 500-lb bombs in the bomb bays - 21 in all; the mechanics were giving a final check on the engines, whilst the sergeant in charge, was polishing the Perspex. She had been refuelled – 1,296 gallons of petrol, and now was ready for us to run the engines up for a final check.

"'Contact', and the four powerful Bristol Hercules engines were ticking over at 1,000 rpm. They were perfect, and an hour later at 15.35 hours (3.35pm), we were airborne, and on our way.

"As we crossed the Channel the weather was perfect - not a cloud in the sky - and just ahead of us was the coast of France. Soon we came nearer, and over it - just two squadrons of Stirlings at 10,000 feet, in broad daylight without a fighter escort!

"I will admit that as we crossed over those French cliffs, with Dieppe on our port bow, I expected all hell to break loose at us, in the way of flak. But, nothing happened; it was just like crossing the English coast - it all looked so peaceful with the brilliant sun shining down on the French countryside.

"Then the bomb doors open - still no flak, and what a sight as every Stirling simultaneously sent down its string of high explosive. Before the bombs hit the ground one or two puffs of flak appeared amongst the formation - not more than a dozen bursts altogether and that was all we saw.

"What a sight as those bombs hit the ground - the wood, in which the ramp was hidden, was almost immediately obliterated in smoke. So we had drawn our first blood! All the time, though, I expected those German fighters to pounce, but nothing happened, and 15 minutes after the first crossing the French coast we were leaving it behind again, without incident.

"Our first taste of enemy territory was finished. Three-and-a-half hours later we were touching down again at base. If all our Ops were to be as easy as that, I don't think there would be any complaints - but, how easy! We had had worse trips on practice flights, with bad weather.

"The 2nd of August 1944 had been an eventful day but not as exciting as we had imagined it would be. We realised now that flying with Bomber Command was just a job of work that had to be done, whether there was excitement or not - perhaps we'd get some excitement on our next trip; or at some later time."

Another mining operation in July, sending four Stirlings to the Bordeaux area and a further four to Ile de Ré area on the 14th/15th, a burst of flak hitting one of the aircraft on the Bordeaux mission. On this same day, Methwold received visitors in the form of five Lancasters from No.550 Squadron returning from a raid on Révigny which was aborted following failure to identify the target which were the railway yards. Other activities for No.149 Squadron in July included two days of air/sea rescue search, unfortunately without success, and various operational and diversion exercises.

A further attack on a V-1 launching site on 2nd/3rd August, known as 'Ramrod 1152', sent fourteen of No.149 Squadron's Stirlings to Mont Candon in Northern France in daylight. There was very little flak, 290 500-lb bombs being dropped. All fourteen aircraft landed within 18 minutes.

On 4th August, No.218 Squadron left Woolfox Lodge and joined No.149 Squadron at Methwold; these being the last two Stirling bomber squadrons it was the most convenient arrangement for maintenance and repair. No.218 Squadron would stay at Methwold for several months, operations now treating the squadrons as twin squadrons and often sending them on the same missions together. However, No.218 was simultaneously converting to Lancasters, flying its last mission with Stirlings in August, defeating the basic aircraft maintenance objective of the move and leaving No.149 as the last squadron in the RAF to fly Stirlings as bombers. It would be only a short time before No.149 followed No.218, being taken off operations mid-month and assigned only air-sea rescue searches, but returning to operations by September. Meanwhile small parties of ground crew were sent over to Mildenhall to attend courses in Lancaster maintenance in preparation for the conversion of the Squadron to Lancasters.

Mining operations by eleven of No.149's Stirlings off Brest on 6th/7th August resulted in the loss of LK383, 'OJ-A' piloted by Flying Officer Adams, which was shot down and seen crashing in flames into the English Channel. Low cloud over Methwold forced the remaining aircraft to land away at Chivenor. Again on the following night, eleven aircraft laid mines off Bordeaux, and once again the poor weather conditions at Methwold resulted in three of the aircraft landing at Chivenor and eight at Colerne on return. Just previously, five Lancasters from Mildenhall landed at Methwold following an attack on a military target south of Caen, ahead of the advancing Allied army, due to the low cloud conditions over Mildenhall.

After one or two more minelaying operations, mainly in the La Rochelle area, and air-sea rescue searches involving a total of fourteen aircraft, finally, on 25th August, No.149 Squadron converted to Lancasters, six Lancasters arriving, being flown in by women ferry pilots of the Air Transport Auxiliary, returning together to West Bromwich in an Avro Anson which accompanied them to Methwold. That night nineteen more Lancasters arrived but these were temporary visitors from No.115 Squadron who were unable to land at their own base at Witchford due to weather conditions. The following day nine more Lancasters arrived for No.149 and by the 29th the Squadron had its full complement of Lancasters. Most of the Stirlings were still at Methwold and on the evening of the 30th five of them were sent out on an air-sea rescue search over the North Sea. That same day, the RAF Film Unit arrived at Methwold with all of the necessary equipment to shoot the Squadron Lancasters for sequences in a movie titled 'Journey Together'. Great pains were taken to exclude No.149's Stirlings from any of the shots.

September for No.149 saw training beginning in earnest to convert the crews from Stirlings to Lancasters. However operations continued with Stirlings, with a raid on Le Havre to support the attacking Allied army by five aircraft from No.149 Squadron, 'OJ-Q' making it to the target on three engines. Two Stirlings repeated this the following day, attacking enemy troop concentrations in Le Havre. There was low cloud cover, so the Master Bomber instructed the attacking aircraft to go below the cloud and bomb on markers. There was slight flak and negligible opposition. The 8th of September saw the last use of Stirlings on operations by No.149 Squadron and the end of the Stirling's role as a bomber. This was a repeat raid on the enemy troop concentrations at Le Havre and involved four of No.149's aircraft, LK401 'OJ-G', aborted its mission and jettisoned its bomb load in the Channel, landing away at Wethersfield. LK396, 'OJ-M' landed away at Tempsford due to the extremely bad weather. LJ632 'OJ-P', and LJ481 'OJ-U', returned at base. Bombing was from 2,000 to 5,000 feet due to low cloud, twenty-two 500-lb bombs being dropped. The two Stirlings returned to base at 09.25 hrs, Flying Officer J J McKee, RAAF making the last Stirling touchdown at 09.31 hrs. It was on this same day that Germany fired its first V-2 rocket at Britain.

On 11th September, two of No.149 Squadron's Lancasters were scheduled for 'Operation Bullseye', which were anti-aircraft exercises. 'OJ-S' returned after 30 minutes with a defect in the navigational equipment, while 'OJ-R' completed the exercise but was late in returning, mistaking Feltwell for Methwold and landing there. The 13th marked the last day when No.149 Squadron flew a Stirling for any purpose. During the Stirlings' service with No.149 Squadron, there were four aircraft worthy of note, having the fifth, sixth, seventh and eighth highest number of operations flown by a Stirling. EJ122 'OJ-Q' flew 57 operations, EJ109 'OJ-M' flew 46, BK781 'OJ-L' flew 45, while EH993 'OJ-D' flew 44.

No.149 Squadron had pioneered the 4,000-lb bomb. The beginning of October would bring it full circle and now the Squadron would take what was now one of Bomber Command's deadliest weapons, an updated version of the early version dropped from a Mark II Wellington, known as the 'Blockbuster'.

*No.149's Stirlings lined up at Lakenheath during a Royal Review.*

*'OJ-K' (EF411) arrives at Methwold from overhaul in almost-new condition.* [L Kearns]

## Chapter 10: Lakenheath and Stirling Stories

What it was like for someone in air crew to go on his first Stirling mission is described by Peter Rowland, a flight engineer, the year being 1943:

"Perhaps the 5th of May has some deeper significant influence in my life for I see in my old diary that it was the birthday of a little Welsh WAAF girlfriend I'd left behind at St.Athan and it was also the birthday of my dear wife who I was to marry years later on, and our two lovely daughters were also born within two weeks of that same date. I never realised the earlier connection with the date in all these years.

"Having ascertained that we were on Squadron Battle Orders for the coming night everyone concerned was of course 'confined to camp', voluntarily in practice but it would be a damn fool who disappeared, or was absent at any time thereafter. You were an integral part of a team, a member of an aircrew of seven 'bods' and of a Squadron. It was all about an intense honour and an overriding sense of duty drummed into us, the penalty of failure being severe in the extreme and absolutely dishonourable.

"All one knew from the detail was the particular aircraft allocated to the individual crew, or with whom in the case of a crew requiring a 'stand-in' for any reason, and the times for meals and briefings. Those flying would then report to their Station Offices, each aircrew trade had its own Section HQ, presided over by an experienced officer, one who has already completed a tour or even two tours, his title being Navigation Leader, Gunnery Leader, Bombing Leader and so forth. He dealt in detail with all aspects relevant to that trade, exercised discipline - to the direction of competence, efficiency and the consolidation in practice of one's largely theoretical training, especially for the newly-qualified, his would be the voice of wisdom and he has been through 'it all', and here he is, right in front of you.

"For the Flight Engineers, we would get advice on engine handling and fuel consumption factors and general aircraft serviceability, modifications of systems and equipment or changes of procedures in the light of experience. Details of weight and fuel loadings are given and log sheet forms issued for the operation in hand.

"In the time to ourselves, until attending the Squadron briefing, I found time to write home and a postcard to a girl I'd met at the HCU at Stradishall (known to all of us as 'Strad'); as I recall, there were also a letter to me from my parents and from a WAAF girlfriend back at St.Athan. Motor insurance proposal forms to fill in from my brokers and post off with a renewal of my driving licence now that I was permanently stationed. I intended getting my motor cycle on the road, private vehicles not being allowed on training stations so it had been laid up some 16 months.

"At the early evening main briefing, the Navigators and Captains being called to their own, secret, meeting a half-hour previously for issue of maps and to copy routes onto them, we were collectively told of our tasks for that night. Twelve crews were on individual efforts with single aircraft on these 'Specials' (supply dropping to French Resistance groups), some laying sea mines. The briefing was in the nature of a general resume of the RAF's efforts that night, Met conditions, current and expected, in the various areas of operation, signals info, colours of the day, restricted or dangerous areas to avoid, heights and the rest of the flight patterns to be flown. It was stressed to the several crews that would be mining individually in the La Rochelle area that its flight over enemy-occupied France had to be plotted and navigated very carefully to avoid crossing over defended areas, of which there were plenty in that area. Time to assemble for transport to aircraft dispersals around the airfield, start up, taxying and take-off times, synchronise watches, Pilots and Navigators having issue wrist watches. Then best wishes and safe trip from the Commanding Officer and it was over.

"Our task was 'Gardening', the code name for mining, off the La Rochelle area in the Bay of Biscay on a course in line with San Sebastian in Spain. The route out was over Selsey Bill, across the Channel to the French Coast then a lengthy penetration right across the Brest Peninsula to its southern coastline to pin-point a nominated visual landmark, and thence a time and distance run to the 'garden', such an innocent and apt description for sowing of 'vegetables', as sea mines were likewise referred to in the air force.

"The Skipper, Netherlander Gerald Tenduis, Navigator Alex Crisp, and Canadian Bomb Aimer Roy Lawrence, responsible between them for the navigation and route finding, went into a huddle with the details with Al who plotted the courses, bearings, times and distances on the maps whilst in the Flight Engineers' Section I received details of the loading weights, fuel to be carried and quantities in the tanks; the Stirling had a rather complex fuel system with no less than 14 tanks in the wings with capacities varying from only 63 gallons to over 300 to juggle with. Obviously the amount carried depended upon bomb load and the distance - so we had the fuel load and the endurance figures and given some servicing details for 'R' Roger, EF161, a Mk III Stirling, which had been allocated to us and I prepared a Log Sheet for the flight on which was to be recorded continuously all the engine power settings used and the times from which the petrol consumption figures are calculated and monitored. Thereby the fuel tanks were systematically drained (before an engine stopped) as the flight progressed. Yes, the F/E's job was quite a busy one - no computers in those days or microchip things!

"After our 'flying supper', which lent us a feeling of, just a little perhaps, superior privilege and the issue of flight rations, coffee, sandwiches, chocolate and barley-sugar sweets, we were 'bussed' back over to the flights to collect our gear, the last item being the queue at the counter of the parachute store. It was then that I can remember a sudden queasy feeling in the belly, picking up the pack; it was a momentary spasm of anxiety and fear that something might go wrong, produced I suppose by the action of accepting that article which represented the ultimate and last resort of survival, a feeling that was to be repeated on every subsequent operational flight. It quickly disappeared in the next moment with the excitement and the concentration to the duties that followed.

"'R' Roger's turn to take off came at ten minutes before 10 pm (21.50hrs). It was now quite dark after the sun had set an hour or so earlier; she soared off the runway with her load of fuel to keep us airborne over seven hours and four 1,500-lb parachute mines under our feet. We circled the airfield and set off on the first course that Al called for us to take us down to the South Coast; it was then that Alex found that the 'Gee' set was u/s, so he had lost a major navigation aid but it did not seem to deter him much.

"There is a note in my diary confessing that I felt distinctly nervous at the prospect of leaving the country for the very first time in my life. Lawrence, laying prone on his bomb- aiming couch in the nose, called out the precise time of crossing the coast and identified Selsey spot-on and I glanced back out of the astro-dome to see the waterline and murky smudge of land slowly retreating behind the tail, as the aircraft moved relentlessly over the greyish rippled surface of the sea and 'home' disappeared into the distance. Gerry called for the guns to be tested and there was a reassuring clatter as Bob and Jack fired off a short burst into the sea from the six machine guns between them.

"Eventually the Bomb Aimer called that the enemy coast was coming up, gave again the precise time of crossing and confirmed our position on his map. We lifted up to 3,000 feet to map-read our way across France; there was plenty of light as it was only two nights from a full moon. Tension eased a little when we reached the Southern Coast of the Peninsula, where we stooged around for a little while until Lawrence was sure of exactly where we were before striking off upon a carefully calculated time and distance run dropping down low to some 1,500 feet above the water, there would be about 150 miles to run - almost another hour.

"As we neared the end of the run, Gerry lifted up a little, Alex counted down the last minutes and the Bomb Aimer called for 'Bomb doors open', and shortly afterwards sung out in some alarm that we were about to pass over a line of four small boats on the same course, just for a moment I thought quite ridiculously 'Christ, the sods are in the bloody way'.

"The Skipper didn't deviate a fraction from his attention glued to airspeed and altitude with Alex calling out the last few seconds of the run. As the boats slipped away astern Bob in the rear turret called out that tracer was coming; Gerry acknowledged and told everyone to 'hold tight' ordered the gunner not to fire back and give our position to them and held onto his straight and level.

"I bobbed up in the astro-dome and took a look at the light flak hosing up out of the darkness in bright colours of broken dots and streams of light, there was quite a packet of it, but it was now some distance astern and we were rapidly drawing away; thank goodness we were flying low and presumably had overtaken them before the guns were manned and trained.

"Our load was deposited smack in front of them and we all felt suddenly very elated and jubilant and had a quick laugh about it with a babble of excited comment on the intercom, except for the Navigator working away at his desk plotting the reciprocal long haul home, I thought it was a bit like stealing a goal when the other chap was looking the other way.

"I noted in my diary later on that I'd felt quite okay watching that flak come up and almost invincible perhaps, and they won't be able to hit us in this great sturdy Stirling; nonsense of course, but that was my personal reaction to our baptism of fire on our very first trip.

"The return to base was uneventful and the round trip was accomplished in 6½ hours. We felt satisfied with a job done well, in our estimation, and seven happy but rather weary airmen, after debriefing and an early breakfast, plodded back to our billets in the early dawn light to crawl thankfully to bed."

Pilot Charles Lofthouse, DFC continues with his own story:

"The conversion to the Stirling brought changes in the crew structure. Geoff Ising was posted to India; Sgt Austin was given Captaincy and his own crew; two new posts were to be filled with the addition of a Flight Engineer and a Mid-Upper Gunner. Sgts Borley and Martins thus joined the crew. The new Navigator was Dennis Pebworth. With three new members joining us, Michael, the two French Canadians and I agreed that we would undertake a further thirty operations, in order to see through the three new members joining. Second Pilots would join experienced crews until such time as they attained Captaincy.

"Michael was again available for Ops on 3rd March, when we visited the Renault Works at Billancourt, Paris. Great care was taken to limit spread, and No.3 Gp aircraft concentrated on the small island in the Seine which held part of the factories. The plan called for the massed use of flares and a very low bombing level. Most aircraft made two runs. Air Commodore 'Dolly' Gray, from Gp HQ, visited us the next day.

"'What did you think of it?' he asked. I said that if he had arranged to turn daylight on for a second or two, nobody would want to fly ever again!

"I think Michael and Georges fired their guns in anger only once during our tour. On 24th March, the Navy came to brief us on a projected minelaying operation in the Lorient area.

"'Find the Ile de Groix', they said. 'On the northern tip there's a white house. Set course over the house, on such and such heading, at 400 feet; fly up the river mouth towards Lorient and drop your four mines, singly, at set intervals, then come home'.

"We did just that. There were searchlights, on wide beam settings, and light tracer being fired both sides of the river mouth.

"'Permission to fire down the beams?' asked both gunners, and for the first time we could smell our own cordite inside the fuselage. I see that we landed at Predannack, but I can't recall why.

"We went to Rostock in April. On the 26th, in good weather, and with a coastline to assist, we established the target, overflew at 10,000 feet, trying to ignore the defences. We circled for the bombing run, now at 6,000 feet, and when 'Bomb doors open' was called, we were disappointed to realise that the electrics/hydraulics were u/s. Round again, still prudently losing height, and released the bomb load directly on to the target. Two photographs were obtained. This resulted in the immediate award of the DFC for one Lofthouse, willingly shared, and dutifully celebrated by the whole crew in the 'Bird in Hand', Beck Row.

"Perhaps I should mention our minelaying trip to Kiel Bay, on the night of 17th May. Nine aircraft were despatched. We were briefed to overfly Denmark on both outward and return flights at 200 feet, don't ask why, and given a forecast barometric pressure reading to be set on altimeters before each transit. I chose to fly at 300 feet. The dropping area for the mines was a critical aspect of the operation, and shipping lanes had to be established by reference to land masses. The area was littered with Flak ships, all very active. We were unable to establish the dropping area, and eventually off-loaded over open sea, and began the homeward flight. Over Denmark, and all quiet, we suddenly hit an obstruction, pulled the nose up, and sorted ourselves out. The front gunner reported some strands of wire, presumably, around his guns and reaching along the fuselage, where the outside noise was somewhat disturbing. Having decided that we had struck telephone wire, the worry was that we would lose the evidence before we got home! Cpl Vesey, the NCO i/c ground crew, told me off for low flying at night and having little regard for his chaps who now had the job of respraying the sides of the aircraft fuselage, now stripped of paint. 'It might not be ready for you tonight,' he said ruefully.

"Each crew member took a length of the wire; mine has been lost over the years, but Leo Langlois still had his skein when I visited him at Port Daniel, some six years ago.

"The Squadron lost three aircraft that night. One belly-landed very comfortably in Danish countryside. All the crew walked away and became POWs. The other two crew were shot down by Flak ships in the 'Gardening' area. Five of one crew were taken prisoner after recovery from the sea. Two of this crew have no known grave. All members of the third crew lost their lives, five of them being washed ashore subsequently and were buried in Vaerlose churchyard. Two are also on the RAF Memorial at Runnymede, having no known grave. Such details become known long after the events which triggered them were planned and executed. We have to wonder at the choice of words such as 'planned' and 'executed'. But had we known of the ineptitude, no doubt we would still have gone.

"Of Michael's twenty-eight operations, three, in later years, would have been categorised 'Non-OP', being early returns due to equipment failures. Those trips not specifically mentioned in this review, involved Brest and 'Happy Valley'. Brest was always covered with a smoke screen, but there was a coastline. Duisburg and Essen, part of the great Ruhr complex, were always covered in thick haze, and at this stage of the Bomber Command Offensive provided statistics for the War Cabinet Secretariat's Mr Butt and his investigation of our 1941 efforts.

"'Of those aircraft recorded as attacking their targets, only one in three got within five miles. Over the French ports, the proportion was two in three; over Germany as a whole the proportion was one in four; over the Ruhr, it was only one in ten'…and…'whereas over thick haze it was only one in fifteen'. All deduced from photographs, which wouldn't have been available had we not gone to get them!

"I end this F540/541 review with the entry notifying my posting in June 1942. Pebworth, Borley and Martins still required eight more operations to complete their tour. A member of Group HQ Staff came to see me at Lakenheath. I was playing Shove Halfpenny in the Mess. 'You've completed your tour, Lofthouse, and we have a job for you,' he said.

"I explained our wishes and our contentment with continuation. 'I know all about that.' he said, 'but there's a war on. You will be given Squadron Leader rank, and take over No.214 Squadron Conversion Flight at Stradishall - with almost immediate effect'.

"So a wonderful relationship expired, with a devastating effect on those left behind. F/O Pebworth remained with No.149 Squadron (now at Lakenheath), taking the post of Squadron Navigation Officer. He had some eight more trips to undertake to finish his tour of operations. On 24th August 1942, he flew with P/O E P Wynn, on operations. The aircraft caught fire very soon after take-off and crashed one mile SE of the airfield. All crew were killed.

*Flight Lieutenant Dennis Pebworth.*

"Sgt Martins also continued his tour. On 29th July he was a crew member with P/O Hulse, and crashed NW of Saarbrücken. All were killed.

"Sgt Borley continued with No.149 Squadron and completed his tour. He was subsequently commissioned and joined No.90 Squadron.

"These three above joined the Lofthouse crew on conversion to Stirling aircraft. Following conversion, Sgt Ising, the Wellington Observer, was posted to India in August 1941, still flying in the Wellington. The Public Record Office confirms that he, too, lost his life on operations.

"Alan Austin, on completion of his operational tour as Captain, and commissioned, was posted to Woolfox Lodge, to instruct on Stirlings. He was killed in an aircraft accident in the autumn of 1942.

"Leo Langlois, and Georges (Gaspe) Langlais, both French-Canadian and of the RCAF, returned to Canada. Leo soon returned to complete a second tour with a Canadian squadron serving in the UK. They both survived the war."

Two tales of what it is like to fall into enemy hands. First, Stan Burnett, a wireless operator/air gunner. Stan remembers doing one more raid to either Essen or Emden before their Stirling N9163 'A' was taken from them and they were presented with a brand-new aircraft BF312:

"At this time, even before delivery of this new 'kite', F/O Forward's crew along with two more senior crews had been practising low flying. Of course, this gave way to speculation why this was necessary. All was revealed on the morning of the 16th July. The three crews were called to briefing and told that they were a specialised dusk attack on the U-boat building yards just 4 miles NE of Lübeck. Twenty-one experienced crews had been chosen from No.3 Group for this raid, and No.149 Squadron was to be the leading 'vic', with F/O Forward as leader.

*'OJ-N' running up while apparently awaiting its bomb load.*

"The operation was code named 'Pandemonium'. Each aircraft was to be loaded with six 1,000-lb GP RDX filled bombs with enough fuel for the trip (about 2,000 gallons). For 'A' for Apple take-off was at 1845 hours. The aircraft were to fly in 'vics' of three and on approaching the target, they would proceed individually to drop their bombs. When 'A' Apple's 'vic' of three reached the turning point for approaching the target, the cloud cover was now only 3/10ths and dispersing, instead of the expected 8/10ths. Of course visibility was excellent and the target was quickly identified. F/O Johnny Forward prepared for his run in and turned on to the heading given to him by Bunny Austin, now in the bomb aiming position. Reducing height to 600 feet he levelled out. Flak was exploding all around and 'A' Apple and its crew took a great pounding. The Skipper kept to his course, guided by 'Bunny', and after what seemed a lifetime, there was a cry of 'bombs gone'.

"Over the intercom Johnny Forward shouted that he was getting down to roof top level, to try to avoid more flak damage. By this time, I was in the front turret, and firing at anything that moved, and saw at least one gun crew put out of action. It was now obvious that 'A' Apple was in a bad way and the skipper called to each member of the crew in turn. There was no reply from Sgt Les Duckworth, the Flight Engineer, or from Sgt Dickie Shepherd, the mid-upper gunner, and Sgt Clifford Turner reported being hit in the face and sounded distressed. Sgt John Locke, a Canadian, flying with the crew as second pilot, and on his first operational trip, was asked to go back to check. He reported that Sgt Turner had head injuries and possibly more, and that the other two lads were dead, their bodies riddled with flak. He had only just returned to his seat when Flt Lt Mace reported that the rear section of the aircraft was on fire. At the same time Sgt Turner cut in to say that there was also a fire in the front centre section. The Skipper immediately told the rest of the crew that he would try to get enough height for them to bale out. In the space of only what seemed like a few seconds, there was an explosion and the Skipper said that he could no longer control the aircraft and gave the order to abandon. I alighted from my turret and opened the front escape hatch, in the nose of the aircraft.

"I assisted Sgt Locke and F/O Austin out, and heard Flt Lt Mace over the intercom say he was going out at the back. I then climbed out of the nose to check on F/O Forward and Sgt Turner. They were both ready to come down and gave the thumbs up sign, and the Skipper indicated to me to get out next. Losing no time, I turned around and dived head first through the hatch. I wasted no time in pulling the ripcord, as I knew that height was in short supply. I felt the pull of the 'silk' as it opened above me, and for a moment imagined I was being jerked back up again. As I gathered my thoughts, I looked up and could see two more 'chutes just above and in front of me, and knew then that the other two had made it. Below and to the left I saw 'A' Apple hit the deck and a great pall of black smoke rise skywards.

"However, before I could dwell further on their fate, I realised that I was only a few feet from the ground and landed in a small field of grazing bullocks. I quickly collapsed my parachute, and hid it in a hedge. As I climbed over a gate, I saw two men running up the lane towards me shouting, one of them waving a rifle. I could not understand what they were saying, but it was crystal clear that they were hostile. Being still daylight, the rest of the crew were soon captured and all taken to a nearby fighter drome for interrogation. Sgt Turner was taken direct to hospital where it was found that he had lost his left eye and some fingers on his right hand. The following day we were entrained for Dulagluft. After six days the three officers were sent to Stalagluft 3, at Sagan, and a few days later Sgt Locke and I were sent to Stalag 8b, at Lamsdorf.

"Whilst we were at Lamsdorf, John and I made arrangements to swap identities with two Army lads. This was to enable us to get out on a working party, where we had a greater chance of escape. Within twelve months we were transferred to Stalagluft 3, Sagan, where we met the rest of the crew. I was there until after the 'Great

Escape' in March '44, and then shortly afterwards the news that 50 of the escaped officers had been shot in cold blood by the Gestapo. I was moved, along with a few hundred others, to a new camp five miles away from Sagan, called Belaria. January '45 found the Russians advancing with great speed, and on the Sunday evening of 28th January, we were all given notice to evacuate the camp. The temperatures were minus 20 degrees Centigrade and the blizzards horrific. I, like many of my fellow POWs, survived mainly by will-power until we reached another camp called Luckenwald, nearly a month later, which was 20 miles south of Berlin. We stayed until the Russians liberated us on 21st April. It was not until the 20th May that we were handed over to the Americans at Wittenburg. Within three days I was flown back to England via Brussels. In consequence of my experiences I weighed just over 84 pounds."

Then the story of Gerry Grant, also a wireless operator/air gunner, with No.149 Squadron at the same time period as Stan Burnett, and reporting his fateful thirteenth mission in Stirling R9320, OJ-S:

"On the Stirling we carried two wireless operators/air gunners and my co-WOp/AG operated the radio, whilst I was in the front turret on the nose guns. On 17th May 1942, we were briefed for a minelaying trip to the Baltic, 'somewhere out there'. This was to be my 13th operational flight; on the previous 12, I had flown as front gunner. At the briefing I was told that on this flight I would be in the mid-upper turret, which was about half-way down the aircraft, mounted on top of the fuselage. While 13 is considered an unlucky number by many people, as I tell my story you will realise that for me it was a lucky one. The front turret was left empty to be manned by the navigator, if necessary.

"We took off from Lakenheath at 2200 hours, I think it was a Sunday, with a crew of seven, and set course in an easterly direction, out across the North Sea, and if I remember correctly, the weather was not too good. We approached Denmark, reducing altitude as we did so, and crossed the coast just north of Sylt, where the Germans had a fighter station. We flew on quite low, down across Denmark to our target area, which I can only remember as 'somewhere out there'. As I mentioned earlier, we were carrying sea mines as our load, and these we dropped on the target and then turned about, setting course to cross Denmark and head for home,. As it turned out, getting back home was to take three years.

"Still in this area, and still at a very low altitude, we were fired at either by a flak ship or a land-based unit on one of the islands. It was a very dark night and we could see nothing as we flew on at low level at around 165 mph. Suddenly, and without warning, we hit the water; the time 0130 hours, 18th May. Later, we found that all of our watches had stopped at this time. I was lucky in that at the time of impact I had my turret turned so that I was facing back over the tail of the aircraft. My shoulders and back took the full force of the very sudden stop, from 165 mph to zero. If I had been facing in the other direction, it would have been a different story. On impact the aircraft broke into two pieces, the fuselage tearing just in front of the tail, which fell away into the water. In the tail section was the rear turret with the rear gunner Mike Wootton. Immediately the nose of the aircraft, which must have been smashed on impact, started to fill with water and the plane started to settle. I remember releasing myself and half-jumping, half falling out of the top turret into the dark fuselage, which by now had already quite a slope to it. I pulled off my flying helmet, and released my 'chute' harness, and could hear the water lapping up through the aircraft, but no voices. As I climbed up to the broken end of the aircraft I made my way through the broken cables and belts of ammunition, and there above me was the night sky.

"At this time I had many things going through my mind. As I stood on the broken end of the aircraft, I could hear the rear gunner, Mike, calling out of the darkness, his voice appearing to come from some distance away. By now the aircraft was really filling with water. I stood on the ripped and torn metal and looked around the outside of the fuselage and down towards the starboard wing. There in the dark I could make out the outlines of our large yellow dinghy,

and could see there was someone in it. This dinghy had self-inflated when our aircraft had crashed on the water. Ours had been tested only the previous day, back at Squadron. From their position in the dinghy, my fellow crew members could see the angle of the aeroplane, and that at any moment it was going to slide beneath the water. My 'Skipper' shouted words which might sound a little profane, but they brought an immediate reaction from myself. The words he shouted were something like, 'Jump, Gerry, for Christ's sake jump!' Obeying the last orders, I jumped and at the same time the aircraft slid down and under the water.

"As it went down it created something like the same effect as when water runs from the bath. I was pulled or sucked down with it. I was wearing a life jacket and rose to the surface near the dinghy. Our second pilot, who was on his first operational flight, jumped from the dinghy to help me aboard. At this point, as far as I can remember, not many words were spoken. Now from seven we were five, we heard no more calls from the darkness. The rear gunner and our Flight Engineer, Gordon Locke, we presumed, had gone down with the aircraft. About this time another one of our Squadron aircraft approached, flying very low, and we fired off one of the distress rockets, which we had in the dinghy. This I think fired thirteen red stars, then there was silence, but for the sound of the water lapping against rubber. As time passed we got ourselves organised, we had paddles, which fitted over the arm, but as for steering, a round dinghy is not the easiest thing to steer. Our Captain had been cut across the forehead and nose, but all round we five survivors were very lucky as regards injury.

"Time passed and came the dawn. I do not know what time; as I have said, our watches had stopped at 0130 hours. Then a Danish fishing boat approached and we were taken aboard. It was good to feel something solid under our feet again. Sometime later we were transferred to a Danish Navy or Customs boat. I do remember that on one of these two boats we were given some very welcome refreshment. We were then brought into the port of Rødby, where a German Army escort was waiting for us as we climbed onto the jetty. As we were taken towards the town, there were a few local people about and I remember how some raised their hats as we passed. We were taken to a house where the Germans later brought our dinghy. Then our Captain was taken away for treatment to his injuries. When he rejoined us, he brought with him a large box of chocolates. These had been left for him in the hospital. We did not stay long at the house, but were taken to an airfield which I understand was Avnø, where we stayed for, I think, two days. Then, with an escort, we were taken to Naestved, where we boarded a train for Gedser. There we took a ferry to Warnemünde and the start of a three-year stay at various POW camps. We were released and returned to England in April 1945."

Air crew always ran the risk of being brought down by 'friendly fire', and this was not only Allied anti-aircraft fire and fighters, but can also include mid-air collisions, and also being hit by a bomb. When a 4,000-lb bomb hits an aircraft from above, the chances of survival are nil. As Bomber Command raids often used all three types of heavy bomber on a given raid, each type flew at its own service ceiling, the Lancasters in the 'top bunk', then the Halifaxes below, who could be bombed by the Lancasters, and finally the Stirlings, who could be bombed by either of the other two. What such an experience is like is best described by Peter Rowland, Flight Engineer, on their raid in 'OJ-P', one of thirteen No.149 Squadron Stirlings, to a V-1 launching site at Mont-Candon, five miles south of Dieppe, on 17th July 1944:

"Crossing our coastline I took up station in the astro-dome, a bubble of Perspex in the cabin roof which afforded a splendid view all round, I'd have a grandstand view of the events and lend another pair of eyes to my mates in the three gun turrets.

"We spotted suddenly the tiny black spots in the far distance to the north which rapidly grew into aircraft at about our height on a converging course, then into four-engine Halifax bombers and the sky seemed full of them, actually only twenty, but a most impressive sight as they slid relentlessly onto us on the same heading at the rendezvous point; we were all in the right place at the right time and we had actually seen other RAF aircraft, which was unusual. It had been a tense moment as other aircraft had sort of 'jockeyed' into position at random, mid-air collisions were not at all unknown and one shivered at the thought of what was happening unseen about you during the night raids when one never actually sees another aircraft, hopefully!

"Before the run in to the target I have to check over all the engine instruments and gauges, everything is fine. I calculate the present fuel position and enter up my log sheet before going into the astro-dome again. The aircraft is now passing into the control of Ted Lukey, our Bomb Aimer from New Zealand, laying prone in the nose calling up directions to the Skipper; we have reached the left-left-right-right-back a bit, situation!

"It is at this point that I became aware one of the Halifaxes was jinking about directly above us only 400 to 500 feet away, I suppose, and I felt a dreadful fear that this was going to be a very dodgy situation and waited to see that our tracks would separate slightly but he seemed to be following with deadly precision every move we made.

"By now the bomb doors are opening and I can see very clearly the neat rows of bombs hanging in the belly of the aircraft right above my head, Gerry and Lukey were in intense concentration as we came up to the aiming point in perfect bombing conditions, an intercom silence was the strict rule for the rest of the crew during this critical stage regardless of anything until 'bombs gone', so I had to keep silent, pray and put my faith in fate which all aircrew had to trust and live with one way or the other, and thought surely the other Bomb Aimer must see us right underneath.

"At the very moment I heard 'Bombs away - bomb doors closed', with heart-stopping suddenness I spotted the other load drop away lazily from the aircraft above and in an instant grow much larger. On September 18th 1983, when having dinner together, I was able to ask our Navigator, Alex Crisp, what immediate effect the next few moments had on him over the target. He of course, together with the Wireless Operator, Felix Martin, were the only ones effectively shut off in the aircraft without a view outside; he said he cannot really remember much except that I called something like, 'Watch out! We're going to be hit by a bomb!', and he thought 'Hit by a bomb?'. The bloke's gone bloody potty or something.

"In fact I'd forgotten after all these years that I'd actually switched on and yelled out, but I still vividly remember grabbing my chute and banging it on the clips feeling great remorse and guilt at not warning earlier but I know the Skipper wouldn't have tolerated interference in the bombing run-in and would have pressed on anyway.

"I simply crouched there standing by my panel expecting at the best that the aircraft would break up and with luck I'd find myself thrown clear and then a flash of abject dismay that we were over enemy ground and even if I drifted out over the sea the Germans would get me before our ASR launches; I wouldn't get 'home'; so near - yet ...... I wonder now at the speed with which these thoughts had passed through my mind in just an instant and are still extremely clear today, I must also reflect that not one thought of actually dying entered my head, only of danger and survival.

"The bombs struck us with a most sickening crunch that was to haunt me for many years after. Jack and Bob in their turrets got the fright of their lives as dirty great bombs swooped past. One of them, I think it was Bob in the tail, sounded most indignant when he exclaimed with some emotion that, 'A bomb's just passed me', and Jack said they were passing between the wing and tail.

"The great huge Stirling was practically torn out of Gerry's hands and we plunged down as he struggled to regain control; the outer part of the port main plane had been hit, smacking it down, coupled with a lot of drag and loss of lift. Gerry pushed open the throttles of the two port engines and applied opposite aileron and compensating rudder to lift up that wing.

"As he got his breath he called out to ask if everyone was okay and getting the affirmative answers ordered us to stand by to abandon the aircraft and called Lukey to come up and help him hold her. Now this was something else, a few moments before I had learnt that I actually would have been able to jump out of the stricken aeroplane, no trouble at all given the chance in despair and panic of catastrophe, but to wilfully leave when necessity might be doubtful and a shred of hope remained, was a different matter."

The Squadron records finish the story very matter-of-factly. 'One aircraft landed away at Woodbridge after successfully bombing the target, as a result of three bombs going through the mainplane, dropped from an aircraft flying above in the target area'.

The Stirling stories end on a comical note with Lawrence Kearns's story of him and his pal, Geoff Thompson, both ground crew:

"We had been stood down because of thick fog, 'airmen's sunshine', as it was known. So during the evening we made our way down to Methwold to one of the pubs and spent a jolly evening drinking what passed for beer in those days. Then we set off around the airfield guided by the taxi-way blue lights. The fog was pretty thick as we got up near to 'A' Flight dispersal. We could hear singing – above us – and realised we were under one of the Stirlings. The happy individual was singing, 'Oh! God Our Help In Ages Past', and we both thought he would need some help in the present, let alone the past! On climbing into the plane, we found our very 'happy' comrade had made his way along the wing and was sitting with his legs dangling over the edge, on the very tip of the wing. The Stirling wing would have been about 18 feet above ground level. With difficulty we got him down through the fuselage to the ground, and onto his own bike, still singing, and back to the billet. He wouldn't believe us the next day until he saw all of the anti-icing paste on the back of his trousers. He went pale and swore he would sign the pledge! Of course, he did not."

*Airmens' Mess Staff, 1943.*
*[Nellie Friend]*

*'OJ-E' (NG381) flying over the Suffolk countryside on a flight from Tuddenham.* [Don Mayston]

# Chapter 11: Lancasters!

The era of the Lancaster had finally arrived for No.149 Squadron, with 'OJ-A' scheduled for a Combined Operation Exercise on 12th September, then three Lancasters taking part in diversionary exercises on the 15th in support of a main operation by Bomber Command. 'OJ-Q' returned early, one of the crew members suffering from a lack of oxygen. The first Lancaster bombing mission took place on the 17th when nine aircraft attacked German strong-points at Boulogne in daylight, bombing below low cloud at the Master Bomber's instructions. This was together with No.218 Squadron Lancasters, which would usually be the case until No.218 left Methwold.

The gun positions and enemy strong-points at Calais were scheduled to receive No.149's attention in support of the Allied ground forces on the 20th, 25th, 26th and 28th of September. However low cloud obscuring the target caused the Master Bomber to abandon both the 25th and the 28th mission for No.149. On the 20th and 26th, they bombed below the low cloud on target markers. This was interspersed with an attack on the industrial area at Neuss on 23rd/24th September. Of the nine Lancasters scheduled, seven of the aircraft bombed on the glow of the target indicators as the target was covered with 10/10th cloud. 'OJ-A' and 'OJ-R' brought their bombs back, not being able to see the target. In order to protect the approaches to Antwerp, gun batteries had been set up on the island of Walcheren. Most of the island lay below sea level. If the sea walls could be breached, the island would be flooded, putting the guns out of action. On 3rd October, ten Lancasters from No.149 Squadron, plus those of other squadrons, 240 in all, carried out a daylight attack on the sea wall at Westkapelle in support of the Allied battle for the sea approaches. After one hour's bombing, the sea wall was breached, the sea then flooding a good deal of the sixteen square miles of the island and several big gun positions. Opposition was negligible but two No.149 aircraft were hit by flak. Each No.149 Lancaster carried a 4,000-lb bomb together with six 1,000-lb and two 500-pounders.

It was back to night raids on 5th October, eighteen No.149 aircraft taking part in the raid on Saarbrücken. Due to questionable positioning of the target markers, the Master Bomber called the raid off, but radio interference resulted in eleven of the aircraft already having dropped their bombs. The remaining aircraft jettisoned part of their load and brought the rest back. Another night raid followed on the 6th, this one to Dortmund, with fourteen aircraft hitting the target, 'OJ-C' having to return early with trouble with its port inner engine; the load per aircraft was one 4,000-lb bomb, the remainder being 4-lb incendiaries.

Back to a daylight raid on the 7th, this one being a concentrated attack on Kleve by ten of No.149 Squadron's aircraft. Then it was preparation for Operation Hurricane, a combined operation between Bomber Command and the 8th Air Force to demonstrate to Germany the overwhelming superiority of Allied air power. This began on 14th October with over 1,000 RAF bombers attacking Duisburg in daylight, while the 8th Air Force sent over 1,000 bombers to the Cologne area. Eighteen of No.149 Squadron's Lancasters were involved. The target was obscured by dense smoke and there were no target indicators. However the Master Bomber decided to go ahead with the raid and gave the code word 'Freehand' to the bombers, indicating that they should bomb visually. There was moderate anti-aircraft fire over the target.

That night twenty of No.149's Lancasters returned to Duisburg, this time bombing on ground markers. Fires were still burning from the morning's raid. Again there was moderate anti-aircraft fire.

Next night, on the 15th, it was a raid to Wilhelmshaven with eight of No.149's Lancasters. 'OJ-L' was unable to find the target and brought its bombs back but the other aircraft bombed the target successfully despite the thick haze partially obscuring the target indicators. The defences were rather weak, with a few searchlights and fighters, and some moderate anti-aircraft fire.

By this time, 'G-H' radar equipment had been fitted to about one in every three Lancasters in No.3 Group, with the Radar School in Feltwell training the Group radar mechanics in the maintenance and repair of the equipment, the navigators being trained on ground trainers. 'G-H' was an extension of the 'Gee' principle, but instead of using the master 'A' station ground transmitter, the transmitter was carried in the aircraft, while the 'B' and 'C' stations necessary to derive the co-ordinates were either in Britain, or in mobile units, advancing into Europe with the Allied front. This system could handle as many as 50 to 100 aircraft at a time, and allowed individual aircraft to precision bomb on 'Gee'-style co-ordinates. It also allowed the attack on targets well beyond

Posed in front of 'OJ-B' at Methwold in March 1945 are the air and ground crews of 'TK-C' (HK699). Back row, left to right: 'Ches' Halford (Navigator), 'Al' Lovett (Bomb Aimer), Jack Wilkinson (Flight Engineer), 'Oak' Jones (Pilot), Arthur Gray (W/Op), Chris Walsh (Air Gunner), 'Tosh' Templeman (Air Gunner), Peter Dempster (Air Gunner). Front row, left to right: 'Taffy' Thomas, 'Tubby' Baker, Arthur Learner, 'Tosh' Williams, Reg Taylor, Reg Newman, 'Sandy' Smith.

the range of 'Gee', now that the slave station transmitters were on the European mainland. To identify 'G-H' carrying Lancasters, two broad horizontal yellow bands were painted across the fins. In this way, non-'G-H' carrying aircraft could formate on a 'G-H' aircraft, and they could all drop their bombs in unison.

With more and more of its Lancasters being equipped with 'G-H', 18th October heralded independent action by No.3 Group from the other Groups. No longer did No.3 Group need to rely on No.8 Group Pathfinders as target markers. With its newly acquired 'G-H', No.3 Group would pinpoint its own targets and also guide its non-'G-H' No.3 Group aircraft. Many raids from now on until the end of the war would become sole No.3 Group raids. On this day, No.3 Group carried out a night 'G-H' raid on Stuttgart, seventeen aircraft from No.149 Squadron being in the second wave. However not all aircraft bombed on 'G-H', some of the aircraft bombing visually on target markers dropped by No.3 Group aircraft or on the glow of the fires from the first wave.

The 22nd of October brought a further all-3 Group 'G-H' raid, this one with 100 aircraft on a daylight raid to Neuss, twenty of the aircraft being from No.149 Squadron. The following night brought another No.3 Group 'G-H' raid, this one to Essen, with eight of the eighteen No.149 Squadron aircraft using 'G-H'. 'OJ-H' was withdrawn, and 'OJ-V' returned early, with an electrical short in the 'Gee" set causing a fire. Several of No.149's Lancasters received minor flak damage. There were 1,055 aircraft on the raid, the biggest number of aircraft on any one target so far, the non-'G-H' aircraft bombing on sky markers. 4,538 tons of bombs were dropped.

The 25th of October sent seventeen of No.149 Squadron's Lancasters to join 754 other bombers on a further raid to Essen, this one being in daylight. There was moderate flak, with 'OJ-B' receiving slight damage and the mid-upper gunner of 'OJ-A' receiving injuries. The damage to Essen was even greater than the previous raid. A further all-3 Group 'G-H' raid with 105 aircraft the following day sent fifteen of No.149's Lancasters to Leverkusen, 'OJ-K' receiving slight flak damage.

The flooding of Walcheren had not eliminated all of the gun positions on the island and so five of No.149's Lancasters joined 272 other bombers in attacking five gun positions at Dishoek in daylight on the 28th. The bombing was accurate, and two large explosions were seen. On that same day, one of No.149 Squadron's Lancasters joined the 733 aircraft which bombed Cologne, causing enormous damage.

Each of the last two days of October sent No.149 Squadron's Lancasters to oil refineries, Wesseling on the 30th, with twelve aircraft acting as 'G-H' leaders, and Bottrop on the 31st, thirteen of No.149's Lancasters acting as 'G-H' leaders, the 'G-H' aircraft dropping red target markers. The remaining Lancaster crews were not idle in that the 30th sent seven aircraft, and the 31st eight aircraft, on night raids to Cologne, this time the target marking being by 'Oboe' for the aircraft involved, the target being totally obscured by cloud. 'OJ-W' returned slightly damaged by flak on the 31st.

The 2nd of November sent 184 aircraft of No.3 Group, 22 of them from No.149 Squadron, on a 'G-H' daylight attack on the Meerbeck synthetic oil plant at Homberg. Two large explosions were seen in the target area, followed by black smoke up to 1,000 feet. There was intense anti-aircraft fire and several of the aircraft were damaged. 'OJ-S' was badly shot up and landed away at Newmarket, Pilot Officer VR Jamieson RNZAF suffering minor flak injuries.

Three more No.3 Group 'G-H' attacks followed on each of the next three days, 17 aircraft each day joining daylight raids to Solingen on the 4th and 5th, and five joining a night raid to Koblenz on the 6th, the raid destroying 58% of the town. This latter raid originally called for fifteen of No.149's Lancasters, but ten were then withdrawn as they were not able to be bombed up in time for the mission. It may well have been an incident in the bomb dump on that day which closed down activities there. Some technical problem had developed with a 500-lb delayed action bomb, which was eventually transferred as a safety measure to the sand pits at the old bomb dump. There it exploded prematurely, killing Aircraftmen H Hamer and W Day, two RAF Regiment personnel from Feltwell on guard duty, and wounding three others, LACs K Corfield, E Smithers, and A Payne. The civil inquest held by the local coroner, G E K Burke Esq., at Station Sick Quarters on the 9th returned a verdict of 'death by misadventure', followed by a Court of Inquiry on the 10th to investigate the accident and 'allocate responsibility'.

Word came down from Headquarters No.3 Group on the 7th, via Administrative Instruction No.44, that No.218 Squadron sharing Methwold's airfield with No.149 Squadron was to be moved to Chedburgh. To this point in time the two Lancaster squadrons had operated like twins, accompanying each other on all raids, as if they had been a single squadron.

Germany's oil refineries once again received No.3 Group's attention, with 'G-H' daylight raids to the Meerbeck synthetic oil plant at Homberg on 8th November, the synthetic oil refinery at Castrop-Rauxel on the 11th and the oil plant at Dortmund on the 15th, fifteen, sixteen and twenty of No.149's Lancasters respectively accompanying each raid. Several aircraft were damaged by heavy flak on the 8th.

The 12th of November brought the news, in a letter dated the 10th, that No.149 Squadron was to be raised to a three-flight Squadron, confirmed by Administrative Instruction No.49 on the 26th, 'C' flight to carry the Squadron code 'TK'. No.218 Squadron was to be similarly expanded.

The American First and Ninth Armies in Europe were about to begin an offensive and a directive was sent to both the 8th Air Force and Bomber Command to cut the German communications behind the German lines. Accordingly, on 16th November, 1,188 aircraft from Bomber Command attacked Düren, Julich and Heinsberg, while 1,239 bombers from the 8th Air Force attacked targets in the same area prior to the American advance. No.3 Group was assigned to Heinsberg with 182 Lancasters, including nineteen from No.149 Squadron, the target being marked by 'G-H'. The weather conditions were very bad on the return journey, with only one of No.149's aircraft being able to land at Methwold. One aircraft landed at Woodbridge, while the other seventeen aircraft landed at Oakley. Flight Sergeant W Scott was hit in the thigh by flak, a tourniquet being successfully applied, but he died before he returned to base. His loss of blood was not exceptional so he most probably died of shock.

On 17th November, various Bomber Squadron equipment, including radar equipment, was loaned by No.149 Squadron to the RAF College at Cranwell for an exhibition there. A message was received from the College Commandant, signed by Group Captain H Nelson, AFC, which stated that this was 'the best exhibition that the College had ever been able to produce'.

More base excitement was added to the bomb dump incident, when a fire occurred in the Motor Transport Workshops on the 18th, but this was extinguished without further incident.

No.3 Group was back with another 'G-H' attack on the Meerburg synthetic oil plant at Homberg on the 20th with 183 Lancasters after a pause of only twelve days. However the weather was stormy, making it difficult for the non-'G-H' carrying Lancasters to formate on the twin yellow-striped tails. This sent them back the next day with 160 Lancasters, bombing through cloud on 'G-H' coordinates. The raid culminated in a vast sheet of yellow flame which was followed by black smoke rising to a great altitude. It was the Nordstern oil plant at Gelsenkirchen which received No.3 Group's 'G-H' attention only two days later on the 23rd, with 168 aircraft bombing through cloud.

The limiting factor for the range of 'G-H' was the location of the two ground 'B' and 'C' slave stations. It was decided to see just

*Bombing the dykes at Westkapelle to flood the German defences of Walcheren before the landing craft arrived, 3rd October 1944.*

what the maximum practical range was by sending 75 Lancasters of No.3 Group on a raid to Fulda on 26th November. Unfortunately the distance was just too great, resulting in very scattered bombing results. Not so the 'G-H' raids on the Kalk Nord railway yards at Cologne, when very good results were obtained by a 'G-H' raid carried out by 169 Lancasters of No.3 Group.

The month ended for No.3 Group with a 145-Lancaster mostly 'G-H' night raid to Neuss on the 28th then a daylight 60-Lancaster 'G-H' raid to the Osterfeldt benzol coking plant near Oberhausen. Of the ten No.149 Squadron aircraft on the raid, 'OJ-H' was hit by flak but returned to base.

The necessary extra Lancasters for 'C' Flight were flown in to Methwold so that by early December, No.149 could be upgraded to a three-flight Squadron with a complement of thirty aircraft plus spares. Most of the all-3 Group attacks during December were 'G-H' daylight attacks on railway marshalling yards and on the Rhine synthetic oil plants. A breakthrough by General Rundstedt in the Ardennes meant that the German supply lines to their forward troops had to be cut, hence the attacks on the railway marshalling yards.

The first oil plant attacked in December was the Hansa coking plant at Dortmund on the 3rd, with six Lancasters from No.149 Squadron being part of the 93 total. The bomb load on this raid was all 1,000-lb bombs, including delayed action. The following day, fourteen aircraft from No.149 Squadron made up the 160 Lancasters which attacked the railway marshalling yards at Oberhausen, resulting in one large explosion being seen. Leaflets were also dropped in an attempt to persuade the German people that continuing the war was a useless exercise. More than half of the bombs dropped were delayed action. 'OJ-X' received slight flak damage, but no fighters were seen.

Hamm was No.3 Group's next 'G-H' target, with 94 Lancasters, fourteen being from No.149 Squadron, attacking in daylight. 'OJ-U' was attacked by a Messerschmitt Bf 109G, but it was itself attacked by an Allied fighter giving cover, sending the Messerschmitt on fire into the clouds. HK653 'OJ-Y' received flak damage. The raid was very successful, 39% of Hamm's built-up area being destroyed. To this point, most of No.218 Squadron's personnel had remained at Methwold, but on the 5th most were transferred over to Chedburgh, the rear party following on the 7th.

The first major raid on an oil target in eastern Germany took place on 6th December, when 425 Lancasters from three different Groups attacked the oil refinery at Leuna in Merseburg at night. This called for fourteen of No.149 Squadron's aircraft to accompany. However 'OJ-V' was withdrawn and no less than four aircraft, 'OJ-O', 'OJ-P', 'OJ-S' and 'OJ-T', were forced to return to base due to various technical problems.

Then on 8th December it was back to No.3 Group acting independently again, with a 163-aircraft 'G-H' daylight raid on the railway marshalling yards at Duisburg. Fourteen of the aircraft were from No.149 Squadron, 'OJ-C' having to abort due to severe icing. The weather over Methwold on return was bad, forcing 'OJ-A', 'OJ-N', and 'OJ-R' to land at Newmarket, 'OJ-Y' to Waterbeach, and one other to Feltwell. 'OJ-P' received slight flak damage on the raid. An enemy fighter attempting to attack the Squadron's Lancasters was shot down by fighter cover. A similar all-No.3 Group 'G-H' daylight attack on the marshalling yards at Osterfeld took place on the 11th, with No.149 Squadron supplying fifteen of the 150 Lancasters involved.

The 12th of December was another sad day for No.149 Squadron. It was on a No.3 Group 'G-H' raid to the Ruhrstahl Steel Works at Witten that the Squadron lost two of its aircraft. Ten of the 140 Lancasters were from No.149 Squadron, with Mustangs escorting the bomber stream. The formation was attacked by about 30 Messerschmitt Bf 109 fighters over the target area, the ensuing fight resulting in eight of the bombers being shot down and also a number of the fighters. HK653 'OJ-R', piloted by Flying Officer E H S Dorey, was shot down, five of the crew being killed, the other two being taken prisoner. HK697 'OJ-Y' was also shot down, all of the crew including its pilot, Flying Officer K A W Miller, being killed. 'OJ-G' was hit by a fighter and landed away at Woodbridge. 'OJ-E' was also damaged by a fighter, the pilot and the flight engineer being slightly wounded, the aircraft landing away at Manston. 'OJ-T' claimed a Messerschmitt Bf 109 shot down while 'OJ-K' claimed one Messerschmitt Bf 109 damaged. 'OJ-P' and 'OJ-W' were damaged by anti-aircraft fire while 'OJ-T' and 'OJ-L' were hit by fighters This was the first major raid on Witten and the steelworks was not hit, the bombs falling all over town.

The breakthrough by the German troops in the Ardennes master-minded by General Rundstedt began on 16th December, sending 108 Lancasters of No.3 Group to the Siegen railway yards to cut off enemy supplies in a 'G-H' daylight attack, fourteen of the aircraft being from No.149 Squadron. Six enemy fighters attacked on the return journey, but with little success. 'OJ-N' returned early with severe icing trouble, while 'OJ-M' and 'OJ-X' received slight flak damage, 'OJ-M' landing away at Wendling. The raid was not too successful.

Another daylight attack on railway yards, this one at Trier, was carried out by 32 of No.3 Group's Lancasters on the 19th, twenty of them being from No.149. The weather over Methwold on return was bad, so eighteen of the aircraft were diverted to Manston, while 'OJ-D' and 'J' landed at Benson. Several aircraft received slight flak damage. Two of No.149's Lancasters formed part of the 113-aircraft 'G-H' daylight attack on the same target two days later. Once more bad weather on return diverted both returning aircraft, this time to Dishforth. All of the aircraft which had landed away on the 19th and 21st returned to Methwold on the 23rd, when the crews received their usual interrogation.

The 24th of December saw the planning of a daylight attack on Hangelar airfield near Bonn, but this was later changed to a night raid. Twenty-one of the 104 No.3 Group Lancasters were from No.149 Squadron, two of No.149's aircraft engaging enemy fighters.

Another attack on marshalling yards took place on the 27th, this time at Rheydt in daylight by 200 Lancasters and eleven Mosquitoes, scheduling nine of No.149's Lancasters to take part, but the bad weather at Methwold permitted only five of them to take off and then they were unable to return to base, landing away at Tuddenham.

The continuing bad weather sent one flight of No.149 Squadron's aircraft to Woodbridge to operate from there as a detachment and Advanced Striking Force, 240 ground crew accompanying them. The facilities at Woodbridge were such that the ground crew had to live and work under the most punishing of conditions, sleeping on the ground in open-ended hangars. The first raid from Woodbridge sent eleven of No.149's Lancasters as part of a 167-Lancaster 'G-H' force in a daylight attack on the Cologne/Gremburg marshalling yards. A large column of black smoke was seen, which penetrated the 10/10 cloud over the target.

The No.3 Group daylight 'G-H' attack on Koblenz/Lutzel on 29th December put 85 Lancasters in the air, including seven of No.149's from the Woodbridge detachment plus a further nine from Methwold. Seven of the Woodbridge aircraft and seven from Methwold hit the primary target. The whole railway system was blocked and the Koblenz/Lutzel railway bridge was put out of action for the rest of the war. 'OJ-N's' rear gunner's electrical suit caught fire and, running short of fuel, the aircraft aborted, landing at Manston. The starboard inner engine of 'TK-C' proved u/s on take-off, so the bombs were jettisoned in The Wash. Five of the Woodbridge aircraft reported slight flak damage, the pilot of 'OJ-O' being wounded in the hand.

The year closed with a No.3 Group 'G-H' daylight raid with 155 Lancasters, 21 of them from No.149, fifteen being from Woodbridge, the other six from Methwold, attacking the railway marshalling yards at Vohwinkel on 31st December. A 40-mph error in the wind prediction carried the bombs south of the target. All of the aircraft landed back at Methwold.

The new year, 1945, brought little change in No.3 Group philosophy, with the Group still operating largely independent of the other Groups and bombing by its own 'G-H' target-marking technique, the primary targets still being railway marshalling yards to hinder German troop movements and supplies, and attacks on the oil plants which provided the fuel supply to the rapidly-dwindling *Luftwaffe*. The loss of fuel following these attacks was claimed later by Albert Speer to have brought German industry to a halt through its inability to move raw materials.

Bad weather continued to hinder Allied efforts and thirteen planned raids in January were cancelled because of 'the most severe (weather) in England for many years'. Snow remained on the ground for almost the entire month with frosts and fogs common. The heroes of the day were the flight line ground crews who, working outside and in the bitter cold, continually maintained the aircraft in fighting condition.

While the *Luftwaffe* was but a shell of its original strength, it still had a trick or two up its sleeve and January saw the formation of *Jagdverband* 44, the first Messerschmitt Me 262 jet fighter squadron in defence of Germany, with the famed German 'fighter ace' *Generalleutnant* Adolf Galland in command, and the best of Germany's fighter pilots, including Steinhoff and Lutzow, gathered into a single squadron, ready for combat against both the British and American bomber streams.

However, the German advance in the Ardennes had been halted, and the Russians were advancing into Silesia, Czechoslovakia, and Western Germany, and were now within 50 to 60 miles of Berlin. The first day of the New Year saw an all-No.3 Group 'G-H' day raid with 146 Lancasters on the railway marshalling yards at Vohwinkel, seventeen of the Lancasters being from No.149 Squadron. Due to an incorrect wind forecast most planes were late over the target. Although there was very little flak, there were two combats with enemy aircraft in the target area.

The 3rd of January brought a Nos.1, 3, 6 and 8 Group night raid with 514 Lancasters and seven Pathfinder Mosquitoes to Nuremberg, fifteen of the Lancasters being from No.149 Squadron.

A large explosion was seen, followed by smoke and fires. Two four-engined aircraft and one single-engined fighter were seen to go down in the target area. (Note 1)

While returning from the raid, NG362, 'OJ-S' overshot the runway on landing at Methwold, crashed and burnt, two of the crew, the rear gunner and the mid-upper gunner being injured. That same day there was also a No.3 Group 'G-H' attack, bombing through 10/10 cloud, on both the Castrop-Rauxel benzol plant and the Hansa benzol plant at Dortmund, three of No.149's Lancasters forming part of the 99-Lancaster force and assigned to the former target. No fighters were seen but there was moderate flak over the target area.

Two days later, eighteen Lancasters from No.149 Squadron were part of the all-3 Group 'G-H' daylight attack on the railway yards at Ludwigshafen, postponed from the previous day. Two aircraft returned early, 'OJ-M' with a sick upper gunner and 'OJ-R' with a failed starboard outer engine. Intense accurate anti-aircraft fire into a clear sky made precision bombing impossible and so the bombs were scattered. 'OJ-G' received 21 flak hits and landed away at Woodbridge while 'OJ-D' received 15 flak hits. Two aircraft from other squadrons were seen going down over the target area, five parachutes being seen. No enemy fighters were encountered.

The following night, 6th January, Nos.1 and 3 Groups held a combined 'G-H' raid on the railway marshalling yards at Neuss with 147 Lancasters, thirteen of them being from No.149 Squadron. The attack was concentrated and a large explosion was seen. An unidentified aircraft was seen to fall in flames at Louvain, Belgium. Only one enemy fighter was seen on the raid.

The 7th of January brought a combined Nos.1, 3, 5, 6 and 8 Group night raid to Munich, involving nine Pathfinder Mosquitoes which used 'Oboe' for target marking, and 645 Lancasters, five of them from No.149. The target was bombed through 10/10 cloud, the slight flak over the target area bursting well below. Several enemy fighters were seen west of Wurm Lake including three jets. Two 'Scarecrows' were seen in the target area, and as eleven Lancasters were lost on the raid, these were most likely aircraft which had received direct hits, exploding in the air.

There was then a four-day respite for No.149 Squadron, but not for Methwold in that a detachment from No.3 Lancaster Finishing School at neighbouring Feltwell flew over on the 8th, on detachment for two weeks.

The 11th sent fifteen of No.149 Squadron's Lancasters on a 152-Lancaster No.3 Group 'G-H' day raid on an attack on the railway marshalling yards at Krefeld, bombing through 10/10 cloud. There was only slight anti-aircraft fire below over the target and no fighters were seen. This was followed two days later by a 158-Lancaster No.3 Group daylight 'G-H' raid on the railway marshalling yards at Saarbrücken, thirteen of the aircraft being from No.149, 'OJ-B' returning early with trouble in one engine. There was no flak or fighters but the aircraft met bad weather on return, eight of them being diverted to St Mawgan, the other four to St Eval.

Another attack on an oil plant, this one the Robert Muser benzol plant at Langendreer near Bochum took place on the 15th, with 63 Lancasters, ten from No.149, on an all-No.3 Group 'G-H' daylight raid through 10/10 cloud. The flak over the target was moderate to intense, sufficient for six of No.149 Squadron's aircraft to return with flak damage, HK 657 sufficiently damaged to be sent on to No.46 Maintenance Unit for repair..

The next night, No.3 Group carried out a 'G-H' raid through 10/10 cloud with 138 Lancasters, ten of them from No.149, to attack the benzol plant at Wanne-Eickel. There was moderate flak over the target with some enemy fighter activity, including combat between 'OJ-N' and a Messerschmitt Bf 110, 'OJ-N' returning to base.

While no raids took place for the next four days, 'G-H' training on air exercises continued,. and to keep up the excitement on the base, an RAF truck collided with the NAAFI mobile unit that went out daily to the dispersal sites to supply the flight line crews with a hot cup of tea and a 'wad'. The No.3 Lancaster Finishing School Lancaster Detachment returned to Feltwell on the 21st. However it was replaced by Lancasters of the Feltwell 'G-H' Training Flight the following day, beginning training five days later. That night 286 Lancasters from Nos.1, 3 and 8 Groups, eleven of them from No.149, together with sixteen Mosquitoes, attacked the benzol plant in the Bruckhausen district of Duisburg in clear moonlight. The Thyssen steel works nearby was also hit. Moderate to intense heavy flak was met over the target with several of No.149's aircraft being coned by searchlights, together with attacks by enemy fighters, 'OJ-N' claiming hits.

The WW I ingenuity of the No.149 personnel continued in WW II, a test of "window light", a No.149 Squadron/Methwold invention to facilitate the dropping of 'window', was carried out and demonstrated to the Chief Signals Officer, Headquarters, No.3 Group, Wing Commander J A Chorlton, on 26th January,

A further No.3 Group 'G-H' daylight attack on railway yards, these being at Cologne/Gremburg, took place on 28th January, with 153 Lancasters including twelve from No.149 Squadron, 'OJ-F' returning early with port outer engine failure, followed by a similar attack the next day on the railway marshalling yards of Krefeld-Verdingen involving 148 Lancasters, again twelve from No.149; this time 'OJ-L' returning early, again with failure of the port outer engine. In both cases the flak was slight or moderate with no sign of enemy fighters.

February began for No.3 Group with a 160-Lancaster daylight 'G-H' attack on the railway marshalling yards at Mönchen-Gladbach on the 1st, fifteen of them from No.149 Squadron. Then out again on the next night to Wiesbaden, the only large raid on this target, in company with Nos.1, 6 and 8 Groups, bringing the Lancaster total up to 475, sixteen from No.149, with twelve Pathfinder Mosquitoes marking the target with 'Oboe', although No.3 Group still bombed on their 'G-H', the 'G-H' in this case proving superior. NN708, 'OJ-Q', with Wing Commander L H Kay, DFC on board was shot down, crashing in France.

The next night it was back to a No.3 Group 'G-H' raid with No.149 Lancasters, fourteen of them from No.149 Squadron, on the Hansa benzol plant at Dortmund. The target area was cloudless, with many searchlights and moderate flak, also evidence of fighter activity but none of them engaged any No.149 aircraft. A four-day rest, then No.3 Group was back in action with a daylight raid on the oil plant at Wanne-Eickel with 100 Lancasters, thirteen of them from No.149, 'OJ-E' having to return early due to problems with the oxygen system. The weather was poor, resulting in only 75 of the aircraft bombing and with scattered results. The flak was slight but accurate, 'OJ-L' and 'TK-B' returning to base with flak damage.

The next night, No.3 Group attacked the railway marshalling yards at Hohenbudberg near Krefeld with 151 Lancasters, fifteen of them from No.149 Squadron. 'TK-F' was not included, having to return early with a failed air speed indicator and other instruments. While the crews believed that the attack was very successful, no new damage could be seen by photographic evidence. PB483 'TK-B' returned with slight flak damage. 'OJ-B' and NF976 'OJ-O' were engaged in combat with enemy fighters, 'OJ-O' being attacked twice. Due to failure of the interrupter gear mechanism, machine gun fire from 'OJ-O's' own mid-upper fatally injured the rear gunner, Sergeant R E Tootell. In the second attack the mid-upper gunner claimed a Messerschmitt Bf 109 as probably destroyed.

'Operation Thunderclap' was the Allied attempt to end the war early, demonstrating the air power of the Allies by the total destruction of Berlin, Dresden and Chemnitz from the air, and to warn Germany that organised resistance after the war would be futile. It was also a show of force to Russia of the Allies' superior air power. The rapid advance of the Soviet army changed the basic plan.

It began with a two-wave attack on Dresden on the night of 13th February. The first wave consisted of 244 Lancasters, all from No.5 Group. The second wave, three hours later, with Nos.1, 3, 6 and 8 Groups, consisted of 529 Lancasters, sixteen of them from No.149, and nine Mosquitoes. 'OJ-V' attacked a target of last resort while the rest of No.149 Squadron attacked the primary target. The 1,478 tons of explosives and 1,182 tons of incendiaries resulted in a firestorm in which 50,000 people died. Flak was slight, and no fighters or searchlights were seen. (Note 2)

The following night, continuing with 'Operation Thunderclap', the target was Chemnitz, with aircraft from Nos.1, 3, 4, 6 and 8 Groups taking part, consisting of 218 Halifaxes and 499 Lancasters, ten of the Lancasters being from No.149. 'OJ-D' was engaged by a fighter on the return journey, with no return of fire.

It was back to all-No.3 Group activities on the 16th, with a 100-Lancaster daylight 'G-H' raid on Wesel, seventeen from No.149 Squadron. There was accurate flak over the target, with NF972 'OJ-H', HK577 'TK-H', PB838 'OJ-M', NN756 'OJ-R', and NF971 'OJ-S' all being hit once by flak. The weather over Methwold was poor on return resulting in 'OJ-A', 'OJ-D', 'OJ-E', and 'OJ-R' all having to land away at Tempsford.

Two days later it was a return to Wesel for No.3 Group with a 160-Lancaster 'G-H' daylight attack, including thirteen from No.149, and back again to the same target in daylight on the 19th with 168 Lancasters, eighteen of them from No.149. It appears that this time the job was done to Headquarters' satisfaction, with concentrated bombing in the railway area. No fighters were seen and though the flak was slight, 'OJ-Q', NG409 returned to base with flak damage. Once again bad weather over Methwold sent all of the returning aircraft to Bottesford.

The last major raid on Dortmund took place on 20th February when No.3 Group joined Nos.1, 6 and 8 Groups in a night raid, consisting of 514 Lancasters, seven of which were from No.149 Squadron, and fourteen Pathfinder Mosquitoes, virtually destroying the southern half of the city. There was negligible flak, but considerable night fighter activity. Back to a No.3 Group 'G-H' daylight attacks on an oil plant two days later, this being on the benzol plant at Osterfeld. The 82 Lancasters on the raid were accompanied by the RAF film unit with No.463 Squadron. No.149 Squadron's contribution was twenty Lancasters. There was moderate flak in and around the target area, several aircraft receiving flak damage. NG244 'OJ-J' received three flak hits, HK793 'TK-A' received two, and HK649 'TK-F', HK654 'TK-G', PB838 'OJ-M', and PB509 'OJ-C' each received one.

The next day it was another 'G-H' raid on an oil plant, No.3 Group attacking the Alma Pluto benzol plant in Gelsenkirchen with 133 Lancasters, twenty from No.149 Squadron. There was no opposition from either flak or fighters. The 'G-H' Training Flight detachment returned to Feltwell this day. Another oil plant attack within two days, on the 25th, the synthetic oil refinery at Kamen with 153 Lancasters, twenty from No.149, resulting in dense black smoke and flames seen in the target area. PB506 'OJ-B' was slightly damaged by flak, and the bomb aimer injured. One aircraft returned with its bombs. Once again, the next day, it was the Hoescht benzol plant near Dortmund, with No.149 Lancasters, seventeen from No.149 Squadron, and again, two days later back to the Alma Pluto synthetic oil plant at Gelsenkirchen, again with 149 Lancasters, this time with nine from No.149 Squadron.

The Flying Fortresses of the 8th Air Force would regularly overfly Methwold, either on their way out or returning from a daylight raid, and it became common practice to see their Fortresses return with war damage, smoke streaming from a dead engine, or popping red or red and green Very lights to alert their field ahead that there were wounded on board. As the pressure and direction of the war was now fully in Allied hands, and the end was in sight, exchange visits were arranged between the American 8th Air Force personnel from the 452nd Group, 3rd Air Division, 45th Combat Wing, consisting of the 728th, 729th, 730th and 731st Boeing B-17G Flying Fortress squadrons at Deopham Green, Norfolk, and No.149 Squadron air crew personnel, each visiting the other's stations on the 27th.

The 'G-H' attacks by No.3 Group on the German oil plants continued at their hectic pace, the Nordstern oil plant at Gelsenkirchen on 28th February, and the oil plants at Kamen on 1st

*'OJ-P' (NF971) at Methwold.* [Flt Lt D R Bull]

*Lancaster III 'OJ-C' (PB509).* [Philip Jarrett collection]

March, seventeen of No.149's Lancasters being on the first raid and fifteen on the second.

A No.3 Group organisational change took place in March which directly affected Methwold in that the airfield no longer acted independently but was now part of No.32 Base, Mildenhall, from where much of its future would be directed.

The last RAF raid on Cologne, which was in daylight and in two waves, took place on 2nd March, with 155 Lancasters of No.3 Group making up the second wave, eleven from No.149 Squadron. However, on the run-up to the target, there was a 'G-H' station failure and only fifteen Lancasters bombed before the attack was aborted. Cologne was captured by American forces only four days later. (Note 3)

Back to the railway marshalling yards as targets, this time on 4th March to Wanne-Eickel, with a No.3 Group 'G-H' daylight raid through 10/10 cloud, involving 128 Lancasters, twenty of them from No.149 Squadron. There was some confusion, causing poor formating over target, but there was very little flak and no fighters. The flaps of 'OJ-F' were u/s and with no radio they landed away at the crash drome at Woodbridge. Back on the same oil target mission and the same technique the next day, this time the Consolidated benzol plant at Gelsenkirchen with 170 Lancasters, twenty of them from No.149, again through 10/10 cloud. While there were no fighters seen, there was accurate flak all of the way from Wesel to target, five of No.149's aircraft being damaged by flak. NF 972, 'OJ-H'. with pilot Flying Officer T S M Williams, was shot down, being seen to go down following a fire and explosion on board over the Wesel area. There was another similar raid on the 6th, this time with 115 Lancasters, fifteen from No.149 Squadron, to the benzol plant at Salzbergen; again no fighters, but this time with only slight flak.

That night No.3 Group returned to Wesel with 97 Lancasters and 51 Mosquitoes from No.8 Group to attack the German troop concentrations there, only three of the Lancasters being from No.149 Squadron. Instead, twelve of them were supporting a combined Nos.1, 3, 6 and 8 Group Pathfinder target-marked night raid to Dessau, with 526 Lancasters and five 'Oboe' Mosquitoes. The raid was very successful, with negligible flak, but *Luftwaffe* fighters caused the loss of eighteen Lancasters.

Back to 'G-H' daylight raids on oil plant targets for No.3 Group, with twenty Lancasters from No.149 Squadron supporting a 159-Lancaster attack on the North and South Emscher Lippe benzol plant at Datteln near Recklinghausen on the 9th, then nineteen of No.149's supporting a 55-Lancaster raid on the Scholven/Buer synthetic oil plant at Gelsenkirchen on the 10th. While the flak was negligible on the first raid, accurate flak in the target area on the second raid resulted in three of No.149's Lancasters returning with shrapnel damage. No fighters were seen in either raid.

The 11th of March brought an all-Group day raid to Essen, with a total of 1,079 aircraft, 750 of them being Lancasters, thirteen of them from No.149 Squadron acting as leaders for No.3 Group, also 293 Halifaxes and 36 Mosquitoes. While the target was marked by 'Oboe' sky markers, No.3 Group aircraft, with No.149 leading the way, used their own 'G-H' equipment through 10/10 cloud. This was the largest number of aircraft on any raid so far, with 4,661 tons of bombs being dropped. This paralysed Essen until the American troops arrived and captured the town. Air Commodore A McKee CBE DSC, DFC, AFC was at Methwold when No.149's Lancasters returned, observing the landing, afterwards expressing much satisfaction and congratulating No.149 on their excellent leading of the Group.

Flying Officer 'Sam' Fox, a Canadian and the radar officer for No.149 Squadron, took the typical radar equipment carried by No.149 Squadron aircraft to the RAF College, Cranwell for demonstration. The visit was very successful and much appreciated.

Another major raid followed on the 12th, with 1,108 aircraft, including 748 Lancasters, 292 Halifaxes, and 68 Mosquitoes on daylight raid to Dortmund. Eighteen of the Lancasters were from No.149 Squadron. No.3 Group and No.149 Squadron once again bombed on 'G-H'. 4,851 tons of bombs were dropped which stopped production there so effectively that it never recovered before the war ended. (Note 4)

A copy of a letter to Air Chief Marshal Sir Arthur T Harris, KCB, OBE, AFC from Dwight D Eisenhower, Allied Commander-in-Chief, was received by the Squadron, passed on by Air Vice Marshal R Harrison, KCB, OBE, AFC. Air Officer

Commanding No.3 Group, congratulating Bomber Command on the support they had given to the advancing ground troops in Europe.

Once again it was oil targets for No.3 Group, with a 'G-H' daylight attack involving 169 Lancasters, sixteen from No.149, to the benzol plant at Hattingen/Heinrich Shutt near Bochum on the 14th in 10/10 cloud cover. The flak before the target was quite accurate, four of No.149's Lancasters being damaged by shrapnel. The day after, the Air Officer Commanding No.3 Group, Air Vice Marshal R Harrison, KBE OBE AFC together with Air Commodore A McKee visited Methwold. Then on the 17th, it was a No.3 Group G-H daylight attack through 10/10 cloud on the benzol plant at Gneisenau near Dortmund, with 167 Lancasters, seventeen of them from No.149 Squadron and, two days later, a similar attack on the Consolidated benzol plant at Gelsenkirchen, this time with 79 Lancasters, almost a quarter of them, twenty-one, being from No.149 Squadron. The flak was intense, and eleven of No.149's Lancasters returned with flak damage. NG244 'OJ-J' received a shrapnel hit directly through the bomb aimer's clear panel, hitting bomb aimer Flight Sergeant G A Dane in the face, killing him instantly. No fighters were seen in any of these three raids.

A change in pace occurred on the 21st when No.3 Group attacked the railway yards and nearby railway viaduct at Munster in daylight with 160 Lancasters, nineteen of them from No.149, then a daylight 'G-H' attack on the town of Bocholt the next day in support of the Allies' advance, with eighteen of No.149's Lancasters being part of the 100 Lancasters of No.3 Group on the raid. The bomb load was one 4,000-lb bomb, the rest being made up of 4-lb incendiaries. The raid was very successful, the town being set on fire with black smoke rising to 15,000 feet. The German strongpoints at Wesel also needed some attention in order to assist the British ground forces and so it received No.3 Group's attention on the 23rd, with No.149 Squadron sending ten Lancasters.

Then back to the oil targets on the 27th, thirteen of No.149's Lancasters accompanying 137 other from No.3 Group on a daylight 'G-H' attack on the benzol plant at Hamm/Konigsborn. A mushroom of black smoke pushed through the 10/10 cloud following the attack.

The Officer Commanding Methwold, Group Captain B C Yarde, was taken ill this day and Wing Commander P L Chilton DFC, AFC took temporary command until the Group Captain recovered. The day after, on the 28th, reporters from the *Daily Herald* arrived on the base and interviewed air and ground crews. The benzol plant and the coke ovens of the Hermann Goering concern at Hallendorf received No.3 Group's attention on the 29th, with 130 Lancasters, fourteen of them from No.149 Squadron. The 'G-H' responses were poor and the 10/10 cloud, topping at 22,000 feet, prevented formating and cohesion in bombing, so alternative bombing techniques were used instead.

By now the Allies had crossed the Rhine and were advancing towards Berlin. The number of No.149 Squadron sorties for March at 306 was a monthly record for the Squadron, the attacks through the month being mainly on the railway yards and oil plants, paralysing German troop movements. A signal of appreciation was received from Field Marshal Montgomery's HQ regarding the attack on Wesel, by which the lives of many British troops were saved. The town was captured with only slight opposition.

*Aircrew members congregate in front of 'OJ-Q' (NG355) at Juvincourt during Operation 'Exodus'.* [Hal Birch]

*'OJ-M' at Juvincourt during Operation 'Exodus'.* [Hal Birch]

*Lancasters lined up at Juvincourt collecting released prisoners-of-war during Operation 'Exodus'.* [Hal Birch]

The target of the combined Nos.3, 6 and 8 Group night attack on the synthetic oil plant at Leuna near Merseburg on 4th April was marked by 'Oboe' from the fourteen Pathfinder Mosquitoes, but the target markers covered a wide area and so the bombing was scattered. Flak was moderate and dummy target markers were much in evidence. The twenty No.149 Squadron Lancasters added to the other 307 on the raid, 'TK-E' having various problems and jettisoning its bombs in the southern part of the target area, then landing at Manston on return. 'TK-K' lost its brake pressure and also landed away, but at Woodbridge.

The Allied advance in Europe had overrun a number of German prisoner-of-war camps and ways had to be found to return the freed prisoners back to England. So 'Operation Exodus' began, flying the prisoners back in whatever aircraft could be used, and that meant the aircraft of Bomber Command. The first batch of prisoners was picked up by No.149 Squadron's Lancasters on 5th April; this consisting of 80 men of the Indian Army and one civilian Channel Islander. Their arrival was greeted by a large group of senior officers from the Headquarters of No.3 Group. This repatriation of Indian Army personnel was repeated on the 6th, but only a small group of five were flown in.

It was back in action again on the 9th, with a combined Nos.1, 3 and 8 Group night attack on the Kiel naval base with 591 Lancasters, virtually every aircraft of No.149 Squadron, twenty-nine of them, taking part. The target was marked by eight Pathfinder Mosquitoes and proved to be a highly successful raid, all three shipyards being hit. The Deutsche Werke U-boat yard was severely damaged and the pocket battleship *Admiral Scheer* hit and capsized. The *Admiral Hipper* and *Emden* were also severely damaged. While there was no night fighter activity (in fact very little fighter activity had been seen for some time), the anti-aircraft fire was moderate, one aircraft being hit by flak. Fires were seen in the target area by No.149 crews when they were crossing the island of Sylt on the return home. 'OJ-P', 'OJ-Q' and 'OJ-U' returned early.

While the number of raids by No.149 Squadron was now lowered by the reduction of potential targets as the Allies advanced, the No.149 crews were still kept up to a high standard of performance with flying exercises laid on for a number of the crews every non-combat day.

It was back to the U-boat yards at Kiel on the night of the 13th through 10/10 cloud, to insure that the target was well and truly put out of action, using 105 Halifaxes and 377 Lancasters from Nos.3, 6 and 8 Groups. However because of inaccurate wind forecasts, the twenty aircraft of No.149 Squadron were over the target before the target markers were placed, and the bombing was poor, 'OJ-V', 'OJ-S' and 'TK-C' aborting in the target area.

A combined Nos.1, 3 and 8 Group raid took place the following night, with 500 Lancasters including twenty-five from No.149, and twelve Pathfinder Mosquitoes, the target being Potsdam and the mission to destroy the army barracks and railway facilities there. This was the first time since March 1944 that four-engined aircraft had entered the Berlin defence zone, flying across recently captured German territory. This also proved to be the last major raid by Bomber Command on any German city. The sky was clear with good visibility, with moderate flak plus fighter activity, two of No.149 Squadron's Lancasters being in combat with enemy fighters. Eight Indian ex-prisoners-of-war were recovered by a No.149 Squadron Lancaster this day, and a further 35 on the 17th.

The following day, the 18th, saw an all-Group daylight raid with 969 aircraft, 617 of them being Lancasters, twenty-six of them from No.149 Squadron, 332 Halifaxes and twenty Pathfinder Mosquitoes, for an attack on the naval base, the airfield and the town on the island of Heligoland. The bombing was controlled by a master bomber, the island still being covered with smoke from a previous raid. No fighters or flak were encountered and the bombing was very accurate, the numerous bomb craters making the territory seem like the surface of the moon. (Note 5)

The war was rapidly drawing to a close and the traditional all-No.3 Group daylight 'G-H' raids were almost over. However there were still two more. On 19th April, 49 Lancasters, ten of them from No.149 Squadron, attacked the Pasing railway yards and the transformer station at Munich with concentrated bombing. The flak was slight, and no fighters were seen. Meanwhile, behind the scenes, 25 more Indian ex-prisoners-of-war were recovered. The last raid on an oil target since the June 1944 policy of making them primary targets took place the following day on the 20th, when the oil storage depot at Regensburg was attacked by 100 Lancasters of No.3 Group, seven of them from No.149 Squadron. The black smoke issuing from the target seemed to indicate that the raid was successful. The Indian ex-prisoner-of-war recovery continued with 15 being brought back to Britain.

The British XXX Corps was about to attack the city of Bremen and so once again a request was made to Bomber Command to see what could be done to weaken the enemy defences prior to the attack. Accordingly, Nos.1, 3 and 6 Groups carried out a daylight raid on the 21st, with a total of 767 aircraft, 651 being Lancasters (including twenty-one from No.149 Squadron), 100 Halifaxes, and sixteen Pathfinder Mosquitoes. While it was said that the German anti-aircraft batteries were now being operated by old men and young boys, the flak over Wilhelmshaven was accurate, thirteen of No.149's Lancasters being damaged by shrapnel. Wing Commander Chilton's aircraft, PD284 'OJ-N', landed away at Woodbridge due to flak damage. This turned out to be the last bombing operation for No.149 Squadron. From here on it was air exercises and repatriating ex-POWs for No.149's Lancaster crews.

On 30th April, Adolf Hitler committed suicide in his bunker in Berlin. The Dutch people had been taken to the point of starvation so in a humanitarian gesture, and by agreement with the German military, it was arranged that Allied aircraft without gunners would fly along a controlled corridor to drop food to them. So 'Operation Manna' began, using the bomber aircraft of Nos.1, 3 and 8 Groups and the bombers of the 8th Air Force. Makeshift panniers were rigged into the bomb bays to carry the food packages and immediately prior to the operation, No.149's Lancasters could be seen making practice runs over the airfield, dropping sacks of sand on suitable markers. Then 'Pathfinder' Mosquitoes marked the dropping zones outside Rotterdam and food packs were dropped from the panniers at 500 feet into the prescribed marked-out area. There were technical failures, in that some panniers did not release, but most dropped successfully. The Dutch civilians were very enthusiastic towards the low aircraft flying both in and out of Holland. The vacant gunners' positions were taken by flight line ground crew who could now see personally where their charges had been flying throughout the war. In all, there were 2,835 Lancaster and 124 Mosquito flights. This first day of 'Operation Manna', No.149 Squadron sent twenty-one of its Lancasters on their mission of mercy, dropping 80 food packs.

The Americans and Russians had linked up at Torgau on 25th April, the Russians having surrounding Berlin. Group Captain B C Yarde, who had been the Commanding Officer of No.149 Squadron since 15th May 1944, was posted to the Air Ministry, Group Captain D H Burnside, DFC, after having just completed a tour of operations with No.195 Squadron, becoming the new C.O. As April ended, No.149 Squadron had recovered 224 Indian ex-POWs, fed them and sent them on to the Army Reception Centre.

For the first five days in May, No.149's Lancasters made 75 food drops at the Hague, involving 279 packages. Then the drop zone was changed on the 7th to Site 2 at Gouda, near Rotterdam, twenty-four of No.149's Lancasters dropping 80 packages. The war was obviously about to end and word spread throughout the flight line ground staff that the air crew had a 'thank you' in store for them, and to 'stand by' for their return from the food drop.

The Squadron returned low and to the east of the airfield. Contrary to their usual practice of returning singly, they were in a tight formation that would have done any 8th Air Force Fortress Group proud. They circled once around the field, then the

Lancasters peeled off one by one like fighters for their landing. No.149 was noted for how fast they could get the Squadron down. This day must have broken all records. One aircraft followed the other down the runway so that there were always two on the runway at any one time, and sometimes three, one landing at one end as another taxied off the other. Flying control went wild, with red Verys being fired one after the other over the landing aircraft. But you can't court martial every air crew member of a whole Squadron. They had left a visual and spectacular 'thank you' that would last a lifetime with each and every ground crew member who had been lucky enough to see it.

The following day six aircraft were detailed to drop food packages at site 1E at Delft, south-east of the Hague, 29 packages being dropped. Then Winston Churchill made the announcement over the radio that everybody had been waiting for, which was relayed over every loudspeaker at Methwold. Germany had surrendered unconditionally and the war was over. It was VE-Day. Naturally everyone went wild, with a dance and celebration party, the hangar being decorated with banners and 'window' in strips and loops, the 'window' being willingly donated by the radar section.

No.149 Squadron had a most enviable World War Two operational record. It was one of only two squadrons to remain with Bomber Command throughout the war, flying on the first and last day. Nearly 16,000 tons of high explosive and incendiary bombs had been dropped by its aircraft, together with a considerable quantity of mines. No.149 Squadron had paid in full measure the ultimate price for victory, as its Roll of Honour demonstrates, and decorations for heroism were continually in evidence throughout the war, including one Victoria Cross to Flight Sergeant Middleton RAAF.

---

**Notes for Chapter 11**
1. No.149 Squadron aircraft on the raid – PB509 OJ-C, NG361 OJ-E, PB506 OJ-B, NG244 OJ-J, PB487 OJ-N, NG362 OJ-S, HK699 TK-C, HK652 TK-E.
2. No.149 Squadron aircraft on the raid – OJ-aircraft: PB506-B, PB509-C, NG361-E, NF972-H, NG244-J, NF973-K, NG355-L, PD284-N NF970-R, NG356-V; TK-aircraft: HK645-D, HK654-G, HK577-H.
3. Aircraft scheduled for raid – OJ-aircraft: PB483-B, NF972-H, PB838-M, PD284-N, NN756-R, NF791-S; TK-aircraft: HK793-A, HK654-G, NG356-V
4. No.149 Squadron aircraft on the raid – OJ-aircraft: PB509-C, NF927-D, NG361-E, NF972-F, NG244-J, PB838-M, PD284-N, NF970-O, NG356-V, NN760-W; TK-aircraft: HK795-B, HK645-D, HK649-F, HK654-G, HK577-H, HK546-K.
5. No.149 Squadron aircraft on the raid – OJ-aircraft: PP684-A, PP673-B, PP681-C, NF927-D, NG361-E, PP-685-G, PB902-H, NG387-L, PA838-M. PD284-N, NF971-P, NG355-Q, NF970-(R?), NF953-S, NG299-T, PA166-U, NN760-W, PA186-X, NN576-(R?); TK-aircraft: HK695-B, HK699-C, HK645-D, HK649-F, HK577-H, HK546-K.

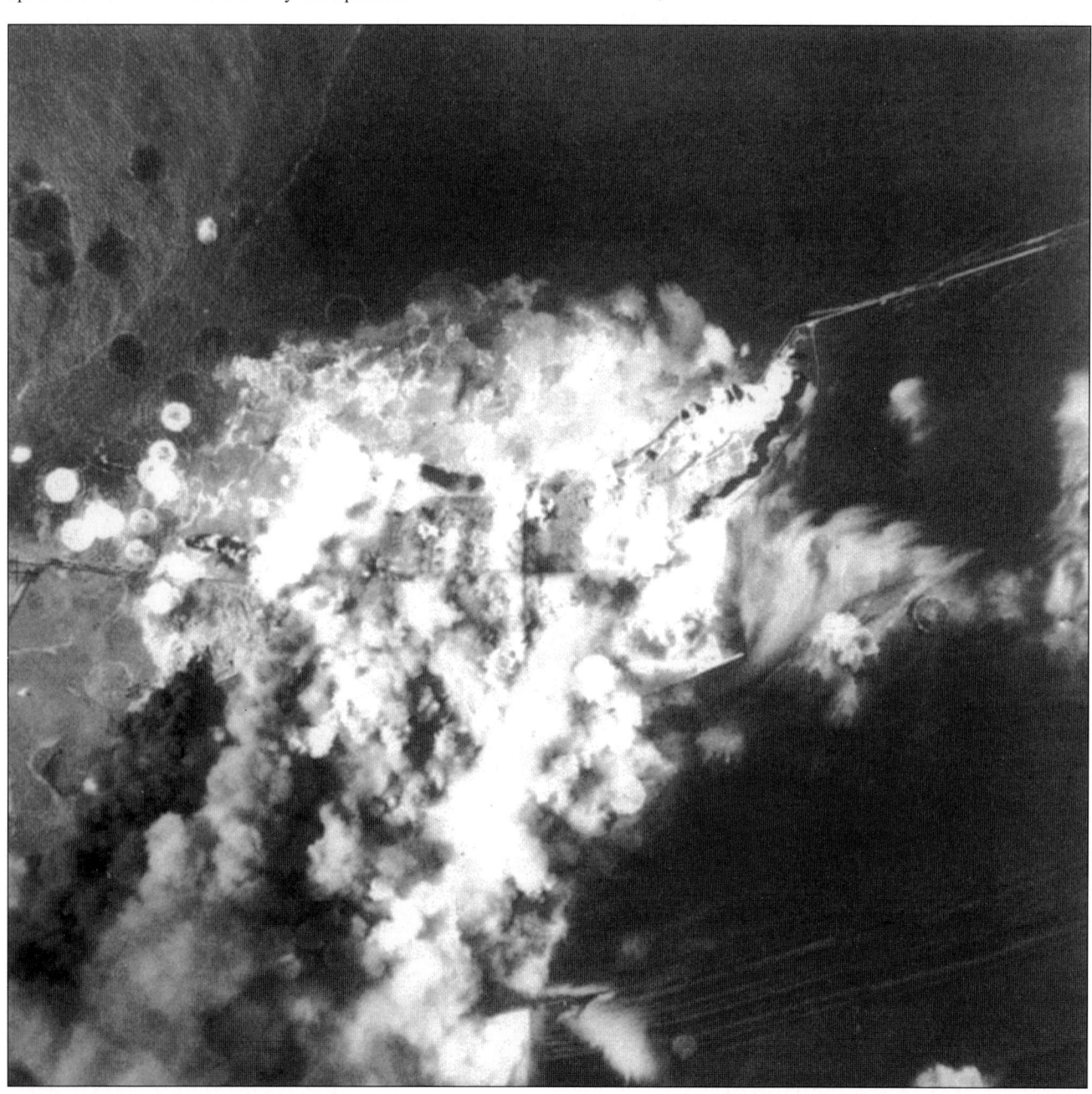

*Heligoland under attack on 18th April 1945, photographed from 'OJ-C'.*

*Loading food onto a Lancaster during Operation 'Manna' for dropping on the Netherlands.*

# Chapter 12: Methwold stories

Observer 'Spud' Taylor kept a fairly accurate diary of events throughout his service life. He served a second tour, back with No.149 Squadron, but this time it was Lancasters at Methwold. His diary speaks for itself:

"**22.2.45.** Did our first Op - a daylight trip, flying in 'X'. Target Osterfeld - Benzene factory. Flak pretty accurate - holes in nose, wings and fuselage. As bomb doors opened flak cut the main cable so couldn't release the bombs. Flying back over North Sea went into a steep dive which made the cables touch and then able to release the load. Didn't fancy landing with them still on. Lovely clear day.

**23.2.45.** To Gelsenkirchen (Happy Valley) and bombed in cloud at 21,000 feet. Diverted to Acklington near Newcastle. Just in time for free beer, dance and binge.

**25.2.45.** Went to oil refinery just West of the Ruhr and in the process did a grand tour of 'Happy Valley'. Flying 'W'. Target Kamen. Fair amount of flak. Terrific fighter escort.

**26.2.45.** Up early and bombed oil refinery, Dortmund. Saw Cologne Cathedral, clear as crystal on the way back. 'Happy Valley' uncannily peaceful these days.

**28.2.45.** Ops Gelsenkirchen.

**1.3.45.** Ops Kamen. Very different technique. We fly in loose formations, in boxes or 'V's, each formation with a 'G-H' leader, the 3 behind bomb on the leader.

**4.3.45.** Woken up early (2.30am) and were briefed to bomb the railway yards at Wanne-Eickel. Trying out a new formation, more compact than usual. A thick layer of cloud covered the target, with brilliant sunshine above. Certain amount of flak and we were nearly bombed by some damn fool! I took some snaps of the 'kite' and the flak on the way back. Crossing English coast ran into blinding rain till we reached base, where we made one of our good old 'split arse landings'.

**6.3.45.** Salzbergen. Quiet trip.

**7.3.45.** In the afternoon we were briefed for a night trip to Dessau, about 40 miles south-west of Berlin. Set out over France in bright daylight and it became dark as we cut through the Ruhr. Cologne was ablaze and gun flashes were reflecting on the cloud. Passed by a number of attacks going on in 'Happy Valley'. Quite like old times, to see the flak and planes over the target. Our "H2S" and 'Gee' were both u/s, so we went round on dead reckoning. Target ablaze when we left it. Saw a number (about 15) 'kites' shot down, all told, and saw one fighter ourselves. Felt worn out when we got back - 9½ hour trip 39 'kites' shot down last night.

**10.3.45.** Ops Buer. Went deaf on the way back; u/s for flying for three days.

**17.3.45.** Bombed factory at Gneisenau, near Dortmund.

**19.3.45.** A perfectly clear day. Skirted Düsseldorf and Essen, and came in for a heavy pasting from all the guns there. Target, Gelsenkirchen. Every 'kite' in the Squadron had at least one hole in it. One of the bomb aimers was 'smacked' through the head on the 'run up', and 'pegged out' before they could get him back.

**21.3.45.** Munster.

**22.3.45.** Bocholt. We were one of the first 'Vees' to bomb and I saw them burst smack in the centre of the town. We left a pall of smoke rising to about 15,000 feet. Noticed a tremendous smoke screen stretching from Arnhem to Duisburg, along the west bank of the Rhine. (*Note: on the night of 23/24 March our Army crossed the Rhine and now had three good bridgeheads*).

**18.4.45.** Fine clear day. Set out for Heligoland, flying straight there across the North Sea. About 1,000 'kites' took part. The Island guards the entrance to Bremen and Hamburg, which the Germans are defending against British troops. Next to Heligoland is a smaller island almost entirely taken up by an aerodrome. The aerodrome was bombed first, then the main island. A huge column of smoke rose up, and a continuous series of red flashes showed where the bombs were exploding.

**21.4.45.** Bremen this afternoon. About 3/10th cloud. No.149 Squadron leading the group and our Wing Commander leading the Squadron, with our aircraft on his starboard side. Over Wilhelmshaven we ran into an accurate barrage of flak causing damage to every 'kite' in the Squadron. Our Army is lining the west bank of the River Weser, facing the Germans on the east bank. Absolute accuracy of bombing was required - pleased to say not one bomb landed on our troops.

**22.4.45.** With the war in Europe coming to a close we have started practising supply dropping by flying low across the aerodrome and dropping sandbags on to a white cross on the perimeter.

**1.5.45.** Holland, from Rotterdam to the north is still held by the Germans. To stop our advance they have flooded half the country with the result that large towns are packed full of homeless and hungry Dutch people. By some special arrangement we are dropping food with no opposition. Set out about eleven, this morning, with 6,000 lbs of food in the bomb bay, for a place just outside The Hague. Crossed the Dutch coast at low level, just north of Overflakee. The whole coastline and the banks of the rivers are covered in defence posts and gun positions but never saw a German the whole time. I daresay they had orders to keep under cover in case we fired at them. The population turned out in strength and waved at us. Some of them were madly waving flags (mostly French but red, white and blue). One little man had an enormous flag in each hand and when he caught sight of our Lancaster he leaped off the ground in his excitement. A woman perched perilously on a rooftop was waving like mad and shouting something. I should think every person in The Hague turned out to cheer us. Our dropping ground was in a sports field north of The Hague, complete with grandstand, which was packed, and someone looking remarkably like a 'mayor' was there in his robes of office! The grandstand was only a stones-throw from our dropping point, which was marked by a white cross. Came back at nought feet above the sea, very pleased with ourselves.

**7.5.45.** Went to a village east of The Hague over a lot of flooded country, with only the roof-tops showing. We took a groundstaff 'bod' with us who was hopping up and down with excitement.

**8.5.45.** VE-day! The war has lasted so long I can hardly believe it is over. Stayed in the flat in Clapham, which was my wife's home; we married in November 1944. Stayed in the flat as the West End was very crowded and got through two bottles of wine. Went to the roof afterwards where we watched people lighting bonfires and letting off Very lights. Singing and shouting went on to the early hours.

**21.5.45.** Flew to Juvincourt this afternoon to pick up some of our lads, ex-POWs. The weather was duff, and we stood in the rain with our 24 men waiting for take-off. Two German POWs were serving in the canteen.

The weather got worse and we crowded into a large lorry with a load of Army lads and went to Rheims, about 10 miles away. The road lined with trees and the country well wooded and hilly. At Rheims the crew split up. Tried to get a meal with Jim, our Navigator, but the café only served Frenchmen! Ended up getting sandwiches at an American canteen.

**2.5.45.** The weather cleared and we took off in the morning. One Army lad shared the bombing compartment with me and I pointed out the 'White Cliffs of Dover' to him soon after we crossed the French coast. Most of our POWs are speechless - they just look at you and smile.

**23.5.45.** The crew split up today.

In June I joined a fresh crew and we flew over France, Germany and Denmark for map making from the photographs we took, and one day the Russians took a 'pot shot' at us when we got too close to their lines."

Frank Mann, and instrument mechanic with No.149 Squadron at Methwold tells a story in a lighter vein:

"In January 1945 I was delegated to check 'George' (autopilot), on I think 'D' for Dog, on the North East dispersal. I was the duty instrument 'basher'. Arriving at the dispersal I was informed by the Flt/Lt, Skipper, that 'George' kept jamming. Climbing aboard I said, 'Take it up to 10,000 feet'. 'Too bloody cold', he said, 'We will do it at 5,000 feet'. Having survived from 1940, I decided to work with my parachute still securely attached to my chest. Although 'out-ranked', my sense of survival was still to the fore. I took note of the 'quick exit' hatch to my right. Looking at the plates and 'Bowden' cables, I could see nothing wrong. At 5,000 feet I said, 'Switch 'George' on', which he did.

"We went into a dive, which I swear I could see the cows getting bigger in the field below. The 'Skipper' did not help by shouting, 'It's jammed again'. I would not have needed 'Ex-Lax' but in the panic I could see the problem. The 'Bowden' cable joints were catching the stay of the fuselage. I do not know, to this day, whether I dislodged the offender. Anyway, he pulled her up and we finished doing the 'job' at 10,000 feet. His crew said that I had called the 'Skipper', to his face, a part of the female anatomy, but I was not disciplined. The aftermath of this misadventure took place a week later.

"It was the 'Liberty' wagon run to Wisbech, a dance hall and a chance to do some drinking and 'wenching'. As I climbed aboard the lorry, who should be there to give me a hand aboard but the 'Skipper', who was about to shorten my life span. Among the convivial mixed crowd of ground and aircrew, I loudly pointed out that we would not stand a chance with the 'wenches' with all the 'wings' and 'gongs' being flashed. The aforesaid 'Skipper' then said, 'It's not the man; I owe you for that bit of excitement last week'.

"He then said, 'We will switch togs for the night' and then peeled off his uniform and hat! There I was, a Flt/Lt Pilot complete with DFC. What a night I had in Wisbech; if only I had a photo done at 'Jeromes'. I was in the dance with a lovely blonde female as my partner; about 9.30p.m., my blonde said, 'There is an airman by the door trying to attract your attention'. It was of course the 'Skipper', by the toilet. I said to my partner, 'You will have to excuse me, but one of my men wants to borrow my uniform to impress a girlfriend'; this I duly did. When I came back to her she said, 'Won't that get you into trouble?'. I had a vision then of what would have happened to me if I had been caught out. We finished the evening more than friends, but that's another story."

Deryck Thurman, Flight Engineer, talks of a 'special trip' to Dortmund:

"Many of our trips were mundane or routine but occasionally something special would happen, as on March 12th, 1945. Early morning, crews on the battle order for that day's trip. It was breakfast in the Officers' Mess.

"The 'Winco', Wing Commander Chilton, calls for the senior captain and my skipper replies 'I am the senior captain, sir!' The Winco 'Right! I am going today.' (I assume that he was one of the few who knew the target) 'I will take your crew'. Skipper- 'Will you require me?' Winco- 'Is your engineer any good?' Skipper- 'He is very good'. Winco- 'Well, I won't need you, will I?'

"I must confess that I was a little over-awed, as a 19-year-old, flying with the Winco. Briefing reveals the target as Dortmund, 1,000 plus aircraft. We are at the dispersal when the 'Winco' arrives

*The crew of Lancaster 'OJ-F' (PP687), recorded as Flt Sgt Les Turner (Flight Engineer), Flt Lt Colin Facey (Pilot), Flt Sgt Tom Jack (Bomb Aimer), Flt Sgt Glyn Davies (Mid-Upper Gunner), Flt Sgt Jack Goodwin (W/Operator), Flt Sgt George York (Rear Gunner), Flt Lt George Haynes (Navigator). The front row consists of four un-named ground staff.*

with the Station Commander, Group Captain Yarde, in his chauffeur-driven car. The Group Captain shakes his hand. 'Have a good trip, and be sure to come back'. Our first Winco went missing on our first trip with No.149 Squadron. Not a good omen, we all thought. This for me was followed up by, prior to start-up. 'It's some time since I flew a Lanc. I shall need all your help.' But he proved to be an excellent pilot.

"We were a 'G-H' leader and flew in some sort of formation. I don't remember much about the trip, but running up to the target - 'Gentlemen, I suggest you have your parachutes ready. There appears to be a lot of flak ahead!' I exchanged glances with the Nav. No words were spoken but 'what's he on about?' The return was uneventful but back at dispersal, the Group Captain was there to greet Winco, who shakes hands with all of us. 'Thanks chaps - bang on!'

"This was our 26th trip out of 33. I've often wondered how many Winco had done. 40-plus years on, my skipper told my wife - 'This was the longest trip I ever did'. Bomb load, cookie, fourteen 500-lbs, one green puff target marker. Take off at 12.31. Landed 18.54. It was for me a special trip, not routine as some were."

The first 'Operation Manna' mission is related by Hugh Fraser, a bomb aimer:

"At a briefing on April 30th, the crews were told that the target was Rotterdam and the 'bomb load' was, in fact, food for the starving Dutch. More than 50 years have passed, but much of what my logbook tells me, that it was a two-hour thirty-five minute flight, remains clear. Our Lancaster was NN760, with the bomb bay loaded with food. Some ground staff 'wag' had chalked on the doors: 'Here lies the body of little Sam, hit on the head by falling Spam'.

"Bright weather for take-off. Skimming low over the North Sea. The Dutch coast appearing like magic. The exhilaration of low flying. Land flashing by below. Glimpses of people waving their national flag. From what hidden recesses had these suddenly been retrieved? After all, most of the country was still occupied by the Germans. Somehow the euphoria of the Dutch was transmitted to us in the air.

"Suddenly the 'target' area was upon us. Below was a milling mass of people. 'Bombs gone', edible ones, and we're heading for home. No enemy fighters. No flak. No problems. Another Operation in the 'bag'. Well - almost! The RAF hierarchy were to decree later that a 'Manna' flight would be down graded to one-third of an 'Op'.

"Rumour has it that one crew had been one 'Op' short of a complete tour and after Rotterdam had retired to the Mess to celebrate in style. Whether or not they made up the missing two-thirds and had a second celebration is lost in the mists of time. I did one more 'Manna' trip - to The Hague on May 3rd - when the format was the same as before.

"End of story? Not quite. Fate was to add a twist some 50 years on. I took part in a Ladies and Gents competition at the golf club where I am a member. While having the customary drink with one's opponent thereafter, it transpired that the lady was of Dutch extraction, married and settled in Scotland and somehow our conversation turned to the 'Manna' from heaven. Yes, she remembered the Lancasters and their more than welcome food. At the time she was a young girl living on a diet of tulip bulbs."

Hugh continues with the next task assigned to Bomber Command, 'Operation Exodus':

"I did one of these operations on the 21st May 1945, when based at Methwold. Much of the detail is lost in the 'mists of time' but I do recall our Skipper, Dennis Johns, making hardly a text-book landing on a Juvincourt runway, not best suited for Lancasters. Moreover, there had been heavy rain, so it was more of a 'splash down' than a touch down!

"We taxied round to a group of soldiers who looked somewhat bedraggled and a touch apprehensive. It transpired that this was our contingent of 24 or so who had been lined up waiting our arrival. I discovered a group of fellow Scots amongst them. I'd like to think I made them feel more at ease and heard one relate his experience as a POW, which I feel is worth recording.

"He'd been a prisoner for about four years, mostly on the German/Poland border. War news was scarce, but early in 1945, when they heard gunfire to the East, and saw anxious looks on their guards' faces, the POWs deduced that the Russians were coming. One morning they woke to find the Germans had fled and soon after the Russians did arrive. However, they didn't reciprocate to the British cheers, were downright hostile and didn't relax until they were satisfied that no German was lurking in the British ranks. Had one done so, his chance of survival would have been slim, very slim. Thereafter the British were treated reasonably well and eventually handed over to the Americans.

"I remember too, being asked by a POW why we dropped 'all that silver paper' on bombing raids. I gave a short lecture on the efficiency of "window" on the German radar defences, but could understand how puzzling it must have been to the POWs to see the ground festooned with the stuff after a raid.

"Back to 'Exodus'. That day the weather closed in and take-off was postponed till the morrow. The POWs boarded trucks to take them about 15 kilometres back to an American-run barracks on the outskirts of Rheims. Nothing daunted, the RAF clambered aboard to do some unexpected sight-seeing, leaving behind some skeleton crews to look after the Lancs.

"I was one of the unofficial sightseers. By this time it was mid-afternoon and transport for the aircrew return journey was to leave Rheims railway station at midnight. We were there in good time, kicked heels for about an hour, then with our navigator, Peter Thomas, and the rear gunner, Ian Drummond, I went to pay my respects to the station lavatory. When we returned, the transports had been and gone. Consternation! No way could we 'hoof it' back to Juvincourt. For a start, poor Ian's shoes were at Methwold – he was lumbered with his knee high, fleece lined flying boots. After a council of war we decided to track down the POW camp and hitch a lift back to the airfield in the morning. Easier said than done! Streets were blacked out. Few people were around. Luckily we passed a US barracks where a sentry gave us rough directions. My next recollection is sitting on a bench in a small park when a Gendarme loomed out of the darkness, an astonished gendarme I may say.

"In schoolboy French I explained our predicament and mercifully he gave us a specific route. To the best of my recollection it was about 4 am when we more or less staggered into the camp and asked for a bed. 'Sure buddy' were the unforgettable words of a US soldier at reception, who issued us with blankets and pillows. Scarcely had my head hit the pillow when there was a 'rise and shine' over the tannoy. As luck would have it, my erstwhile Scottish POW pals were in the same billet and after they recovered from their surprise, lent us soap, towels, etc., so we could at least freshen up. An outdoor breakfast at 6 am served by German POWs (what stick they took from the British lads!), then on to the trucks and back to Juvincourt where we reported to a very relieved pilot.

"The journey to some airfield in the South of England was uneventful. Our 'cargo', knowing they were on the last lap home, sat huddled in the fuselage mostly in silence. What I'll never forget was watching them set foot again on British soil. No one actually kissed the tarmac, but at least one turned a somersault in delight. As the saying goes, 'it would have brought tears to a glass eye'.

"Back at Methwold some time in the afternoon, we found we were down for a week's leave. Ian Drummond and I caught an over-night train from Peterborough to Edinburgh. The journey is a complete blank. If we'd gone through an earthquake, we wouldn't have known!"

Lancaster B.1(FE) SW305 'OJ-V' at the end of the Lancaster's service with No.149 Squadron.  [A Thomas collection]

# Chapter 13: No.149 Squadron post-war

With the war in Europe now over, No.149 Squadron continued to return repatriated prisoners of war and also provide tours over Germany for those few chosen lucky No.149 ground crew members, who were each given a hand-out giving the route and the targets they would visit. Meanwhile it was being decided in Whitehall what should be done with the now-incongruous massive British fighting arm that had been generated. Like thoughts were being generated in the minds of those who had signed on for the duration of the war, in that they were now looking forward to returning to their lives as civilians. A system of reverse points was developed for everyone, based on service life, family status, overseas service and so on, the lowest numbers being demobilised first and on June 18th demobilisation began, with airmen and women being sent to demobilisation depots for separation from the service, handing in most of their service kit and being issued the bare minimum of civilian clothes in return.

However, as the Royal Air Force is made up almost entirely of trade skills of one sort or another, another phrase crept into the demobilisation system... 'the exigencies of the Service', which meant that a balance of trades was to be maintained in order to keep the Royal Air Force as a continually-functioning fighting force. Each month a list of the demobilisation numbers for release in the following month was posted in each trade section, but also grouped by trades, one trade being released with demobilisation numbers higher than the average, while another would be well below the average.

Aircraft losses in an operational squadron regrettably do not end as the war ends, and No.149 Squadron was to lose another three aircraft in the next three months, Lancaster PP673, 'OJ-B', being the first, suffering a major wing structural failure and crashing near Arras in France on 5th June on one of the prisoner-of-war repatriation flights. PA166, also 'OJ-B' suffered a severe airframe stress on 16th July when the pilot temporarily lost, then recovered, control of the aircraft due to severe icing build-up, and was eventually struck off charge on 10th October.

With the war against Japan continuing, it had been arranged that at the cessation of hostilities in Europe, Lincolnshire-based No.5 Group would be re-formed to become 'Tiger Force', intended as the striking arm of Royal Air Force Bomber Command in the Far East. Tiger Force already had two Australian Squadrons, Nos.460 and 467, and now No.75 New Zealand Squadron was moved out of No.3 Group to join Tiger Force, changing places with No.44 Squadron. However, the dropping of the two atom bombs on Japan, the first on Hiroshima on 6th August, and the second on Nagasaki three days later, resulting in Japan's total surrender on the 14th, eliminated the need for Tiger Force. One day before, Lancaster PB902, 'OJ-H', met an untimely end at Trondheim/ Vaernes in Norway, when it overshot the runway and the undercarriage collapsed.

There was no longer any need for the remaining massive air armada in Britain and so the reduction in air power began, with aircraft being sent to Maintenance Units for storage until turned to scrap, and squadron sizes being shrunk until they consisted of only six aircraft. Many squadrons were disbanded, five sister Squadrons in No.3 Group, Nos.186, 195, 218, 514 and 622 not even seeing the end of 1945, No.75 Squadron with an even earlier fate at the disbanding of Tiger Force. The remaining bomber squadrons spent their days disposing of the build-up of bomb stocks by dropping them in the North Sea. No.149 Squadron was given an added duty, the 'H2S' cupola and scanner being removed from their aircraft and 12-inch lens twin cameras were fitted in their place. Then the Squadron was assigned the task of aerial mapping, covering the whole of Europe, with flights being detached to France and to Norway, three aircraft being assigned to the Photographic Reconnaissance Headquarters which was at RAF Benson in Oxfordshire. The slimming down of No.149 Squadron began in earnest in October and November, when aircraft after aircraft was flown to Maintenance Units for storage before disposal, or to other squadrons, No.44 Squadron being a major recipient.

'OJ-S' and 'OJ-T' in white tropical paint scheme devised for 'Tiger Force' flying from Tuddenham.  [Don Mayston]

*Washington B.1 WF491 devoid of codes in 1952.* [G Brown]

September 15th 1945 heralded the first 'Open Day' at Methwold and other RAF airfields, which would become the annual 'Battle of Britain' celebrations. Several aircraft were flown in for static display, including an Anson, Dakota, Dominie, Halifax, Harvard, Horsa glider, two Lancasters, Mosquito, Mustang, Proctor, Spitfire, Stirling, Warwick and Wellington, the two Lancasters allowing visitors to inspect their interiors. In addition, static displays were set up showing a broad range of the equipment, arms and bombs used by the Squadron.

The final Air Ministry objective was to whittle RAF bomber squadron strength down to six aircraft, the remaining No.149 Squadron Lancasters finally being exchanged for B.I(FE)s, the 'FE' indicating 'Far East' but equally applicable to most overseas duties involving high heat and humidity. With peace having been brought to Europe, it was envisaged that any future Squadron military activities would most probably be overseas, and so the Squadron and its aircraft had to be ready for such an exigency. With the number of aircraft rapidly decreasing, on 30th October No.149 was joined at Methwold by No.207 Squadron, as an early move in the consolidation of No.3 Group Squadrons. No.149's role as a ferry Squadron was not yet over when the repatriation of prisoners-of-war from France came to an end. From 7th November until 8th December 1945, No.149's Lancasters joined 'Operation Dodge' in bringing British servicemen and women located in Italy back to Britain in place of the usual slow troopship, particularly those who were due for demobilisation. The outward trip took as full a complement as possible of ground crew, sixteen to an aircraft, together with their kit and tools, to ensure that the Lancasters would be serviced adequately while in Italy. The pick-up was from two sites, Pomigliano near Naples and the other on the east coast, near Bari, where No.2 Lancaster Servicing Unit was set up, using No.149's ground crew and others. The Squadron completed thirteen sorties, discharging their passengers at Glatton, near Peterborough. No.149 would become very familiar with Pomigliano in later years when detached there.

While 'Sunny Italy' might appear so from the travel posters, Peter Russell, who was posted there, remembers the mud-filled road to the airfield, the cold winter nights, and even the snow, the ground crew keeping warm from primitive heaters. These were made from oil drums with a row of holes around the top and a layer of sand across the bottom, the fuel being a petrol drip fed from outside; it became both a heat source and a cooking stove. Leave in Sorrento or Rome helped to make up for the 'inconvenience'. Pick-up was completed by the end of winter, when the ground crew were flown home from Naples after travelling overland by train.

Just as squadrons were being disbanded, and swords beaten into ploughshares, but more often into pots and pans, so the need for airfields shrunk, and naturally the wartime dispersed airfields were the first to go, often having the runways torn up and returning once more to ploughed fields. However the new owners often found uses for some of the buildings, hangars making excellent barns and the Motor Transport buildings still serving their purpose, but now for trucks and tractors. So it was that on 26th April 1946, No.149 Squadron, together with No.207 Squadron, was moved from the dispersed airfield of Methwold to the more formalised airfield of Tuddenham, Suffolk, to join Nos.90 and 138 Squadrons already based there, to wait for an even more permanent station. With only six aircraft per Squadron, the 24 Lancasters of No.3 Group could easily be accommodated. One more Lancaster accident occurred when PD370 crash-landed on 13th July 1946 and was officially struck off charge on 17th October.

In keeping with the role of a squadron capable of immediate operation overseas, a detachment of No.149 Squadron was sent to Pomigliano, Italy, in 1946 to gain experience in working under sub-tropical conditions. In November of that same year a further move took place, when both No.149 and 207 Squadrons transferred from Tuddenham to Stradishall in Suffolk to join Nos.35 and 115 Squadrons, also of No.3 Group, and also fitted with Lancaster B.I(FE)s. In that same month, detachments of No.149 Squadron were sent on 'Sunray' flights to Shallufa in Egypt with the same purpose as the Pomigliano mission, to be joined at one time or another by similar detachments from the other three Stradishall squadrons, taking part in joint exercises with Canal Zone squadrons.

On 29th February 1949, No.149 Squadron once again moved, this time back to its old base in Mildenhall, Suffolk together with Nos.35, 115 and 207 Squadrons, all with Lancaster B.I (FE)s. No.149 again maintained detachments to Shallufa, Egypt, as did Nos.35 and 207 Squadrons, until February 1949 when all four squadrons moved simultaneously to Mildenhall in Suffolk, No.149 Squadron moving on the 28th. This was No.149 Squadron's original base in the late 1930s and early 1940s. February brought with it another Lancaster loss when 'OJ-X', PA410 had two engines cut out, the pilot making a forced belly-landing at Shepherd's Grove, Suffolk.

By the end of the decade, the Lancaster had outlived its usefulness in Bomber Command and so No.149 Squadron was to join the other Squadrons of No.3 Group including the three sister squadrons at Mildenhall in converting to Avro Lincoln B.2s. This meant recalling the detachment at Shallufa, which returned to Mildenhall in September 1949, the conversion to Lincolns taking place in October. True to form, as for the Stirlings, No.149 Squadron was the last Squadron in No.3 Group to convert.

No.149's only Lincoln loss was on 29th December when RA688 undershot the runway on landing at Mildenhall, belly-landing. Afterwards it was scrapped. No.149's career with Lincolns was short-lived as it was recognised that the Lincoln was essentially an overgrown Lancaster and did not fill the demands of a bomber faced with the challenge of the cold war with Russia. The British jet bomber was not yet on the horizon and no fill-in, pressurised, high altitude, all-weather, long range bomber was available from British aviation manufacturers.

At that time hundreds of World War II B-29s sat cocooned out in various deserts in the United States and met the necessary requirements, this being the most modern bomber around, even with remote-controlled gun barbettes. So in its Air Estimates for 1949-1950 Britain decided that funds could be raised to purchase enough Boeing B-29 Superfortresses from the United States to equip eight squadrons, to be assigned to No.3 Group, as a stop-gap until the jet bombers arrived on the scene. With Britain as its closest ally, it was to the United States' advantage to have Britain well-armed and so, on 27th January 1950, under the Military Defence Aid Program, it was agreed that 70 aircraft be taken from storage, modernised and brought to flying condition. The Air Ministry decided in July 1950 that the British name should be the 'Washington B Mark I', and the number of aircraft ordered was later stepped up to 85.

The first four Washingtons were received at Marham on 22nd March 1950 and were used as the nucleus for the Washington Conversion Unit, to be commanded by Squadron Leader B H Foster DSO DFC, the instructors being RAF personnel who had been detached to the US Air Force on B-29s, together with American Air Force staff. It had been decided that No.3 Group would be the RAF's Washington bomber group, and so on the 1st March 1950, No.149 Squadron was disbanded as a Lincoln squadron, most of crews being posted to Marham in Norfolk to begin initial training as Boeing Washington crews. Training included everything from long-range flights and navigation exercises, both day and night procedures, and emergency procedures, to gunnery exercises and high level bombing. It also called for a change in language, British port and starboard being replaced by the American left and right, the gunners at the side blisters now being the 'left and right scanners', the top gunner became the Central Fire Controller, and it was no longer '....skipper' it was '...Captain, sir!'. The air crews certainly appreciated the pressurised, quiet, heated cabins in contrast to the noisy cold Lincolns. While the crew in an American B-29 was eleven, the RAF found a way to reduce that number in a Washington to eight, Captain or First Pilot, Second Pilot, Flight Engineer, Signaller, Navigator/Bombardier, Radar Navigator, and two Air Gunners. In addition to flying training, individual trades attended specialist classes in their own profession. The biggest concern was that the Washington was essentially an electrical/electronic aircraft and there was an acute shortage of both electricians and radar technicians in the RAF at that time. However enough were found to keep the programme going. Once No.149's crews had been brought up to full efficiency it was now time to re-form the Squadron and call for enough aircraft to equip. So the Squadron was officially re-formed at Marham on 14th August 1950 as a Washington squadron, under the command of Squadron Leader H Canton.

Unanticipated problems come to even the best-made plans. The Korean War began on June 25th 1950, and the United States needed every B-29 being returned to flying condition to face North Korea. It wasn't until this primary objective had been achieved that the flow of B-29s to Britain could be re-initiated. So No.149 Squadron was without aircraft for six weeks, the Squadron moving from Marham to Coningsby during this time, on 17th October. Coningsby, which until then had been closed for renovation, had been chosen, together with Marham, to be the other Washington-based station. The first two aircraft arrived on November 17th in USAF markings and with US serials 44-62074, renumbered with the RAF serial WF490 as 'OJ-S', and 44-62198, renumbered WF491 and 'OJ-T'. No.149 Squadron was the second squadron, following No.115 Squadron, to be equipped with Washingtons, and received their first aircraft in October.

Les Feakiss, an air gunner with No.149 Squadron at this time, recalls that the aircraft Captains were F/O Garretts (later Flt Lt), F/O Fruen (later Flt Lt), Flt Lt Penning (later Sqn Ldr), Flt Lt Smith (later Sqn Ldr), Flt Lt Care (later Sqn Ldr), Flt Lt Edwards, Ft Lt Collins and Flt Lt Corney.

The first Washington flight from Coningsby followed only three days later when WF490, 'OJ-S' with Flight Lieutenant Edwards at the controls, and Flight Lieutenant Shuster from the Washington Conversion Unit as check pilot, took to the air for a five-hour check flight, including take-offs and landings and air-to-sea firing. On 6th December four more Washingtons flew in, becoming WF492 to WF495, and on the 8th, 11th and 13th December another two, one, and three respectively, continuing in sequence as WF496 to WF 501, giving No.149 Squadron a complement of eleven. The B-29s received by No.149 were in their natural metal finish, except for WF498 which was still in its wartime black anti-searchlight under-finish. The 5th and 7th of April 1951 brought two more Washingtons, WF546 and WF547, bringing the Squadron up to full flight strength of six aircraft for each flight, with one spare. WF547 was one of the very few B-29s to have been built with an elongated forward top turret.

Coningsby was fortunate to have as its Commanding Officer, Group Captain 'Gus' Walker, the well-known World War II bomber pilot who had lost an arm in trying to rescue the crew from a crashed and burning bomber when it blew up. No.15 Squadron with its Washingtons joined No.149 Squadron at Coningsby in February 1951, then No.57 Squadron in April and finally No.44 Squadron in May, giving Coningsby its full Washington complement. Spring 1951 brought another group to Coningsby, National Service Air Gunners who swelled the ranks of the air crew providing one to each aircraft, increasing the crew from eight to nine, the added crew member being considered 'in training'. Later in 1951, a massive flypast of RAF aircraft over London was planned for the forthcoming Battle of Britain celebrations, and so No.149's and the other Coningsby Washingtons spent some time in practising large formation flying. In any event bad weather cancelled the plan, and No.149 had to be satisfied with a static display for the Battle of Britain open day at Coningsby, with No.149 Washingtons also being flown to other airfields as static display for their own open days.

Among the other duties which No.149 Squadron carried out was that of National Air/Sea rescue cover, the B-29 Squadrons

*The twin 0.50-inch guns in the tail turret of a Lincoln.*

undertaking this on a rotational basis. Les Feakiss recalls being sent out to search for a Vampire that had ditched in the sea off the Scottish coast. Wreckage was found and photographed and the film dropped off at RAF Kinloss for development, ending a mission of over 12 hours.

Activities on the ground which Les recalls included dinghy drill at Cranwell, various sports, weekend escape and evasion exercises, and especially shooting for the air gunners. The escape and evasion involved the Army, who had the task of capturing aircrew on the run, interrogating them and incarcerating them. Needless to say inter-service relationships were not the best, particularly when capture consisted of touching the escaper on the shoulder accompanied by the words 'Squadron Flit'. Two of our number avoided all the unpleasantness upon being dropped off near Skegness by discarding their denims, and instead of finding their way cross-country to Coningsby, booked into Butlin's Holiday Camp for the duration of the exercise!

The island of Heligoland was still being used as a bombing range and so a number of 'Bullseye' raids were carried out by the Squadrons on Heligoland until the island was returned to the German government, the last bombing practice taking place in February 1952, with nine Washingtons from Nos.15, 44 and No.149 Squadrons, when five aircraft each dropped twelve 500-lb bombs while the other four aircraft dropped twelve 1,000-lb bombs just before the hand-over. Long-distance flying exercises were high on the training program, with non-stop flights up to fifteen hours in duration. Various defence exercises including NATO exercises were carried out in which No.149 Squadron took part, notably 'Ombrelle' (Umbrella) in May and 'Pinnacle' in September and October, both in 1951, and 'Ardent' in October 1952, 'Ardent' being the biggest. These exercises were to test the defences in Britain and the latter included every branch of the services including the RCAF, the USAF units based in Britain and European forces, involving no less than 200,000 personnel, and 6,000 sorties of both defence and attack aircraft. The Washingtons were among the aggressor aircraft which, in addition, saw the first Western Powers operational jet bomber on the scene, the English Electric Canberra. The lessons learned showed clearly how well the Canberra had proven itself as an attack bomber and, in contrast, that propeller-driven aircraft, including the Lincoln and the Washington, were obsolete.

No.149 Squadron was not without its Washington accidents. On one occasion the nose gear of one of its Washingtons was damaged when landing at Bassingbourn during a ground-controlled landing approach, which is best described by Jeff Brown, an air gunner and crew member:

"The year was 1951. Very few RAF Stations had 'ground control approach' (GCA) equipment, in those days - I think only two airfields had it, Manston and one other - possibly Binbrook. However, many of the American bases in the UK had GCA, Bassingbourn being one of them, and we (RAF) were permitted to use them, with prior booking, for practice approaches. On 31st May 1951 I flew in the crew of Washington WF498, Captain F/O Fruen, co-pilot Sgt Sowerby; part of the flight included practice GCA runs at Bassingbourn.

"It was a nice Spring evening with good visibility and we were the only aircraft in the circuit. I observed the first few approaches from the top gunner's position and listened to the 'patter' from the American controller and our own pilots on the R/T, everything went off fine. Later I decided to drink more coffee and climbed down out of the gunner's seat. I left my headset switch in the same position and continued to listen to the R/T. The Controller talked us down, giving minor corrections, and ended with the words, 'You are six feet above the runway threshold - look ahead and land visually'.

"We flew on - seconds later there was an almighty crash, as 50 tons of bomber bounced off the runway and I was flung to the floor. The aeroplane had flown itself into the ground and landed on only the nose wheel. This came about because of a misunderstanding between the two pilots. Each thought the other was flying the plane. The co-pilot, who sat in the right seat, had flown the approach, at the end of which he let go of the controls and looked out to his right, thinking that the Captain had taken over control of the aircraft. The captain, sitting on the left seat, was looking out to his left and thought that the co-pilot was still flying the plane - consequently the plane flew itself for a few seconds before landing on the nose wheel.

"As the plane bounced up, the captain applied full power to the engines, quickly raised the flaps to 'take-off' position and we staggered up into the air. Damage to the plane was considerable -

*The First Annual Reunion Dinner of No.149 Squadron, 21st April 1951.*

the nose undercarriage was 'knocked' backwards and upwards, it was ten degrees out of alignment and the pivot attachment at the top was shattered, as was the cockpit console between the two pilots, which was mounted directly above it. It was not possible to retract the undercarriage, so we flew around with it still down.

"We flew low and slow, passing the Control Tower, where the staff examined us externally with binoculars and then advised us to return to base. On arrival back at Coningsby, the same examination was carried out again, and it was decided that we would try a landing on the main wheels and 'tail skid'. Inside the plane we took up 'crash positions' and padded parachutes and ourselves with seat cushions. We came in low and slow and by holding the nose high to keep the nose wheel off the ground the pilot landed the plane dragging the 'tail skid' along the runway. The noise inside was deafening.

"Our predicament at Coningsby had created quite a stir and an 'audience' had gathered to watch the performance; they later told us that the sparks from the 'tail skid' looked like a giant 'Guy Fawkes Day' rocket! The hefty steel shoe of the skid was worn down about two inches when we examined it later, and we made a huge score mark several hundred yards long down the runway. The pilot managed to hold up the nose until we had slowed right down and then gently lowered the nose wheel onto the runway; luckily it did not collapse and we all quickly scrambled out, none the worse for our adventure. A mobile trestle was attached under the nose of the plane to support it and it was carefully towed off the runway.

"Next morning the plane was being moved and it stopped near the Squadron crew room, whilst several American civilians (aircraft company reps who were permanently stationed there) walked out to examine the aircraft. Someone spotted them and called out to the pilot F/O Fruen 'Hey, Freddie, the Yanks are looking at your plane'. A 'joker' called out from behind his newspaper, 'Perhaps they want to buy the bugger back' - much laughter all round. As it was, the plane was tucked away, out of sight, behind the hangars and a civilian working party from the Bristol Aircraft Company carried out extensive repairs, which took three months to complete.

"On another occasion the fin of one of the Washingtons had a neat 0.5 inch hole drilled in it from a bullet during an air-to-sea firing exercise."

It was soon decided that the Washingtons would be traded for Canberras at the first opportunity and so, in March 1953, No.149 Squadron, while still at Coningsby, entered the jet age by trading their Washingtons for Canberra B.2s, beginning with a factory-fresh WH711, all but two of the succeeding Canberras coming direct from the factory. No.44 Squadron followed suit in April, while Nos.15 and 57 Squadrons converted in May, bringing Coningsby to an all-Canberra base. This also disposed of the historic air gunner's position as a crew member in RAF aircraft. No.149's Washingtons were moved on, either to an existing Washington squadron or to a Maintenance Unit prior to their being returned to the United States. Jeff Brown describes the hand-over:

"On March 16, 1954, the formal ceremony to mark the handing back of the Washingtons to the American authorities took place at RAF Marham. Aircraft WF438 (44-27342) of the Washington Conversion Unit was 'on parade' to represent the type, and the inspection of a 'guard of honour' and salute at a march-past was taken by Air Marshal Sir George Mills, AOC-in-C, Bomber Command, and Brigadier General P H Robey, USAF Chief of the Military Assistance Advisory Group for the UK.

"At the end of March most of the Washingtons had been flown back to America, except for five which went to the Ministry of Supply and were later used as gunnery targets at Shoeburyness. These were, WF434 (44-61599), WF435 (44-61787), WF436 (44-61792), WF441 (44-61714), and WW355 (44-62239).

"Four others, WW346 (44-61937), WZ966 (44-62283), WZ967 (44-62282) and WZ968 (44-62296) of No.192 Squadron in No.90 (Signals) Group, which were used for Radio Counter Measures training, soldiered on until 1958 before they were finally retired. They also finished their days at Shoeburyness, thus ending the era of the Washington in the RAF."

The stay at Coningsby was soon to end. In preparation for the four-engined V-bombers about to join the RAF, plans for upgrading the airfield by extending the runway and for other reconstruction work had already been laid. So the tenants were moved out and No.149 Squadron, together with Nos.15, 44 and 57 Squadrons, were transferred to Cottesmore in May 1954.

The stay at Cottesmore for No.149 was brief. Life moves in cycles and following its post-World War I course, on 24th August 1954, the Squadron was moved to Ahlhorn in West Germany, with Squadron Leader R E R Adams as Commanding Officer, No.149 becoming the first Canberra squadron to be based permanently overseas, and the first British bomber squadron to be based in Germany since World War I. The first of No.149's Canberras to land on German soil was WJ626, landing at Ahlhorn on 25th August. Then less than a month later, on 17th September, the Squadron was moved to Gutersloh, to join No.102 Squadron and become part of the eventual four-squadron Canberra B.2 light bomber wing, No.551 Wing, of the Second Tactical Air Force, still under the control of Bomber Command. They were joined later by Nos.103 and 104 Squadrons, whose primary task was as a night bomber intruder wing. With ten Canberras on strength, No.149 Squadron was seen as the core, providing experience on which the other No.551 Wing squadrons would build and rely, using G-H as their primary bombing aid. No.149 Canberras carried the horseshoe and lightning flash from the Squadron badge on the fin, with the No.551 Wing motif on the nose.

*Seen in silhouette, Canberras during the Royal Review flypast. No.149 formed the centre trio of the final nine aircraft.* [Peter Newman]

Activities were primarily navigation and bombing exercises, the latter both visual and using 'G-H', with 25-lb practice bombs or 1,000-lb bombs. One aircraft from each squadron of the Wing was also routinely assigned on 'Lone Ranger' exercises, which ranged from the Middle East to Kenya. But their stay at Gutersloh was not to be for long. As efficiency in equipment grew and the need for such a strong Air Force lessened, more and more squadrons were pruned from the Royal Air Force rolls, with No.149 Squadron being selected as one of those to go. It was disbanded on 13th August 1956, while still on service at Gutersloh, ending the service career of one of the Royal Air Force's most outstanding bomber squadrons, with a combat record few could equal.

*Above left: Canberra B.2 WH713 undergoing maintenance at Gutersloh in July 1956. Note the lightning flash and horseshoe from the Squadron badge on the fin and the No.551 Wing motif on the nose.* [A Thomas collection]

*Above right: No.149's emblem on the fin of Canberra WJ567.* [A Thomas collection]

*Left: Master Pilot Duvall and crew.* [Peter Newman]

*Below: A quartet of Canberra B.2s in September 1954: WJ564, WJ576, WJ612, WJ626.* [A Thomas collection]

# APPENDIX I
# Roll of Honour No.149 (East India) Squadron 1939-1945

*The 'Roll of Honour', completed by Leslie Belton, is situated in St George's Church, Methwold. Leslie was a former member of No.149 (East India) Squadron based at Methwold.*

Extract from *The London Gazette* of 15th January 1943

### Rawdon Hume Middleton, RNZAF - No.149 Squadron

Aus.402745 Flight Sergeant Rawdon Hume Middleton, Royal Australian Air Force (Missing), No.149 Squadron.

"Flight Sergeant Middleton was captain and first pilot of a Stirling aircraft detailed to attack the Fiat works at Turin one night in November 1942. Great difficulty was experienced in climbing to 12,000 feet to cross the Alps, which led to excessive consumption of fuel. So dark was the night that the mountain peaks were almost invisible.

During the crossing Flight Sergeant Middleton had to decide whether to proceed or turn back, there being barely sufficient fuel for the return journey. Flares were sighted ahead and he continued the mission and even dived to 2,000 feet to identify the target despite the difficulty of regaining height. Three flights were made over Turin at this low altitude before the target was identified. The aircraft was then subjected to fire from light anti-aircraft guns.

A large hole appeared in the port main plane which made it difficult to maintain lateral control. A shell then burst in the cockpit, shattering the windscreen and wounding both pilots. A piece of shell splinter tore into the side of Flight Sergeant Middleton's face, destroying his right eye and exposing the bone over the eye. He was probably wounded also in the body or legs. The second pilot received wounds in the head and both legs which bled profusely. The wireless operator was also wounded in the leg.

Flight Sergeant Middleton became unconscious and the aircraft dived to 800 feet before control was regained by the second pilot, who took the aircraft up to 1,500 feet and released his bombs. There was still some light flak and the aircraft was hit many times. The three gunners replied continuously until the rear turret was put out of action.

Flight Sergeant Middleton had now regained consciousness and, when clear of the target, ordered the second pilot back to receive first aid. Before this was completed the latter insisted on returning to the cockpit, as the captain could see very little and could speak only with loss of blood and great pain.

Course was set for base and the crew now faced an Alpine crossing and homeward flight in a damaged aircraft with insufficient fuel. The possibilities of abandoning the aircraft or landing in Northern France were discussed but Flight Sergeant Middleton expressed the intention of trying to make the English coast, so that his crew could leave the aircraft by parachute. Owing to his wounds and diminishing strength, he knew that, by then, he would have little or no chance of saving himself. After four hours, the French coast was reached and here the aircraft, flying at 6,000 feet, was once more engaged and hit by intense light anti-aircraft fire. Flight Sergeant Middleton was still at the controls and mustered sufficient strength to take evasive action.

After crossing the Channel there was only sufficient fuel for five minutes' flying. Flight Sergeant Middleton ordered the crew to abandon the aircraft while he flew parallel with the coast for a few miles, after which he intended to head out to sea. Five of the crew left the aircraft safely, while two remained to assist Flight Sergeant Middleton. The aircraft crashed in the sea and the bodies of the front gunner and flight engineer were recovered the following day. Their gallant Captain was apparently unable to leave the aircraft and his body has not been traced.

Flight Sergeant Middleton was determined to attack the target regardless of the consequences and not allow his crew fall into enemy hands. While all the crew displayed heroism of a high order, the urge to do so came from Flight Sergeant Middleton, whose fortitude and strength of will made possible the completion of the mission. His devotion to duty in the face of overwhelming odds is unsurpassed in the annals of the Royal Air Force".

The body of Flight Sergeant Middleton was not recovered until 1st February 1943 when washed ashore at Shakespeare Cliff, Dover. He was buried on 5th February 1943 in the War Graves Plot of St John's, Beck Row, Mildenhall, UK. He was awarded the Victoria Cross posthumously.

### Squadron Leader Lloyd Watt Coleman DFC and Bar: Killed in Action 11th March 1942

On 20th November 1940 Squadron Leader Lloyd Watt Coleman was awarded the Distinguished Flying Cross (London Gazette 26th November 1940).

"In November 1940 this officer was Captain of an aircraft detailed to attack the railway and locomotive sheds at Munich. In spite of the fact that on his arrival he found considerable anti-aircraft activity and that he had been warned of the presence of balloons, he glided down to a height of 3,500 feet and straddled the target with his bombs. He then circled the town and ordered his air gunners to put out as many searchlights as possible. Since June 1940 Flight Lieutenant Coleman has carried out twenty-five raids, fifteen of them as captain of aircraft, during which he has displayed skill, persistent determination and devotion to duty and has set a magnificent example to his Squadron".

On 10th May 1941 Squadron Leader Coleman was awarded a Bar to his DFC (The first New Zealander to be so awarded):

"One night in May 1941, this officer was captain of aircraft which carried out an attack on the aerodrome at Benina in the Western Desert. He displayed great skill and tenacity in locating his target and carried out his attack with great determination, bombing and machine gunning the aerodrome from different heights, sometimes less than 1,000 feet. He destroyed at least two Junkers 52s on the ground and damaged others. Just after he returned from his attack an incoming aircraft crashed and caught fire. Though the petrol tanks and bombs on the crashed aircraft were exploding, Squadron Leader Coleman ran to another aircraft, started the engines and taxied to safety. He has continuously displayed outstanding courage and devotion to duty"

### Sergeant Louis Victor Fossleitner: Killed in Action 10th November 1942

### Pilot Officer John Philp: Killed in Action 8th December 1942

Sergeant Louis Victor Fossleitner and Pilot Officer John Philp were both awarded the British Empire Medal (London Gazette 29th December 1942):

"Pilot Officer Philp and Sergeants Reardon and Fossleitner were Captain, front gunner and navigator respectively of Stirling BF334, which attacked Munich on the night of 19th September 1942. On the return flight the engineer reported that there would only be sufficient fuel to operate for 15 minutes. Pilot Officer Philp, therefore, obtained permission to land at a nearby airfield. When nearing the airfield, however, one of the engines failed and it was necessary to come down in the sea off the English coast. Although the aircraft was kept level, it broke into four parts on impact with the water. Pilot Officer Philp, who was a strong swimmer, volunteered to swim ashore to get help. He abandoned his intention, however, as it was necessary to help the mid-upper gunner. Pilot Officer Philp and Sergeant Reardon started to swim ashore taking the mid-upper with them. They were picked up by a fishing boat after swimming for $3^{1}/_{2}$ hours. Unfortunately the mid-upper gunner was found to be dead. In the meantime Sergeant Fossleitner, although badly shaken, had volunteered to remain behind to support the wireless operator whose spine was fractured. He supported him for $2^{1}/_{2}$ hours before being picked up by an Air-Sea rescue Launch. The courage and fortitude shown by Pilot Officer Philp and Sergeants Reardon and Fossleitner were of the highest order."

## Personnel of No.149 Squadron Killed or Died in Service

|  |  |  |
|---|---|---|
| 15th Sept 1918 | Lt A J G King<br>2/Lt W Hogan | F.E.2B<br>Raid on Menin<br>Clairmarais North |
| 13th Dec 1937 | P.O. Aitken<br>Sgt Ross<br>Cpl Roberts<br>LAC Sillence | Heyford K4039<br>Night training<br>Stopham, Sussex |
| 4th Sept 1939 | AC2 T Thomson | Wellington L4270 |
| 13th Dec 1939 | LAC E J Naylor | Motor accident |
| 16th Dec 1939 | LAC I J T Smith | Bicycle hit by car, 15 December |
| 18th Dec 1939 | F.O. M F Briden<br>P.O. W S F Brown<br>Sgt V H G Richardson<br>AC1 I D Leighton<br>AC1 P J Warren<br>AC2 A G Foster | Wellington N2961 OJ-P<br>Operation Heligoland<br>Crashed into the North Sea |
| 18th Dec 1939 | F.O. J H C Spiers<br>P.O. F N Lines<br>Sgt R R Hammond<br>LAC J H Sinton<br>AC W J Ellis | Wellington N2962 OJ-B<br>Operation Heligoland<br>Crashed into the North Sea |
| 2nd Jan 1940 | F.O. H L McBulloch<br>Sgt R Ballantyne<br>Sgt D J Kirkness<br>LAC A A Brown<br>LAC W Greig DFM<br>AC2 D H Grove | Wellington N2943<br>Operation Heligoland<br>Crashed into the North Sea |
| 2nd Jan 1940 | Sgt J Morrice<br>Sgt W H C Kidd<br>Sgt H R B Wareham<br>LAC A J Mantle<br>AC2 D J Drury<br>AC2 A Hinchcliffe | Wellington N2946<br>Operation Heligoland<br>Crashed into the North Sea |
| 18th Jan 1940 | AC2 W A Colebourne | Wellington N2944;<br>Airfield accident, hit by aircraft propeller |
| 2nd Mar 1940 | F.O. L R Field<br>Sgt J C Murdoch<br>Sgt M Wiffen<br>LAC E H Prior<br>AC2 L B Hughson<br>AC2 T E Smith | Wellington N2984<br>Operation Bremen<br>Crashed at Burnt Fen nr Mildenhall, Suffolk |
| 4th Apr 1940 | P.O. J D Hargreaves<br>F.O. J P M Hewitt<br>Sgt R M Nelson<br>AC2 L F Foster | Wellington P9267<br>Training mission<br>Crashed near Mildenhall, Suffolk |
| 12th Apr 1940 | Sgt H J Wheller<br>Sgt W C Parker<br>Sgt L C Wakeling<br>LAC R Coalter<br>AC2 H Gillott<br>AC2 F Tootle | Wellington P9246<br>Operation Norwegian coast<br>Crashed into the sea off Norway |
| 12th Apr 1940 | Sgt G E Goad<br>Sgt F A Woodcock<br>Sgt R F Vickery<br>Cpl J H Langridge RNZAF<br>AC1 E B Doherty<br>AC2 J Henry | Wellington P9266<br>Operation Norwegian coast<br>Aircraft crashed into the sea off Norway |
| 24th May 1940 | Fl Lt I D Grant-Crawford<br>AC2 J Burton<br>AC2 E S Hewitt | Wellington P9270 OJ-G<br>Overseas operation<br>Crashed near Barton Mills, Suffolk |
| 11th June 1940 | F.O. J S Douglas-Cooper<br>P.O. M B Dawson<br>P.O. J R Swift<br>Sgt R Donaldson<br>Sgt G B Fleming<br>Sgt M Murphy | Wellington L7800<br>Operation Soissons<br>Crashed into the English Channel |
| 11th June 1940 | AC2 A F Moss | Wellington R3161.<br>Struck by propeller while aircraft was taxiing |
| 12th July 1940 | P.O. J S Torglason<br>P.O. C W Howie<br>P.O. J A Rose<br>Sgt J W Craig<br>Sgt J V Futcher<br>Sgt C Suggett | Wellington L7805<br>Operation Bremen<br>Lost on Operations |
| 23rd July 1940 | P.O. R C Sterling | Wellington T2459<br>Operation in troop combat area, Europe<br>Aircraft attacked by fighter on outward journey.<br>Observer killed.<br>Aircraft returned |
| 12th Aug 1940 | P.O. J G Miller<br>P.O. J Body<br>P.O. R E Houseman<br>Sgt R J Cocks<br>Sgt J J Scott<br>Sgt J H Swift | Wellington P9244 OJ-E<br>Operation Gelsenkirchen<br>Crashed Beck Row near Mildenhall, Suffolk |
| 17th Aug 1940 | Sqn Ldr E H T Thwaites AFC<br>P.O. D E S Charles<br>P.O. J Wilk | Wellington R3174 OJ-A<br>Operation Koleda<br>Lost on mission |
| 8/9th Sept 1940 | P.O. J L Leeds<br>Sgt W W Crooks<br>Sgt H G Gledhill<br>Sgt S C Grant<br>Sgt R A Jerritt<br>Sgt A C Martin | Wellington R3175 OJ-V<br>Operation Boulogne<br>Crashed into the sea off Clacton, Essex |
| 8/9th Sept 1940 | Sq Ldr L V Andrew<br>P.O. W G Searles<br>Sgt J L Brown<br>Sgt N G Bull<br>Sgt D M Payne | Wellington P9245 OJ-W<br>Operation Boulogne<br>Crashed into the English Channel |
| 18th Sept 1940 | P.O. J S Pay<br>P.O. D S Cox<br>P.O. G R M Ford<br>P.O. D R Tuppen<br>Sgt H H Harrison<br>Sgt W R Pope | Wellington R3160 OJ-E<br>Operation Le Havre<br>Crashed into the English Channel |
| 29th Sept 1940 | Sgt W T Hallam | Wellington R3164 OJ-E<br>Operation Hanau<br>Lost on Operations |
| 10th Oct 1940 | F.O. R G Furness<br>Sgt P T Catto<br>Sgt K McN Davidson<br>Sgt F G R McDonald<br>Sgt M P Reynolds<br>Sgt K Shimmells | Wellington P9273 OJ-V<br>Operation Herringen<br>Lost on mission |

|  |  |  |
|---|---|---|
| 27th Oct 1940 | AC A E Batchelor<br>Cpl F A Lacey | Airfield accident<br>Killed by enemy bombs from lone bomber |
| 20th Nov 1940 | P.O. K J Hide<br>Sgt A J Mitchell<br>Sgt H W Third<br>Sgt G O Webster<br>Sgt H Whitworth<br>Sgt N E Vince | Wellington N2774 OJ-A<br>Operation Berlin<br>Crashed Prussia |
| 16th Dec 1940 | Sgt R S W Lloyd<br>Sgt G G Matthews<br>Sgt D S Roberts<br>AC1 N J Cross<br>AC1 H W Little<br>AC2 J I Henderson<br>AC2 N Morton | Wellington R1294<br>Air Test<br>Crashed near Mildenhall, Suffolk |
| 12th Feb 1941 | Sgt F F Early | Wellington P9247 OJ-M<br>Operation Hannover<br>Crashed near Digby Airfield, Lincolnshire |
| 21st Feb 1941 | F.O. I S Henderson<br>Sgt W P Jinks<br>Sgt W H Macleod<br>Sgt F May<br>Sgt J P Redmond<br>Sgt J Stewart | Wellington R1045 OJ-M<br>Operation Wilhelmshaven<br>Lost on Mission |
| 6th Mar 1941 | LAC R H Waters | Cycle accident |
| 14th Mar 1941 | Sgt L R Hawley<br>Sgt W G Marett<br>Sgt C B Rodgerst<br>Sgt E G Prettyman<br>Sgt C G H Ward<br>Sgt E White | Wellington L7858 OJ-A<br>Operation Gelsenkirchen<br>Crashed at Sevenum, Netherlands |
| 18th Mar 1941 | Sgt R Warren<br>Sgt D J Capel<br>Sgt H Chapman<br>Sgt E R Cooke<br>Sgt W J Greaves<br>Sgt E A Lown | Wellington R1474 OJ-M<br>Operation Bremen<br>Crashed at Beck Row, Mildenhall, Suffolk |
| 1st Apr 1941 | Sgt P E Butler | Wellington R1229 OJ-H<br>Operation Bremen<br>Crashed on return to Mildenhall, Suffolk |
| 9th Apr 1941 | Sgt J B C Jago<br>Sgt A J Coster<br>Sgt J A Graham RNZAF<br>Sgt F M Jarret<br>Sgt P E M Mertens<br>Sgt A W Rose | Wellington R3167 OJ-H<br>Operation Kiel<br>Crashed into the North Sea |
| 10th Apr 1941 | Sgt J K Moseley<br>Sgt R J Uhrig RAAF | Wellington R1181 OJ-W<br>Training Mission<br>Crashed at Holmsey Green, Mildenhall, Suffolk |
| 13th Apr 1941 | P.O. R R Morrison<br>Sgt E J Holland DFM<br>Sgt R Hutchinson<br>Sgt J L G Westley<br>Sgt W H Wilkinson | Wellington T2897 OJ-O<br>Operation Merignac<br>Crashed near St Sever-Calvados, France |
| 16th Apr 1941 | Sgt P R B Maynell<br>Flt Sgt T E Evans<br>Sgt L G Gillam<br>Sgt A G Humphries<br>Sgt R C Payne<br>Sgt H W Patten | Wellington R1439 OJ-U<br>Operation Kiel<br>Lost on Mission |
| 18th Apr 1941 | Sgt J Peel<br>P.O. K E Platt<br>Sgt A A Allnatt<br>Sgt T C C Clifton<br>Sgt H S Walters<br>Sgt J Wood | Wellington P9248 OJ-G<br>Operation Cologne<br>Lost on Mission |
| 4th May 1941 | Sgt A A Wood | Wellington T2899<br>Operation Brest<br>Aircraft returned. |
| 9th May 1941 | Flt Sgt C R Burch<br>P.O. D Martin<br>Sgt W G H Dauncey<br>Sgt J A Keates | Wellington R1506 OJ-D<br>Operation Hamburg<br>Crashed into sea off Heligoland, Germany |
| 10th May 1941 | Sgt R J Keymer<br>P.O. G R N Adams<br>Sgt T N Menage<br>Sgt F C Ockenden<br>Sgt T C Pugh<br>Sgt L G Sutherland | Wellington R1512 OJ-H<br>Operation Hamburg<br>Crashed into the North Sea |
| 17th May 1941 | Sq Ldr A W J Clark<br>P.O. G H Cotton<br>Sgt C E Bushford<br>Sgt D J Gray<br>Sgt A Pepper<br>Sgt R A Petter | Wellington R1587<br>Training mission<br>Crashed near Ely, Cambridgeshire |
| 1st July 1941 | P.O. J E Horsefield<br>P.O. G F Burbidge<br>P.O. J F Philpot<br>Sgt F T Kearney<br>Sgt B D J Kennedy RNZAF<br>Sgt J C Robertson | Wellington R1408 OJ-J<br>Operation Brest<br>Crashed at Plouzane, France |
| 2nd July 1941 | P.O. S L St Vincent-Welch RAAF<br>Sgt R H Crafts RCAF<br>Sgt A R J Harrison<br>Sgt W J Megran<br>Sgt C C Reidmuller<br>Sgt W M Symmons RAAF | Wellington R1343 OJ-B<br>Operation Brest<br>Crashed in the target area |
| 18th July 1941 | Sgt P G Gibbins | Wellington N2853 OJ-R<br>Operation Cologne<br>Crashed near Sudbury, Suffolk |
| 5th Aug 1941 | Sgt E D Fowler<br>Sgt H Hale RCAF<br>Sgt S Morris<br>Sgt B A J Richardson<br>Sgt V Scholey<br>Sgt E A R Thomson | Wellington R1524 OJ-P<br>Operation Mannheim<br>Crashed at St Martens-Voeren, Belgium |
| 7th Aug 1941 | Sgt G T Farmer<br>Sgt D E G Denier RAAF<br>Sgt F S Ellis<br>Sgt G Lickley<br>Sgt V B Quinlan RCAF<br>Sgt A Yoxall | Wellington X9633 OJ-R<br>Operation Mannheim<br>Crashed at Thorembais St Trond, Belgium |
| 12th Aug 1941 | F.O. F H Beemer RCAF<br>P.O. F W J Scott RCAF<br>Sgt P E H Dangerfield<br>Sgt E W Hall<br>Sgt J R Littlefield<br>Sgt C F Young | Wellington R1024 OJ-V<br>Operation Hannover<br>Crashed into the sea off Sylt, Germany |

|  |  |  |
|---|---|---|
| 13th Aug 1941 | Sgt A N Hampson<br>Sgt G Morris RCAF | Wellington T2716 OJ-W<br>Operation Hannover<br>Crashed at Elvedon, Suffolk |
| 18th Aug 1941 | P.O. J C Lynn<br>P.O. P I A Mendoza | Wellington X9704 OJ-B<br>Operation Duisburg<br>Crashed at Haelen, Germany |
| 7th Sept 1941 | Sgt J W Fenton<br>Sgt S D Chamberlin<br>Sgt J M Dixon<br>Sgt E C Hatton<br>Sgt M McL Keswick RCAF<br>Sgt W R Malkemus RCAF | Wellington X9705 OJ-J<br>Operation Mannheim<br>Lost on mission |
| 12th Sept 1941 | Flt Sgt D W Bennett RCAF<br>Flt Sgt I P Graham RCAF<br>Sgt P M Kenvin<br>Sgt P M Wakefield<br>Sgt D G Willis<br>Sgt D J Wyatt | Wellington X9879 OJ-V<br>Operation Kiel<br>Crashed near Kiel, Germany |
| 20th Oct 1941 | P.O. A C L Hodge<br>F.O. B W Brubacker RCAF<br>Sgt F L Capstick RCAF<br>Sgt J W Horrocks<br>Sgt J St G Johnston<br>Sgt L E Scantlebury | Wellington Z8795 OJ-C<br>Operation Bremen<br>Crashed in the River<br>Schelde, Belgium |
| 8th Nov 1941 | Sgt S W Dane<br>P.O. H R Crowe RCAF<br>Sgt A C A Davies<br>Sgt P I Leeman<br>Sgt J C Pengelly | Wellington X9878 OJ-A<br>Operation Berlin<br>Lost on mission |
| 16th Nov 1941 | Sgt R Bramhall<br>Sgt R V Bawden<br>Sgt B Ferguson<br>Sgt J E King<br>Sgt J K Moss<br>Sgt C Northcott | Wellington R1627<br>Operation Emden<br>Crashed into the North Sea |
| 10th Mar 1942 | F.O. C L Pilkington<br>Sq Ldr L W Coleman DFC*<br>Flt Sgt L Kowalski RCAF<br>Sgt D A Graham<br>Sgt J Millichip<br>Sgt R A Shea<br>Sgt H Skelton | Stirling R9295 OJ-G<br>East India III<br>Operation Ruhr<br>Crashed at Hollywell Row,<br>Mildenhall, Suffolk |
| 10th Mar 1942 | P.O. L W Bailey RAAF<br>Sgt G B Daines<br>Sgt R W Hunt<br>Sgt T E Jordan<br>Sgt T J Sherriff<br>Sgt S N N O L B Smart<br>Sgt G R Williams | Stirling N6126 OJ-U<br>Operation Ruhr<br>Crashed near Kleve,<br>Germany |
| 16th Apr 1942 | P.O. M L Field<br>P.O. A L Ellis RNZAF<br>Sgt S Briggs<br>Sgt P S Brunsden<br>Sgt N C Hutson<br>Sgt E A Kirk<br>Sgt C Moynes<br>Sgt C V Phillips | Stirling N6068 OJ-T<br>Operation Dortmund<br>Crashed at Steene, Belgium |
| 27th Apr 1942 | P.O. J H Thomson RCAF<br>P.O. P C Budd RCAF<br>Sgt G Baker<br>Sgt J D Burnley<br>Sgt A J V Homan<br>Sgt C H Johnson<br>Flt Sgt H F Jordan<br>Sgt A Pope | Stirling W7512 OJ-A<br>Operation Rostock<br>Crashed into the North Sea |
| 5th May 1942 | P.O. A F Cheetham<br>F.O. K W B Moodie RCAF<br>Flt Sgt F D Jago<br>Sgt V Carriline<br>Sgt P B Pomeroy<br>Sgt J A Shaw<br>Sgt B E Smith | Stirling N6124 OJ-R<br>Operation Stuttgart<br>Crashed at Aguilcourt,<br>France |
| 18th May 1942 | Flt Sgt J M Wootton<br>Sgt G J V Lock | Stirling R9320 OJ-S<br>Mining off Copenhagen<br>Crashed off Copenhagen,<br>Denmark |
| 18th May 1942 | P.O. A J Frost<br>P.O. G W Coldwell RCAF<br>P.O. R P Gent<br>Sgt W Collins<br>Sgt J Currie<br>Sgt J H Baille<br>Sgt A H Smith | Stirling R9310 OJ-P<br>Mining off Copenhagen<br>Crashed in Great Belt,<br>Denmark |
| 6th June 1942 | Sq Ldr R B Harris<br>Flt Sgt J S Flockhart<br>Flt Sgt F D Lindsey RCAF<br>Sgt J Eastin<br>Sgt S D England<br>Sgt N H Kortwright<br>Sgt J Parris | Stirling R9321 OJ-T<br>Operation Essen<br>Crashed at Wanheimerort,<br>Germany |
| 6th June 1942 | P.O. P L Clayton<br>Sgt T A George<br>Sgt J F Gwyther<br>P.O. D M P Jones<br>Sgt M J Kelleher<br>Sgt J H Mouat | Stirling W7508 OJ-D<br>Operation Essen<br>Crashed near Tienen,<br>Belgium |
| 6th June 1942 | Sgt K Roderick | Stirling R9314 OJ-T<br>Operation Essen, Turret torn<br>away by impact with<br>Bf 110. Ditched in the North<br>Sea off Belgium |
| 9th June 1942 | Flt Sgt H L Davis<br>F.O. V W J Mansell RAAF<br>P.O. E A Phillips<br>Sgt E F W Booth<br>Sgt N Peake<br>Sgt E Ward<br>Sgt T Whittle | Stirling N6084 OJ-C<br>Operation Essen<br>Crashed at Hassel, Germany |
| 30th June 1942 | P.O. C W Simmons<br>F.O. K White<br>Sgt R E Barr<br>Sgt L S Lloyd<br>Sgt W C Scarlett<br>Sgt F Squires<br>Sgt W E Thomas | Stirling BF310 OJ-H<br>Operation Bremen<br>Crashed into the IJsselmeer,<br>Netherlands |
| 30th June 1942 | Sq Ldr G W Alexander<br>Flt Lt W G Barnes DFC<br>F.O. C W Dellow<br>Flt Sgt L Wilshire<br>Sgt R Gallagher<br>Sgt P F Hickley<br>Sgt L Shearer | Stirling N6082 OJ-Q<br>Operation Bremen<br>Crashed at Wons,<br>Netherlands |
| 16th July 1942 | Sgt H L Duckworth<br>Sgt C T Shepherd | Stirling BF312 OJ-A<br>Operation Lübeck<br>Crashed at Steinfeld,<br>Germany |
| 16th July 1942 | Sgt M V Cato RNZAF<br>Sgt R A Hawkins<br>Sgt H P Johnson RNZAF<br>Sgt E Mores | Stirling R9299<br>Training operation<br>Crashed at Swaffham<br>Bulbeck, Cambridgeshire |

|  |  |  |
|---|---|---|
| | Sgt J N Nichol RNZAF | |
| | Sgt L E Pole RNZAF | |
| 24th July 1942 | F.O. A J L Bowes<br>P.O. P H Basson<br>Sgt N Acton<br>Sgt G Blatherwick<br>Sgt E H Boumphrey<br>Sgt E C Isted<br>Sgt D Morris | Stirling W7580 OJ-D<br>Operation Duisburg<br>Crashed at Geffen,<br>Netherlands |
| 30th July 1942 | P.O. T M F Hulse<br>Flt Sgt W V Pickering RCAF<br>Flt Sgt C R Spratt RCAF<br>Sgt E J Buckton<br>Sgt R G P Capham<br>Sgt G Martins<br>Sgt R B Randell<br>Sgt G K Sutherland RCAF | Stirling BF320 OJ-H<br>Operation Düsseldorf<br>Crashed at Rodenhof,<br>Germany |
| 30th July 1942 | Flt Lt F G Neate<br>Flt Lt R R Graham RCAF<br>Flt Sgt E J Le Blanc RCAF<br>Sgt A Alsop<br>Sgt J T Avedisian RCAF<br>Sgt H W Sampson RNZAF | Stirling R9161 OJ-T<br>Operation Saarbrücken<br>Crashed at Regniowez,<br>France |
| 11th Aug 1942 | Sgt C W S Oliver RAAF<br>P.O. W C Sutton<br>Flt Sgt G F Smith RCAF<br>Sgt N P Gregson<br>Sgt L R Sims<br>Sgt J H Storey<br>Sgt W B Streater | Stirling R9162 OJ-Q<br>Minelaying in the Kattegat<br>Crashed in the Baltic |
| 21st Aug 1942 | P.O. G E Robertson<br>Sgt C J Bond<br>Sgt F S Clarke<br>Sgt D H Harris<br>Sgt P E J Jenkins<br>Sgt L H Nicholson<br>Sgt D R Simpson | Stirling R9329 OJ-V<br>Mining off the coast of France<br>Crashed on return,<br>Cornwood, Devon |
| 24th Aug 1942 | P.O. E P Wynn RCAF<br>Flt Lt D A Pebworth DFC<br>P.O. J A Trooter<br>Flt Sgt A N Charlton<br>Sgt W Green<br>Flt Sgt S Martin<br>Sgt R F Raphael | Stirling N6083 OJ-N<br>Operation Frankfurt<br>Crashed near Eriswell,<br>Suffolk |
| 29th Aug 1942 | W.Cmdr C Charlton-Jones<br>F.O. C D Dobson RNZAF<br>Sgt E D Butler<br>Sgt J W Gray<br>Sgt T Hickman<br>Sgt D McNamee | Stirling N6081 OJ-H<br>Operation Nuremburg<br>Crashed at Arlenbach,<br>Odenwalde, Germany |
| 10th Sept 1942 | Flt Sgt A F Potts<br>Sgt J F Lumsden RNZAF<br>Sgt G E Martin RNZAF<br>Sgt F Roberts<br>Sgt R F Swindlehurst RNZAF<br>Sgt J Mc R Wallace | Stirling R9170 OJ-H<br>Operation Düsseldorf<br>Crashed at Oud Beijrland,<br>Netherlands |
| 17th Sept 1942 | Flt Sgt M J Kynstan<br>Sgt E D Booty<br>Sgt J Collumbell<br>Sgt A C Rault<br>Sgt R A Russell<br>Sgt W Walker<br>Sgt J A Waterman | Stirling R9164 OJ-Q<br>Operation Essen<br>Crashed at Tongrinne,<br>Belgium |
| 20th Sept 1942 | Sgt A J Ottaway<br>Sgt R Spencer<br>Sgt F H King | Stirling BF334 OJ-R<br>Operation Munich<br>Crashed into the North Sea |
| 30th Sept 1942 | Flt Sgt S D Wells RNZAF<br>W.O.2 L J Tighe RCAF<br>Flt Sgt G F McHugh RCAF<br>Sgt M H Elliott RNZAF<br>Sgt R B L Flint<br>Sgt E H C Phillips<br>Sgt E G Souter | Stirling BF328 OJ-D<br>Minelaying in the Friesians<br>Crashed into the North Sea |
| 2nd Oct 1942 | Sq Ldr W R Greenslade DFC AFC<br>Flt Sgt R F McIntyre RCAF<br>Flt Sgt W Orange<br>Sgt E L More<br>Sgt B F Goldsmith<br>Sgt F L Hughes<br>Sgt M K Smith | Stirling R9167 OJ-N<br>Operation Krefeld<br>Crashed at Kronenberg,<br>Netherlands |
| 6th Oct 1942 | F.O. R Lonsdale RNZAF | Stirling N3755 OJ-S<br>Operation Aachen<br>Crashed at Eastling, Kent |
| 10th Oct 1942 | Sgt H J Hart<br>Sgt H I F Connelly RNZAF<br>Sgt A W Corker<br>Sgt K G McKenzie RNZAF<br>Sgt H C Whitwell RNZAF<br>Sgt L G Warren RNZAF | Stirling BF348 OJ-P<br>Mining off the mouth of the Gironde<br>Crashed at Great<br>Cressingham, Norfolk |
| 15th Oct 1942 | Flt Sgt J C Brocket RNZAF<br>Flt Sgt R G Blair RCAF<br>Sgt T B Bywaters<br>Sgt J Denny<br>Sgt M J Howe<br>Sgt T C B Pike RNZAF<br>Sgt F W O Sullivan RNZAF | Stirling W7526 OJ-V<br>Operation Cologne<br>Crashed near Tiel,<br>Netherlands |
| 16th Oct 1942 | W.O.2 J H Ekelund RCAF<br>F.O. M S Gilberd RNZAF<br>Flt Sgt E H Howell RNZAF<br>Sgt J C Leach<br>Sgt A Martin RNZAF<br>Sgt M A Torrance RNZAF<br>Sgt E H Uzzell | Stirling BF392 OJ-D<br>Mining in the Gironde Estuary<br>Crashed near<br>Ile d'Yeu, France |
| 24th Oct 1942 | Flt Sgt A H Siwak RCAF<br>F.O. R K Randell<br>Sgt L J Barnard RCAF<br>Sgt R A Blake<br>Sgt D J Bowden<br>Sgt E C C Holmes<br>Sgt S F Taylor | Stirling W7628 OJ-B<br>Operation Genoa<br>Crashed at Cliffe, Kent |
| 10th Nov 1942 | Sq Ldr W C Hutchings DFC<br>Flt Sgt J A Clough<br>Sgt L V Fossleitner BEM<br>Sgt C Hill<br>Sgt F Hughes<br>Sgt J D Pickup RAAF<br>P.O. J D Seigne | Stirling W7582 OJ-S<br>Training mission<br>Crashed at Mildenhall,<br>Suffolk |
| 16th Nov 1942 | Sgt T A West<br>Flt Sgt C R McMullin RCAF<br>Flt Sgt T H Short RCAF<br>Sgt B D Allen<br>Sgt H Carter<br>Sgt W R St G Fairfield<br>Flt Sgt K S Gunning RCAF | Stirling W7566 OJ-C<br>Mining off the French Coast<br>Crashed into the sea off<br>Vielle St-Girone, France |

|  |  |  |
|---|---|---|
| 29th Nov 1942 | P.O. R H Middleton VC RAAF<br>Sgt J E Jeffrey<br>Sgt J W Mackie | Stirling BF372 OJ-H<br>Operation Turin<br>Crashed into the English Channel |
| 30th Nov 1942 | Sgt V T Bowie RNZAF<br>Sgt G N Beames<br>Sgt A Carter<br>Flt Sgt P M Everson<br>Sgt N A MacLeod<br>Sgt C Smith<br>Sgt L H Smith<br>Flt Sgt W M Wright RCAF | Stirling R9202 OJ-K<br>Operation Turin<br>Crashed at Irasco-Finerola, Italy |
| 7th Dec 1942 | Sgt W F D Rogers | Domestic accident |
| 8th Dec 1942 | P.O. J Philp BEM<br>P.O. C W Higgins<br>Flt Sgt T H Harris<br>Flt Sgt G E Hills<br>Flt Sgt T G Williams<br>Sgt F Craven<br>Sgt W S Hughes | Stirling W7639 OJ-Q<br>Mining off Warnemünde<br>Crashed at Brandon, Suffolk |
| 8th Dec 1942 | F.O. M H Good<br>Flt Sgt P H Murray<br>Sgt J A Clough<br>Sgt L P J French<br>Sgt C R Long<br>Sgt W T Taylor<br>Sgt H T Williams | Stirling BF391 OJ-T<br>Mining in Fehmarn Channel<br>Crashed at Dobersdorf, Germany |
| 8th Dec 1942 | P.O. L T Izzard RCAF<br>Flt Sgt S H Hopkinson<br>Sgt P W Ditchburn<br>Sgt D P McAleese<br>Sgt W Osborn<br>Sgt J L Stracham<br>Sgt F H K Watt<br>Sgt R H Williams | Stirling R9253 OJ-K<br>Mining off Warnemünde<br>Crashed at Westermarsch, Germany |
| 19th Dec 1942 | F.O. E A R Hunt<br>Flt Sgt G E Tait RNZAF<br>Sgt J F Alpe RNZAF<br>Sgt R Macaulay<br>Sgt I N J Macnaughton RNZAF<br>Sgt L E Neary<br>Sgt H S Taylor<br>Sgt G W Williams | Stirling R9265 OJ-N<br>Air Test<br>Crashed at Great Gransden, Bedfordshire |
| 3rd Jan 1943 | Sgt T Whitelock | Stirling R9334 OJ-G<br>Training mission<br>Crashed at Lakenheath, Suffolk |
| 14th Feb 1943 | Flt Sgt J G Gow RNZAF<br>Sgt P C T Oldham<br>Sgt W A Summerson<br>Sgt J C Brigden | Stirling W7638 OJ-R<br>Operation Cologne<br>Crashed near Boxmeer, Netherlands |
| 2nd Mar 1943 | Flt Lt R E Richman DFM<br>Sgt D A Crofts<br>Sgt R A Nunn | Stirling BK692 OJ-W<br>Operation Berlin<br>Crashed near Gueutteville, France |
| 12th Mar 1943 | Flt Sgt F A Pearson<br>F.O. G W Sellers RCAF<br>P.O. L H R Binning<br>W.O.2 G W Miller RCAF<br>Flt Sgt R H Skinner RNZAF<br>Sgt W H Clayton<br>Sgt J Misseldine<br>Sgt V Page | Stirling EF330 OJ-P<br>Operation Essen<br>Crashed at Beek, Netherlands |
| 30th Mar 1943 | P.O. I T S Fulton (USA)<br>Sgt A J Crosson<br>Sgt E D Edwards<br>Sgt J W Houlgrave<br>Sgt E Hunt<br>Sgt R P T Saunders | Stirling BK708 OJ-P<br>Operation Berlin<br>Crashed at Lindenberg, Germany |
| 4th Apr 1943 | Sgt K A Way<br>Sgt R P Bilham<br>Sgt E G King<br>Sgt N MacLeod<br>Sgt W E Norman<br>Sgt J Palmer<br>Sgt R G Woodfield | Stirling R9327 OJ-M<br>Operation Kiel<br>Crashed at Obbekaer, Denmark |
| 15th Apr 1943 | P.O. T G Ogle<br>P.O. E M Merritt RCAF<br>Flt Sgt W Stephen<br>Sgt L Jones<br>Sgt D Lenehan<br>Sgt V J Upson<br>Sgt H Walters | Stirling BK759 OJ-X<br>Operation Stuttgart<br>Crashed at Studernheim, Germany |
| 15th Apr 1943 | P.O. D B White RCAF<br>F.O. L G Vallance RCAF<br>W.O.2 R R Stover RCAF<br>Flt Sgt T W Foran RCAF<br>Sgt E Farnen<br>Sgt K S A Payne<br>Sgt A J White | Stirling BF500 OJ-M<br>Operation Stuttgart<br>Crashed at Belval, France |
| 20th Apr 1943 | Flt Lt G I Ellis RNZAF<br>F.O. D McNarey RNZAF<br>P.O. E Booth<br>P.O. I A M Holloway<br>Sgt E R Ginn<br>Sgt P L C Kelly<br>Sgt P B Mills<br>Sgt F Sheppard | Stirling BK698 OJ-O<br>Operation Rostock<br>Crashed into the sea off Denmark |
| 21st Apr 1943 | Sgt E Lewis | Stirling BK714 OJ-L<br>Operation Rostock<br>Crashed near Esbjerg, Denmark |
| 5th May 1943 | Flt Lt W E Davey<br>P.O. T C Timney<br>Flt Sgt E H Finch RAAF<br>Flt Sgt R F Whitaker<br>Sgt G J C Hall<br>Sgt D R Higgs<br>Sgt C W E Leach<br>Sgt J J O Niell | Stirling EF343 OJ-B<br>Operation Dortmund<br>Crashed near IJpecolsga, Netherlands |
| 13th May 1943 | Sgt E G Bass<br>F.O. R F Kingham<br>Sgt R D Evans<br>Sgt J G Newall<br>Sgt K G Roots<br>Sgt D B Sach<br>Sgt F G Salter | Stirling EF357 OJ-V<br>Operation Duisburg<br>Crashed near Rotterdam, Netherlands |
| 14th May 1943 | P.O. H E Forsyth RCAF<br>P.O. D E Sharpe<br>W.O.2 Y J B Guepin RCAF<br>Flt Sgt D F McDonald RCAF<br>Sgt L P Barnett<br>Sgt W McCall<br>Sgt J J Ryan | Stirling BK726 OJ-Z<br>Operation Bochum<br>Crashed at Immerath, Germany |
| 14th May 1943 | F.O. L C Martin<br>F.O. G R Royde DFC<br>Sgt N H Frank<br>Flt Sgt R C Ferguson RCAF | Stirling BK479 OJ-E<br>Operation Bochum<br>Crashed at Kasterlee, Belgium |

|  |  |  |
|---|---|---|
|  | Flt Sgt H P Fudge RCAF<br>Sgt H A J Berry<br>Sgt J E Butt<br>Sgt E Hazelden-French |  |
| 18th May 1943 | Sgt S Biddulph<br>Sgt J E Boyes<br>Sgt C C D Scotney<br>Sgt T Smith | Stirling BK701 OJ-G<br>Mining off La Rochelle, France<br>Ditched in the Loire Estuary, France |
| 21st May 1943 | Sgt C E Tomlin<br>Sgt A Camps<br>Sgt G T Cook<br>Sgt E W Hall<br>Sgt A James<br>Sgt W H A Shelvington<br>Sgt J S Warburton | Stirling BF510 OJ-P<br>Mining in the Bay of Biscay<br>Crashed into the English Channel |
| 26th May 1943 | Sgt J H Uden<br>F.O. W E L Morse<br>Sgt L D Hadden<br>Sgt H S Scott<br>Sgt C J Percival<br>Sgt F A Williams<br>F.O. H S Winchester | Stirling BK710 OJ-A<br>Operation Düsseldorf.<br>Crashed into the North Sea |
| 30th May 1943 | P.O. A W Flack RNZAF<br>P.O. J Shepherd<br>W.O.2 H Sponsler RCAF (US)<br>W.O.2 R W Stanley RCAF<br>Sgt F C Detley<br>Sgt H Lloyd<br>Sgt T B Morris | Stirling BF507 OJ-S<br>Operation Wuppertal<br>Crashed at Dormagen, Germany |
| 22nd June 1943 | P.O. J Lowrie<br>F.O. D H Lyne<br>Sgt J Atkinson<br>Sgt A Coull<br>Sgt D C H Fudge<br>Sgt E G Hird<br>Sgt E C Wait | Stirling BK799 OJ-O<br>Operation Krefeld<br>Crashed into the IJsselmeer, Netherlands |
| 29th June 1943 | F.O. W R Booker<br>Sgt K Broadhurst<br>Sgt D W B Channing<br>Sgt L Franklin<br>Sgt B J Herbert<br>Sgt A D Hall<br>Sgt C V Howden RCAF | Stirling BK703 OJ-K<br>Operation Cologne<br>Crashed at Netersel, Netherlands |
| 29th June 1943 | Sgt R K Scott<br>F.O. R J Peattie RNZAF<br>Flt Sgt A B Parton RNZAF<br>Flt Sgt T R-A-H Tomoana RNZAF<br>Sgt R J Cockshott<br>Sgt L A Cooper (17, among youngest lost)<br>Sgt J Douglas | Stirling BF483 OJ-C<br>Operation Cologne<br>Crashed into the North Sea |
| 29th June 1943 | F.O. A R Porter<br>Sgt P Butterworth<br>Sgt A Derbyshire<br>Sgt L B McCallum RNZAF<br>Sgt B S Swainston | Stirling EE880 OJ-O<br>Operation Cologne<br>Crashed near Aarschot, Belgium |
| 4th July 1943 | P.O. G A Cozens DFM<br>F.O. E G Redman DFC<br>P.O. L W Curtis<br>Sgt R F Hathaway<br>Sgt P Hodgkinson<br>Sgt W J Williams | Stirling BF530 OJ-C<br>Operation Cologne<br>Crashed at Geetbetz, Belgium |
| 9th Aug 1943 | Flt Sgt J W Cumming RCAF<br>A.C.2 R W Cooper<br>Sgt J Dabbs<br>Sgt G Jones<br>Sgt A McStirling<br>Sgt S L Noakes<br>Sgt R W Poole<br>Sgt G H Riley | Stirling BF512 OJ-E<br>Training Flight<br>Crashed near Lakenheath, Suffolk |
| 12th Aug 1943 | Sgt A L Mason | Stirling EH904<br>Operation Turin<br>Aircraft returned to Lakenheath |
| 24th Aug 1943 | Flt Sgt A E May<br>Flt Sgt H J French<br>Sgt F W R Day<br>Sgt R A Freeman<br>Sgt J A Hobbs<br>Sgt T J Lucy | Stirling EE894 OJ-R<br>Operation Berlin<br>Crashed near Hannover, Germany |
| 28th Aug 1943 | Flt Sgt G S Steer<br>Flt Sgt D G Booth RCAF<br>Sgt G V Cook<br>Sgt V A Deacock<br>Sgt P H Johnson<br>Sgt H R J Richardson<br>Sgt W C Havercroft | Stirling EE877 OJ-E<br>Operation Nuremberg<br>Crashed near Cologne, Germany |
| 31st Aug 1943 | Flt Sgt E W Bower<br>Sgt L J D Bristow (US)<br>Sgt T C Cassidy<br>Lt H A Deviney USAAF<br>Sgt J Collins<br>Sgt P O Fletcher<br>Sgt J G Golden | Stirling EF438 OJ-D<br>Operation Mönchen-Gladbach<br>Crashed in the target area |
| 1st Sept 1943 | P.O. H A More<br>Flt Sgt W D Clark RNZAF<br>Flt Sgt R W Lower RNZAF<br>Sgt T Birkby<br>Sgt T Collier<br>Sgt L R Fisher<br>Sgt R J H Hitchmough | Stirling EE879 OJ-G<br>Operation Berlin<br>Crashed at Sputendorf, Germany |
| 5th Sept 1943 | Sgt L Gaffee<br>Sgt R J Humbles | Stirling BF477 OJ-B<br>Operation Mannheim<br>Crashed at Sorbon, France |
| 6th Sept 1943 | Flt Sgt D H W Badcock RNZAF<br>Flt Sgt A A Brown<br>Sgt D A P Guest<br>Flt Sgt A H Holms RNZAF<br>Sgt H A Saunders<br>W.O. A V Douglas RNZAF | Stirling EE872 OJ-N<br>Operation Mannheim<br>Crashed Germany |
| 6th Sept 1943 | Flt Lt B Cottrell<br>Sgt J Cowap<br>Sgt A R Crowther<br>Sgt W L Smith | Stirling BK711 OJ-O<br>Operation Mannheim<br>Crashed near Hockenheim, Germany |
| 23rd Sept 1943 | P.O. W J Leedham<br>W.O.2 W Ness RCAF<br>Sgt W A Beales<br>Sgt E Magson<br>Sgt I Thomlinson | Stirling EH883 OJ-A<br>Operation Mannheim<br>Crashed near Herxheim bei Landau, Germany |
| 27/28th Sept 1943 | Flt Sgt G S Hotchkiss RAAF<br>F.O. C J W Bevan<br>Sgt R B Andrews RNZAF<br>Flt Sgt B J Schollum RNZAF | Stirling EF495 OJ-R<br>Operation Hannover<br>Crashed into the North Sea |

| Date | Crew | Aircraft / Operation |
|---|---|---|
| 7th Oct 1943 | Flt Sgt J G McInnes RCAF<br>Flt Sgt T P Walton RAAF<br>Sgt D E Ashton<br>Sgt R A Barr RCAF<br>Sgt J E McQuade<br>Sgt A Robinson<br>Flt Sgt A D Steels RCAF | Stirling EJ106 OJ-O<br>Mining in the Friesians<br>Crashed into the North Sea |
| 17th Nov 1943 | P.O. G T Lowe RNZAF<br>Sgt R A Nicholls<br>Sgt A B Pilbeam<br>Sgt L J Somers | Stirling MZ260 OJ-C<br>Training Flight<br>Crashed at Lakenheath,<br>Suffolk |
| 19th Nov 1943 | Sgt E C Beacock<br>Sgt J D Scott | Stirling EH903 OJ-L<br>Operation Mannheim<br>Crashed in the target area |
| 20th Dec 1943 | Flt Sgt R J Ayers RAAF<br>Flt Sgt C W M Corkhill RAAF<br>Flt Sgt J R Martin RCAF<br>Sgt V Mandy<br>Sgt W McAdie<br>Sgt S J Lunn<br>Sgt W M Power RCAF | Stirling BK798 OJ-Q<br>Mining off the Friesians<br>Crashed into the North Sea |
| 27th Jan 1944 | P.O. E Wood<br>F.O. R W Heal<br>Flt Sgt E H Paton<br>Sgt S Allan<br>Sgt A F Brett<br>Sgt H Cookman<br>Sgt A J Manthorpe | Stirling EE969 OJ-E<br>Mining in the Kattegat<br>Crashed into the sea |
| 6th Feb 1944 | Flt Lt H J Colenutt<br>F.O. D H Mills<br>F.O. G H Mulligan RCAF<br>W.O. G N Gosling<br>Sgt J J Cassels (18)<br>Sgt D G Davies<br>Sgt R J S Waller | Stirling EF187 OJ-C<br>SOE Operation near<br>Dijon, France<br>Crashed at Cussy-les-<br>Forges, France |
| 24th Feb 1944 | Flt Lt A V Collins<br>F.O. J B Blencowe<br>F.O. E E C Davies<br>F.O. G T Raymond<br>W.O.2 A J Long RCAF<br>Sgt J G Gowans<br>Sgt G J MacPherson | Stirling EF307 OJ-E<br>Mining in the Kiel Bay<br>Crashed into the sea |
| 25th Feb 1944 | Flt Lt R N Johnstone RNZAF<br>F.O. G H Fowler RNZAF<br>F.O. W G Tibbits<br>Flt Sgt V G Tunnicliffe RNZAF<br>Sgt A Hartley<br>Sgt F R Jeffcoate<br>Sgt F R Webster | Stirling EF308 OJ-R<br>Mining in the Baltic<br>Crashed into the sea |
| 15th Mar 1944 | P.O. D J Munro RAAF<br>F.O. M F Culling<br>Flt Sgt N A McAllister RAAF<br>Sgt R S Barratt<br>Sgt R B Priestley<br>Sgt A McL Reid<br>Sgt A R Skelton | Stirling EJ124 OJ-C<br>Operation Amiens<br>Crashed near Boves, France |
| 10th Apr 1944 | Flt Lt R V Sanders<br>P.O. D McGregor<br>P.O. J W Patrick RCAF<br>Flt Sgt S Lindhard<br>Sgt T Hardman<br>Sgt C R Kemp<br>Sgt T Warden | Stirling LK382 OJ-Q<br>SOE Operation in France<br>Crashed near Esmery-<br>Hallon, France |
| 11th Apr 1944 | P.O. D Bray<br>Sgt A E Bristow<br>Flt Sgt G Cameron<br>P.O. D L Northover DFC<br>Flt Sgt J Turner | Stirling EF502 OJ-G<br>SOE Operation in France<br>Crashed at St-Jean-le-Vieux,<br>France |
| 19th Apr 1944 | Flt Sgt E Jeal<br>P.O. R W Lowther RCAF<br>F.O. G Watson<br>Sgt J F Brunton<br>Sgt J N Elliott<br>Sgt A McR Geddes<br>Sgt W Wigham | Stirling LJ504 OJ-K<br>Mining Kiel Bay<br>Crashed into the sea off<br>Jutland |
| 23rd Apr 1944 | P.O. H E Billens RNZAF<br>Flt Sgt S P Dullaghan<br>Flt Sgt G E Longley RNZAF<br>Sgt F L Dawson<br>Sgt S S J Haines<br>Sgt J Nichols<br>Sgt K A Harper<br>Sgt J Nicholls | Stirling EH943 OJ-B<br>Operation Laon<br>Crashed at Cuissy-et-Geny,<br>France |
| 23rd Apr 1944 | Flt Lt R J Freeman<br>P.O. R H Cameron RCAF<br>P.O. D Hughes<br>P.O. J M Ronahan RCAF<br>Sgt A R Redfearn<br>Sgt J L Stean<br>Flt Sgt R T Walker RAAF | Stirling LJ526 OJ-P<br>Minelaying in the Baltic<br>Crashed at Oster Skerninge,<br>Denmark |
| 1st June 1944 | P.O. J R McWade RCAF<br>Flt Sgt J Hodgkins<br>Sgt F Cartwright<br>Sgt S Dickinson<br>Sgt F C Pallett<br>Sgt E R Searles | Stirling LJ501 OJ-H<br>Mining operation to Knocke,<br>Belgium<br>Crashed at Zeebrugge,<br>Belgium |
| 6th June 1944 | P.O. W H Mayo<br>W.O. G C C Holmes<br>Flt Sgt J MacFarlane<br>Flt Sgt H F Munday RAAF<br>Flt Sgt R Parker<br>Sgt H J Mather | Stirling LJ621 OJ-M<br>Support to D-Day operations<br>Crashed at Marcelett, France |
| 6th June 1944 | Sq Ldr C J K Hutchins<br>F.O. J B Hornby<br>P.O. W C McCoy<br>W.O. W A Hannaford<br>Flt Sgt R H S Hart<br>Sgt R W Abrams<br>Sgt F W Bellamy<br>Sgt A H Brown<br>Sgt A R Wincott | Stirling LK385 OJ-C<br>Support to D-Day operations<br>Crashed near Baudre, France |
| 24th June 1944 | P.O. E J Lincoln RAAF<br>P.O. H W G Fox RCAF<br>Flt Sgt F P J Brady RAAF<br>Flt Sgt R J McQuitty RAAF<br>Flt Sgt L R Richards<br>Sgt E R Duckworth<br>Sgt E D Eaton | Stirling EF188 OJ-M<br>Minelaying off Brest, France<br>Crashed near Plougonvelin,<br>France |
| 25th June 1944 | Flt Lt G R B Roe RCAF<br>P.O. I W Harland<br>F.O. H R Murray<br>W.O. R W G Bryant<br>Sgt W A McDougall<br>Sgt T H Williams | Stirling EF140 OJ-B<br>Operation Ruisseauville<br>Crashed in the English<br>Channel off Boulogne |
| 25th June 1944 | F/O V F Wunsch RCAF<br>F/O W L Baker RCAF<br>F/O L E Owen RCAF | Stirling LK394 OJ-D<br>Operation Ruisseauville<br>Crashed at Lisbourg, France |

|  |  |  |
|---|---|---|
|  | Sgt G Harrison<br>Sgt K A Horswell<br>Sgt P A Budd<br>Sgt D D Munson RCAF |  |
| 6th July 1944 | Flt Sgt F L A White | Stirling LJ477 OJ-M<br>SOE Operation in France<br>Crashed at Thorney Island, Sussex |
| 17th July 1944 | Sgt D Davidson<br>Sgt D E W Jones | Stirling LK388 OJ-L<br>Training mission<br>Crashed at Methwold, Norfolk |
| 7th Aug 1944 | F.O. D A M Adams<br>P.O. E S Cary RCAF<br>Sgt J E A Cuthbert<br>Sgt T Kilcoyne<br>Sgt L H Mercer<br>Sgt J A Prior<br>Sgt J W Robinson | Stirling LK383 OJ-A<br>Minelaying off Brest<br>Crashed into the English Channel |
| 24th Nov 1944 | Flt Sgt W Scott | Lancaster NF971<br>Operation Cologne<br>Aircraft returned to Methwold |
| 12th Dec 1944 | F.O. K A M Miller<br>W.O. G N Bury RAAF<br>Flt Sgt J Cass<br>Sgt C M Hanna<br>Sgt R Middleton<br>Sgt H L Richamn<br>Sgt D Ward | Lancaster HK653 OJ-Y<br>Operation Witten<br>Crashed into the North Sea |
| 12th Dec 1944 | F.O. E H S Dorey<br>Flt Sgt N A L Green RAAF<br>Flt Sgt D Wham RAAF<br>Sgt L A V Hunt<br>Sgt W L Taylor | Lancaster HK653 OJ-R<br>Operation Witten<br>Lost on mission |
| 2nd Feb 1945 | Wg Cmdr L H Kay<br>Flt Lt L E Button RAAF<br>P.O. J C Botting<br>W.O. P H Wales RAAF<br>Sgt C S Bowers | Lancaster NN708 OJ-Q<br>Operation Wiesbaden<br>Crashed in France |
| 9th Feb 1945 | Sgt R E Tootell | Lancaster NF976<br>Operation Hohenbudberg<br>Aircraft returned to Methwold |
| 5th Mar 1945 | Flt Sgt A E London RAAF<br>Flt Lt B M Williams RAAF | Lancaster NF972 OJ-H<br>Operation Gelsenkirchen<br>Crashed near Wesel, Germany |
| 19th Mar 1945 | Flt Sgt G A Dane | Lancaster NG244<br>Operation Gelsenkirchen<br>Aircraft returned to Methwold |
| 5th June 1945 | F.O. P Tottle<br>Flt Sgt J Dyer<br>Flt Sgt K Hird<br>Flt Sgt L Jones<br>Flt Sgt E Paige<br>Flt Sgt P C Wyatt<br>Sgt R E Tilley<br>LAC W Spark<br>LAC W H Wardle<br>AC2 W Quinn | Lancaster PP673<br>Repatriation of ex-prisoners-of-war<br>Crashed at Arras, France |

**No.149 Squadron casualties are as follows:**

702 of the Royal Air Force
 28 of the Royal Australian Air Force
 76 of the Royal Canadian Air Force
 53 of the Royal New Zealand Air Force
  1 of the United States Army Air Force

**Total: 860**

263 have no known grave and are commemorated on the Runnymede Memorial.
157 are buried in Germany
124 in France
 89 in Netherlands
 54 in Belgium
130 in England
  9 in Scotland
  3 in Ireland
  6 in Wales
  4 in Norway
  1 in Sweden
 22 in Denmark
  8 in Italy

## Injuries / Evaders / Prisoners-of-war No.149 (East India) Squadron

| *Date* | *Name* | *Fate* | *A/c serial* | *Mission* |
|---|---|---|---|---|
| 22nd/23rd June 1918 | Lt J W Thomson<br>2/Lt L J W Ingram | POW<br>POW | D9777 | Op: Armentières |
| 19th/20th July 1918 | Lt Vosper<br>Lt Smith | POW<br>POW | D3779 | Op: Warneton |
| 4th/5th November 1918 | Lt F Marsh<br>Lt Cuffe | POW<br>POW | D9903 | Op: Renaix |

## 1940

| Date | Name | Fate | A/c serial | Mission |
|---|---|---|---|---|
| 21st/22nd April 1940 | F.O. F T Knight<br>Sgt W G McDonald<br>Sgt G E Forsyth<br>AC2 J J Eldridge<br>AC2 Blackburn<br>AC1 W J Thew | POW<br>POW<br>POW<br>POW<br>POW<br>POW | P9218 OJ-O | Op: Aalborg |
| 23rd/24th May 1940 | F.O. Holdsworth<br>Sgt Mundell<br>AC1 Crook | Inj<br>Inj<br>Inj | P9270 OJ-G | Op: Battle Area |

| Date | Crew | Status | Aircraft | Operation |
|---|---|---|---|---|
| 16th/17th August 1940 | Flt.Lt. Fisher | POW | R3174 OJ-A | Op: Koleda |
| | Sgt N J V Conway | POW | | |
| | Sgt F J Pennicott | POW | | |
| 27th/28th August 1940 | Flt.Lt. P F R Vaillant | POW | P9272 OJ-A | Op: Kiel |
| | Sgt R W Saywood | POW | | |
| | Sgt L F Mabey RNZAF | POW | | |
| | Sgt J Fender | POW | | |
| | Sgt D H G Connolly | POW | | |
| | P.O. M G Butt | POW | | |
| 5th/6th September 1940 | F.O. H Burton | POW/Escaped | R3163 OJ-G | Op: Black Forest |
| | P.O. G M R Smith | POW | | |
| | Sgt A R Peacock | POW | | |
| | Sgt H R Barnes | POW | | |
| | Sgt J Bailey | POW | | |
| | P.O. D A McFarlane | POW | | |
| 8th/9th September 1940 | Sq.Ldr. L V Andrews | POW | P9245 OJ-W | Op: Boulogne |
| | P.O. C W Parish | POW | | |
| | Sgt J L Brown | POW | | |
| | Sgt N J Bull | POW | | |
| | Sgt D M Payne | POW | | |
| | P.O. W G Searles | POW | | |
| 18th/19th September 1940 | P.O. J S Pay | POW | R3160 OJ-E | Op: Le Havre |
| | P.O. D R Tuppen | POW | | |
| | P.O. D S Cox | POW | | |
| | Sgt W R Pope | POW | | |
| | Sgt H H Harrison | POW | | |
| | P.O. G R M Ford | POW | | |
| 28th/29th September 1940 | P.O. H R Petersen | POW | R3164 OJ-B | Op: Hanau |
| | Sgt K Holden | POW | | |
| | Sgt K Hallam | POW | | |
| | Sgt A Botten | POW | | |
| | Sgt C McKlaird RNZAF | POW | | |
| | Sgt A B Witton RNZAF | POW | | |
| 19th/20th November 1940 | P.O. K J Hide | POW | N2774 OJ-A | Op: Berlin |
| | Sgt G O Webster | POW | | |
| | Sgt N E Vince | POW | | |
| | Sgt A J Mitchell | POW | | |
| | Sgt H Whitworth | POW | | |
| | Sgt H W Third | POW | | |

## 1941

| Date | Crew | Status | Aircraft | Operation |
|---|---|---|---|---|
| 12th/13th January 1941 | Sgt R A Hodgson | POW/Escaped | T2807 OJ- | Op: Italy |
| | P.O. L K S Wilson | POW | | |
| | Sgt L W Hatherly | POW | | |
| | Sgt E E Harding | POW | | |
| | Sgt J McAnnally | POW | | |
| | Sgt C F Plummery | POW | | |
| 11th/12th February 1941 | Sgt Pates | Inj | P9247 OJ-M | Op: Bremen. Aircraft crashed, Digby, Lincs. |
| 1st April 1941 | Sgt P E Butler | Inj | R1229 OJ-H | Op: Emden. Aircraft returned to Mildenhall. Sgt Butler died of his injuries. |
| 10th April 1941 | P.O. J H Fisher | Inj | R1181 OJ-W | Op: Training. Aircraft crashed, Holmsey Green, Mildenhall, Suffolk. |
| | Sgt D C Smallbone | Inj | | |
| | Sgt H J F Kerr | Inj | | |
| | Sgt C Inglesby | Inj | | |
| | Sgt G H Goodwing | Inj | | |
| | Sgt R L Clark | Inj | | |
| | Mrs M Brightwell | Civilian (Fatal) | | |
| 8th/9th May 1941 | Sgt G D K Jones | POW | R1506 OJ-D | Op: Hamburg |
| | Sgt D Westmacott | POW | | |
| 11th/12th June 1941 | Sgt W Harrison | POW | W5439 OJ-X 'Wizard of Oz' | |
| | Sgt G A Johnstone | POW | | Op: Düsseldorf |

|  |  |  |  |  |
|---|---|---|---|---|
|  | Sgt C Morgan | POW |  |  |
|  | F/S M T Kenny | POW |  |  |
|  | F/S V G Anderson | POW |  |  |
|  | W.O. T E Schofield RNZAF | POW |  |  |
| 14th/15th July 1941 | P.O. P L Dixon RAAF | POW | T2737 | Op: Bremen |
|  | Sgt M E Adams | POW |  |  |
|  | Sgt J M Grace RNZAF | POW |  |  |
|  | Sgt A Lawson | POW |  |  |
|  | Sgt F J Woods | POW |  |  |
|  | Sgt F W Price | POW |  |  |
| 17th/18th July 1941 | Sgt D C Stewart RNZAF | Inj | N2853 | Op: Cologne |
|  | Sgt Jordan | Inj |  | Aircraft crashed, Cockfield. |
|  | Sgt Brookes | Inj |  |  |
|  | Sgt Main | Inj |  |  |
|  | Sgt J M Dixon RCAF | Inj |  |  |
| 12th/13th July 1941 | F/S Batten | Inj | T2716 OJ-W | Op: Hannover |
|  |  |  |  | Aircraft crashed Elvedon, Suffolk |
| 18th/19th July 1941 | Sgt W J R Culpan RNZAF | POW | X9704 OJ-B | Op: Duisburg |
|  | P.O. R R Henderson RNZAF | POW |  |  |
|  | Sgt C G Jones | POW |  |  |
|  | Sgt K K Sterrett | POW |  |  |
| 18th/19th July 1941 | Sgt Reed | Inj | X9746 OJ-A | Op: Duisburg |
|  | P.O. Raffaelli | Inj |  | Aircraft coned by searchlights over Venlo, Netherlands. Aircraft landed safely. |
| 7th/8th November 1941 | Sgt F Jenkinson | POW | X9878 OJ-A | Op: Berlin |

# 1942

|  |  |  |  |  |
|---|---|---|---|---|
| 10th/11th March 1942 | Sgt Harris | Inj | R9295 OJ-G 'East India III' | Op: Essen Aircraft crashed Hollywell Row, Mildenhall |
| 10th/11th March 1942 | Sgt D H Munro | POW | N6126 OJ-U | Op: Essen |
| 17th/18th May 1942 | Sgt J A Jerman | POW | N3752 OJ-O | Op: Minelaying |
|  | Sgt S H Butcher RNZAF | POW |  |  |
|  | Sgt A Lauriston | POW |  |  |
|  | Sgt A M A Brittle | POW |  |  |
|  | Sgt J E Sloane | POW |  |  |
|  | Sgt A T Lewis | POW |  |  |
|  | Sgt F Hoyland | POW |  |  |
| 17th/18th May 1942 | F/S G H R Woodhouse | POW | R9320 OJ-S | Op: Minelaying |
|  | Sgt G D Anderson | POW |  |  |
|  | Sgt R J Nason | POW |  |  |
|  | Sgt R H P Waite | POW |  |  |
|  | Sgt G Grant | POW |  |  |
| 5th/6th June 1942 | Sgt D J Poynter | POW | W7508 OJ-D | Op: Essen |
|  | Sgt B F Goldsmith | Evaded |  |  |
| 29th/30th June 1942 | Sgt L C Collins RAAF | POW | N6082 OJ-Q | Op: Bremen |
| 29th/ 30thJune 1942 | Sgt C Caiger | Inj | R9330 OJ-O | Op: Bremen Aircraft crashed on return to Lakenheath |
| 16th July 1942 | P.O. J M P Forward | POW | BF312 OJ-A | Op: Lübeck |
|  | Sgt J B Locke RCAF | POW |  |  |
|  | P.O. F J Austin | POW |  |  |
|  | Sgt G S Burnett | POW |  |  |
|  | P.O. A W Mace RAAF | POW |  |  |
| 29th/30thJuly 1942 | Sgt C W Hazell | POW | R9161 OJ-T | Op: Saarbrücken |
| 24th/25th August 1942 | Sgt D A Baker | Evaded | W7572 OJ-R | Op: Frankfurt |
|  | Sgt J B Downing | POW |  |  |
|  | Sgt F J Berthelsen RNZAF | Evaded |  |  |

|  |  |  |  |  |
|---|---|---|---|---|
| | Sgt S E Robinson | POW/Escaped | | |
| | Sgt H Williams | Evaded | | |
| | F/S V S Wood | POW | | |
| | Sgt T J Jenkins | POW/Escaped | | |
| 28th/29th August 1942 | Sgt W M Hughes | POW | N6081 OJ-H | Op: Nuremberg |
| | Sgt C Steel | POW | | |
| 10th/11th September 1942 | Sgt A Yates | POW | R9170 OJ-H | Op: Düsseldorf |
| 19th/20th September 1942 | Sgt I G Davies | Inj | BF334 OJ-R | Op: Munich |
| | Sgt F H King | Inj | | Aircraft ditched off Ramsgate, Kent |
| | Sgt King did not survive his injuries. | | | |
| 28th/29th November 1942 | F/S L A Hyder | Inj | BF372 OJ-H | Op: Turin |
| | P.O. N E Skinner | Inj | | Ditched off Dymchurch, Kent |
| | Sgt H W Gough | Inj | | F/S Middleton's crew |
| 6th/7th December 1942 | P.O. M Keeting | Inj | N3723 OJ-E | Op: Mannheim |
| | Sgt L Jones | Inj | | Aircraft crashed, Ascot, Berkshire |

# 1943

|  |  |  |  |  |
|---|---|---|---|---|
| 3rd January 1943 | F/S J L Blair RNZAF | Inj | R9334 OJ-G | Op: Training |
| | Sgt W F Johnson | Inj | | Overshot runway at Lakenheath |
| | Sgt F G Giacomelli RCAF | Inj | | |
| | Sgt W H Clayton | Inj | | |
| | Sgt R Zambra | Inj | | |
| | Sgt J C Barker RCAF | Inj | | |
| 14th/15th February 1943 | F/S C Loughlin RNZAF | POW | W7638 OJ-R | Op: Cologne |
| | Sgt V W Tulley | POW | | |
| | Sgt G S S Reynolds RNZAF | POW | | |
| 1st/2nd March 1943 | P.O. R J Taylor RCAF | POW | BK692 OJ-W | Op: Berlin |
| | Sgt D R Clayton | POW | | |
| | Sgt R H Hale | POW | | Evaded capture for nine months |
| | Sgt H J Gillingham | POW | | |
| | Sgt N Thornley | POW | | |
| 29th/30th March 1943 | W.O. C L Blackford | POW | BK708 OJ-P | Op: Berlin |
| 20th/21st April 1943 | Sq.Ldr. T L Howell | POW | BK714 OJ-L | Op: Rostock |
| | Sgt G W Herring | POW | | |
| | Sgt F L Parker | POW | | |
| | Sgt A W Dowie | POW | | |
| | P.O. M S Winston | POW | | |
| | Sgt G A C Carter | POW | | |
| 1st/2nd May 1943 | F/S N K Sunderland RCAF | Inj | BK696 OJ-L | Op: Minelaying |
| 17th/18th May 1943 | P.O. J E Hill | POW | BK701 OJ-G | Op: Minelaying |
| | Sgt J A Boland | POW | | |
| | Sgt S R Shankster | POW | | |
| 28th/29th June 1943 | Sgt D C Foster | Evaded | EE880 OJ-O | Op: Cologne |
| | Sgt I A Mears RNZAF | POW | | |
| 3rd/4th July 1943 | F.O. J J Needham RCAF | POW | BF530 OJ-B | Op: Cologne |
| | F/S R A Hodge RNZAF | POW | | |
| 23rd/24th August 1943 | Sq.Ldr. J J E Mahoney | POW | BK765 OJ-P | Op: Berlin |
| | P.O. J F S Hood | POW | | |
| | Sgt J Branford | POW | | |
| | F.O. A J McKirdy | POW | | |
| | F/S T D Dixon RCAF | POW | | |
| | P.O. L Van-Aardt | POW | | |
| 23rd/24th August 1943 | Sgt W A Long | POW | EE894 OJ-R | Op: Berlin |
| 5th/6th September 1943 | F.O. C D Farmer | POW | BF477 OJ-B | Op: Mannheim |
| | Sgt N H Clark | Evaded | | |
| | Sgt J R Lilley | POW | | |
| | F.O. D A Luzmoor RNZAF | POW | | |
| | Sgt J B MacNeill | POW | | |

| Date | Name | Status | Aircraft | Operation |
|---|---|---|---|---|
| 5th/6th September 1943 | Sgt P Bates | POW | BK711 OJ-O | Op: Mannheim |
| | F.O. C K McLean RNZAF | POW | | |
| | Sgt R Wall | POW | | |
| 5th/6th September 1943 | Sgt H G Barnard | POW | EE872 OJ-N | Op: Mannheim |
| 23rd/24th September 1943 | F/S K F Lear RAAF | Evaded | EH883 OJ-A | Op: Mannheim |
| | Sgt N E Mathenson RCAF | POW | | |
| 27th/28th September 1943 | Sgt F D Tweedie | POW | EF495 OJ-R | Op: Hannover |
| | Sgt J W Crowe | POW | | |
| | Sgt P Lyons | POW | | |
| 18th/19th November 1943 | F/S R L L Smith | POW | EH903 OJ-L | Op: Mannheim |
| | Sgt D G Keay | POW | | |
| | Sgt M M Cross | POW | | |
| | F/S E F L Crow | POW | | |
| | P.O. A A Sharrock RNZAF | POW | | |
| 25th/26th November 1943 | Sgt K C Richardson | Evaded | EF202 OJ-L | Op: Minelaying |
| | Sgt H W Hitchman | Evaded | | |
| | Sgt E C Powell | Evaded | | |
| | F/S K B Wootton | Evaded | | |
| | Sgt W Cross | POW | | |
| | Sgt A J Rooney | Evaded | | |
| | Sgt J A O'Brien | POW | | |

## 1944

| Date | Name | Status | Aircraft | Operation |
|---|---|---|---|---|
| 10th/11th April 1944 | Sgt D E Cadge | Evaded | EF502 OJ-G | Op: SOE |
| | F/S N C H Pilgrim | Evaded | | |
| 1st June 1944 | F/S H V Cutts | POW | LJ501 OJ-H | Op: Minelaying |
| 5th/6th June 1944 | Sgt F C Heal | POW | LJ621 OJ-M | Op: D-Day Support |
| | Sgt J A W Nind RCAF | Evaded | | |
| | Sgt B Wynne-Cole | POW | | Sgt Heal was admitted to hospital with a broken leg. Freed on 4th August 1944 by the Americans. |

The total number of POWs, escapers/evaders and injuries to aircrew are:

POW          – 148
POW/Escaped – 4
Evaded     – 12
Injured      – 35

# APPENDIX II
# Individual Aircraft Histories

## Royal Aircraft Factory F.E.2b

| | | |
|---|---|---|
| A6438 | June 1918 | |
| A6439 | May 1918 | Not taken to France |
| A6496 | June 1918 | |
| A6497 | June 1918 | Damaged in forced landing during raid on Armentières, 25th June 1918; to 1 ASD |
| A6594 | May 1918 | Not taken to France |
| B469 | By April 1918 | Not taken to France |
| B1855 | By May 1918 | Not taken to France |
| C9701 | By May 1918 | Not taken to France |
| C9779 | By July 1918 | Missing on raid to Warneton Dump 18th/19th July 1918; crew prisoners-of-war |
| C9799 | June 1918 | Engine cut on raid on Comines; crash-landed near Neuve Eglise, 16th Sept 1918 |
| C9801 | 22 June 1918 | To 15th Sept 1918 |
| C9808 | June 1918 | Engine cut during raid on Warneton dump; forcelanded at Droglandt, 16th August 1918; to 1 ASD for repair |
| C9815 | 6th July 1918 | Wheel damaged; crashed on landing, Alquines, on return from raid on Bac St Maur dump, 15th Aug 1918; to 1 ASD |
| C9816 | 19th July 1918 | Engine seized during raid on Courtrai; crash-landed near Cassel., 29.9.18 |
| C9827 | 14th Aug 1918 | |
| D3779 | 25th June 1918 | Missing on night raid 18th July 1918; crew prisoners-of-war |
| D3825 | 18th Sept 1918 | |
| D9089 | June 1918 | |
| D9091 | June 1918 | |
| D9106 | 5th July 1918 | Engine cut after take-off for raid on Menin; stalled and nosedived; blew up, Clairmarais North, 15th Sept 1918; both crew killed; to 1 ASD 18th Sept 1918 |
| D9740 | June 1918 | Engine cut on training flight; stalled and dived into ground, 7th July 1918 |
| D9741 | June 1918 | Overshot flarepath and hit fence, Clairmarais North on return from reconnaissance to Messines, 12th Aug 1918; to 1 ASD |
| D9742 | June 1918 | Throttle cable snapped on reconnaissance mission; force-landed Fauquembergues, 4th July 1918; to 1 RP for repair |
| D9743 | June 1918 | Hit hedge on take-off, Houtain-le-Val, 9.12.18 |
| D9744 | June 1918 | Stone shattered prop on take-off and airframe damaged, Clairmarais, 19th August 1918; to 1 ASD 22nd Aug 1918 for repair |
| D9745 | June 1918 | Engine cut; force-landed near Poperinghe, 9th Sept 1918; repaired at 1 RP; crashed 16th Sept 1918 |
| D9746 | 18th Aug 1918 | |
| D9750 | June 1918 | |
| D9751 | June 1918 | |
| D9761 | 2nd July 1918 | |
| D9777 | June 1918 | Missing on night raid to Armentières 23rd June 1918; crew prisoners-of-war |
| D9778 | June 1918 | Prop blades damaged by stones on take-off; tail booms damaged, 30th June 1918; to 1 RP for repair |
| D9901 | 18th Aug 1918 | |
| D9903 | | Missing from night raid on Renaix sidings, 4th Nov 1918; crew prisoners-of-war |
| D9909 | 8th July 1918 | Engine cut during raid on Warneton dump; forcelanded at Arneke, 2nd Sept 1918; to 1 RP for repair |
| D9925 | 16th Aug 1918 | Crashed on landing on bad ground, Le Quesnoy/Ste Marguerite returning from Grammont, 1.11.18. Lt Bull, Lt Osborne unhurt |
| D9939 | 4th Sept 1918 | |
| F5862 | Jan 1919 | Force-landed and caught fire on ferry flight to 149 Squadron, Olne, between Liège and Verviers, 16.1.19 |

## Handley Page Heyford
*('A' Flight red markings, 'B' Flight yellow markings)*

**Non-standard**

| | | |
|---|---|---|
| K3489 | Aug 37 | Modified to Mk III. From Aeroplane and Armament Experimental Establishment. To Royal Aircraft Establishment for de-icing trials 16 Sep 38. |

## Heyford Mark Is and IIs

| | | |
|---|---|---|
| K3494 | Aug 37 | from 99 Sqn; to 148 Sqn |
| K3495 | July 37 | from 99 Sqn. Struck off charge 29th Aug 39 |
| K3502 | 3rd Aug 37 | from 99 Sqn, code 'F'. Struck off charge 25th Aug 38 |

## Heyford Mark IIA

| | | |
|---|---|---|
| K4021 | | Converted to Mk III. Ran out of fuel. Wrecked on landing in bad visibility at Mildenhall, 30th April 1938 |
| K4025 | May 37 | From 10 Sqn. Struck off charge 6th Sep 37 |
| K4031 | | From 99 Sqn, code 'B'. To 19 MU. Struck off charge 28th Aug |
| K4032 | May 37 | From 10 Sqn, code 'D'. Taxied into wall, Evanton, 1st Mar 38. Repaired on site. Undershot flarepath and hit fence at Mildenhall, 8th Sep 38. Damage beyond repair. |
| K4033 | May 37 | From 10 Sqn. To 19 MU. Struck off charge June 39. |
| K4037 | May 37 | From 99 Sqn. Engine cut and aircraft forced to land in a field at Shotton Farm, near Sedgefield, Co.Durham; hit hedge and tipped on its nose, 15th Feb 38. Struck off charge 18th Feb 38. |
| K4039 | From 99 Sqn. | Flew into the ground on a rainy night at Stopham, near Pulborough, Sussex, 13th Dec 37. Four crew killed. Struck off charge 15th Mar 38. |
| K4043 | June 37 | From Handley Page after repair. Code 'C'. To 19 MU. Struck off charge 28th Aug 39. |
| K4865 | July 38 | From 7 Sqn. Brakes failed, hit hangar at Mildenhall. Struck off charge 16th Jan 39 |
| K4866 | July 38 | From 9 Sqn. Brakes failed, ran into hangar door at Mildenhall. Struck off charge 2nd Dec 38 |
| K4867 | Apr 37 | From 7 Sqn. Code 'D'. To 19 MU. Struck off charge 29th Aug 39 |
| K4870 | Jan 38 | From 78 Sqn. Struck off charge 29th Aug 38 |
| K4875 | Apr 38 | From 7 Sqn. To 19 MU. Struck off charge 29th Aug 39 |
| K4877 | Aug 38 | From 7 Sqn. Code 'H'. To 19 MU. Struck off charge 29th Aug 39 |
| K4878 | Aug 38 | From 78 Sqn. Code 'M'. To 19 MU. Struck off charge 29th Aug 39 |
| K5180 | | From 7 Sqn. To 19 MU. Struck off charge 29th Aug 39 |

## Heyford Mark III

| | | |
|---|---|---|
| K5187 | | From 102 Sqn. Code 'M'. To 19 MU. Struck off charge 18th May 40 |

| Serial | Date | Notes |
|---|---|---|
| K5191 | 12th Apr 37 | From 99 Sqn. To 99 Sqn 31st May 37 |
| K5199 | 12th Apr 37 | From 148 Sqn. To 99 Sqn 31st May 37 |
| K6857 | 12th Apr 37 | From 99 Sqn. To 99 Sqn 31st May 37. Later returned to No.149 Sqn, then back to 99 Sqn |
| K6858 | 12th Apr 37 | From 99 Sqn. To 99 Sqn 31st May 37 |
| K6859 | 6th Dec 38 | From 102 Sqn. To 102 Sqn 31st May 37 |
| K6871 | Apr 37 | From 99 Sqn. To 99 Sqn May 37 |
| K6876 | 12th Apr 37 | From 99 Sqn. To 99 Sqn 31st May 37 |
| K6877 | 12th Apr 37 | From 99 Sqn. To 99 Sqn 31st May 37 |
| K6897 | 28th Jun 37 | From No 2 Aircraft Storage Unit. To 99 Sqn |
| K6901 | | From 102 Sqn after accident and repair. To 19 MU. Struck off charge 29th Aug 39 |
| K6903 | Jun 37 | From No 2 Aircraft Storage Unit. Code 'E'. To 99 Sqn |
| K6904 | Jun 37 | From No 2 Aircraft Storage Unit. To 9 Sqn Dec 38 |

## Vickers Wellington

*1st batch of 16 Wellington aircraft (two flights, even serial numbers to 'A' Flight, odd numbers to 'B' Flight) delivered between 20th Jan 39 and 20th Feb 39.*

## Wellington Mark I/IA

| Serial | Date | Notes |
|---|---|---|
| L4214 | From Vickers 17th July 39 | To Vickers 6th Oct 39 |
| L4229 | From 99 Sqn 10th Mar 39 | To 214 Sqn 6th Oct 39 |
| L4249 | New 6th Feb 39 | To 75 Sqn 24th Sep 39 |
| L4252 | New 20th Jan 39 | To Vickers 5th Dec 39 |
| L4253 | New 20th Jan 39 | To 215 Sqn 20th Apr 40 |
| L4254 | New 20th Jan 39 | To 75 Sqn 24th Sep 39 |
| L4255 | New 24th Jan 39 | To 22 MU 16th Apr 40 (One of first converted to transport role. To Air Transport Auxiliary, converted to flying ambulance. Served until struck off charge 19th Nov 44) |
| L4256 | New 24th Jan 39 | To 75 Sqn 10th Sep 39 |
| L4257 | New 24th Jan 39 | 'OJ-P'. Flew into the sea in bad visibility, 5 miles southeast of the Happisburgh Light Vessel, 29th Aug 39. |
| L4258 | New 24th Jan 39 | Missing over the North Sea on a night flight, bad visibility and low cloud, 9th Aug 39 |
| L4259 | New 6th Feb 39 | To 8 MU 16th Oct 39 |
| L4262 | New 7th Feb 39 | To 10 MU 28th Nov 39 |
| L4264 | New 7th Feb 39 | To 23 MU 31st Mar 40 |
| L4265 | New 10th Feb 39 | To 24 MU 12th Nov 1939 |
| L4266 | New 10th Feb 39 | To 24 MU 8th Nov 39 |
| L4270 | New 9th Mar 39 | To 19 MU 16th Oct 39 |
| L4271 | New 17th Feb 39 | To 19 MU 16th Oct 39 |
| L4272 | New 17th Feb 39 | Coded 'LY-G', then 'OJ-C'. To 19 MU 16th Oct 39 |
| L4356 | From 214 Sqn 30th Nov 39 | To 4 MU 19th Jan 40 |
| L4374 | New 12th Jul 39 | To Royal Aircraft Establishment 8th Jan 40 |
| N2866 | New 1st Sep 39 | To 215 Sqn 5th May 40 |
| N2867 | New 1st Sep 39 | To 214 Sqn 13th Dec 39; retd to 149 Sqn 8th Jun 40; to Vickers 21st Nov 40 |
| N2868 | New 1st Sep 39 | To 75 Sqn 1st Mar 40 |
| N2869 | New 3rd Sep 39 | To 75 Sqn 1st Mar 40 |
| N2891 | New 30th Sep 39 | To 99 Sqn 18th Jan 40 |
| N2892 | New 30th Sep 39 | To 7 Sqn 20th Jan 40 |
| N2893 | New 2nd Oct 39 | To Central Gunnery School 15th Mar 40 |
| N2894 | New 2nd Oct 39 | To 215 Sqn 30th Mar 40 |
| N2943 | New 2nd Oct 39 | Shot down by enemy fighter whilst on a reconnaissance patrol near Sylt. All crew killed 2nd Jan 40 |
| N2944 | New 8th Nov 39 | To Central Gunnery School 18th Mar 40 |
| N2945 | New 6th Nov 39 | To 215 Sqn 6th Jun 40 |
| N2946 | New 6th Nov 39 | Shot down by enemy fighter whilst on reconnaissance patrol near Sylt. All crew killed, 2nd Jan 40 |
| N2960 | From 99 Sqn 16th Nov 39 | To 215 Sqn 9th Apr 40 |
| N2961 | From 99 Sqn 16th Nov 39 | Badly shot up on a raid to Wilhelmshaven. Ditched in the North Sea off Cromer. All crew killed, 18th Dec 39. |
| N2962 | From 99 Sqn 6th Dec 39 | Shot down on raid to Wilhelmshaven. All crew killed, 18th Dec 39 |
| N2980 | New 20th Nov 39 | To 37 Sqn 30th May 1940. Raised from Loch Ness 1985; now on display at the Brooklands Museum, Weybridge, Surrey |
| N2984 | From 99 Sqn 22nd Nov 39 | Engine failure shortly after take-off for leaflet raid on Bremen. Crashed at Burnt Fen, Norfolk. All crew killed 2nd Mar 40 |
| N3012 | New 22nd Dec 39 | To 215 Sqn 7th May 40 |
| N3013 | New 27th Dec 39 | To 99 Sqn 24th Jan 40 |
| P2517 | From Yeadon | Became 'OJ-F' for movie 'Target for Tonight'. To No.3 Group Training Flight. |
| P2527 | New 9th Jan 40 | To 215 Sqn 5th May 40 |
| P2528 | New 9th Jan 40 | To 215 Sqn 10th Apr 40 |
| P9225 | New 15th Feb 40 | Hit by 'friendly fire' near Dunkerque following reconnaissance patrol. Crew baled out near Belgian border and returned to UK by boat train/Channel ferry 26th Mar 40. |
| P9234 | New 26th Feb 40 | To 99 Sqn 5th Mar 40 |

## Wellington Mark IC

| Serial | Date | Notes |
|---|---|---|
| L7800 | From 148 Sqn 16th May 40 | Missing from raid on Soissons. Crashed into sea. All crew lost 10th/11th Jun 40 |
| L7805 | From 23 MU 1st Jun 40 | Lost on raid to bomb naval installations at Bremen. All crew killed 12th Jul 40 |
| L7806 | From Vickers 14th Jan 41 | To 311 Sqn 6th Mar 41 |
| L7811 | From 24 MU 5th Oct 40 | Abandoned near Conksbury, returning from a raid on Bremen, 11th/12th Feb 41 |
| L7812 | From 115 Sqn 1st Jun 40 | To 30 MU 12th Feb 41 |
| L7817 | From 300 Sqn 26th Aug 41 | To 9 Sqn 31st Aug 41 |
| L7845 | From 24 MU 21st Jun 40 | To 115 Sqn 23rd Jun 40 |
| L7846 | New 21st Jun 40 | To Vickers 2nd Jan 41 |
| L7855 | 22 MU 9th Sep 40 | 'OJ-W'. To Vickers 12th Dec 40 |
| L7858 | From 22 MU 31st Aug 40 | 'OJ-A'. Shot down by night fighter on raid to Gelsenkirchen. All crew lost 14th/15th Mar 41 |
| N2769 | From 9 MU 10th Sep 40 | 'OJ-N'. Damaged 30th Jan 41; to 30 MU 12th Feb 41 |
| N2774 | From 99 Sqn 3rd Oct 40 | 'OJ-A'. Missing on a raid on Berlin. All crew lost. 20th Nov 40 |
| N2775 | From 18 MU 1st Oct 40 | To 311 Sqn 6th May 41 |
| N2783 | From 57 Sqn 21st Apr 41 | 'OJ-W'. To Vickers 27th Jun 41 |
| N2853 | From 57 Sqn 21st Apr 41 | Hit by flak on raid on Cologne. Blinded by searchlights in attempting to land. Crashed into trees at Cockfield, Suffolk. One crew member killed, others injured. 17th/18th Jul 41. |
| P9240 | From 24 MU 11th Mar 40 | To 99 Sqn 19th Mar 40 |
| P9241 | From 24 MU 11th Mar 40 | To 99 Sqn 19th Mar 40 |

| Serial | History | Fate |
|---|---|---|
| P9244 | New 3rd Mar 40 | Hit radio mast at Mildenhall and crashed at Beck Row, returning from a raid on Gelsenkirchen. All crew lost, 12th Aug 40 |
| P9245 | New 3rd Mar 40 | Ditched in North Sea off Clacton, Essex, returning from a raid on Boulogne. All crew lost, 9th Sep 40 |
| P9246 | New 5th Mar 40 | Shot down by enemy fighter on anti-shipping sweep off Stavanger, Norway. All crew lost, 12th Apr 40 |
| P9247 | New 5th Mar 40 | 'OJ-M'. Flew into the ground while trying to get below very low cloud near Digby airfield, Lincolnshire, returning from a raid on Hannover. One crew member killed, 12th Feb 41 |
| P9248 | New 6th Mar 40 | 'OJ-D' then 'OJ-G'. Lost on a raid to Cologne. All crew lost, 18th Apr 41 |
| P9266 | New 9th Mar 40 | Shot down by enemy fighter on anti-shipping sweep off Stavanger, Norway. All crew lost, 12th Apr 40 |
| P9267 | New 11th Mar 40 | Aircraft stalled whilst attempting an overshoot during a training exercise at Mildenhall. Five crew lost, 4th Apr 40 |
| P9268 | New 11th Mar 40 | 'OJ-A'. Overshot during landing at Mildenhall on return from a raid on Mannheim, and ran into the bomb dump, 17th Dec 40 |
| P9270 | New 13th Mar 40 | Wing hit trees on return from a raid on German troop concentrations at the battlefront; aircraft crashed, Barton Mills, Suffolk. Three crew members lost, 24th May 40 |
| P9272 | From 99 Sqn 5th Mar 40 | 'OJ-A'. Shot down on a raid to Kiel. Crew became Prisoners of War, 28th Aug 40 |
| P9273 | From 99 Sqn 15th Mar 40 | 'OJ-V'. Lost on a raid to Grevenbroich. All crew members lost, 9th/10th Oct 40 |
| P9289 | New 2nd Apr 40 | To Vickers 3rd Jul 40 |
| R1024 | From 9 MU 11th Oct 40 | 'OJ-V'. Crashed into the North Sea off Sylt, following a raid on Hannover. All crew lost, 13th Aug 41 |
| R1045 | From 9 MU 11th Oct 40 | Lost on raid to Wilhelmshaven. All crew lost, 22nd Feb 41 |
| R1159 | From 5 MU 15th Jan 41 | 'OJ-N'. Hit trees at Peaseland Green, Suffolk, returning from raid on Cologne, in poor visibility, 20th Mar 41 |
| R1181 | From 99 Sqn 20th Nov 40 | 'OJ-W'. Lost height during take-off from Mildenhall; crashed into trees and cottage at Holmsey Green, Suffolk. Two crew and one occupant of the cottage killed, 10th Apr 41. |
| R1229 | From 24 MU 27th Nov 40 | 'OJ-H'. Bounced, stalled, and then caught fire on landing after completing a raid on Bremen. One crew member died of injuries, 1st Apr 41 |
| R1294 | From 23 MU 7th Dec 40 | Lost wing fabric on air test; stalled while landing and crashed at Mildenhall. All crew lost, 16th Dec 40 |
| R1296 | – | Coded 'OJ-F' for 'Freddie' in the movie 'Target for Tonight', (the pilot Sqn Ldr, later Group Captain, Percy Pickard, never flew with No.149 Sqn) |
| R1339 | From 22 MU 1st Feb 41 | To 218 Sqn 3rd Feb 41 |
| R1343 | From 24 MU 21st Dec 40 | 'OJ-B'. Shot down on a raid to Brest. All crew lost, 1st/2nd Jul 41 |
| R1391 | From 24 MU 15th Jan 41 | To Vickers 14th Feb 41 |
| R1408 | From 23 MU 6th Feb 41 | 'OJ-J'. Shot down at Plouzane on a raid to Brest. All crew lost 1st/2nd Jul 41 |
| R1439 | From 8 MU 23rd Feb 41 | 'OJ-W' then 'OJ-U'. Shot down by anti-aircraft fire on a raid to Kiel. All crew lost, 16th Apr 41 |
| R1449 | From 8 MU 23rd Feb 41 | To Vickers 28th Mar 41 |
| R1469 | From 8 MU 14th Feb 41 | To Vickers 26th Jun 41 |
| R1474 | From 115 Sqn 22nd Feb 41 | 'OJ-M'. Shot down by Junkers 88 intruder, crashing into a bungalow at Beck Row near Mildenhall, on return from a raid on Bremen. All crew members lost, 18th Mar 41 |
| R1506 | From 48 MU 4th Mar 41 | 'OJ-D'. Shot down by enemy fighter, crashing into the North Sea off Heligoland while returning from a raid on Hamburg. Four crew members lost. Two prisoners-of-war, 9th May 41 |
| R1512 | From 18 MU 20th Apr 41 | 'OJ-H'. Shot down on a raid to Hamburg. All crew lost, 11th May 41 |
| R1514 | From 18 MU 12th May 41 | To 30 MU 10th Dec 41 |
| R1524 | From 37 MU 12th May 41 | 'OJ-P'. Crashed at St.Martens Voeren, near Liège, Belgium, following raid on Mannheim. All crew lost, 6th Aug 41 |
| R1587 | From 33 MU 18th Mar 41 | Collided with 1401 Met Flight Hurricane V7225 near Ely, Cambridgeshire. All crew lost, 17th May 41 |
| R1593 | From 24 MU 23rd Mar 41 | 'OJ-N'. To 1483 Flight (No 3 Group Gunnery Flight) 6th Dec 41 |
| R1627 | From 18 MU 13th Apr 41 | Shot down on raid to Emden. All crew lost 16th Nov 41 (Last Wellington lost on operations by No.149 Sqn) |
| R1629 | From 18 MU 15th Apr 41 | To Royal Aircraft Establishment 3rd Jun 41 |
| R1802 | From 44 MU 19th May 41 | To 311 Sqn 11th Dec 41 |
| R3150 | From 37 Sqn 27th Jul 40 | To 37 Sqn 15th Sep 40 |
| R3160 | From 115 Sqn 22nd Apr 40 | 'OJ-E' Lost on a raid to Le Havre. All crew lost, 19th Sep 40 |
| R3161 | From 9 Sqn 22nd Apr 40 | To Vickers 2nd Jun 41 |
| R3163 | New 25th Apr 40 | 'OJ-G'. Lost on a "Razzle" raid to Schwarzwald (Black Forest), Germany. All crew taken prisoner-of-war, 6th Sep 40 |
| R3164 | New 22nd Apr 40 | 'OJ-B'. Lost on raid to Hanau. One crew member killed, remainder taken prisoner-of-war, 29th Sep 40 |
| R3165 | New 25th Apr 40 | To 75 Sqn 29th Apr 40 |
| R3174 | From 148 Sqn 17th May 40 | 'OJ-A'. Lost on a raid to Koleda. Three crew members lost, three taken prisoner-of-war, 17th Aug 40 |
| R3175 | From 148 Sqn 16th May 40 | 'OJ-V'. Lost over the sea following a raid on Boulogne. All crew lost, 9th Sep 40 |
| R3206 | From 22 MU 3rd Jul 40 | 'OJ-M'. Damaged 24th Feb 41; to 20 MU 17th Mar 41 |

| | | |
|---|---|---|
| R3212 | From 24 MU 19th Jun 40 | To Vickers 5th Nov 40 |
| R3280 | From 12 MU 14th Jul 40 | To Brooklands Avn 29th Aug 40 |
| R3285 | From 24 MU 21st Jul 40 | To Brooklands Avn 27th Nov 40 |
| T2458 | From 9 Sqn 9th Sep 40 | To Brooklands Avn 20th Jan 41 |
| T2459 | From 10 MU 30th Jun 40 | To Vickers 18th Jul 40 |
| T2460 | From 99 Sqn 20th Aug 40 | To Brooklands Avn 1st May 41 |
| T2713 | From 57 Sqn 21st Apr 41 | To 115 Sqn 15th Oct 41 |
| T2716 | From 40 Sqn 11th May 41 | 'OJ-W'. Hit by flak and night fighter while on a raid to Hannover. One crew member lost. Crashed whilst making a forced landing at Elvedon, Suffolk. One crew member died of injuries, 13th Aug 41 |
| T2737 | From 9 MU 17th Sep 40 | 'OJ-A'. Lost on a raid to Bremen. All crew members taken prisoner-of-war, 15th Jul 41 |
| T2739 | From 9 MU 19th Sep 40 | To 99 Sqn same day as arrival |
| T2740 | From 9 MU 19th Sep 40 | 'OJ-E'. Damaged in action. Crashed whilst making a forced landing at St.Osyth, Essex, 24th Oct 40 |
| T2747 | From 33 MU 9th Jan 41 | Damaged in action 6th Nov 41; to Brooklands Avn 16th Nov 41 |
| T2807 | From 10 MU 21st Nov 40 | Lost on operations to Italy. All crew members taken prisoner-of-war, 12th Jan 41 |
| T2846 | From 22 MU 13th Dec 40 | To 9 MU 4th Apr 41 |
| T2881 | From 33 MU 9th Jan 41 | Named 'Ceylon III'; to Brooklands Avn 21st Jan 41 |
| T2897 | From 9 MU 21st Nov 40 | 'OJ-O'. Lost on a raid to Merignac. Crashed near St.Sever-Calvados, France. Five crew members lost, one taken prisoner-of-war, 13th Apr 41 |
| T2898 | From 9 MU 21st Nov 40 | Damaged in action 19th Jun 41; to Brooklands Avn 1st Jul 41 |
| T2899 | From 38 MU 7th Dec 40 | To 27 OTU 14th Aug 41 |
| T2994 | From 10 MU 10th Mar 41 | To 23 OTU 12th Aug 41 |
| W5718 | From 33 MU 11th May 41 | 'OJ-O'. To 75 Sqn 17th Nov 41 |
| W5724 | From 33 MU 12th May 41 | To 27 OTU 10th Nov 41 |
| X3165 | From Vickers 23rd Mar 41 | To 30 MU 28th Oct 41 |
| X3167 | New 29th Mar 41 | 'OJ-H'. Lost on a raid to Kiel. All crew members lost, 9th Apr 41 |
| X3174 | From 40 Sqn 29th Mar 41 | To 27 OTU 5th Dec 41 |
| X3176 | From 24 MU 14th Apr 41 | To 75 Sqn 17th Nov 41 |
| X3201 | From 8 MU 25th Oct 41 | To 419 Sqn 9th Jan 42 |
| X9633 | From 12 MU 22nd Jul 41 | 'OJ-R' Lost on a raid to Mannheim; crashed near Wavre, Belgium. All crew members lost, 6th Aug 41 |
| X9663 | From 115 Sqn 22nd Jul 41 | To 218 Sqn 29th Jul 41 |
| X9679 | From 301 Sqn 26th Aug 41 | To 218 Sqn 29th Aug 41 |
| X9704 | From 9 MU 25th Jul 41 | 'OJ-B'. Lost on a raid to Duisburg. Crashed near Roermond, Netherlands. Two crew members lost. Four taken prisoner-of-war, 19th Aug 41 |
| X9705 | From 9 MU 5th Jul 41 | 'OJ-J' Lost on a raid to Berlin. All crew members lost, 8th Sep 41 |
| X9746 | From 44 MU 22nd Jul 41 | Struck off charge 29th Sep 41 |
| X9758 | From 46 MU 24th Jul 41 | 'OJ-N' To 214 Sqn 6th Dec 41 |
| X9817 | From 46 MU 20th Aug 41 | 'OJ-N' To 214 Sqn 6th Dec 41 |
| X9823 | From 45 MU 17th Aug 41 | Damaged in action 1st Oct 41; to Brooklands Avn 16th Oct 41 |
| X9824 | From 45 MU 18th Aug 41 | To 40 Sqn for seven days and back to No.149 Sqn; to 40 Sqn 12th Nov 41 |
| X9878 | From 8 MU 24th Aug 41 | 'OJ-A' Lost on a raid to Berlin. Five crew members lost, one taken prisoner-of-war, 8th Nov 41 |
| X9879 | From 8 MU 24th Aug 41 | 'OJ-V' Shot down over the target, Kiel. All crew members lost, 11th Sep 41 |
| X9880 | From 8 MU 24th Aug 41 | To 40 Sqn 6th Dec 41 |
| Z1052 | From 45 MU 12th Oct 41 | 'OJ-R' To 40 Sqn 5th Dec 41 |
| Z8795 | From 9 MU 27th Jul 41 | 'OJ-C' Shot down on a raid to Bremen; crashed into River Schelde. All crew members lost, 21st Oct 41 |
| Z8837 | From 33 MU 14th Aug 41 | To 40 Sqn 12th Nov 41 |
| Z8838 | From 33 MU 14th Aug 41 | To 40 Sqn 17th Oct 41, back to No.149 Sqn 23rd Oct 41; to 311 Sqn 9th Dec 41 |

## Wellington Mark II

| | | |
|---|---|---|
| W5399 | From 12 MU 3rd Mar 41 | 'OJ-Q' Damaged in action 3rd Jul 41; to Vickers 1st Aug 41 |
| W5439 | From 12 MU 6th Mar 41 | 'OJ-W', 'The Wizard of Oz'. Shot down by flak whilst on a raid to Düsseldorf. Crashed near Bergharen, Netherlands. All crew members taken prisoner-of-war, 12th Jun 41 |
| W5567 | From 33 MU 12th Jul 41 | To 305 Sqn 2nd Aug 41 |
| W5573 | From 33 MU 1st Jul 41 | To 305 Sqn 2nd Aug 41 |

## Short Stirling Mark I

| | | |
|---|---|---|
| N3638 | From 15 Sqn 24th Nov 41 | To 106 Sqn Conversion Flight 3rd Jan 42. |
| N3680 | New 27th Oct 41 | To 7 Sqn 7th Nov 41 |
| N3682 | New 23rd Nov 41 | 'OJ-F'. To No.149 Conversion Flight, to 1657 Conversion Unit 23rd Apr 42 |
| N3684 | New 15th Mar 42 | Flying accident, 26th Mar 42. To Sebro 4th May 42 for repair |
| N3719 | New 1st Apr 42 | 'OJ-S'. Swung on rough ground returning from a raid on Cologne. Undercarriage collapsed, 23rd Apr 42 |
| N3723 | New 8th Mar 42 | 'OJ-E' Anti-aircraft shell shrapnel severed elevator control cables during a raid on Mannheim. Crew abandoned aircraft near Ascot, Berkshire. Aircraft crashed near the racecourse, 6th Dec 42 |

| | | |
|---|---|---|
| N3726 | New 18th Mar 42 | 'OJ-G' Attacked by fighter during a raid on Essen; severe right wing damage and engine out. Undercarriage collapsed on landing at base, 7th Apr 42 |
| N3752 | New 1st May 42 | 'OJ-C' then 'OJ-O'. Shot down whilst on a mining operation off Copenhagen. Crashed at Risegaard, Denmark. All crew members taken prisoner 18th May 42 |
| N3755 | New 14th Jun 42 | 'OJ-S' Used by No.149 Conversion Flight. Ran out of fuel on return from a raid on Aachen. Crashed at Eastling, Kent. Pilot lost, 6th Oct 42 |
| N3766 | New 3rd Jun 42 | To 214 Sqn 5th Jun 42 |
| N6065 | From 15 Sqn 8th Jul 42 | 'OJ-Z' Used by No.149 Conversion Flight, then 1657 CU 4th Oct 42 |
| N6066 | New 23rd Nov 41 | To 26 Conversion Flight 25th Nov 41 |
| N6068 | New 29th Jan 42 | 'OJ-T' Shot down whilst on a raid to Dortmund, crashing at Steene, Belgium. All crew members lost, 16th Apr 42 |
| N6070 | New 20th Mar 42 | 'OJ-F' To No.149 Conversion Flight then 1657 Conversion Unit 16th Aug 42 |
| N6080 | New 23rd Mar 42 | 'OJ-G' To 1657 Conversion Unit |
| N6081 | New 25th Mar 42 | 'OJ-H' then 'OJ-G' Shot down by night fighter whilst on a raid to Nuremberg, crashing at Arlenbach, Germany. Six crew members lost, two taken prisoner, 29th Aug 42 |
| N6082 | New 25th Mar 42 | 'OJ-Q' Shot down by night fighter during raid on Bremen and crashed, Wons, Friesland, Netherlands 30th Jun 42 |
| N6083 | New 27th Mar 42 | 'OJ-N' Engine failure followed by fire just after take-off for a raid on Frankfurt. Aircraft crashed just south of Lakenheath. All crew members lost, 24th Aug 42 |
| N6084 | New 27th Mar 42 | 'OJ-C' Shot down whilst on a raid to Essen, crashing at Hassel, Germany. All crew members lost, 9th Jun 42 |
| N6093 | New 12th Oct 41 | Crashed on landing, 23rd Jan 42; to repair unit |
| N6094 | New 22nd Oct 41 | To 7 Sqn 23rd Oct 41 |
| N6095 | New 24th Oct 41 | To 7 Sqn 8th Nov 41 |
| N6099 | New 2nd Jan 42 | 'OJ-C' To 1651 Conversion Unit 28th Mar 42 |
| N6100 | New 3rd Nov 41 | To 26 Conversion Flight 6th Nov 41 |
| N6101 | New 3rd Nov 41 | To 26 Conversion Flight 6th Nov 41; retd to 149 Sqn 31st Dec 41; to 1651 CU 22nd Mar 42 |
| N6102 | New 8th Nov 41 | 'OJ-G' Damaged in action 12th Feb 42; to Sebro 14th Mar 42 |
| N6103 | New 23rd Nov 41 | 'East India I'. To 1651 Conversion Unit 10th May 42 |
| N6104 | New 25th Nov 41 | To 26 Conversion Flight 11th Dec 41 |
| N6122 | New 9th Dec 41 | 'OJ-Q' 'East India II'. To 149 Conversion Flight 15th Jun 42. Swung on landing at Mildenhall and undercarriage collapsed, 21st Jun 42 |
| N6123 | New 7th Dec 41 | 'OJ-F' To No.149 Conversion Flight 3rd Sep 42 |
| N6124 | New 11th Dec 41 | 'OJ-R- Lost on a raid to Stuttgart, crashing at Aguilcourt, France. All crew members lost, 5th May 42 |
| N6125 | New 13th Dec 41 | To No.149 Conversion Flight 18th Jan 42 |
| N6126 | From 218 Sqn 14th Feb 42 | 'OJ-U' Lost on a raid to Essen, crashing at Kleve, Germany, 14th Feb 42 seven crew members lost, one taken prisoner-of-war, 11th Mar 42 |
| N6127 | From 218 Sqn 15th Feb 42 | To 1651 CU 28th Mar 42 |
| R9142 | New 27th Jun 42 | 'OJ-R' Undercarriage collapsed 17th Aug 42. To 1651 Conversion Unit 12th Mar 43 |
| R9143 | From 7 Sqn 1st Jul 42 | 'OJ-O' To 1665 Conversion Unit 6th Jul 43 |
| R9161 | New 22nd Jun 42 | 'OJ-T' Lost on raid to Saarbrücken, crashing at Regniowez, France. Six crew members lost, one taken prisoner-of-war, 30th Jul 42 |
| R9162 | New 6th Jul 42 | 'OJ-Q' Lost on mining operation in the Kattegat; crashed into the sea in mining area. All crew members lost, 11th Aug 42 |
| R9163 | New 1st May 42 | To Sebro 10th Jul 42 |
| R9164 | New 21st Aug 42 | 'OJ-Q' Shot down by fighter whilst on a raid to Essen, crashing at Tongrinne, Belgium. All crew members lost, 17th Sep 42 |
| R9167 | New 27th Aug 42 | 'OJ-N' Shot down by night fighter whilst on a raid to Krefeld, crashing at Kronenburg, Netherlands. All crew members lost, 3rd Oct 42 |
| R9170 | New 31st Aug 42 | 'OJ-H' Shot down by night fighter whilst on a raid to Düsseldorf, crashing near Oud Beyerland, Netherlands. Six crew members lost, one taken prisoner-of-war, 11th Sep 42 |
| R9200 | From 214 Sqn 9th Oct 42 | 'OJ-P' To 75 Sqn 23rd Mar 43 |
| R9202 | New 13th Oct 42 | 'OJ-K' Lost whilst on a raid to Turin, crashing at Irasco-Finerola, Italy. All crew members lost, 30th Nov 42 |
| R9203 | New 11th Oct 42 | 'OJ-D' To 218 Sqn 18th Feb 43 |
| R9242 | New 21st Oct 42 | 'OJ-B' To 214 Sqn 23rd Feb 42 |
| R9253 | New 17th Nov 42 | 'OJ-K' Lost on mining operation, Warnemünde, crashing on the mud flats at Westermarsche, Germany. All crew members lost, 9th Dec 42 |
| R9265 | New 1st Dec 42 | 'OJ-N' Wings came off on pulling out from a dive during height test with load, crashing at Gransden, Bedfordshire. All crew members lost, 19th Dec 42 |
| R9271 | New 20th Dec 42 | 'OJ-K' To 90 Sqn 23rd Feb 43 |
| R9276 | New 29th Dec 42 | 'OJ-F' To 90 Sqn and lost 20th Feb 43 |
| R9287 | New 22nd Jan 43 | To 218 Sqn 4th Mar 43 |
| R9295 | From 7 Sqn 14th Feb 42 | 'OJ-G' 'East India III'. Damaged whilst on a raid to Essen; made belly-landing on return, overshot and hit trees, Hollywell Row, Mildenhall. Seven crew members lost, one injured, 11th Mar 42 |
| R9296 | From 7 Sqn 13th Feb 42 | 'OJ-D' To No.149 Conversion Flight 26th Mar 42 |
| R9299 | New 11th Feb 42 | To No.149 Conversion Flight, 19th Feb 42. Caught fire in the air, spun in and crashed at Swaffham Bulbeck, Cambridgeshire, 16th Jul 42 |
| R9307 | New 29th Mar 42 | Swung on take-off for raid on Le Havre and undercarriage collapsed, 22nd Apr 42 |
| R9310 | From 15 Sqn 12th Apr 42 | 'OJ-P' Lost on mining operation off Copenhagen, crashing in the Great Belt near Asnaes Peninsula, Denmark. All crew members lost, 18th May 42 |
| R9314 | From 15 Sqn 12th May 42 | 'OJ-T' Collided with Messerschmitt Bf 110 following a raid on Essen, which cut off the rear turret, killing the rear gunner. Aircraft ditched off the Belgian Coast, crew picked up by Air-Sea Rescue from Ramsgate, 6th Jun 42 |
| R9320 | New 29th Apr 42 | 'OJ-S' Shot down by flak on a mining operation off Copenhagen, crashing in Ferne Belt, near Lolland, Denmark. Two crew members lost, remainder taken prisoner-of-war, 18th May 42 |
| R9321 | New 1st May 42 | 'OJ-R' Shot down by night fighter whilst on a raid to Essen, crashing at Duisburg, Germany. All crew members lost, 6th Jun 42 |

| | | |
|---|---|---|
| R9327 | From 44 MU 26th Jan 43 | 'OJ-M' Lost on raid to Kiel, crashing at Obbekaer, Denmark. All crew members lost, 5th Apr 43 |
| R9329 | From 214 Sqn 29th May 42 | 'OJ-V' Damaged by anti-aircraft fire in the target area, crashing Cornwood, Devon, on return. All crew members lost, 21st Aug 42 |
| R9330 | New 24th May 42 | 'OJ-O' Starboard outer engine failed on take-off for a raid on Bremen. Ground-looped and undercarriage collapsed, 29th Jun 42 |
| R9334 | New 29th May 42 | 'OJ-G' Overshot runway on returning from practice bombing, resulting in second attempt at landing. Faulty altimeter, aircraft crashed at Lakenheath village. One crew member lost, rest injured, 3rd Jan 43 |
| R9358 | New 19th Jun 42 | To 214 Sqn 24th Jun 42 |
| W7448 | New 12th Oct 41 | To 7 Sqn 14th Oct 41 |
| W7449 | New 15th Oct 41 | To 7 Sqn 19th Oct 41 |
| W7450 | New 20th Oct 41 | To 15 Sqn 21st Oct 41 |
| W7451 | New 26th Oct 41 | To 7 Sqn 8th Nov 41 |
| W7452 | New 31st Oct 41 | 'OJ-A' 'East India IV' Landed at Ayr on training mission. Ground-looped to avoid running through fence, one undercarriage leg collapsed, 9th Mar 42 |
| W7453 | New 3rd Nov 41 | To 26 Conversion Flight 6th Nov 41 |
| W7455 | New 9th Nov 41 | 'OJ-B' To 149 Conversion Flight 19th Feb 42; damaged 15th Jun 42 and to Sebro for repair |
| W7456 | New 15th Nov 41 | Fire in one engine on training mission, force-landed at Boxworth, Cambridgeshire. First Stirling loss by No.149 Sqn, 22nd Nov 41 |
| W7457 | New 18th Nov 41 | To 149 Conversion Flight. Starboard undercarriage collapsed on landing from training mission, 11th Feb 42 |
| W7458 | New 23rd Nov 41 | On training mission, undercarriage collapsed following a heavy landing at Mildenhall, aggravated by the sun's reflection from the wet runway, 28th Jan 42 |
| W7459 | New 25th Nov 41 | To 26 Conversion Flight, 11th Dec 41 |
| W7460 | New 9th Feb 41 | To 15 Sqn 23rd Dec 41; back to 149 Sqn Jan 42, then No.149 Conversion Flight, then to 1657 Conversion Unit 25th Jun 42 |
| W7461 | New 5th Dec 41 | 'OJ-N' Engine failure over Hamburg, poor visibility. On return all but the pilot baled out, then force-landed at Toderick Bar, Yorkshire, 16th Jan 42 |
| W6462 | New 12th Feb 41 | 'OJ-T' Skidded on ice and overshot runway, landing in a ditch, at Lossiemouth on return from an attack on the Tirpitz, 29th Jan 42 |
| W 7463 | New 9th Dec 41 | To 15 Sqn 31st Dec 41 |
| W7465 | From 19 MU 2nd Jan 43 | To 214 Sqn 28th Feb 43 |
| W7469 | From 19 MU 21st Jan 43 | To 75 Sqn 28th Jan 43 |
| W7508 | New 23rd Mar 42 | 'OJ-D' Shot down by night fighter during raid on Essen, crashed in Brabant, Belgium. Six crew members lost, one taken POW. Sgt Goldsmith evaded capture, 6th Jun 42 |
| W7509 | New 13th Mar 42 | 'OJ-U' To 1651 Conversion Unit 24th May 42 |
| W7510 | New 13th Mar 42 | 'OJ-B' To 90 Sqn 18th Feb 43 |
| W7512 | New 17th Mar 42 | 'OJ-A' Lost on raid to Rostock, crashing at Schönhagen, Germany. All crew members lost, 27th Apr 42 |
| W7513 | From 10 MU 21st Jan 43 | To 75 Sqn 4th Mar 43 |
| W7526 | New 17th Apr 42 | To 214 Sqn 19th Apr 42, back to 149 Sqn 28th Aug 42, then 149 Conversion Flight 20th Sep 42, then back to No.149 29th Sep 42. 'OJ-V' Shot down by night fighter on raid to Cologne, crashed near Tiel, Netherlands. All crew members lost 16th Oct 42 |
| W7530 | New 30th Apr 42 | To 214 Sqn, back to No.149 Sqn, then No.149 Conversion Flight, and back to No.149 Sqn. To 218 Sqn, 8th May 42 |
| W7566 | From 10 MU 22nd Jun 42 | 'OJ-C' Lost while mining off the coast of France. Crashed off Vielle St.Girons, France. All crew members lost, 17th Nov 42 |
| W7567 | From 10 MU 20th Jun 42 | To 214 Sqn 24th Jun 42 |
| W7572 | From 10 MU 23rd Jun 42 | 'OJ-R' Shot down by night fighter on raid to Frankfurt, crashing at Thieulain, Belgium. Three crew members taken prisoner-of-war, four crew members evaded capture, 25th Aug 42 |
| W7580 | New 2nd Jul 42 | 'OJ-D' Shot down by night fighter on raid to Duisburg, crashing at Geffen, Netherlands. All crew members lost, 24th Jul 42 |
| W7582 | New 2nd Jul 42 | 'OJ-F' Fire in starboard outer engine whilst on a training flight, crashing at Mildenhall, Suffolk. All crew members lost, 10th Nov 42 |
| W7589 | New 21st Jul 42 | 'OJ-P' Fighter attack on return from raid on Osnabrück, knocking out two engines. Crashed near Sothery, Norfolk, 18th Aug 42 |
| W7619 | New 15 Aug 42 | 'OJ-A' To Sebro 9th Dec 42 |
| W7628 | New 29th Aug 42 | 'OJ-B' Ran out of fuel on return from Genoa; crashed at Cliffe, Kent. All crew members lost, 24th Oct 42 |
| W7638 | New 19th Sep 42 | 'OJ-R' Shot down by night fighter on a raid to Cologne, crashing near Boxmeer, Netherlands. Four crew members lost, three taken prisoner-of-war, 15th Feb 43 |
| W7639 | New 19th Sep 42 | 'OJ-Q' Returned early from a mining operation, crashing at Hockwold, Norfolk. All crew members lost, 8th Dec 42 |
| BF310 | New 20th Jun 42 | 'OJ-H' Shot down by night fighter whilst on a raid to Bremen, crashing into the IJsselmeer, Netherlands. All crew members lost, 29th Jun 42 |
| BF311 | New 22nd Jun 42 | 'OJ-G' To 75 Sqn, 20th Oct 42 |
| BF312 | New 23rd Jun 42 | 'OJ-A' Hit by anti-aircraft fire whilst on a raid to Lübeck, crash-landed at Steinfeld, Germany. Two crew members lost, five taken prisoner-of-war, 17th Jul 42 |
| BF320 | New 6th Jul 42 | 'OJ-H' Hit by anti-aircraft fire on a raid to Saarbrücken, crashing near target. All crew members lost, 30th Jul 42 |
| BF323 | New 11th Jul 42 | To 1651 Conversion Unit 13th Jul 42 |
| BF325 | New 20th Jul 42 | 'OJ-A' To Sebro 13th Aug 42 |
| BF328 | New 30th Jul 42 | 'OJ-D' Crashed in North Sea returning from minelaying, 1st Oct 42. All crew members lost |
| BF334 | New 4th Aug 42 | To 149 Conv Flt 26th Aug 42. Ditched off Margate, Kent, returning from Munich, 20th Sep 42 |
| BF348 | New 28th Aug 42 | 'OJ-P' Technical problems on take-off for mining operation in Gironde area, attempted landing at Watton. Aircraft hit trees and crashed. Six crew members lost, one injured, 10th Oct 42 |
| BF349 | New 28th Aug 42 | 'OJ-R' To 218 Sqn 4th Mar 43 |
| BF357 | New 6th Sep 42 | 'OJ-T' To 214 Sqn 23rd Feb 43 |

| Serial | History | Notes |
|---|---|---|
| BF372 | New 11th Sep 42 | 'OJ-H' Damaged by anti-aircraft fire over the target whilst on a raid to Turin, then again over Boulogne. Pilot and co-pilot badly injured, but pilot insisted on bringing the aircraft back, to allow four of the crew to bale out. Crashed in the Channel off Dymchurch, Kent. Pilot and two crew lost. Pilot Flt Sgt Middleton awarded VC, 29th Nov 42 |
| BF389 | From 15 Sqn 6th Oct 42 | Swung on take-off and undercarriage collapsed, Lakenheath, 27th Oct 42 |
| BF391 | New 5th Oct 42 | 'OJ-T' Lost on mining operation in Fehmarn Channel. Crashed at Dobersdorf, Germany. All crew members lost, 9th Dec 42 |
| BF392 | From 15 Sqn 8th Oct 42 | 'OJ-D' Lost on mining operation in Gironde Estuary. Crashed at Ile d'Yeu, France. All crew members lost, 17th Oct 42 |
| BF416 | From 115 Sqn 1st Jan 43 | To 218 Sqn 18th Feb 43 |
| BF444 | New 13th Jan 43 | 'OJ-G' To 214 Sqn, 3rd Mar 43 |
| BK597 | From 15 Sqn 6th Oct 42 | 'OJ-F' To 218 Sqn 2nd Oct 43. |
| BK598 | New 1st Oct 1942 | To 90 Sqn 16th Nov 1942 |
| BK601 | from 214 Sqn 8th Oct 42 | 'OJ-N' To 1657 Conversion Unit 10th May 43 |
| BK612 | New 4th Dec 42 | 'OJ-E' To 214 Sqn 28th Mar 43 |
| BK665 | New 24th Feb 1943 | To 90 Sqn 3rd Mar 43 |
| DJ972 | New 13th Apr 1942 | 'OJ-T' Attacked by night fighter on raid to Stuttgart. Swung on landing at base, undercarriage collapsed, 7th May 42 |
| EF327 | From 75 Sqn 29th Feb 43 | 'OJ-M' Engine failure when landing from raid on Stuttgart. Undercarriage collapsed, 12th Mar 43 |
| EF328 | From 90 Sqn 4th Mar 1943 | 'OJ-R' Starboard engines cut on return from raid on Nuremberg, crash landed at Sudbury 9th Mar 43 |
| EF330 | New 18th Jan 43 | 'OJ-P' Shot down by night fighter whilst on a raid to Essen. Crashed at Bergh, Netherlands; all crew members lost, 13th Mar 43 |
| EF332 | From 214 Sqn 16th Feb 1943 | To 75 Sqn 24th Mar 43 |
| EF335 | From 214 Sqn 28th Feb 43 | 'OJ-E' then 'OJ-H' To 1665 Conversion Unit 21st Jun 43 |
| EF336 | From 90 Sqn 4th Mar 1943 | To 620 Sqn 21st Jun 43 |
| EF337 | From 75 Sqn 2nd Mar 43 | To 1657 Conversion Unit 17th May 43 |
| EF338 | New 16th Feb 43 | 'OJ-O' To 620 Sqn 21st Jun 43 |
| EF340 | From 40 Sqn 16th Feb 43 | To 75 Sqn 17th May 43 |
| EF341 | New 10th Feb 43 | To 1665 Conversion Unit 17th May 43 |
| EF342 | New 7th Feb 1943 | To 1665 Conversion Unit 17th May 43 |
| EF343 | New 13th Feb 43 | 'OJ-B' Shot down by night fighter while on raid to Dortmund, crashed near Smallebrugge, Netherlands. All crew members lost, 5th May 43 |
| EF344 | New 16th Feb 43 | 'OJ-R' To 1657 Conversion Unit, 18th Jul 43 |
| EF357 | New 14th Mar 43 | 'OJ-V' Shot down by night fighter on raid to Duisburg, crashing at Rotterdam, Netherlands. All crew members lost, 13th May 43 |
| EF360 | New 14th Mar 43 | 'OJ-H' To 1651 Conversion Unit, 5th Oct 43 |
| EF389 | New 22nd April 43 | 'OJ-Q' To 1651 Conversion Unit, 7th August 43 |
| EF395 | New 21st Apr 43 | 'OJ-L' Swung on landing, undercarriage collapsed; repaired; to 1651 Conversion Unit |
| EF396 | New 20th May 43 | 'OJ-E' To 1651 Conversion Unit, 28th Sep 43 |
| EF400 | From 75 Sqn 30th Jun 43 | 'OJ-C' Engine failed while taking-off for a raid on Cologne. Swung on landing undercarriage collapsed, 4th Jul 43 (Last Mk I lost) |

## Stirling Mark III

| Serial | History | Notes |
|---|---|---|
| BF477 | New 13th Mar 43 | Engine failure whilst on raid to Mannheim, crashing at Sorbon, France. Two crew members lost, four taken prisoner-of-war, one evaded capture, 6th Sep 43 |
| BF479 | New 13th Mar 43 | 'OJ-E' Shot down by night fighter on raid to Bochum, crashing at Kasterlee, 14th May 43 |
| BF483 | New 13th Mar 43 | 'OJ-C' Lost on raid to Cologne. All crew members lost, 29th Jun 43 |
| BF500 | New 7th Apr 43 | 'OJ-M' Lost on raid to Stuttgart, crashing near Tounes, France. All crew members lost, 15th Apr 43 |
| BF503 | New 23rd Mar 43 | 'OJ-U' To 90 Sqn 5th Apr 43 |
| BF507 | New 31st Mar 43 | 'OJ-S' Shot down by night fighter on raid to Wuppertal, crashing at Dormagen, Germany. All crew members lost, 30th May 43 |
| BF509 | New 31st Mar 43 | 'OJ-N', 'OJ-B', 'OJ-R'. To 1653 Conversion Unit 16th Feb 44 |
| BF510 | New 31st Mar 43 | 'OJ-P' Lost on mining mission to the south-west coast of France, crashing in the Bay of Biscay. All crew members lost, 22nd May 43 |
| BF512 | New 31st Mar 43 | Undershot the runway after compass adjustment flight, opened up one outboard engine in error as well as the two inboards, swung and crashed near Lakenheath. All crew members lost, 9th Aug 43 |
| BF520 | New 12th Apr 43 | 'OJ-Y' Crashed on take-off, repaired. To Sebro 18th May 43 |
| BF530 | New 1st May 43 | Shot down by night fighter whilst on a raid to Cologne, crashing at Geetbetz, Belgium. Six crew members lost, one taken prisoner-of-war, one evaded capture, 4th Jul 43 |
| BF531 | New 21st Apr 43 | 'OJ-M' Tyre burst on landing from a 'Bullseye' exercise with anti-aircraft searchlight batteries. Swung off the runway and the undercarriage collapsed, 14th Jun 43 |
| BF570 | New 25th May 43 | 'OJ-T', OJ-H' 'OJ-J' To 1651 Conversion Unit, 11th Aug 43 |
| BF573 | From 75 Sqn 20th May 43 | 'OJ-W' To 620 Squadron, 21st Jun 43 |
| BF576 | New 13th May 43 | To 620 Sqn 21st Jun 43 |
| BF580 | New 24th May 43 | To 620 Sqn 21st Jun 43 |
| BK692 | New 27th Feb 43 | 'OJ-W' Hit by night fighter over target area, killing two crew on raid to Berlin, then hit by anti-aircraft fire crossing the French coast, crashing Gueuteville. Three crew members lost, five taken prisoner-of-war, 2nd Mar 43 |
| BK696 | New 27th Feb 43 | 'OJ-L' Hit by both anti-aircraft fire from a flak ship and by a fighter, whilst on a mining mission to the south-west coast of France. With the compass out and low on fuel, hit by an electrical storm. Crew baled out. Aircraft crashed at Havant, Hants., 2nd May 43 |

| | | |
|---|---|---|
| BK698 | From 15 Sqn 10th Mar 43 | 'OJ-O' Lost on a raid to Rostock, crashing into the North Sea. All crew members lost, 21st Apr 43 |
| BK701 | New 16th Feb 43 | 'OJ-G' Lost on mining operation to the west of La Rochelle, crashing in the Loire Estuary, sinking so rapidly that only three crew members could escape. Taken prisoners-of-war. Four crew drowned, 18th May 43 |
| BK703 | From 15 Sqn 10th Mar 43 | 'OJ-K' Shot down by night fighter whilst on a raid to Cologne, crashing at Netersel, Netherlands. All crew members lost, 29th Jun 43 |
| BK708 | New 14th Mar 43 | 'OJ-P' Lost on raid to Berlin, crashing Lindenberg, Germany 30th Mar 43 |
| BK710 | New 31st Mar 43 | 'OJ-A' Shot down by night fighter whilst on a raid to Düsseldorf, crashing into the North Sea. All crew members lost, 26th May 43 |
| BK711 | New 12th Apr 43 | 'OJ-O' Hit by both night fighter and anti-aircraft fire whilst on a raid to Mannheim, crashing at Hockenheim, Germany. Four crew members lost. Three taken prisoner-of-war, 6th Sep 43 |
| BK713 | New 15th Mar 43 | 'OJ-N' To 620 Sqn, 21st Jun 43 |
| BK714 | New 15th Mar 43 | 'OJ-L' Flew into the ground whilst flying low to avoid anti-aircraft fire whilst on a raid to Rostock, crashing Broendum, Denmark. One crew member lost, six taken prisoner-of-war, 21st Apr 43 |
| BK715 | New 15th Mar 43 | 'OJ-D' Starboard outer engine caught fire whilst taking off for air test. Fire initially died down on return to dispersal, but then re-ignited; aircraft burnt out, 31st Mar 43 |
| BK726 | New 24th Mar 43 | 'OJ-Z' Shot down by night fighter on raid to Bochum, crashing at Immerath, Germany. All crew members lost, 14th May 43 |
| BK759 | New 24th Mar 43 | 'OJ-X' Lost on a raid to Stuttgart, crashing at Studernheim, Germany. All crew members lost, 15th Apr 43 |
| BK765 | New 17th May 43 | 'OJ-P' Hit by anti-aircraft fire on a raid to Berlin; crew baled out except for one, aircraft crashing in the target area. One crew member missing, six taken prisoner-of-war, 24th Aug 43 |
| BK772 | New 27th Mar 43 | 'OJ-T' To 199 Sqn, 6th Jul 43 |
| BK781 | From 90 Sqn 13th Jul 44 | 'OJ-L' To 1651 Conversion Unit, 17th Aug 44. 45 Ops. |
| BK798 | New 13th Mar 43 | 'OJ-Q' Shot down by night fighter whilst mining in the West Friesians, crashing into the North Sea. All crew members lost, 21st Dec 43 |
| BK799 | New 21st Apr 43 | 'OJ-O' lost on a raid to Krefeld, crashing in the IJselmeer, Netherlands. All crew members lost, 22nd Jun 43 |
| BK806 | New 17th Jun 43 | To 199 Sqn 2nd Aug 43 |
| BK812 | New 29th Apr 43 | Aircraft taking-off to be flown to 15 Sqn at Mildenhall in high cross-wind; aircraft swung and undercarriage collapsed, 11th May 43 |
| BK816 | From 90 Sqn 6th Jun 44 | To 1657 CU 17th Oct 44 |
| EE872 | New 26th May 43 | 'OJ-N' Shot down by night fighter whilst on a raid to Mannheim, crashing Ludwigshaven, Germany. Six crew members lost, one taken prisoner-of-war, 6th Sep 43 |
| EE875 | New 24th May 43 | To 620 Sqn 21st Jun 43 |
| EE877 | From 15 Sqn 14th Jun 43 | 'OJ-E' Lost on raid to Nuremberg, crashing between Langel and Weiss, Germany. All crew members lost, 28th Jun 43 |
| EE879 | New 29th May 43 | 'OJ-G' Lost on raid to Berlin, crashing Sputendorf, Germany. All crew members lost, 1st Sep 43 |
| EE880 | New 31st May 43 | 'OJ-O' Shot down by night fighter whilst on a raid to Cologne, crashing at Houwaart, Belgium. Five crew members lost, one taken prisoner-of-war, one evaded capture, 29th Jun 43 |
| EE894 | New 16th Jun 43 | 'OJ-R' Shot down whilst on a raid to Berlin, crashing Hannover, Germany. Six crew members lost, one taken prisoner-of-war, 24th Aug 43 |
| EE953 | From 199 Sqn 11th Jul 43 | To 19 MU 29th Nov 44 |
| EE963 | From 32 MU 27th Aug 43 | 'OJ-N', Titled 'The Nuthouse'. To 1653 Conversion Unit, 29th Aug 43 |
| EE969 | New 27th Aug 43 | 'OJ-E' Lost on mining operation in the Kattegat, 28th Jan 44 |
| EF124 | From 218 Sqn 17th Aug 43 | To 1653 Conversion Unit 12th Sep 43 |
| EF133 | From 218 Sqn 17th Aug 44 | To 1651 Conversion Unit 13th Sep 44 |
| EF140 | New 8th Sep 43 | 'OJ-A' Lost on raid to Ruisseauville, crashing into the sea off Boulogne, France, 25th Jun 44 |
| EF161 | From 199 Sqn 5th May 44 | To 1657 Conversion Unit 13th Sep 44 |
| EF185 | From 218 Sqn 17th Aug 44 | 'OJ-D' To 1653 Conversion Unit 23rd Aug 44 |
| EF187 | New 5th Oct 43 | Lost on SOE mission to Mont de Cras, France, crashing at Cussy les Forges, 5th Feb 44 |
| EF188 | From 90 Sqn 12th Jun 44 | 'OJ-M' Lost on mining operation to Brest, crashing at Plougonvelin, France, 24th Jun 44 |
| EF192 | From 199 Sqn 5th May 44 | 'OJ-F' To 1653 Conversion Unit 17th Aug 44 |
| EF193 | From 90 Sqn 31st May 44 | 'OJ-D' To 1653 Conversion Unit 11th Aug 44 |
| EF202 | New 8th Oct 43 | 'OJ-L' Shot down by night fighter on mining operation in Gironde Estuary, crashing at St.Etienne-de-Montluc, France. Two crew members taken prisoner-of-war, five evaded capture, 26th Nov 43 |
| EF207 | From 218 Sqn 7th Aug 44 | 'OJ-F' To 1654 Conversion Unit 29th Aug 44 |
| EF233 | From 218 Sqn 17th Aug 44 | To 1657 Conversion Unit 18th Sep 44 |
| EF238 | From 10 MU 1st Mar 44 | 'OJ-H' Hit by anti-aircraft fire whilst on SOE mission, but completed mission, crashed on landing at Methwold due to damaged undercarriage, 9th May 44 |
| EF262 | From 214 Sqn 21st Jan 44 | 'OJ-G' To 199 Sqn 2nd Feb 44, back to 149 Sqn 25th Apr 44, then to 1653 Conversion Unit 11th Aug 44 |
| EF307 | New 27th Dec 43 | Lost on mining operation in Kiel Bay, crashing into the sea, 25th Feb 44 |
| EF308 | New 31st Dec 43 | 'OJ-R' Lost on mining operation in the Baltic, crashing into the sea, 26th Feb 44 |

| Serial | History | Notes |
|---|---|---|
| EF411 | From 15 Sqn 21st Jun 43 | 'OJ-M', OJ-K' To 1653 Conversion Unit 29th Aug 44. This aircraft recorded the most operational flights by a Stirling in Bomber Command, 74 ops. |
| EF412 | From 15 Sqn 14th Jun 43 | 'OJ-F' Swung on take-off during training flight. Wheel hit sodium flare and undercarriage collapsed, 13th Nov 43 |
| EF431 | From 90 Sqn 2nd Jun 44 | 'OJ-B' To 1651 Conversion Unit 25th Aug 44 |
| EF438 | New 14th Jun 43 | 'OJ-D' Lost on raid to Mönchen-Gladbach crashing in the target area. All crew members lost, 31st Aug 43 |
| EF450 | New 3rd Jul 43 | To 199 Sqn 6th Jul 43 |
| EF495 | New 12th Aug 43 | 'OJ-R' Lost on a raid to Hannover, crashing into the North Sea, 28th Sep 43 |
| EF502 | New 27th Aug 43 | 'OJ-G' Shot down by anti-aircraft fire whilst on SOE mission, crashing at St.Jean le Vieux, France, 11th Apr 44 |
| EH879 | From 15 Sqn 22nd May 43 | To Sebro 26th May 43 |
| EH883 | New 20th May 43 | 'OJ-A' lost on a raid to Mannheim, crashing Herxheim, Germany. Five crew members lost, one taken prisoner-of-war, one evaded capture, 24th Sep 43 |
| EH885 | New 17th May 43 | 'OJ-V' Swung on take-off for wireless homing test; undercarriage collapsed, 9th Jun 43 |
| EH903 | New 12th Jun 43 | 'OJ-L' Lost on raid to Mannheim, crashing in the target area. Two crew members lost. Five taken prisoner-of-war, 19th Nov 43 |
| EH904 | New 17th Jun 43 | 'OJ-K', 'OJ-P' Landed at Pembrey airfield in bad visibility while on training mission, swung to avoid obstruction, undercarriage collapsed, 16th Dec 43. Aircraft sent as training airframe 4445M to No 1 Air Gunners School, 27th Dec 43 |
| EH909 | New 24th Jun 43 | To 199 Sqn, 6th Jul 43 |
| EH922 | New 24th Jun 43 | 'OJ-O' To 1653 MU, 4th May 44 |
| EH927 | New 3rd Jul 43 | To 199 Sqn 6th Jul 43 |
| EH934 | New 7th Jul 43 | To 199 Sqn, 29th Jul 43 |
| EH943 | New 4th Sep 43 | 'OJ-B' Lost on raid to Laon, France, crashing at Cuissy-et-Geny. All crew killed, 23rd Apr 44 |
| EH982 | From 218 Sqn 14th Jul 44 | 'OJ-S' To 1653 Conversion Unit, 17th Aug 44 |
| EH987 | New 14th Aug 43 | 'OJ-P' New undercarriage failed to lock on landing after gas exercise and collapsed, 4th Oct 43 |
| EH993 | New 1st Sep 43 | 'OJ-D' Damaged on operations, 4th Jun 44; to Sebro 16th Jul 44 |
| EJ106 | New 8th Sep 43 | 'OJ-O' Lost on mining operation to Kattegat, crashing into the North Sea. All crew members lost, 8th Oct 43 |
| EJ107 | New 4th Sep 43 | 'OJ-K' Belly-landed at Coltishall, following a raid on Augsburg, 26th Feb 44. To Sebro 12th Mar 44 |
| EJ109 | New 8th Sep 43 | 'OJ-G' 'OJ-H', 'OJ-M' To 1657 Conversion Unit 23rd Sep 44. 46 Ops. |
| EJ115 | From 90 Sqn 18th Jul 44 | To 1653 CU 11th Aug 44 |
| EJ122 | From 90 Sqn 14th Jun 44 | 'OJ-Q' To 1657 Conversion Unit, 29th Aug 44. 57 Ops |
| EJ124 | From 214 Sqn 27th Jan 44 | 'OJ-C' Lost on raid to Amiens, crashing at Boves, France. All crew members killed, 15th Mar 44 |
| LJ447 | From 218 Sqn 17th Aug 44 | 'OJ-C' To 1657 Conversion Unit 29th Aug 44 |
| LJ449 | From 218 Sqn 11th Aug 44 | To 1651 CU 23rd Aug 44 |
| LJ472 | From 218 Sqn 11th Aug 44 | To 1651 CU 14th Sep 44 |
| LJ477 | From 90 Sqn 14th Jun 44 | 'OJ-X' Crashed on return from SOE mission to site 'Gondolier 15', in France, crashing Thorney Island. One killed, six injured,, 6th Jul 44 |
| LJ481 | From 218 Sqn 17th Aug 44 | 'OJ-U' To 1653 Conversion Unit, 15th Sep 44 |
| LJ501 | From 199 Sqn 15th May 44 | Lost on mining operation off Knocke; crashed Zeebrugge, Belgium. Six killed, one prisoner-of-war, 1st Jun 44 |
| LJ504 | From 10 MU 1st Dec 43 | 'OJ-K' Lost on mining operation to Kiel Bay. All crew lost, 19th Apr 44 |
| LJ511 | From 10 MU 13th Apr 44 | 'OJ-Q' Swung on take-off and undercarriage collapsed, 7th Jul 44. To Sebro 7th Jul 44 |
| LJ522 | from 218 Sqn 27th Jul 44 | 'OJ-N' To 1657 Conversion Unit, 25th Aug 44 |
| LJ526 | New 5th Jan 44 | 'OJ-P' Lost on mining operation in Fehmarn Channel, crashing at Oster Skerninge, Denmark. All crew lost, 24th Apr 44 |
| LJ568 | From 218 Sqn 28th Jul 44 | 'OJ-A" To 199 Sqn, 23rd Aug 44 |
| LJ577 | New 21st Feb 44 | 'OJ-E' To 1651 Conversion Unit 23rd Aug 44 |
| LJ580 | New 29th Feb 44 | To 199 Sqn, 11th Mar 44 |
| LJ582 | New 29th Feb 44 | To 199 Sqn, 11th Mar 44 |
| LJ621 | New 19th Apr 44 | Lost on SOE mission, crashing at Marcelet, France. Six killed, two prisoners-of-war and one evaded, 6th Jun 44 |
| LJ623 | New 22nd Apr 44 | 'OJ-P' To 1661 Conversion Unit, 12th Sep 44 |
| LJ625 | From 218 Sqn 26th Jul 44 | To 1657 Conversion Unit 25th Aug 44 |
| LJ632 | From 218 Sqn 26th Jul 44 | 'OJ-P' To 1653 Conversion Unit 12th Sep 44 |
| LK382 | New 6th Oct 43 | 'OJ-Q' Lost on SOE mission, crashing Esmery-Hallon, France. All crew lost, 10th Apr 44 |
| LK383 | From 90 Sqn 14th Jun 44 | 'OJ-A' Lost on mining operation to Brest; seen crashing in flames into the sea. All crew lost, 7th Aug 44 |
| LK385 | From 199 Sqn 5th May 44 | Lost on SOE mission to Caen, crashing at Baudre, France. All nine of crew killed, 6th Jun 44 |
| LK386 | From 15 Sqn 27th Nov 43 | 'OJ-J' Damaged by anti-aircraft fire on mining mission to Brest. Made emergency landing at Hartfordbridge but overshot the runway due to failure of brake pressure. Undercarriage collapsed, 24th Jun 44 |
| LK388 | New 9th Oct 43 | 'OJ-L' Starboard undercarriage collapsed due to heavy landing at Methwold, following practice bombing exercise. Aircraft overturned 17th Jul 44 |
| LK392 | From 90 Sqn 14th Jun 44 | 'OJ-O' Overshot runway, undercarriage collapsed, 19th Jul 44; to Sebro for repair |
| LK394 | New 20th Oct 43 | 'OJ-D' Shot down by night fighter during raid on Ruisseauville and crashed, Lisbourg, Pas-de-Calais, 25th Jun 44. All seven crew members killed |

| | | |
|---|---|---|
| LK396 | From 218 Sqn 17th Aug 44 | 'OJ-M' To 1657 Conversion Unit 14th Sep 44 |
| LK397 | From 218 Sqn 26th Apr 44 | 'OJ-K' Belly-landed at Methwold 23rd Jun 44; to Sebro 16th Jul 44 |
| LK401 | From 218 Sqn 17th Aug 44 | 'OJ-G' To 1653 Conversion Unit, 12th Sep 44 |
| LK445 | From 214 Sqn 30th Jan 44 | 'OJ-C' To 1657 Conversion Unit, 5th May 44 |
| LK499 | New 24th Feb 44 | 'OJ-R' To 1653 Conversion Unit 8th May 44 |
| LK500 | New 29th Feb 44 | 'OJ-F' 'OJ-S' Swung on take-off for SOE mission and hit mound, undercarriage collapsed, 11th May 44. Recovered and re-serialled TS262 |
| LK516 | New 29th Feb 44 | To 90 Sqn, 11th Mar 44 |
| LK568 | From 218 Sqn 26th Jul 44 | To 1653 Conversion Unit 13th Sep 44 |
| MZ260 | New 31st May 43 | 'OJ-C' Overshot runway with one engine out, 17th Nov 43 (September 8th 1944, last Stirling Operation by No.149 Sqn) |

## Avro Lancaster

*August 25th 1944, 6 Lancasters arrived at Methwold to begin replacing the Stirlings, 9 more on the 26th and by the 29th, No.149 Sqn had a full complement; all B.Is except B.IIIs shown* *

| | | |
|---|---|---|
| HK546 | From 115 Sqn 7th Nov 44 | 'TK-K' To 10 MU, 19th Jun 45 |
| HK549 | From 115 Sqn 6th Nov 44 | To 1653 Conversion Unit 15th Nov 44 |
| HK551 | From 115 Sqn 7th Nov 44 | 'TK-J' To 10 MU 29th Jun 45 |
| HK555 | From 115 Sqn 6th Nov 44 | To 115 Sqn on unspecified date |
| HK572 | From 115 Sqn 6th Nov 44 | To 10 MU 19th Jun 45 |
| HK577 | From 115 Sqn 28th Aug 44 | 'TK-H' To 10 MU 29th Jun 45 |
| HK578 | From 115 Sqn 6th Nov 44 | To 115 Sqn 3rd Mar 45 |
| HK598 | From 115 Sqn 6th Nov 44 | To 1654 CU 23rd Jan 45 |
| HK624 | New 30th Sep 44 | To 115 Sqn 6th Nov 44 |
| HK645 | New 6th Oct 44 | 'TK-D' To 115 Sqn Oct 44 |
| HK649 | New 20th Sep 44 | 'OJ-S' then 'TK-F' To 20 MU 30th Oct 45 |
| HK652 | New 30th Sep 44 | 'OJ-E' To 186 Sqn 30th Jun 45 |
| HK653 | New 5th Oct 44 | 'TK-E' To 115 Sqn 6th Nov 44; retd to No.149 Sqn 'OJ-Y' 18th Nov 44. Lost on a raid to Witten 12th Dec 44; all seven crew members killed |
| HK654 | New 5th Oct 44 | 'TK-G' To 186 Sqn 30th Jun 45 |
| HK655 | New 5th Nov 44 | Damaged in action 21st Oct 44; to 24 MU for repair |
| HK656 | New 6th Oct 44 | To 115 Sqn 6th Nov 44 |
| HK657 | New 7th Oct 44 | Damaged 15th Jan 45. To Avro 12th Feb 45 |
| HK699 | New 21st Nov 44 | 'OJ-H' To 54 MU 26th Mar 45, then back to No.149 Sqn 'TK-C' 5th Apr 45, then to 20 MU 1st Nov 45 |
| HK792 | New 23rd Feb 45 | To 138 Sqn 10th Mar 45 |
| HK793 | New 10th Feb 45 | 'OJ-B', 'TK-A' To 20MU 30th Oct 45 |
| HK795 | New 14th Feb 45 | 'OJ-O', 'OJ-H', 'TK-B' To 20 MU 1st Nov 45 |
| LM240 | From 15 Sqn 30th Apr 46 | 'OJ-O' Struck off charge 25th Mar 48 |
| LM692 * | New 26th Aug 44 | To 90 Sqn 20th Feb 45 |
| LM697 * | New 26th Aug 44 | 'OJ-E' To Avro 29th Nov 44 |
| LM721 * | New 28th Aug 44 | 'OJ-O' To Avro 29th Nov 44 |
| ME350 | From 138 Sqn 26th Jun 45 | 'OJ-W', 'OJ-G', 'OJ-O' Struck off charge 28th Feb 46 |
| ME352 | From 218 Sqn | 'OJ-K', 'OJ-S', 'OJ-T', 'OJ-E' To 207 Sqn date unspecified |
| NF927 | New 27th Aug 44 | 'OJ-D', 'OJ-E' Damaged three times, scrapped 24th Apr 46 |
| NF934 | From 218 Sqn 10th Dec 44 | Struck off charge Jun 47 |
| NF953 | From 15 Sqn Mar 45 | To 10 MU Jun 45 |
| NF969 | New 26th Aug 44 | 'OJ-F' To 10 MU 10th Jun 45 |
| NF970 | New 25th Aug 44 | 'OJ-R' To 207 Sqn 31st Jan 46 |
| NF971 | New 26th Aug 44 | 'OJ-P' To 207 Sqn, date unspecified |
| NF972 | New 26th Aug 44 | 'OJ-H' Shot down by anti-aircraft fire in Wesel area on raid to Consolidated benzol plant at Gelsenkirchen. Fire and explosion on board seen, 5th Mar 45. Two crew members killed; five prisoners-of-war |
| NF973 | New 27th Aug 44 | 'OJ-K' To 207 Sqn Apr 46 |
| NG140 | From 186 Sqn 1st Jul 45 | 'OJ-U' To 38 MU 15th Mar 46 |
| NG148 | From 186 Sqn 4th Dec 45 | To 15 MU 30th Apr 46 |
| NG224 | New 24th Nov 44 | To 138 Sqn 17th Apr 46, back to 149 Sqn 2nd Jul 46, then to 15 MU 27th Jul 46 (As code 'OJ-J', during attack on benzol plant at Gelsenkirchen, shrapnel smashed through bomb aimer's panel, hitting the bomb aimer in the face, and killing him. Aircraft repaired on site) |
| NG248 | From 138 Sqn 2nd May 46 | 'OJ-W' To 10 MU 26th Jul 47 |
| NG299 | From 622 Sqn 14th Mar 45 | 'OJ-A', 'OJ-T' To 207 Sqn 2nd Mar 46 |
| NG355 | New 6th Dec 44 | 'OJ-F', 'OJ-G', 'OJ-Q', 'OJ-U' To 10 MU 24th Apr 46 |
| NG356 | New 25th Nov 44 | 'OJ-O', 'OJ-C', 'OJ-V' To 10 MU 24th Apr 46 |
| NG361 | New 6th Dec 44 | 'OJ-E' To 10 MU 23rd Apr 46 |
| NG362 | New 6th Dec 44 | 'OJ-S' Overshot runway whilst landing at Methwold on return from Nuremberg; crashed and burnt. Two crew members injured, 2nd Jan 45 |
| NG387 | New 2nd Dec 44 | To 10 MU 9th May 46 |
| NG407 | New 2nd Feb 45 | To 138 Sqn 10th Mar 45, then back to 149 Sqn 'OJ-X' 8th Apr 46, then to 10 MU 23rd Apr 46 |
| NG409 | New 2nd Feb 46 | 'OJ-Q' To 138 Sqn 10th Mar 46 |
| NG448 | From 138 Sqn 2nd May 46 | To 10 MU 26th Jul 46 |
| NN708 | New 25th Aug 44 | 'OJ-Q' Missing on raid to Wiesbaden 2nd/3rd Feb 45. Five crew members killed, three prisoners-of-war |
| NN717 | From 138 Sqn 2nd May 46 | To 138 Sqn 2nd Jul 46 |
| NN756 | New 25th Nov 44 | 'OJ-R' To 15 MU 30th Apr 46 |
| NN760 | New 8th Dec 44 | 'OJ-G', 'OJ-W' To 207 Sqn 24th Apr 46 |
| NN781 | From 138 Sqn 26th Jun 46 | To 10 MU 26th Jul 46 |
| PA166 | New 27th Aug 44 | 'OJ-B', 'OJ-G', 'OJ-U' Control lost due to icing; overstressed 19th Jul 45 |
| PA193 | From 138 Sqn 2nd May 46 | To 138 Sqn 26th Jun 46 |
| PA186 | From 514 Sqn 21st Mar 45 | To 10 MU 17th Jun 45 |
| PA410 | From 115 Sqn | 'OJ-X' Two engines cut out over Shepherd's Grove, bellylanded, 14th Feb 49 |
| PA449 | From 32 MU 17th Jun 46 | 'OJ-S' Far East version. To 7 Sqn 27th Oct 48 |
| PB352 * | From 218 Sqn 6th Dec 44 | To 1661 Conversion Unit 24th May 45 |

| | | |
|---|---|---|
| PB483 * | New 26th Aug 44 | To 186 Sqn 31st Mar 45 |
| PB487 * | New 26th Aug 44 | 'OJ-V' To G-H Flt 23rd Jan 45 |
| PB488 * | New 26th Aug 44 | To 90 Sqn 20th Feb 45 |
| PB506 * | New 26th Aug 44 | 'OJ-B' To G-H Flt 4th Apr 45 |
| PB508 * | New 26th Aug 44 | To G-H Flight 31st Apr 45 |
| PB509 * | New 26th Aug 44 | 'OJ-C' To 186 Sqn 3rd Apr 45 |
| PB697 * | From 83 Sqn 24th Feb 45 | To 83 Sqn 13th Dec 45 |
| PB838 * | New 30th Nov 44 | To 138 Sqn 18th Apr 45, back to 149 Sqn 2nd Jul 46. To 15 MU 26th Jul 46 |
| PB902 * | From 514 Sqn 21st Mar 45 | Overshot runway when landing at Trondheim/Vaernes, Norway, and undercarriage collapsed 13th Aug 45 |
| PD284 | New 25th Aug 44 | 'OJ-N' To 138 Sqn 2nd Jul 46 |
| PD334 | From 514 Sqn 26th Jun 45 | To 207 Sqn 31st Jan 46 |
| PD364 | From 218 Sqn 7th Oct 44 | To 218 Sqn 8th Nov 44 |
| PD370 | From 138 Sqn 2nd May 46 | Struck off charge 17th Oct 46 |
| PD426 | From 626 Sqn 11th Oct 45 | 'OJ-H', 'OJ-K' To 15 MU 30th Apr 46 |
| PD440 | From 90 Sqn 2nd May 46 | To 10 MU 26th Jul 46 |
| PP673 | From 5 MU 23rd Mar 45 | Lost wing and dived from 2,000 feet into ground, Arras, France, 5th Jun 45; ten occupants killed |
| PP677 | New 27th Mar 45 | To 44 Sqn 8th Oct 45 |
| PP681 | New 26th Mar 45 | To 44 Sqn 9th Oct 45 |
| PP684 | From 46 MU 26th Mar 45 | To 20 MU 30th Oct 45 |
| PP685 | New 25th Mar 45 | 'OJ-G' To 44 Sqn 9th Oct 45 |
| PP686 | New 29th Mar 45 | To 44 Sqn 9th Oct 45 |
| PP687 | New 26th Mar 45 | To 44 Sqn 9th Oct 45 |
| RA588 | From 207 Sqn 18th May 46 | To 15 MU 18th May 46 |
| RA598 | From 138 Sqn 2nd Jul 46 | To 15 MU 26th Jul 46 |
| RF142 | New 22nd Feb 45 | 'OJ-U' To 138 Sqn 10th Mar 45 |
| RF143 | New 22nd Feb 45 | To 138 Sqn 10th Mar 45 |
| SW299 | From 32 MU 19th Jun 46 | 'OJ-U' Far East version. Struck off charge 21st Dec 49 |
| SW305 | From 32 MU 3rd Sep 46 | 'OJ-V' Struck off charge 13th Dec 49 |
| SW309 | From Wyton 30th Aug 46 | To 90 Sqn 12th Oct 46 |
| TW663 | From 207 Sqn 27th Jul 49 | 'OJ-X' Far East version. To 38 MU 30th Nov 49 |
| TW865 | From 35 Sqn 22nd Sep 49 | Far East version. Struck off charge 24th Nov 49 |
| TW881 | From Wyton 20th Jun 46 | Far East version. To 90 Sqn 12th Oct 46 |
| TW885 | From 7 Sqn 22nd Jan 47 | 'OJ-Y' Far East version. To 115 Sqn 16th Nov 49 |
| TW886 | From Wyton 20th Jun 46 | Far East version. To 115 Sqn 11th Dec 46 |
| TW887 | From Wyton 19th Jun 46 | 'OJ-T' Far East version. To 230 Operational Conversion Unit 12th Apr 47 |
| TW894 | From Wyton 20th Jun 46 | 'OJ-Z' Far East version. To 90 Sqn 12th Oct 46 |
| TW896 | From Wyton 19th Jun 46 | 'OJ-T', 'OJ-V' Far East version, to 230 Operational Conversion Unit 2nd May 47 |
| TW906 | From Wyton 19th Jun 46 | 'OJ-W' Far East version. To 38 MU 21st Dec 49 |

## Avro Lincoln B.2

| | | |
|---|---|---|
| RA688 | From BCAMS 23rd Oct 49 | Undershot landing at Mildenhall and belly-landed, 29th Dec 49 |
| RA709 | From BCAMS 12th Sep 49 | To 214 Sqn 20th Mar 50 |
| RE299 | From 7 Sqn 20th Jan 50 | To 49 Sqn 2nd Mar 50 |
| RF336 | From BCAMS 21st Sep 49 | To 49 Sqn 2nd Mar 50 |
| RF565 | From BCAMS 12th Oct 49 | To 35 Sqn 20th Oct 49 |
| RF570 | From 207 Sqn 14th Oct 49 | To 214 Sqn 21st Mar 50 |
| SX975 | From CBE 15th Feb 49 | To 148 Sqn 28th Feb 50 |
| SX982 | From CBE 11th Feb 49 | To 148 Sqn 28th Feb 50 |

## Boeing Washington (Boeing B-29A)

| | US Serial | |
|---|---|---|
| WF490 | 44-62074 | Received 17th Nov 50, 'OJ-S', 'S'. To 35 Sqn 18th Feb 53 |
| WF491 | 44-62198 | Received 17th Nov 50, 'OJ-T', 'T'. To 90 Sqn 13th Mar 53 |
| WF492 | 44-61895 | Received 6th Dec 50, 'OJ-U', 'U'. To 90 Sqn 20th Feb 53 |
| WF493 | 44-61642 | Received 6th Dec 50, 'OJ-W', 'W'. To Scottish Aviation for maintenance and storage 11th Mar 53 |
| WF494 | 44-62155 | Received 6th Dec 50, 'OJ-X', 'X'. To Disposal Flight for return US 24th Apr 53 |
| WF495 | 44-6228 | Received 6th Dec 50 from 115 Sqn. To Scottish Avn 26th Aug 52 |
| WF497 | 44-62012 | Received 8th Dec 50. To 15 Sqn 17th Jan 51 |
| WF498 | 44-61688 | Received 8th Dec 50. To 35 Sqn 26th Mar 53 |
| WF499 | 44-61889 | Received 11th Dec 50. To 15 Sqn 17th Jan 51 |
| WF500 | 44-62043 | Received 13th Dec 50. To Disposal Flight 24th Apr 53 for return to US |
| WF501 | 44-61982 | Received 13th Dec 50. To Disposal Flight 24th Apr 53 for return to US |
| WF546 | 44-62101 | Received 5th Apr 51. To Disposal Flight 24th Apr 53 for return to US |
| WF547 | 44-62328 | Received 7th Apr 51. To Scottish Avn 13th Mar 53 |

## English Electric Canberra B.2

| | | |
|---|---|---|
| WD957 | From 231 OCU 30th Apr 54 | To EEC 21st Jun 54 |
| WH711 | From BCAMS 28th Apr 53 | To 88 Sqn 21st Aug 54 |
| WH713 | From BCAMS 22nd Apr 53 | To 33 MU 22nd Aug 56 |
| WH855 | From BCAMS 18th Apr 53 | To 15 MU 10th Aug 56 |
| WJ567 | From BCAMS 7th May 53 | To 59 Sqn 1st Sep 56 |
| WJ569 | From BCAMS 20th May 53 | To 59 Sqn 1st Sep 56 |
| WJ570 | From BCAMS 21st May 53 | To 59 Sqn 1st Sep 56 |
| WJ612 | From BCAMS 22nd Apr 54 | To 59 Sqn 1st Sep 56 |
| WJ626 | From 33 MU 7th Jul 54 | To EEC 26th Apr 56 |
| WJ676 | From 15 MU 28th Mar 55 | To 40 Sqn 8th Aug 56 |
| WJ858 | From 33 MU 27th Sep 54 | To 69 Sqn 6th Oct 54 |
| WJ973 | From BCAMS 12th May 53 | To EEC 20th Sep 55 |

# Appendix III
# No.149 Squadron Aircraft Losses

## F.E.2b

**1918**

| | | |
|---|---|---|
| 23rd June | D9777 | Missing on night raid to Armentières. Two crew became prisoners of war |
| 7th July | D9740 | Engine cut; stalled and dived into ground |
| 18th July | C9779 | Missing on night raid to Warneton. Two crew became prisoners of war |

## Heyford

**1937**

| | | |
|---|---|---|
| 13th December | K4039 | (Mk IIA) Flew into the ground on a rainy night at Stopham, near Pulborough, Sussex. Four crew killed. Struck off charge |

**1938**

| | | |
|---|---|---|
| 15th February | K4037 | (Mk IIA) Engine cut, aircraft force landed in a field at Shotton Farm, Durham, hit the hedge and tipped on its nose. Struck off charge three days later. |
| 1st March | K4032 | (Mk IIA) Code 'D', Taxied into wall, Evanton, Scotland. Repaired on site. (See 8 Sept.) |
| 30th April. | K4021 | (Mk IIA) Converted to Mk III. Ran out of fuel. Wrecked on landing in bad visibility at Mildenhall |
| 17th August | K4870 | (Mk IIA) Bounced on landing and tipped, Mildenhall. Struck off charge 29th August 1938 |
| 8th September | K4032 | (Mk IIA) Code 'D' Undershot flarepath and hit fence at Mildenhall. Damaged beyond repair. |
| 2nd December | K4866 | (Mk IIA) Brakes failed; ran into hangar door, Mildenhall. Struck off charge |
| 6th December | K4865 | (Mk IIA) Brakes failed. Hit hangar at Mildenhall. Struck off charge |

## Wellington (W)

**1939**

| | | |
|---|---|---|
| 9th August | L4258 | (W I/IA) Missing over the North Sea on night flight, bad visibility and low cloud, |
| 29th August | L4257 | (W I/IA) 'OJ-P' Flew into the sea in bad visibility, 5 miles southeast of Happisburgh Light Vessel. |
| 18th December | N2961 | (W I/IA) 'OJ-P' Pilot F/O MF Briden. Badly shot up on raid to Wilhelmshaven. Ditched into the sea off Cromer. All crew killed |
| 18th December | N2962 | (W I/IA) 'OJ-B' Pilot F/O JHC Spiers. Shot down on raid to Wilhelmshaven. All crew killed. |

**1940**

| | | |
|---|---|---|
| 2nd January | N2943 | (W I/IA) Pilot F/O HL McL Bulloch. Shot down by enemy fighter while on reconnaissance patrol near Sylt, All crew killed |
| 2nd January | N2946 | (W I/IA) Pilot Sgt J Morrice. Shot down by enemy fighter while on reconnaissance patrol near Sylt, All crew killed |
| 2nd March | N2984 | (W I/IA) Pilot F/O LR Field. Engine failure shortly after take-off for leaflet raid on Bremen. Crashed at Burnt Fen, Norfolk. All crew killed. |
| 26th March | P9225 | (W I/IA) Pilot Sgt SA Williams. Hit by 'friendly' anti-aircraft fire near Dunkerque following reconnaissance patrol. Crew baled out near Belgian border and returned to England by boat train/channel ferry |
| 4th April | P9267 | (W IC) Pilot F/Lt JM Griffiths-Jones. Aircraft stalled while attempting an overshoot during training at Mildenhall. Five crew killed. |
| 12th April | P9246 | (W IC) Pilot Sgt HJ Wheller. Shot down by enemy fighter on anti-shipping sweep off Stavanger, Norway. All crew killed. |
| 12th April | P9266 | (W IC) Pilot Sgt GE Goad. Shot down by enemy fighter on anti-shipping sweep off Stavanger, Norway. All crew killed. |
| 24th May | P9270 | (W IC) 'OJ-G' Pilot F/Lt ID Grant-Crawford. Wing hit trees on return from an attack on German troop concentrations at the battle front, aircraft crashed at Barton Mills, Suffolk, Three crew killed. |
| 10/11th June | L7800 | (W IC) Pilot F/O JS Douglas-Cooper. Missing from raid on Soissons. Crashed into the sea. All crew killed. |
| 12th July | L7805 | (W IC) Pilot P/O JS Torgalson. Lost on raid to bomb naval installations at Bremen. All crew killed. |
| 12th August | P9244 | (W IC) 'OJ-E' Pilot P/O JG Miller. Hit radio mast at Mildenhall and crashed at Beck Row, returning from raid on Gelsenkirchen. All crew killed. |
| 17th August | R3174 | (W IC) 'OJ-A' Pilot S/Ldr EHT Thwaites, AFC. Lost on raid to Koleda. Three crew killed, three prisoners-of-war. |
| 28th August | P9272 | (W IC) 'OJ-A' Pilot F/Lt PFR Vaillant. Shot down on a raid to Kiel, Crew prisoners of war |
| 6th September | R3163 | (W IC) 'OJ-G' Pilot F/O H Burton. Lost on "Razzle" raid to Black Forest, and all crew prisoners of war. |
| 9th September | P9245 | (W IC) 'OJ-W' Pilot S/Ldr LV Andrews. Ditched into the sea off Clacton, Essex, returning from a raid on Boulogne. All crew killed. |
| 9th September | R3175 | (W IC) 'OJ-V' Pilot P/O JL Leeds. Lost over the sea following raid to Boulogne, All crew killed. |
| 19th September | R3160 | (W IC) 'OJ-E' Pilot P/O JS Pay. Lost on raid to Le Havre. All crew killed |
| 29th September | R3164 | (W IC) 'OJ-B' Pilot P/O JR Bjelke-Peterson. Lost on raid to Hanau. One crew killed, remainder prisoners-of-war. |
| 9/10th October | P9273 | (W IC) 'OJ-V' Pilot P/O RG Furness. Lost on raid to Grevenbroich. All crew killed. |
| 24th October | T2740 | (W IC) 'OJ-E' Pilot F/O DW Donaldson. Damaged in action. Crashed while making a forced landing at St. Osyth, Essex. |
| 20th November | N2774 | (W IC) 'OJ-A' Pilot P/O KJ Hide. Missing from a raid on Berlin, All crew killed [Records say raid was to Skoda Works, Plsen, Czechoslovakia, but most aircraft attacked secondary targets] |
| 16th December | R1294 | (W IC) Pilot Sgt RSW Lloyd. Lost wing fabric on air test, stalled while landing and crashed at Mildenhall. All crew killed. |
| 17th December | P9268 | (W IC) 'OJ-A' Pilot Sgt JS Marr. Overshot during landing at Mildenhall on return from a raid on Mannheim and ran into the bomb dump. |

**1941**

| | | |
|---|---|---|
| 12th January | T2807 | (W IC) Pilot Sgt RA Hodgson. Lost on operations to Italy. All crew prisoners of war. |
| 11/12th Feb | L7811 | (W IC) OJ-C Pilot Sgt Turner. Abandoned near Congresbury returning from raid on Bremen. |
| 12th February | P9247 | (W IC) 'OJ-M' Pilot Sgt R Warren. Flew into the ground while trying to get below very low cloud near Digby airfield, Lincolnshire, returning from |

| Date | Serial | Details |
|---|---|---|
| | | raid on Bremen. One crew killed. 22 aircraft crashed due to fog returning from Bremen. |
| 22nd February | R1045 | (W IC) 'OJ-M' Pilot F/O IS Henderson. Lost on raid to Wilhelmshaven. All crew killed. |
| 14/15th March | L7858 | (W IC) 'OJ-A' Pilot Sgt LR Hawley. Shot down by night fighter raid on Gelsenkirchen. All crew killed. |
| 18th March | R1474 | (W IC) 'OJ-M' Pilot Sgt R Warren. Shot down by Junkers 88 intruder, crashing into a bungalow at Beck Row near Mildenhall on return from raid on Bremen. All crew killed. |
| 19th March | R1159 | (W IC) 'OJ-N' Pilot Sgt W Hall. Hit tree at Peaseland Green, Suffolk, and crashed returning from raid on Cologne, poor visibility. |
| 1st April | R1229 | (W IC) 'OJ-H' Pilot Sgt GJP Morhen. Bounced, stalled, then caught fire, on landing from a raid on Bremen, One crew died of injuries. |
| 9th April | X3167 | (W IC) 'OJ-H' Pilot Sgt JBC Jago. Lost on raid to Kiel. All crew killed. |
| 10th April | R1181 | (W IC) 'OJ-W' Pilot P/O JH Fisher. Lost height during take-off from Mildenhall. crashed into trees and cottage at Holmsey Green, Suffolk, Two crew, lady in cottage killed. |
| 13th April | T2897 | (W IC) 'OJ-O' Pilot Sgt RR Morison. Lost on raid to Merignac airfield. Crashed near St Sever-Calvados, France. Five of crew killed one prisoner-of-war. |
| 16th April | R1439 | (W IC) 'OJ-W then U' Pilot Sgt PRB Meynell. Shot down by anti-aircraft fire on raid to Kiel. All crew killed. |
| 18th April | P9248 | (W IC) 'OJ-G' Pilot Sgt J Peel. Lost on raid to Cologne. All crew killed. |
| 9th May | R1506 | (W IC) 'OJ-D' Pilot F/Sgt CR Burch. Shot down by enemy fighter into the sea off Heligoland returning from raid on Hamburg. Four crew killed. Two prisoners-of-war. |
| 11th May | R1512 | (W IC) 'OJ-H' Pilot Sgt JG Keymer. Shot down on raid to Hamburg. All crew killed. |
| 17th May | R1587 | (W IC) Pilot S/Ldr AWJ Clark. Collided with 1401 Meteorological Flight Hurricane V7225 near Ely, Cambridgeshire. All crew killed. |
| 12th June | W5439 | (W II) 'OW-X The Wizard of Oz'. Pilot Sgt W Harrison. Shot down by anti-aircraft fire while on a raid to Düsseldorf. Crashed near Bergharen, Netherlands. 4 Crew prisoners-of-war. |
| 1st/2nd July | R1343 | (W IC) 'OJ-B' Pilot P/O SL St. Vincent-Welch RAAF. Shot down on a raid to Brest, All crew killed. |
| 1st/2nd July | R1408 | (W IC) 'OJ-J' Pilot P/O JE Horsfield. Shot down at Plouzane on a raid to Brest. All crew killed. |
| 15th July | T2737 | (W IC) 'OJ-A' Pilot P/O PL Dixon RAAF. Lost on raid to Bremen. All crew prisoners of war. |
| 17/18th July | N2853 | (W IC). Pilot Sgt DC Stewart RNZAF. Hit by flak on raid to Cologne. Blinded by searchlights in attempting to land. Crashed into trees at Cockfield, Suffolk. One killed, others injured. |
| 6th August | R1524 | (W IC) 'OJ-P' Pilot Sgt FD Fowler. Crashed at St. Martens Voeren, near Liège, Belgium, following raid to Mannheim. All crew killed. |
| 6th August | X9633 | (W IC) 'OJ-R' Pilot Sgt JT Farmer. Lost on raid to Mannheim. Crashed near Wavre, Belgium. All crew killed. |
| 13th August | R1024 | (W IC) 'OJ-V' Pilot P/O FH Beemer RCAF. Crashed in the sea off Sylt following a raid on Hannover. All crew killed. |
| 13th August | T2716 | (W IC) 'OJ-W' Pilot P/O Fox. Hit by flak and night fighter while on a raid to Hannover. One crew killed. Crashed while making a forced landing at Elvedon, Suffolk, one crew died of injuries. |
| 19th August | X9704 | (W IC) 'OJ-B' Pilot P/O JC Lynn. Lost on raid to Duisburg railway yards. Crashed near Roermond, Netherlands. Two crew killed. Four prisoners of war. |
| 8th September | X9705 | (W IC) 'OJ-J' Pilot Sgt GW Fenton. Lost on raid to Berlin. All crew killed |
| 11th September | X9879 | (W IC) 'OJ-V' Pilot Sgt DW Bennett RCAF. Shot down over target on raid to Kiel. All crew killed |
| 21st October | Z8795 | (W IC) 'OJ-C' Pilot P/O ACL Hodge. Shot down on raid to Bremen. Crashed into River Schelde. All crew killed. |
| 8th November | X9878 | (W IC) 'OJ-A' Pilot Sgt SW Dane. Lost on raid to Berlin. Five crew killed, one prisoner-of-war. |
| 16th November | R1627 | (W IC) Pilot Sgt R Bramhall. Shot down on raid to Emden. All crew killed. Last Wellington lost on operations by No.149 Squadron. |

## Stirling

### 1941

| Date | Serial | Details |
|---|---|---|
| 22nd Nov | W7456 | (S I) Pilot P/O C Lofthouse. Fire in one engine on training mission; force-landed at Boxworth, Cambridgeshire. First Stirling loss by No.149. |

### 1942

| Date | Serial | Details |
|---|---|---|
| 16th January | W7461 | (S I) 'OJ-N' Pilot F/O WG Barnes. Engine failure over Hamburg, poor visibility, on return all but pilot baled out, then force landed at Toderick Bar, Yorkshire. |
| 28th January | W7458 | (S I) Pilot F/Lt MR Evans. On training mission, undercarriage collapsed following heavy landing at Mildenhall aggravated by sun reflection from wet runway. |
| 29th January | W6462 | (S I) 'OJ-T' Pilot F/Lt RWA Turtle. Skidded on ice and overshot runway, landing in a ditch, at Lossiemouth on return from attack on the Tirpitz |
| 11th February | W7457 | (S I) To No.149 Conversion Flight. Starboard undercarriage collapsed on landing from training mission. |
| 9th March | W7452 | (S I) 'OJ-A' Titled 'East India IV' Pilot Sgt A Austin. Landed at Ayr on training mission. Ground-looped to avoid running through fence, one undercarriage leg collapsed. |
| 11th March | N6126 | (S I) 'OJ-U' Pilot P/O LW Bailey RAAF. Lost on raid to Essen, crashing near Kleve, Germany, 7 crew killed, one prisoner-of-war. |
| 11th March | R9295 | (S I) 'OJ-G' Titled 'East India III', Pilot F/O CL Pilkington. Damaged on raid to Essen, made belly landing on return, overshot, hit trees, Hollywell Row, Mildenhall. Seven of the crew killed, one injured. |
| 7th April | N3726 | (S I) 'OJ-G' Pilot F/Lt MR Evans. Attacked by fighter during raid to Essen, with severe right wing damage and engine out. Undercarriage collapsed on landing at base. |
| 16th April | N6068 | (S I) 'OJ-T' Pilot P/O ML Field. Shot down while on raid to Dortmund, crashing at Steene, Belgium. All crew killed |
| 22nd April | R9307 | (S I) Pilot P/O AF Cheetham. Swung on take off to raid on Le Havre, undercarriage collapsed. |
| 23rd April | N3719 | (S I) 'OJ-S' Pilot F/Sgt GHR Woodhouse. Swung on rough ground returning from raid on Cologne. Undercarriage collapsed. |
| 27th April | W7512 | (S I) 'OJ-A' Pilot P/O JH Thomson RCAF. Lost on raid to Rostock, crashing at Schönhagen, Germany. All crew killed. |
| 5th May | N6124 | (S I) 'OJ-R' Pilot P/O AF Cheetham. Lost on raid to Stuttgart, crashing at Aguilcourt, France. All crew killed. |
| 7th May | DJ792 | (S I) 'OJ-T' Pilot F/O MA Brogan. Attacked by night fighter on raid to Stuttgart. Swung on landing at base. Undercarriage collapsed. |

| Date | Serial | Details |
|---|---|---|
| 18th May | N3752 | (S I) 'OJ-O' Pilot Sgt JA Jerman. Shot down while on mining operation off Copenhagen, crashing at Risegard, Denmark. All crew prisoners of war. |
| 18th May | R9310 | (S I) 'OJ-P' Pilot P/O AJ Frost. Lost on mining operation off Copenhagen in the Baltic, crashing in Great Belt, near Asnaes Peninsula, Denmark, All crew killed. |
| 18th May | R9320 | (S I) 'OJ-S' Pilot F/Sgt GHR Woodhouse. Shot down by anti-aircraft fire on mining operation off Copenhagen, crashing in Ferne Belt, near Lolland, Denmark. Two crew killed, remainder picked up by Danish fishing boat, then taken prisoners of war. |
| 6th June | R9314 | (S I) 'OJ-T' Pilot F/Sgt EW Whitney. Collided with Messerschmitt 110 following raid on Essen which cut off rear turret, killing the rear gunner. Aircraft ditched near Belgian coast, Crew picked up by Air-sea Rescue from Ramsgate. |
| 6th June | R9321 | (S I) 'OJ-R' Pilot S/Ldr RB Harris. Shot down by night fighter on raid to Essen, crashing at Duisburg. Germany. All crew killed. |
| 6th June | W7508 | (S I) 'OJ-D' Pilot P/O PL Clayton. Shot down by night fighter during raid on Essen. Crashed in Brabant, Belgium. Six of the crew killed, one prisoner-of-war, Sergeant Golsmith evaded capture. |
| 9th June | N6084 | (S I) 'OJ-C' Pilot F/Sgt HL Davis. Shot down while on raid to Essen, crashing at Hassel, Germany. All crew killed. |
| 21st June | N6122 | (S I) Titled 'East India II' To No.149 Conversion Flight. Swung on landing at Mildenhall and undercarriage collapsed. |
| 29th June | R9330 | (S I) 'OJ-O' Pilot F/Sgt R Hockley. Starboard outer engine failure on take-off for raid on Bremen. Ground-looped and undercarriage collapsed. |
| 29th June | BF310 | (S I) 'OJ-H' Pilot P/O CW Simmons RCAF. Shot down by night fighter on raid to Bremen, crashing into the IJsselmeer, Netherlands. All crew killed. |
| 30th June | N6082 | (S I) 'OJ-Q' Pilot S/Ldr GW Alexander. Shot down by night fighter on raid to Bremen, Crashed near Wons, Netherlands. Seven crew killed one prisoner-of-war |
| 16th July | R9299 | (S I) To No.149 Conversion Flight. Caught fire in the air, spun in and crashed at Swaffham Bulbeck, Cambridgeshire. |
| 17th July | BF312 | (S I) 'OJ-A' Pilot P/O JMP Forward. Hit by anti-aircraft fire on raid to Lübeck, crashlanded at Steinfeld, Germany. Two crew killed, five prisoners of war. |
| 24th July | W7580 | (S I) 'OJ-D' Pilot F/O AJL Bowes. Shot down by night fighter on raid to Duisburg, crashing at Geffen, Netherlands. All crew killed. |
| 30th July | R9161 | (S I) 'OJ-T' Pilot F/Lt FG Neate. Lost on raid to Saarbrücken, crashing at Regniowez, France. Six of crew killed, one prisoner-of-war. |
| 30th July | BF320 | (S I) 'OJ-H' Pilot P/O TMF Hulse. Hit by anti-aircraft fire on raid to Saarbrücken, crashing near target. All crew killed. |
| 11th August | R9162 | (S I) 'OJ-Q' Pilot F/Sgt CWS Oliver RAAF. Lost on mining operation in Kattegat, crashed in the sea in mining area. All crew killed. |
| 18th August | W7589 | (S I) 'OJ-P' Pilot Sgt DA Baker. Fighter attack on return from raid on Osnabrück, knocking out two engines. Crashed near Sothery, Norfolk. |
| 21st August | R9329 | (S I) 'OJ-V' Pilot Sgt GE Robertson. Damaged by anti-aircraft fire in target area while mining off French coast, crashing at Cornwood, Devon, on return, all crew killed. |
| 24th August | N6083 | (S I) 'OJ-N' Pilot P/O EP Wynn RCAF. Engine failure followed by fire just after take off for raid on Frankfurt. Aircraft crashed just south of Lakenheath. All crew killed. |
| 25th August | W7572 | (S I) 'OJ-R' Pilot Sgt DA Baker. Shot down by night fighter on raid to Frankfurt, crashing at Thieulain in Belgium. Three crew prisoners of war, four crew evaded capture. |
| 29th August | N6081 | (S I) 'OJ-H' Pilot W/Cdr C Charlton-Jones. Shot down by night fighter on raid to Nuremberg, crashing at Arlenbach, Germany. Six of crew killed two prisoners of war. |
| 11th September | R9170 | (S I) 'OJ-H' Pilot F/Sgt AF Potts. Shot down by night fighter on raid to Düsseldorf, crashing near Oud Beyerland, Netherlands. Six of crew killed, one prisoner-of-war. |
| 17th September | R9164 | (S I) OJ-Q' Pilot F/Sgt MJ Kynaston. Shot down by night fighter on raid to Essen, crashing at Tongrinne, Belgium. All crew killed. |
| 19/20th Sept | BF334 | (S I) 'OJ-R' Pilot Sgt J Philp. No.149 Conversion Flight, ditched into the sea off Ramsgate, Kent after engine failure on return from a raid on Munich, the aircraft breaking into pieces. The pilot, Sgt J Philp and Sgt GK Reardon swam towards shore towing injured Sgt FH King, who died. Picked up after 4 hours by fishing boat. Sgt LV Fossleitner stayed with injured Sgt IG Davies until rescued by Air Sea Rescue launch. Other two crew members never found. Sgts Philp, Fossleitner and Reardon awarded BEM (Gazetted 29 Dec.42) but Philp and Fossleitner killed in separate crashes before announcement |
| 1st October | BF328 | (S I) 'OJ-D' Pilot F/Sgt SD Wells RNZAF. Crashed into the North Sea on mining operations off the Friesian Islands (Nectarines); all crew killed |
| 3rd October | R9167 | (S I) 'OJ-N' Pilot S/Ldr WR Greenslade DFC, AFC. Shot down by night fighter on raid to Krefeld, crashing at Kronenburg, Netherlands. All crew killed. |
| 6th October | N3755 | (S I) 'OJ-S' Pilot P/O R Lonsdale RNZAF. Used by No.149 Conversion flight for a while. Ran out of fuel on return from raid on Aachen. Crashed at Eastling, Kent. Pilot killed. |
| 10th October | BF348 | (S I) 'OJ-P' Pilot F/Sgt HJ Hart. Technical problems on take-off for mining operation in Gironde area, with attempted landing at Watton. Aircraft hit trees and crashed. Six crew killed, one injured. |
| 16th October | W7526 | (S I) 'OJ-V' Pilot F/Sgt JC Brocket RNZAF. Shot down by night fighter on raid to Cologne. Crashed near Tiel, Netherlands. All crew killed. |
| 17th October | BF392 | (S I) 'OJ-D' Pilot F/Sgt JH Ekelund RCAF. Lost on mining operation in Gironde Estuary. Crashed at Ile d'Yeu, France; all crew killed. |
| 24th October | W7628 | (S I) 'OJ-B' Pilot Sgt AA Siwak RCAF. Ran out of fuel on return from raid to Genoa, crashed at Cliffe, Kent. All crew killed. |
| 27th October | BF389 | (S I) 'OJ-S' Pilot F/Sgt JG Gow RNZAF. Overcorrection of swing on take-off at Lakenheath with undercarriage collapse |
| 10th November | W7582 | (S I) 'OJ-S' Pilot S/Ldr WC Hutchings DFC. Fire in the starboard outer engine while on a training flight, crashing in Mildenhall, Suffolk. All crew killed. |
| 17th November | W7566 | (S I) 'OJ-C' Pilot Sgt TA West. Lost while mining off the coast of France. Crashed off Vielle St. Girone, France; all crew killed. |

| Date | Aircraft | Details |
|---|---|---|
| 29th November | BF372 | (S I) 'OJ-H' Pilot F/Sgt RH Middleton RAAF. Damaged by anti-aircraft fire both over target where the pilot and co-pilot were severely wounded, and again over Boulogne on return from raid on Turin. Pilot insisted on remaining at controls and bringing aircraft back to England so crew could bale out. Five complied. Aircraft crashed in the sea off Dymchurch, Kent. Remaining three crew including pilot killed. Pilot, Flt Sgt RH Middleton RAAF awarded Victoria Cross. |
| 30th November | R9202 | (S I) 'OJ-K' Pilot F/Sgt VT Bowie RNZAF. Lost on raid to Turin, crashing at Irasco-Finerola, Italy, All crew killed. |
| 6th December | N3723 | (S I) 'OJ-E' Pilot F/Sgt FHJ Ashley. Anti-aircraft shell shrapnel severed elevator control cables during raid on Mannheim. Crew abandoned aircraft over Ascot, Berkshire. Aircraft crashed near racecourse. |
| 8th December | W7639 | (S I) 'OJ-Q' Pilot P/O J Philp BEM. Returned early from mining operation, crashing at Hockwold, Norfolk. All crew killed |
| 9th December | R9253 | (S I) 'OJ-K' Pilot F/O LT Izzard RCAF. Lost on mining operation, Warnemünde, crashing on the mud flat at Westermarsche, Germany. All crew killed. |
| 9th December | BF391 | (S I) 'OJ-T' Pilot F/O MH Good. Lost on mining operation in Fehmarn Channel. Crashed at Doberdsorf, Germany. All crew killed. |
| 19th December | R9265 | (S I) 'OJ-N' Pilot F/O EAR Hunt. Wings came off on pulling out from a dive during height test with load, crashing at Gransden, Bedfordshire. All crew killed. |

**1943**

| Date | Aircraft | Details |
|---|---|---|
| 3rd January | R9334 | (S I) 'OJ-G' Pilot F/Sgt JL Blair RNZAF. Overshot runway on returning from practice bombing, resulting in second attempt at landing. Faulty altimeter, aircraft crashed at Lakenheath village. One crew killed, rest injured. |
| 15th February | W7638 | (S I) 'OJ-R' Pilot Flt/Sgt JG Gow RNZAF. Shot down by night fighter on raid to Cologne, crashing near Boxmeer, Netherlands. Four crew killed three prisoners-of-war. |
| 2nd March | BK692 | (S III) 'OJ-W' Pilot F/Lt RE Richman DFM. Hit by night fighter over target area killing two crew on raid to Berlin, then by anti-aircraft fire crossing the French coast, crashing at Gueuteville, France. Three crew killed, five prisoners-of-war |
| 9th March | EF328 | (S I) 'OJ-R' Pilot P/O GTP Southall RNZAF. Starboard engines cut on return from raid on Nuremberg. Crash-landed at Sudbury. |
| 12th March | EF327 | (S I) 'OJ-M' Pilot P/O ITS Fulton. Engine failure when landing from raid on Stuttgart, swung and undercarriage collapsed. |
| 13th March | EF330 | (S I) 'OJ-P' Pilot F/Sgt FA Pearson. Shot down by night fighter while on raid to Essen. Crashed at Bergh, Netherlands. All crew killed. |
| 30th March | BK708 | (S III) 'OJ-P' Pilot P/O ITS Fulton. Lost on raid to Berlin, crashing at Lindenburg, Germany. Six of crew killed. One prisoner-of-war. |
| 31st March | BK715 | (S III) 'OJ-D' Pilot F/Lt LH Butler RNZAF. Starboard outer engine caught fire while taking off for air test. Fire initially died down on return to dispersal, but then re-ignited, aircraft burnt. |
| 5th April | R9327 | (S I) 'OJ-M' Pilot Sgt KA Way. Lost on raid to Kiel, crashing at Obbekaer, Denmark; all crew killed. |
| 15th April | BF500 | (S I) 'OJ-M' Pilot P/O DB White RCAF. Lost on raid to Stuttgart, crashing near Tounes, France. All crew killed |
| 15th April | BK759 | (S III) 'OJ-X' Pilot TG Ogle. Lost on raid to Stuttgart, crashing at Studernheim, Germany; all crew killed. |
| 21st April | BK698 | (S III) 'OJ-O' Pilot F/Lt GI Ellis RNZAF. Lost on raid to Rostock, crashing into the North Sea. All crew killed. |
| 21st April | BK714 | (S III) 'OJ-L' Pilot S/Ldr TL Howell. Flew into the ground while flying low to avoid anti-aircraft fire while on raid to Rostock, crashing at Broendum, Denmark. One crew killed, six prisoners of war. |
| 2nd May | BK696 | (S III) 'OJ-L' Pilot P/O PL Blair RNZAF. Hit by both anti-aircraft fire from flak ship and by fighter while on mining mission to the south-west coast of France. With the compass out and low on fuel, hit an electrical storm. Crew baled out. Aircraft crashed at Havant, Hampshire. |
| 5th May | EF343 | (S I) 'OJ-B' Pilot F/O WE Davey. Shot down by night fighter while on raid to Dortmund. Crashed near Smallebrugge, Netherlands, All crew killed. |
| 11th May | BK812 | (S III) Pilot P/O KJ Beetles. Aircraft taking off to be flown to 15 Squadron at Mildenhall. In high cross-wind, aircraft swung and undercarriage collapsed. |
| 13th May | EF357 | (S I) 'OJ-V' Pilot Sgt EG Bass. Shot down by night fighter on raid to Duisburg, crashing at Rotterdam, Netherlands. All crew killed. |
| 14th May | BF479 | (S III) 'OJ-E' Pilot F/O LC Martin. Shot down by night fighter on raid to Bochum, crashing at Kasterlee, Germany. |
| 14th May | BK726 | (S III) 'OJ-Z' Pilot P/O HE Forsyth RCAF. Shot down by night fighter on raid to Bochum, crashing at Immerath, Germany; all crew killed. |
| 18th May | BK701 | (S III) 'OJ-G' Pilot P/O JE Hill. Lost on mining operation to the west of La Rochelle, crashing in the Loire estuary, sinking so rapidly that only three of crew could escape to be taken prisoners-of-war. Four crew drowned. |
| 22nd May | BF510 | (S III) 'OJ-P' Pilot Sgt CE Tomlin. Lost on mining mission to the South West coast of France, crashing in the Bay of Biscay. All crew killed. |
| 26th May | BK710 | (S III) 'OJ-A' Pilot Sgt JH Uden. Shot down by night fighter while on raid to Düsseldorf, the aircraft crashing into the North Sea. All crew killed. |
| 30th May | BF507 | (S III) 'OJ-S' Pilot P/O AW Flack RNZAF. Shot down by night fighter on raid to Wuppertal, crashing at Dormagen, Germany; all crew killed. |
| 9th June | EH885 | (S III) 'OJ-V' Pilot Sgt T Nicholson. Swung on take off for wireless homing test, undercarriage collapsed. |
| 14th June | BF531 | (S III) 'OJ-M' Pilot F/O AR Porter. Tyre burst on landing from a "Bullseye" exercise with anti-aircraft searchlight batteries. Swung off the runway and the undercarriage collapsed |
| 22nd June | BK799 | (S III) 'OJ-O' Pilot P/O J Lowrie. Lost on raid to Krefeld, crashing in the IJsselmeer, Netherlands. All crew killed. |
| 29th June | BF483 | (S III) 'OJ-C' Pilot Sgt RK Scott. Lost on raid to Cologne. All crew killed. |
| 29th June | EE880 | (S III) 'OJ-O' Pilot F/O AR Porter. Shot down by night fighter on raid to Cologne crashing at Houwaart, Belgium. Five crew killed, one prisoner-of-war, one evaded capture. |
| 29th June | BK703 | (S III) 'OJ-K' Pilot F/O WR Booker. Shot down by night fighter on raid to Cologne, crashing at Netersel, Netherlands. All crew killed. |

| | | |
|---|---|---|
| 4th July | EF400 | (S I) 'OJ-C' Pilot Sgt SW Rogers. Engine failed while taking off for raid on Cologne. Swung on landing. Undercarriage collapsed. (Last Mk I lost on operations) |
| 4th July | BF530 | (S III) Pilot P/O GA Cozens DFM. Shot down by night fighter on raid to Cologne, crashing at Geetbetz, Belgium. Six of the crew killed, one prisoner-of-war, one evaded capture. |
| 9th August | BF512 | (S III) Pilot Sgt JW Cumming RCAF. Undershot the runway after compass adjustment test flight, opened up one outboard engine in error as well as the two inboards, swung and crashed near Lakenheath. All crew killed. |
| 24th August | BK765 | (S III) 'OJ-P' Pilot S/Ldr JJE Mahoney. Hit by anti-aircraft fire on raid to Berlin; crew baled out except one, aircraft crashing in target area; one crew killed six prisoners of war. |
| 24th August | EE894 | (S III) 'OJ-R' Pilot F/Sgt AE May. Shot down on raid to Berlin crashing at Hannover, Germany. Six crew killed, one prisoner-of-war. |
| 28th August | EE877 | (S III) 'OJ-E' Pilot F/Sgt GS Steer. Lost on raid to Nuremberg, crashing between Langel and Weiss, Germany. All crew killed. |
| 31st August | EF438 | (S III) 'OJ-D' Pilot F/Sgt EW Bower. Lost on raid to Mönchen-Gladbach crashing in the target area. All crew killed. |
| 1st September | EE879 | (S III) 'OJ-G' Pilot F/Sgt HA More. Lost on raid to Berlin crashing at Sputendorf, Germany; all crew killed. |
| 6th September | BF477 | (S III) Pilot F/O CD Farmer. Engine failure on raid to Mannheim, crashing at Sorbon, France. Two crew killed, four prisoners-of-war, one evaded capture. |
| 6th September | BK711 | (S III) 'OJ-O' Pilot F/Lt B Cottrell. Hit by both night fighter and anti-aircraft fire while on raid to Mannheim, crashing at Hockenheim, Germany. Four crew killed, three prisoners-of-war. |
| 6th September | EE872 | (S III) 'OJ-N' Pilot F/Sgt AA Brown. Shot down by night fighter on raid to Mannheim, crashing at Ludwigshafen, Germany. Six crew killed one prisoner-of-war. |
| 24th September | EH883 | (S III) 'OJ-A' Pilot W/O WJ Leedham. Lost on raid to Mannheim crashing at Herxheim, Germany. Five crew killed, one prisoner-of-war, one evaded capture. |
| 28th September | EF495 | (S III) 'OJ-R' Pilot. F/Sgt GS Hotchkis RCAF. Crashed into North Sea while on raid to Hannover. Four crew killed, three prisoners-of-war. |
| 4th October | EH987 | (S III) 'OJ-P' Pilot. P/O BA Connor RAAF. Undercarriage failed to lock on landing after gas exercise, and collapsed. |
| 8th October | EJ106 | (S III) 'OJ-O' Pilot. F/Sgt JG McInnes RCAF. Lost on mining operation to Kattegat, crashing into the North Sea. All crew killed. |
| 13th November | EF412 | (S I) 'OJ-F' Pilot. P/O GN Knowles. Swung on take-off during training flight. Wheel hit sodium flare and undercarriage collapsed. |
| 17th November | MZ260 | (S III) 'OJ-C' Pilot. P/O GT Lowe RNZAF. Overshot runway with one engine out while on training. Four crew killed. |
| 19th November | EH903 | (S III) 'OJ-L' Pilot. F/Sgt RLL Smith. Lost on raid to Mannheim, crashing in the target area; two crew killed, five prisoners-of-war. |
| 26th November | EF202 | (S III) 'OJ-L' Pilot Sgt KC Richardson. Shot down by night fighter on mining operation in Gironde Estuary, crashing at St. Etienne-de-Montluc, France. Two crew prisoners-of-war, five evaded capture. |
| 16th December | EH904 | (S III) 'OJ-P' Pilot P/O RN Johnstone RNZAF. Landed at Pembrey airfield in bad visibility while on training mission and swung to avoid obstruction; undercarriage collapsed. Aircraft sent as training airframe 4445M to No.1 Air Gunners School December 1943. |
| 21st December | BK798 | (S III) 'OJ-Q' Pilot F/Sgt RJ Ayers RAAF. Shot down by night fighter while mining in the West Friesians, crashing into the North Sea. All crew killed |

**1944**

| | | |
|---|---|---|
| 28th January | EE969 | (S III) 'OJ-E' P/O E Wood. Lost on mining operation in the Kattegat. All crew killed (Lost without trace) |
| 5th February | EF187 | (S III) 'OJ-C' Flight Lieutenant HE Colenutt. Lost on Special Operations mission to Mont de Cras, France, supporting Maquis Henri Bourgogne of Semur-en-Auxois, 50 km west of Dijon, crashing at Cussy-les-Forges. All crew killed |
| 25th February | EF307 | (S III) 'OJ-E' F/O AV Collins. Lost on mining operation in Kiel Bay, crashing into the sea. All crew killed |
| 26th February | EF308 | (S III) 'OJ-R' F/L RN Johnstone RNZAF. Lost on mining operation in the Baltic, crashing into the sea. All crew killed |
| 16th March | EJ124 | (S III) 'OJ-C' P/O DJ Munro RAAF. Lost on raid to Amiens crashing at Boves, France. All crew killed |
| 10th April | LK382 | (S III) 'OJ-Q' F/L RV Sanders. Shot down by night fighter on Special Operations mission crashing at Esmery-Hallon, France. All crew killed |
| 11th April | EF502 | (S III) 'OJ-G' P/O D Bray. Shot down by anti-aircraft fire while on Special Operations mission in south of France, crashing on the roof of a farmhouse at St. Jean-le-Vieux, France. 5 killed. Sgt DE Cadge and Flight Sergeant NCH Pilgrim evaded capture, arriving home on the 9th of July 1944. |
| 19th April | LJ504 | (S III) 'OJ-K' Sergeant E Jeal. Lost on mining operation to Kiel Bay. All crew killed |
| 23rd April | EH943 | (S III) 'OJ-B' Flight Sergeant HE Billens RNZAF. Shot down by night fighter on raid to Laon, France, crashing at Cuissy-et-Geny. All crew killed |
| 24th April | LJ526 | (S III) 'OJ- P' Flight Lieutenant RJ Freeman. Shot down by night fighter on mining operation in Fehmarn Channel crashing at Oster Skerninge, Denmark. All crew killed |
| 29th April | EF238 | (S III) 'OJ-H' Pilot Officer IC McArthur. Hit by anti-aircraft fire while on Special Operations mission, but completed mission, crash landing at Methwold due to damaged undercarriage. Damaged beyond repair. No injuries (First NOT killed in 1944 other than the two evaders) |
| 11th May | LK500 | (S III) Swung on take off for Special Operations mission and hit mound. Undercarriage collapsed. Recovered and re-serialled TS262 but then struck off charge. |
| 1st June | LJ501 | (S III) 'OJ-H' Flight Sergeant HV Cutts. Lost on mining operation to Knocke, crashing off Zeebrugge, Belgium. Pilot taken prisoner-of-war. The other six crew were killed. |
| 6th June | LJ621 | (S III) 'OJ-M' Pilot Officer WH Mayo. Lost on Special Operations mission crashing at Marcelet, France. Nine on board six killed, two prisoners of war. Sergeant JAW Nind, a Canadian, evaded capture returning August the 12th |
| 6th June | LK385 | (S III) 'OJ-C' Squadron Leader CJK Hutchins, also nine on board, lost on Special Operations |

| | | |
|---|---|---|
| | | Mission to Caen, crashing at Baudre, France, near St Lô. All crew killed [Squadron records: 7 Aircraft of No.149 Squadron assigned Special Duties related to D Day. OJ-M and OJ-C failed to return] |
| 24th June | EF188 | (S III) 'OJ-M' Pilot P/O EJ Lincoln RAAF. Hit by ack-ack on mining operation to Brest, crashing at Plougonvelin, France. All crew killed |
| 24th June | LK386 | (S III) 'OJ-O' Pilot P/O SE Lucas. Damaged by anti-aircraft fire on mining mission to Brest. Made emergency landing at Hartfordbridge but overshot runway due to failure of brake pressure. Undercarriage collapsed. Two crew injured |
| 25th June | EF140 | (S III) 'OJ-B' Pilot F/Lt JRB Roe. RCAF Lost on raid to flying bomb site at Ruisseauville, crashing into the sea off Boulogne, France. All crew killed |
| 25th June | LK394 | (S III) 'OJ-D' Pilot F/O VF Wunsche. RCAF Shot down by night fighter on raid to flying bomb site at Ruisseauville, crashing at Lisbourg, France. All crew killed |
| 6th July | LJ477 | (S III) 'OJ-M' Pilot Officer CW Holmes DFC. Hit by anti-aircraft fire, jettisoned its load in the English Channel, and crashed at Thorney Island on return from Special Operations mission to site 'Gondolier 16' in France, catching fire on landing. One crew member killed, others received burns. |
| 17th July | LK388 | (S III) 'OJ- L' Flight Sergeant HM Arnott RAAF. Starboard undercarriage collapsed due to heavy landing at Methwold following practice bombing exercise. Aircraft overturned and caught fire. Two gunners thrown clear and killed, Remainder of crew injured. |
| 7th August | LK383 | (S III) 'OJ-A' Pilot Flying Officer DAM Adams. Lost on mining operation off Brest, seen crashing in flames into the sea. All crew killed |

## Lancaster

### 1944

| | | |
|---|---|---|
| 12th December | HK645 | B.1 'OJ-R' Flying Officer EHS Dorey. Shot down on raid to 3 Group G-H raid to Ruhrstahl Steel Works, Witten. Five crew killed, two taken prisoner-of-war. |
| 12th December | HK653 | B.I 'TK-E', OJ-Y. Flying Officer KAW Miller. Shot down by fighter on 3 Group G-H raid to Ruhrstahl Steel Works, Witten. All crew killed |

### 1945

| | | |
|---|---|---|
| 2nd January | NG362 | B.I, 'OJ-S' Overshot runway while landing at Methwold returning from raid on Nuremberg, crashed and burnt. Two crew injured. |
| 2nd/3rd Feb | NN708 | B.1,'OJ-Q', Pilot W/Cdr LH Kay DFC. Shot down, crashing in France, on raid to Wiesbaden, Germany |
| 5th March | NF972 | B.I, 'OJ-H' Pilot F/O TSM Williams. Shot down by anti-aircraft fire in Wesel area on 3 Group G-H raid to Consolidated Benzol plant at Gelsenkirchen. Fire and explosion on board seen. |
| 5th June | PP673 | B.I Lost wing and dived from 2,000 feet into the ground over Arras |
| 19th July | PA166 | B.I 'OJ-B', G, U, Control lost due to icing, crashed |
| 13th August | PB902 | B.III Overshot runway when landing at Trondheim/Vaernes, Norway, undercarriage collapsed. |

### 1946

| | | |
|---|---|---|
| 17th October | PD370 | B.I Damaged 13 July 1946, struck off charge 17.10.46 |

### 1949

| | | |
|---|---|---|
| 14th February. | PA410 | B.I 'OJ-X' Two engines cut, belly landed at Shepherd's Grove |

## Lincoln

### 1949

| | | |
|---|---|---|
| 29th December | RA688 | B.2. New. Undershot landing at Mildenhall, bellylanded; scrapped |

# Appendix IV
# Operational Statistics – No.149 (East India) Squadron
# No 3 Group Bomber Command 1939-1945

**Operational Statistics - All Aircraft Types**

| | |
|---|---|
| Aircraft losses | 131 (2.2%) |
| Sorties dispatched | 5905 |
| Total Operations | 738 |
| Bombing Operations | 567 |
| Minelaying | 160 |

**Squadron performance by Aircraft Type – Bomber Command**

| | | A/C lost | % Loss | Position* |
|---|---|---|---|---|
| *Avro Lancaster* | | 3 | 0.8% | 55 |
| Sorties Despatched | 1630 | | | 40 |
| Total Operations | 110 | | | 41 |
| | | | | |
| *Short Stirling* | | 87 | 3.3% | 3 |
| Sorties Despatched | 2628 | | | 1 |
| Total Operations | 410 | | | 1 |
| | | | | |
| *Vickers Wellington* | | 40 | 2.4% | 12 |
| Sorties Despatched | 1647 | | | 7 |
| Total Operations | 218 | | | 7 |

*Squadron performance within No 3 Group*

| | | | | |
|---|---|---|---|---|
| Operational Losses | | 130 | 2.2% | 4 |
| Sorties Despatched | 5905 | | | 3 |
| Total Operations | 738 | | | 2 |

*Position within all the Squadrons in Bomber Command or Group

**Bomber Command Sorties and Losses**

No 3 Group

| | Sorties | Lost |
|---|---|---|
| Wellington | 20,584 | 608 (3.0%) |
| Stirling | 15,895 | 577 (3.6%) |
| Lancaster | 26,462 | 380 (1.4%) |
| Other (SD, RCM) | 3,672 | 103 (2.5%) |
| | | |
| Total | 66,613 | 1,668 (2.5%) |

**Bomber Command Yearly Statistics 3 September 1939 to 8th May 1945**

| | | |
|---|---|---|
| 1939 | 333 | 33 (10.0%) |
| 1940 | 20,809 | 527 (2.3%) |
| 1941 | 30,608 | 914 (3.0%) |
| 1942 | 35,050 | 1,400 (4.0%) |
| 1943 | 64,528 | 2,314 (3.6%) |
| 1944 | 57,448 | 2,573 (1.6%) |
| 1945 | 64,738 | 599 (0.9%) |

*Does not include SOE or Minelaying Operations*

**Total Command Sorties and Losses All Types**

| *Sorties* | *Losses* | *Operational Crashes* |
|---|---|---|
| 389,809 | 8,953 (2.3%) | 1,368 (0.35%) |
| Total Bomb Tonnage | 955,044 approx | |
| Nights with Operations | 1,481 (71.4% of nights during the war) | |
| Days with Operations | 1,089 (52.5% of days during the war) | |
| Night Sorties | 307,253 | Losses 7,953 |
| Day Sorties | 80,163 | Losses 1,000 |

**Minelaying and Other Operations Against Shipping**

| | |
|---|---|
| No of Sea Mines laid | 47,307 |
| Approximate Tonnage | 30,000 |
| Vessels Destroyed | 1,102 |
| Approx Tonnage Lost | 1.1 Million |

**Aircrew Casualties**

| | |
|---|---|
| Killed in Action | 47,268 |
| Killed in Accidents | 4,195 |
| Killed in Ground Action | 37 |
| *Total Killed* | 55,500 |
| Prisoners-of-war | 9,838 |
| Wounded on Operations | 4,200 |
| Injured in Accidents | 4,203 |
| **Total Casualties** | 73,743 |

**Aircrew Casualties by Nationality**

| | |
|---|---|
| Royal Air Force | 38,462 (69.2%) |
| Royal Canadian Air Force | 9,919 (17.8%) |
| Royal Australian Air Force | 4,050 (7.3%) |
| Royal New Zealand Air Force | 1,679 (3.0%) |
| Polish Air Force | 929 (1.7%) |
| Other Allied Air Forces | 473 (0.9%) |
| South African Air Force | 34 (0.1%) |
| Other Dominions | 27 |

**Aircrew Casualties by Rank**

| | |
|---|---|
| Officers | 27.6% |
| Warrant Officers | 3.3% |
| NCOs | 69.1% |

**Air Officers Commanding No.3 Group**

| | |
|---|---|
| Air Vice-Marshal J.E.A. Baldwin | 22nd August 1939 |
| Air Vice-Marshal The Hon. R.A. Cochrane | 19th September 1942 |
| Air Vice-Marshal R.Harrison | 27th February 1943 |

**Commanding Officers – No.149 (East India) Squadron RAF**

| | |
|---|---|
| Major B P Greenwood | 3.3.18 |
| Wing Commander E H Richardson | 8.6.37 |
| Wing Commander G H Russell DFC | 22.12.38 |
| Wing Commander R Kellett DFC AFC | 2.11.39 |
| Wing Commander J R Whitley AFC | 10.5.40 |
| Wing Commander J A Powell DSO CBE | 28.11.40 |
| Wing Commander W R Boaman | 9.5.41 |
| Wing Commander G J Spence | 25.11.41 |
| Wing Commander C Charlton-Jones | 17.5.42 |
| Wing Commander K M M Wasse DFC | 1.9.42 |
| Wing Commander G M Harrison (Silver Star) | 23.3.43 |
| Wing Commander C B E Wigfall | 26.10.43 |
| Wing Commander M E Pickford DFC | 7.5.44 |
| Wing Commander Kay | 31.1.45 |
| Wing Commander W D Chilton DSO DFC AFC | 25.2.45 |
| Squadron Leader B C Versey | 5.9.45 |
| Wing Commander J Kennedy | 24.9.45 |
| Squadron Leader K Ruskell DFC | 16.4.46 |
| Wing Commander F R Foster | 22.1.47 |
| Squadron Leader A B Goldie | 7.5.47 |
| Squadron Leader K H Blair | 14.5.48 |
| Squadron Leader Canton MBE DFC | 13.8.49 |
| Squadron Leader J Finch DFC AFC | 12.5.52 |
| Flt Lieutenant K J Ryall DFC | 15.1.53 |
| Flt Lieutenant F Fruin | 4.2.53 |
| Squadron Leader R E R Adams | 16.3.53 |
| Flt Lieutenant K J Ryall DFC | 8.3.54 |
| Squadron Leader R E R Adams | 24.5.54 |
| Squadron Leader J P E Peters | 10.9.55 |

# Appendix V
# Signals, Codes and Frequencies

**RAF 'X' signals (in use until December 1943)**

| | |
|---|---|
| X100 | Affirmative |
| X114 | Negative |
| X194 | Airborne |
| X195 | I am about to reel in trailing aerial |
| X279 | What strength are my signals |
| X291 | Your signals are loud and clear |
| X496 | Closing down now |
| X680 | Your magnetic course to steer to reach me is......... |
| X700 | What is my true bearing in relation to you |
| X702 | What is my position |
| X901 | Landed. |

The RAF abandoned its 'X' signals in late 1943 so as to fall in line with American W/T and R/T procedure, in readiness for the coming Second Front.

**'Q' codes (used from December 1943 onwards)**

| | |
|---|---|
| QBB | The height of base of low cloud at.........is........ |
| QDM | Your magnetic course to steer to reach me is....... |
| QFE | Barometric pressure at your aerodrome level is..... |
| QTF | Your position was.....latitude......longitude....... |
| QMF | How does my frequency check |
| QSY | I am changing frequency to .......................... |
| QRM | Are you being interfered with (used especially to WAAF R/T Operatives) |
| QGP | What is my turn for landing |
| QTG | Send your call sign, followed by 50 sec dash |
| QSA | What is the strength of my signals (1 to 5) |

**RAF H/F D/F Station call signs and frequencies and R/T call signs used by 3 Group Bomber Command.**

| | KC/S | C/S | R/T Call Sign |
|---|---|---|---|
| Abingdon | 3270 | 7DD | Peeloff |
| Benson | 4140 | M5M | Digdeep |
| Boscombe Down | 3355 | K7B | Pugla |
| Chipping Warden | 3720 | CO8 | Payoff |
| Coltishall | 3250 | 8JU | Manlove |
| Downham Market | 3470 | 6CD | Offstrike |
| Feltwell | 3170 | T3C | Dewpool |
| Harwell | 3430 | B6B | Poundweight |
| Market Harborough | 3080 | Q90 | Bigtrout |
| Methwold | 3170 | T3C | Highheel |
| Mildenhall | 3705 | 7UM | Redcoat |
| Pershore | 4110 | AX3 | Sideslip |
| Stradishall | 4055 | K8R | Halma |
| Tempsford | 3630 | 6CA | Brasstray |
| Upper Heyford | 4185 | H3D | Shelllike |
| Waterbeach | 3690 | V9V | Nectar |
| Westcott | 3830 | O7F | Pepsin |
| Wing | 3245 | P5B | Bridsmiles |
| Wyton | 3290 | Q5B | Beachline |

# Appendix VI
# Bombs, Mines and Incendiaries dropped by No.149 Squadron

## World War I

20 lb Cooper Mk I. Fragmentation. Amatol (Ammonium Nitrate/TNT) filled.

112 lb H.E. R.L. (High Explosive, Royal Laboratory) Mk I. TNT or Amatol filled. Could be set with a delay of up to 15 seconds after impact for low level bombing, to give the aircraft sufficient time to clear the area.

230 lb H.E. RFC Mk III. 40/60 Amatol filled. Light casing. Could be delayed up to 15 seconds

40 lb Incendiary. Phosphorus mixture filled.

Michelin Flare, Reconnaissance, designed to be dropped from the Michelin bomb rack.

## World War II

### Bombs

250 lb GP* (General Purpose)
250 lb USA GP (General purpose)
500 lb GP*.(General purpose)
500 lb MC* (Medium Capacity)
500 lb HE (High Explosive)
500 lb SAP (Semi-armour-piercing)
500 lb ANM44 (Medium Capacity)
(US bombs, AN = Army or Navy use, M = Military)
500 lb ANM58 (Semi-armour-piercing)
500 lb ANM64* (Medium capacity)
1,000 lb MC* (Medium Capacity)
1,000 lb SAP (Semi-armour-piercing)
1,000 lb AMN59 (Semi-Armour-piercing)
1,000 lb ANM65 (General purpose)
2000lb AP (Armour-piercing)
4,000lb HC Mark I with drogue 'chute
4,000lb HC. Mark IV Minol (High Capacity) 40% TNT, 40% Ammonium nitrate, 20% Aluminium powder
4,000 lb HC Mark IV, T.N.T.
4,000 lb HC Mark IV, Amatol

*Had possible time delay (TD) followed by the delay time in seconds to hours, up to 144 hours, commonly as little as 0.025 seconds for slight initial penetration before explosion.*

### Incendiaries

4 lb Incendiary, Hexagonal, filled with thermite pellets and magnesium alloy body, with and without explosive charge (Explosive charge type identified by 'X') Possibly in 500lb clusters or in 90s from SBCs (Small bomb containers).

30 lb Incendiary filled with phosphorus and rubberised benzol.

Incendiary leaves (Code name 'Razzle') Phosphorus between celluloid strips 3" x 1", 500 leaves per alcohol/water container, poured down flare chute.

### Mines

1,500 lb A Mk I-IV Sea mine, 750 lb of explosive, Amatol or Minol. Fitted with a number of trigger mechanisms including magnetic and acoustic.

2,000 lb A Mk IV Sea mine, 1,030 lb of explosive. Multiple triggers as for 1,500 lb sea mine.

### Miscellaneous

250 lb. TI (Target Indicator) various colours

Special Operations Executive containers and packages. Arms and supplies to the Resistance. Containers typically 5' 6" long, 14" across, circular cross section, dropped by either centre- or end-mounted parachute.

One-third scale dummy parachutists with equivalent scale parachute, fitted with pyrotechnics to operate on impact. D-day diversionary operation.

# Appendix VII: 'G-H' and No.149 Squadron
## Airborne Radar Navigation and Bombing Aid to Bomber Command

World War Two began with RAF Bomber Command having to navigate and bomb entirely by the navigational skill of the aircraft. 'Observers' later titled 'Navigators', and the number of aircraft which lost their way, could not find the target, or bombed miles away from it as indicated by the Butt Report highlighted only too clearly that alternate means were needed.

The first radar navigation aid was 'Gee' which worked from three ground transmitter stations together with a receiver in the aircraft, and an indicator to display the findings. The method gave two co-ordinates, which with the aid of a 'Gee' map, enabled the navigator to determine where they were within one to four hundred yards, and initially with a range of 400 miles. Germany soon jammed the system but it was still effective up to the European coast. A 'Gee' set was eventually carried in every Bomber Command aircraft and in many bomber aircraft of the 8th Air Force. The second aid was 'H2S', which gave a display on an indicator as to the outline of built-up areas and water masses below, which could aid navigation, with the assistance of an 'H2S' map, and would also allow carpet bombing. The later Marks of 'H2S' were even linked in with the bomb computer.

The third was No.8 Group, the Pathfinder Force of Bomber Command, with skilled navigators, who could mark the target using target markers on which the main force could bomb. No.8 Group needed assistance too, and so they used the latest Mark of 'H2S', and later, 'Oboe', and then the Master Bomber, flying at a much lower altitude, who, like an orchestra conductor, would control the complete operation.

'Oboe' worked from two stations in England some distance apart, known as the 'cat' and the 'mouse', each sending a signal to a high-flying 'Oboe'-carrying Mosquito from 105 or 109 Squadron, who would return the signal. The time taken for each signal could be converted to a precise distance and so the exact position of the Mosquito was known. By pre-determination, the pilot of the Mosquito could be controlled to fly on an arc of a circle passing through the target by one transmitter, while the other transmitter gave instructions to the Navigator/Bomb Aimer to drop the target markers. This system allowed only one Mosquito to be controlled every ten minutes, and to keep the target markers going, Pathfinder Lancasters needed to visually bomb on these with further target markers to keep the target lit. Even with later systems enabling more Mosquitoes to use 'Oboe', it still was limiting. But it was accurate.

Then came 'G-H'. This operated on similar principles to 'Gee', but the transmitter was carried in the aircraft, considerably increasing the range. Like 'Oboe' it would have its limitations as to how many aircraft the two ground transmitters could handle, but by blacking out eight of ten of the trigger pulses, the number of aircraft could be increased considerably. Instead of the two 'Gee' units to make up the airborne radar set this was increased to five, and the equipment was issued to only one Group, No.3 Group, and that included No.149 Squadron. The installation into No.3 Group's Lancasters began in late 1944, and a radar school was opened in Feltwell to bring the No.3 Group radar mechanics up to competency. All 'G-H' trained radar mechanics not only knew the principles on which 'G-H' functioned, they could operate, inspect and maintain this complex equipment even to diagnosing and repairing any electronic faults which developed, and in those days, with the level of unreliability of electronic components, it was often. A Lancaster 'G-H' training flight was also set up at Feltwell, also 'G-H' ground trainers installed at each base for the air crew, and it was common for navigators to occasionally pop into the radar section for a little further education or brush-up from one of the mechanics.

'H2S' was fitted almost entirely throughout the Lancasters of No.3 Group, although not being fitted in the extended bomb bay versions, as this prevented their being fitted with an 'H2S' scanner. 'G-H' could operate as a normal 'Gee' set as needed and so any 'G-H' carrying aircraft had the 'G-H' indicator and receiver in the normal 'Gee' locations, the indicator over the navigator's table, the receiver underneath. The fins of the No.3 Group 'G-H' aircraft carried two broad horizontal yellow stripes to allow non-'G-H'-carrying Lancasters to formate on them and then bomb in unison.

From late 1944 until the end of the war, No.3 Group aircraft were capable of acting as their own Pathfinders, working independently of other Groups and bombing with a precision approaching that of 'Oboe'. Occasionally it was better. The 'G-H' equipment and Air Publication manuals relating to it were naturally top secret, and remained so until 1975.

# Appendix VIII
# Bomber Command Minelaying Area Codes 1940 – 1945

*Below is a table with a list of the codes given to 'sea lanes' and areas that Bomber Command dropped mines in. The codeword for a mining operation was "Gardening", and the area codes used generally followed a horticultural theme, although there were a few exceptions, as can be seen from the list below. We are sure that this list is probably by no means exhaustive. The codes are listed alphabetically below. The 'codeword' used is shown first, with the area or lane name following.*

| | | | | | |
|---|---|---|---|---|---|
| Anemones | – Le Havre | Geranium | – Swinemunde | Rosemary | – Heligoland |
| Artichokes | – Lorient | Gorse | – Quiberon | Scallops | – Rouen |
| Asparagus | – Green Belt | Greengage | – Cherbourg | Silverthorn | – Kattegat Areas |
| Barnacle | – Zeebrugge | Jasmine | – Travemunde | Sweet Peas | – Rostock and Arcona Light |
| Beech | – St Nazaire | Jellyfish | – Brest | | |
| Bottle | – Haugesund | Juniper | – Antwerp | Tangerine | – Pillau |
| Broccoli | – Great Belt | Krauts | – Lim Fjord | Tomato | – Oslo Fjord Approaches |
| Carrots | – Little Belt | Lettuces | – Kiel Canal | Trefoils | – Texel (South) |
| Cinnamon | – La Rochelle | Limpets | – Den Helder | Turbot | – Ostend |
| Cypress | – Dunkerque | Melon | – Kiel Canal | Undergrowth | – Kattegat |
| Daffodil | – The Sound | Mullet | – Spezia | Verbena | – Copenhagen Approaches |
| Deodar | – Bordeaux | Mussels | – Terschelling Gat | | |
| Dewberry | – Boulogne-sur-Mer | Nasturtiums | – The Sound | Vine Leaves | – Dieppe |
| Eglantine | – Heligoland Approaches | Nectarines | – Friesian Islands | Wallflowers | – Kiel Bay |
| Elderberry | – Bayonne | Newt | – Maas and Scheldt | Welks | – Zuider Zee |
| Endives | – Little Belt | Onions | – Oslo | Willows | – Arcona to River Dievenow |
| Flounder | – Maas and Scheldt | Oysters | – Rotterdam | | |
| Forget-me-Nots | – Kiel Canal | Prawns | – Calais | Xeranthemums | – River Jade |
| Furze | – St Jean de Luz | Privet | – Danzig | Yams | – Heligoland Approaches |
| Hawthorn | – Esbjerg Approaches | Pumpkins | – Great Belt | Yewtree | – Kattegat |
| Hollyhock | – Travemunde | Quinces | – Great Belt / Kiel Bay | Zinneas | – River Jade |
| Hyacinth | – St Malo | Radishes | – Kiel Bay | | |

---

# Appendix IX
# Operations 'Manna' and 'Exodus' Statistics

**Operation 'Manna'**

| | |
|---|---|
| 30th April 1945 | 21 aircraft assigned to drop supplies Rotterdam area, 79 2/3 packages dropped |
| 1st May 1945 | 21 aircraft assigned to drop supplies at site 1A – The Hague, 89 packages dropped. |
| 2nd May 1945 | 21 aircraft assigned to drop supplies at site 1A – The Hague, 79 packages dropped. |
| 3rd May 1945 | 21 aircraft assigned to drop supplies at site 1A – The Hague, 57 packages dropped. |
| 4th May 1945 | 6 aircraft assigned to drop supplies at site 1A – The Hague, 30 packages dropped. |
| 5th May 1945 | 6 aircraft assigned to drop supplies at site 1A – The Hague, 24 packages dropped. |
| 6th May 1945 | No flying. |
| 7th May 1945 | 24 aircraft assigned to drop supplies at site 2 – Gouda, 97 packages dropped. |
| 8th May 1945 | 6 aircraft assigned to drop supplies at site 1E – Delft, 29 packages dropped. |

*During Operation 'Manna' the Squadron completed 96 sorties and dropped some 405 packages to the Dutch population.*

**Operation 'Exodus'**

| | |
|---|---|
| 10th May 1945 | 15 aircraft assigned to Juvincourt returned to Westcott, 360 POWs repatriated. |
| 11th May 1945 | 15 aircraft assigned to Juvincourt returned to Tangmere, 384 POWs repatriated. |
| 12th May 1945 | 2 aircraft assigned to Juvincourt returned to Wing, 48 POWs repatriated. |
| 13th May 1945 | 15 aircraft assigned to Juvincourt returned to Oakley, 360 POWs repatriated. |
| 14th May 1945 | 14 aircraft assigned to Juvincourt returned to Oakley, 336 POWs repatriated. |
| 16th May 1945 | 4 aircraft assigned to Juvincourt returned to Wing, 96 POWs repatriated. |
| 21st May 1945 | 21 aircraft assigned to Juvincourt returned to Dunsfold, 333 POWs repatriated. |
| 23rd May 1945 | 15 aircraft assigned to Juvincourt returned to Oakley, 360 POWs repatriated. |
| 27th May 1945 | 10 aircraft assigned to Juvincourt returned to Oakley, 193 POWs repatriated. |

*In total No.149 Squadron flew 106 sorties from Methwold and returned some 2,470 POWs. In addition some 945 POWs were repatriated through Methwold, mostly Indian.*

# Appendix X
# Extracts from The United Services Review 21st October, 1937

**Notes on No.149 Squadron:**

Quite a good book could be written on the subject of the development of night flying during the war and of the achievements of the gallant fellows who, in the words of Tennyson:-

*'......while their companions slept*
*Were toiling upwards in the night'*

One of the Squadrons so employed was No.149, the title of which has now been passed to one of the new bomber formations at Mildenhall.

Its record of service was a fine one and earned a special commendation from Maj-Gen J M Salmond, commanding the RAF in the Field, after the Armistice.

Addressing the officers of the Squadron on 2nd January, 1919, he said,

"I am proud of you, and not I alone but the Air Ministry and England as a whole, for the large part that you and other night-flying Squadrons have played in bringing about the successful conclusion of hostilities".

After the Armistice.No.149 Squadron was the only one equipped with F.E.2b machines, and was chosen to accompany the Army of Occupation, moving up to Bickendorf, Cologne, on Christmas Eve, 1918.

These machines, fitted with 160 hp Beardmore engines, proved reliable in service. Out of the eighteen, which were flown across with the unit, seven were still in service on the day of the Armistice.

The Squadron was formed for night flying at Yapton, Sussex, on 3rd March, 1918, under Maj. B P Greenwood, and the flying officers were trained entirely in the home defence Squadron of 6th Brigade.

Assembling of personnel and equipment was complete by 22nd May; transport and stores left for embarkation at Southampton on the 27th; and three days later these were followed by all personnel not flying across.

The machines flew over in Squadron formation on 2nd June, led by Maj. Greenwood, and landed at Marquise. Two days later the flight was resumed to Quelmes, where the transport and personnel rejoined during the night.

Other stations occupied by the Squadron after joining the BEF were: - Alquines, 16th June - 16th September, Clairmarais, 16th September - 25th October, Quesnoy, 25th October - 26th November, and Fort de Cognelée (Namur), 26th November - 24th December.

A salient feature of every move was that in no case was a single machine lost or left behind, despite the bad weather conditions, which prevailed on each occasion.

For this the excellent training before coming out was no doubt largely responsible. Of the original pilots only one had failed to complete 100 hours or more flying previous to transfer overseas. The number of forced landings on night raids, which were effected safely, was attributed to this fact.

Seventeen aircraft landed without hurt to pilot or observer away from aerodromes, one machine on the night of 16-17th September only just succeeding in re-crossing the lines. Two machines landed safely behind German lines. Only one pilot and one observer were killed.

The period of active service extended from the night of 23rd-24th June until the night of 10-11th November, and machines were actually still in the air when the news of the signing of the Armistice came through.

In these 4½ months a total of just 80 tons of bombs were dropped and 161 reconnaissances were carried out. It should be remembered that during the whole period only on a few nights were the conditions really good. Haze, ground mist, clouds, and rain invariably succeeded each other.

The Squadron may be said to have reached its peak of activity during the Allied advance on the nights of 27-28th September and 28-29th September, when over twelve tons of bombs were dropped in front of the Ypres salient. Two pilots made nine raids on those two nights; two others, eight; and several had seven to their credit.

# Appendix XI
# No.149 (NB) Squadron RFC /No.149 (NB) Squadron RAF/ No.149 (East India) Squadron
# Historical Summary

**Stations and Movements**

| | |
|---|---|
| 1st March 1918 | Formed as No.149 (NB) Squadron RFC at Ford Junction, Sussex (F.E.2b/d) from 148 Squadron RFC. |
| 1st April 1918 | Became No.149 (NB) Squadron RAF at Ford Junction, Sussex |
| 2nd June 1918 | To Marquise, France from Ford Junction |
| 4th June 1918 | Moved to Quelmes |
| 16th June 1918 | Alquines |
| 16th September 1918 | Clairmarais |
| 25th October 1918 | Quesnoy |
| 26th November 1918 | Fort de Cognelée (Namur) |
| 24th December 1918 | Bickendorf, Germany as part of the Army of Occupation |
| 26th March 1919 | Tallaght, Ireland |
| 1st August 1919 | Disbanded at Tallaght, Ireland. (F.E.2b/d) |
| 12th April 1937 | Reformed from 'B' Flt No.99 Squadron at Mildenhall, Suffolk (Heyfords) |
| 6th September 5th October 1939 | Temporarily dispersed to Netheravon, Wiltshire (Wellington) |
| March 1940 | Detachment to Salon-en-Provence, France (Wellington) |
| November 1941 | Detachments at Lakenheath, Suffolk (Stirling) |
| 21st January 1942 | Formed No.149 Squadron Conversion Flight Mildenhall (Stirling) |
| 6th April 1942 | To Lakenheath (Stirling) |
| 7th October 1942 | Disbanded No.149 Conversion Flight at Lakenheath, merged with 7, 101 and 218 Squadron Conversion Flights to become 1657 Heavy Conversion Unit (Stirling) |
| February 1943 | Detachments to Tempsford (SOE Ops/Stirling) |
| 15th May 1944 | To Methwold, Norfolk (Stirling/ re-equipped Lancaster August/Sep 44) |
| December 1944 | Detachment to Woodbridge (Adverse weather/ Lancaster) |
| 29th April 1946 | To Tuddenham; Detachments to Pomigliano, Italy |
| 4th November 1946 | To Stradishall; Detachments to Shallufa, Egypt |
| 1st March 1950 | Disbanded at Mildenhall (Lincoln) |
| 9th August 1950 | Reformed Marham (Washington) |
| 31st August 1956 | Disbanded Gutersloh, Germany (Canberra) |

**Squadron Codes**

| | |
|---|---|
| 1938/9 | LY |
| 1939/50 | OJ |
| 1944 | TK for 'C' Flight. |

**Films in which the Squadron featured**

'The Lion has Wings'
'Target for Tonight'
'Journey Together'

# Bibliography

Ashworth, C. RAF Bomber Command.
Patrick Stephens Ltd. 1995

Barker, R. The Thousand Plan. Chatto and Windus Ltd. 1975

Blake, R, Hodgson, M, and Taylor, W.
The Airfields of Lincolnshire Since 1912.
Midland Counties Publications, 1984.

Bowman, M.W. and Boiten, T. Raiders of the Reich.
Airlife Publishing Ltd. 1996

Bowman, M.W. Wellington, The Geodetic Giant.
Airlife Publishing Ltd. 1989

Bowyer, M.J.F. Action Stations I. Wartime Military Airfields of East Anglia 1939-1945. Patrick Stephens Ltd. 1979

Bowyer, M.J.F. Aircraft for the Few.
Patrick Stephens Ltd. 1991

Bowyer, M.J.F. The Stirling Bomber.
Faber and Faber Ltd. 1980

Bowyer, C. Air War Over Europe, 1939-1945.
William Kimber and Co. Ltd. 1981

Bowyer, C. The Wellington Bomber.
William Kimber and Co. Ltd. 1986

Bowyer, C. Wellington at War. Ian Allan Ltd. 1982

Bruce, J.M. RAF F.E.2b, Windsock Data File 18.
Albatross Publications Ltd. 1989

Caidin, M. The Night Hamburg Died. Ballantine Books. 1960

Chant, C. The Encyclopedia of Code Names in World War II.
Routledge & Keegan Paul Ltd. 1986

Chorley, W.R. Royal Air Force Bomber Command Losses of the Second World War 6 Vols. 1939-1945. 1992-1997

Clutten-Brock, O. Massacre Over the Marne.
Patrick Stephens Ltd. 1994

Cole, C. (ed) Royal Air Force Communiqués 1918.
Tom Donovan Publishing Ltd. 1969

Cooke, R.C. and Nesbit, R.C. Target: Hitler's Oil.
William Kimber and Co. Ltd. 1985

Cooksley, P.G. Wellington, Mainstay of Bomber Command.
Patrick Stephens Ltd. 1987

Cooper, A.W. Air Battle of the Ruhr.
Airlife Publishing Ltd. 1992

Cooper, A.W. Bombers Over Berlin.
William Kimber and Co. 1985

Cross, R. The Bombers. Macmillan Publishing Co. 1987

Delve, K. D-Day, The Air Battle.
Arms and Armour Press. 1994

Delve, K. and Jacobs, P. The Six Year Offensive.
Arms and Armour Press. 1992

Delve, K. The Source Book of the R.A.F.
Airlife Publishing Ltd. 1994

Dring, C.M. A History of RAF Mildenhall.
Mildenhall Museum Publications. 1980

Fairhead, H. and Tuffen, R. Norfolk and Suffolk Airfields and Airstrips Part I. Norfolk and Suffolk Aviation Museum Publications. 1987

Fairhead, H. and Tuffen, R. Norfolk and Suffolk Airfields and Airstrips Part 3. Norfolk and Suffolk Aviation Museum Publications. 1981

Fairhead, H. and Tuffen, R. Norfolk and Suffolk Airfields and Airstrips Part 6. Norfolk and Suffolk Aviation Museum Publications. 1989

Falconer, J. Stirling at War. Ian Allan Ltd. 1991

Falconer, J. Stirling Wings. Alan Sutton Publishing Ltd. 1995

Fopp, M.A. The Washington File.
Air-Britain (Historians) Ltd. 1983

Frankland, N. The Bombing Offensive Against Germany.
Faber and Faber 1965

Franks, N. Forever Strong.
Random Century New Zealand Ltd. 1991

Freeman, R.A. Raiding the Reich.
Arms and Armour Press. 1997

Frere-Cook, G. The Attacks on the Tirpitz. Ian Allan Ltd. 1973

Garbett, M and Goulding, B. The Lancaster at War.
Ian Allan Ltd. 1971

Garbett, M. and Goulding, B. The Lancaster at War 2.
Ian Allan Ltd. 1979

Garbett, M. and Goulding, B. Lancaster at War 3.
Ian Allan Ltd. 1984

Garbett, M. and Goulding, B. Lancaster at War 5.
Fifty Years On. Ian Allan Ltd. 1995

Gomersall, B. The Stirling File (revised Ed.).
Air-Britain (Historians) Ltd. 1987

Goulding, J. & Moyes, P. RAF Bomber Command & Its Aircraft 1936-1940. Ian Allan Ltd. 1975

Goulding, J. & Moyes, P. RAF Bomber Command & Its Aircraft 1941-1945. Ian Allan Ltd. 1978

Halley, J.J. The K File. The Royal Air Force of the 1930s.
Air-Britain (Historians) Ltd, 1995

Halley, J.J. Royal Air Force Aircraft L1000-N9999.
Air-Britain (Historians) Ltd. 1993

Halley, J.J. Royal Air Force Aircraft P1000-R9999.
Air-Britain (Historians) Ltd. 1996

Halley, J.J. The Squadrons of the Royal Air Force & Commonwealth 1918-1988.
Air-Britain (Historians) Ltd. 1988

Halley, J.J. The Lancaster File.
Air-Britain (Historians) Ltd. 1985

Hamilton, A. Wings of Night.
William Kimber and Co. Ltd. 1977

Harris, Sir A.T. Bomber Offensive. Collins, 1947

Harris, Sir A.T. Dispatch on War Operations.
Frank Cass and Co. 1995

Hartcup, G. Camouflage. Charles Schribner's Sons. 1980

Hastings, M. Bomber Command. Michael Joseph Ltd. 1979

Hazard, B. and Dean, D.F.E.C. They're Not Shooting at You Now, Granddad. S.B.Hazard. 1991

Hinchliffe, P. The Other Battle. Airlife Publishing Ltd. 1996

Holmes, H. Lancaster, the Definitive Record.
Airlife Publishing Ltd. 1997

Holt, P. Target for Tonight. Hutchinson and Co. Ltd. (1941?)

Holmes, R. One of Our Aircraft. Quiller Press. 1991

Irving, D. The Destruction of Dresden.
    William Kimber and Co. Ltd. 1963
Jacobs, P. The Lancaster Story. Arms and Armour Press. 1996
Jackson, R. Before the Storm. Arthur Barker Ltd. 1972
Jackson, R. Canberra, The Operational Record.
    Smithsonian Institution Press. 1989
Jefford, C.G. R.A.F. Squadrons. Airlife Publishing Ltd. 1988
Jackson, R. Storm from the Skies. Arthur Barker Ltd. 1974
Jones, N. The Beginnings of Strategic Air Power.
    Frank Cass and Co. Ltd. 1987
Jones, N. The Origins of Strategic Bombing.
    William Kimber and Co. Ltd. 1973
Jones, R.V. Most Secret War. Hamish Hamilton Ltd. 1978
Lacey-Johnson, L. Point Blank and Beyond.
    Airlife Publishing Ltd.. 1991
Lamberton, W.M. et al. Reconnaissance and Bomber Aircraft of the 1914-1918 War. Harleyford. 1962
Liddle, P.H. The Airman's War 1914-1918.
    Blandford Press. 1987
Longmate, N. The Bombers. Hutchinson and Co.Ltd. 1983
Lorain, P. Secret Warfare. Orbis Publishing Co. 1983
Lumsden, A. Wellington Special. Ian Allan Ltd. 1974
MacBean, J.A. and Hogben, A.S. Bombs Gone.
    Patrick Stephens Ltd. 1990
MacMillan, N. The Royal Air Force in the World War
    Vols I to IV. George G. Harrap & Co. Ltd.1950
Mason, F.K. The Avro Lancaster. Aston Publications. 1989
Mayhill, R. Bombs on Target. Patrick Stephens Ltd. 1991
McKee, A. Dresden 1945. Granada Publishing Ltd. 1983
Messenger, C. Cologne, The First 1,000 Bomber Raid.
    Ian Allan Ltd. 1982
Middlebrook, M. The Battle of Hamburg.
    Allen Lane, Penguin Books Ltd. 1980
Middlebrook, M. The Berlin Raids. Viking Penguin Inc. 1988
Middlebrook, M. and Everitt, C. The Bomber Command War Diaries. Midland Counties Publications. 1985
Middlebrook, M. The Nuremberg Raid.
    Allen Lane, Penguin Books Ltd. 1973
Middlebrook, M. The Peenemunde Raid.
    Allen Lane, Penguin Books Ltd. 1982
Morris, A. First of the Many. Jarrolds. 1968
Moyes, P.J R. Bomber Squadrons of the R.A.F.
    and Their Aircraft. Macdonald and Janes 1964
Musgrove, G. Operation Gomorrah.
    Janes Publishing Company Ltd. 1981
Odenwater, H. Operation Manna/Chowhound Romen
    Luchtvaart, Unieboek bv. 1985
Overy, R.J. The Air War 1939-1945.
    Europa Publications Ltd. 1980
Overy, R.J. Bomber Command 1939-1945.
    Harper Collins Publishers. 1997
Phillips, J.A. Valley of the Shadow of Death.
    Air Research Publications. 1991
Price, A. Battle over the Reich.
    Charles Schribner's Sons. 1973

Price, A. The Bomber in World War II.
    Charles Schribner's Sons. 1976
Price, A. The Luftwaffe Handbook, 1939-1945.
    Ian Allan Ltd. 1977
Rickson, P.A. and Holliday, A. Mission Accomplished.
    William Kimber and Co. Ltd. 1974
Robertson, B. et al. Lancaster, the Story of a Famous Bomber.
    Harleyford Publications Ltd. 1964
Rostow, W.W. Pre-Invasion Bombing Strategy.
    Gower Publishing Company Inc. 1981
Searby, J. The Bomber Battle for Berlin.
    Airlife Publishing Inc. 1991
Searby, J. The Great Raids, Essen. The Nutshell Press. 1978
Searby, J. The Great Raids, Peenemunde.
    The Nutshell Press. 1978
Shirer, W.L. Berlin Diary. Alfred A. Knopf. 1942
Smith, D.J. Vickers Wellington Crash Log Vol I. 1937-1942.
    Private Publication.
Smith, P. C. Royal Air Force Squadron Badges.
    Balfour Productions
St. G. Saunders, H. Per Ardua. Oxford University Press. 1944
St. G. Sanders, H. and Richards, D.
    Royal Air Force 1939-1945, Vols 1-3. HMSO 1975
Sweet, T. Enemy Below. Square One Publications. 1991
Taylor, E. Operation Millennium. Robert Hale Ltd. 1987
Taylor, J.W.R. Pictorial History of the RAF Vol I 1918-1939.
    Ian Allan Ltd. 1974
Taylor, J.W.R. Pictorial History of the RAF Vol II 1939-1945.
    Ian Allan Ltd. 1969
Terraine. J. The Right of the Line.
    Hodder and Staughton. 1985
Thetford, O.G. & Riding, E.J. Aircraft of the 1914-1918 War.
    Harborough Publishing Co 1954.
Thorne, A. Lancaster at War 4, Pathfinder Squadron.
    Ian Allan Ltd. 1990
Verrier, A. The Bomber Offensive. B.T.Batsford Ltd. 1968
Webster, Sir C. and Franklin, N. The Strategic Air Offensive Against Germany Vols I-IV. H.M.S.O 1961
Wells, M.K. Courage and Air Warfare.
    Frank Cass and Co. Ltd. 1995
Young, R.A. The Flying Bomb. Ian Allan Ltd. 1978

**Public Record Office, Kew, London**

Air 1 First World War Records

Air 27/1004 No.149 Squadron Record Book

Air 27/1006 Miscellaneous Records, No.149 Squadron

**Miscellaneous References/Organisations**

Imperial War Museum, London – Photographic Department

Bomber Command Museum, Hendon

Mildenhall Museum, Mildenhall, Suffolk, UK

Bomber Command Historical Society, Cardiff, South Wales
    (Independent Organisation)

Air Crew Association

Stirling Association

# Index

*Note: Picture denoted by (p) with page number preceding.*

**PERSONNEL**
Abbott, Roy, 67,75
Abrams, R.W. Sgt, 112
Acton, N. Sgt, 109
Adams, D.A.M., P/O, 134
Adams, G.R.N. P/O, 107
Adams, R.E.R. S/Ldr, 103,135
Adams, F/O, 75,113
Adams, M.E. Sgt, 115
Adams, P/O, 67
Aitken. P/O, 15,106
Alexander, G.W. S/Ldr, 108,131
Alexander, W/Cdr, 56
Allan, S. Sgt, 112
Allen, B.D. Sgt, 109
Allnatt, A.A. Sgt, 107
Alpe, J.F. Sgt, 110
Alsop, A. Sgt, 109
Anderson, G.D. Sgt, 115
Anderson, V.G. F/Sgt, 115
Andrews, L.V. S/Ldr, 29,109,114,129
Andrews, R.B. Sgt, 111
Arnott, H.M. F/Sgt, 134
Ashley, F.H.J. F/Sgt, 58,132
Ashley, George, 'Bird In Hand' landlord, 28
Ashton, D.E. Sgt, 112
Ashton, G.R. S/Ldr, 15,18
Asquith, Lord, 7
Atkinson, J. Sgt, 111
Austin, Alan Sgt, 45,46,52,78,79,80,130
Austin, F.J. P/O, 115
Avedisian, J.T. Sgt, 109
Ayers, R.J. F/Sgt, 66,112,133
Badcock, D.H.W. F/Sgt, 111
Bailey, J. Sgt, 114
Bailey, L.W. P/O, 52,108,130
Baille J.H. Sgt, 108
Baker, D.A. Sgt, 56,115,131
Baker, G. Sgt, 108
Baker, 'Tubby', (74p), (84p)
Baker, W.L. F/O, 112
Balch, 25,26
Baldwin, J.E.A. AVM, 19,50,135
Ballantyne, R. Sgt, 106
Barker, Clark Sgt, 59,60,63
Barker, J. Mrs, 60
Barker, J.C. Sgt, 116
Barnard, H.G. Sgt, 117
Barnard, L.J. Sgt, 109
Barnes, H.R. Sgt, 114
Barnes, W.G. F/O, 51,56,108,130
Barnett, L.P. Sgt, 110
Barr, R.A. Sgt, 112
Barr, R.E. Sgt, 108
Barratt, Arthur, A/M, 28
Barratt, R.S. Sgt, 112
Barrington-Kent, B.H. Lt., 7
Bass, E.G. Sgt, 64,110,132
Basson, P.H. P/O, 109
Batchelor, A.E. AC, 107
Bates, P. Sgt, 117
Batten, F/Sgt, 115
Bauer, Martin Oblt, 62
Bawden, R.V. Sgt, 108
Bayliss, Mr, 38
Beacock, E.C. Sgt, 112
Beales, W.A. Sgt, 111
Beames, G.N. Sgt, 110
Becket, Sgt, 47
Beemer, F.H. P/O, 39,107,130
Beetles, K.J. P/O, 63,132
Bellairs, S/Ldr, 19
Bellamy, F.W. Sgt, 112
Belton, Leslie, 105

Bemrose, F/Sgt, 73
Bennett, D.W. Sgt, 40,108,130
Berry, H.A.J. Sgt, 111
Berry, Jim, 69
Berthelsen, F.J. Sgt, 115
Bettles, Alan F/O, 68
Bevan, C.J.W. F/O, 111
Biddulph, S. Sgt, 111
Bilham, R.P. Sgt, 110
Billens, H.E. P/O, 68,112,133
Billington, Sgt, (32p),38,47
Binning, L.H.R. P/O, 110
Birkby, T. Sgt, 111
Bjelke-Peterson, H.R. F/O, 29,129
Blackburn, AC2, 113
Blackford, C.L. W/O, 63,116
Blair, J.L. F/Sgt, 59,60,62,63,116,132
Blair, K.H. S/Ldr, 135
Blair, P.L. P/O, 63,132
Blair, R.G. F/.Sgt, 109
Blake, R.A. Sgt, 109
Blatherwick G. Sgt, 109
Blencowe, J.B. F/O, 112
Boaman, W.R. W/Cdr, 135
Board, F.E. P/O, 19
Body, J. P/O, 106
Boland, J.A. Sgt, 116
Bond, C.J. Sgt, 109
Booker, W.R. F/O, 64,111,132
Borley, Sgt, 78,79
Booth, D.G. F/Sgt, 111
Booth, E. P/O, 110
Booth, E.F.W. Sgt, 108
Booty, E.D. Sgt, 109
Botten, K. Sgt, 114
Botting, J.C. P/O, 113
Boumphrey E.H. Sgt, 109
Bourdillon, Robert, Lt., 10
Bowden, D.J. Sgt, 109
Bower, E.W. Sgt, 65,111,133
Bowers, C.S. Sgt, 113
Bowes, A.J.L. F/O, 56,109,131
Bowie, V.T. F/Sgt, 58,110,132
Boyes, J.E. Sgt, 111
Bradley, Cpl, 37,39,42,46
Brady, F.P.J. F/Sgt, 112
Bramhall, R. Sgt, 42,108,130
Branford, J. Sgt, 116
Bray, D P/O, 68,112,133
Brett, A.F. Sgt, 112
Briden, M.E. F/O, 26,106,129
Bridgen, Jim, 62,(62p),110
Briggs, S. Sgt, 108
Brightwell, Mrs. M., 114
Bristow, A.E. Sgt, 112
Bristow, L.J.D. Sgt, 111
Brittle, A.M.A. Sgt, 115
Broadhurst, K. Sgt, 111
Brocket, J.C. F/Sgt, 57,109,131
Brogan, M.A. F/O, 54,130
Brookes, Sgt, 115
Brown, A.A. F/Sgt, 65,111,133
Brown, A.A. LAC, 106
Brown, A.H. Sgt, 112
Brown, Geoffrey, 102,103
Brown, J.L. Sgt, 106,114
Brown, W.S.F. P/O, 106
Brubacker B.W. F/O, 108
Brunsden, P.S. Sgt, 108
Brunton, J.F. Sgt, 112
Bryant, R.W.G. W/O, 112
Buckton, E.J. Sgt, 109
Budd, P.A. Sgt, 113
Budd, P.C. P/O, 108
Bull Lt, 118
Bull, N.G. Sgt, 106,114
Bulloch, H.L. F/O, 26,129
Bullock, E.J. Cpl, 18

Bunn, Maurice, (74p)
Burbidge, G.F. P/O, 107
Burch, C.R. F/Sgt, 37,107,130
Burke, G.E.K., 85
Burnley, J.D. Sgt, 108
Burnett, G.S. Sgt, 115
Burnett, Stan, 79,81
Burrows, Tom, 59
Burton, H. F/O, 29,114
Burton, J. AC2, 106
Bury, G.N. W/O, 113
Bushford, C.E. Sgt, 107
Butcher, S.H. Sgt, 115
Butler, E.D. Sgt, 109
Butler, L.H. F/Lt, 63,132
Butler, P.E. Sgt, 37,107,114
Butt, J.E. Sgt, 111
Butt, M.G. P/O, 114
Butterworth, P. Sgt, 111
Button, L.E. F/Lt, 113
Bywaters, T.B. Sgt, 109
Cadge, D.E. Sgt, 117,133
Caiger, C. Sgt, 115
Cameron, G. F/Sgt, 112
Cameron, R.H. P/O, 112
Camps, A. Sgt, 111
Canton, H S/Ldr, 101
Canton, S/Ldr, MBE, DFC, 135
Capel, D.J. Sgt, 107
Capham, R.G.P. Sgt, 109
Capstick, F.L. Sgt, 108
Cardall, Joe, 69,(70p)
Care, F/Lt, 101
Carriline, V. Sgt, 108
Carter, A. Sgt, 110
Carter, G.A.C. Sgt, 116
Carter, H. Sgt, 109
Cartwright, F/Sgt, 112
Cary, E.S. P/O, 113
Cass, J. F/Sgt, 113
Cassels J.J. Sgt, 112
Cassidy, T.C. Sgt, 111
Cato, M.V. Sgt, 108
Catto, P.T. Sgt, 106
Chamberlain, Jack, (74p)
Chamberlain, Neville, 19
Chamberlin, S.D. Sgt, 108
Channing, D.W.B. Sgt, 111
Chapman, H. Sgt, 107
Chappell, F/Lt, 68
Charles, D.E.S. P/O, 106
Charlton, A.N. F/Sgt, 109
Charlton Jones, C. W/Cdr, 54,56,109,131,135
Cheetham, A.F. P/O, 53,54,108,130
Chilton, P.L. W/Cdr, 91,93,96
Chilton, W.D. W/Cdr, 135
Chorlton, J.A. W/Cdr, 88
Churchill, Winston, Rt Hon., 28,36,37,56,94
Churchward, Harry, 69,(70p)
Clark, Anthony W.J. S/Ldr, 37,45,107,130
Clark, N.H. Sgt, 116
Clark, R.L. Sgt, 114
Clark, W.D. F/Sgt, 111
Clarke, F.S. Sgt, 109
Clayton, D.R. Sgt, 116
Clayton, P.L. P/O, 55,108,131
Clayton, W.H. Sgt, 59,60,110,116
Clifton, T.C.C. Sgt, 107
Clough, J.A. Sgt, 110
Clough, J.A. F/Sgt, 109
Coalter, R. LAC, 106
Cobb, John, 44
Cochrane, The Hon. R.A., 135
Cocks, R.J. Sgt, 106
Cockshott, R.J. Sgt, 111

Coldwell, G.W. P/O, 108
Cole, Mr, 42
Colebourne, W.A. AC2, 106
Coleman, Lloyd Watt, DFC S/Ldr, 105,108
Colenut, H.J. F/Lt, 67,112,133
Collett, F/Sgt, 29,42
Collier, T. Sgt, 111
Collins, A.V. F/Lt, 112,133
Collins, J. Sgt, 111
Collins, L.C. Sgt, 115
Collins, Len W/O, 56
Collins, F/Lt, 101
Collins, W. Sgt, 108
Collumbell, J. Sgt, 109
Coman, Jim, 40,50,52,53
Connelly, H.I.F. Sgt, 109
Connolly, D.H.G. Sgt, 114
Connor, B.A. P/O, 65,133
Conway, N.J.V. Sgt, 114
Cook, E.R. Sgt, 44,107
Cook, G.T. Sgt, 111
Cook, G.V. Sgt, 111
Cooke, W/O, 28
Cookman, H. Sgt, 112
Cookson, Sawry, S/Ldr, 43,44,45
Cooper, L.A. Sgt, 111
Cooper, R.W. AC2, 111
Copely LAC, 23
Corfield, K. LAC, 85
Cork, Frank, 35,47
Corker, A.W. Sgt, 109
Corkill, C.W.M. F/Sgt, 112
Corney, F/Lt, 101
Coster, A.J. Sgt, 107
Cotton, G.H. P/O, 107
Cottrell, B. F/Lt, 65,111,133
Coull, A. Sgt, 111
Cowap, J. Sgt, 111
Cox, D.S. P/O, 106,114
Cox, F/Sgt, 73
Cozens, G.A. P/O, 64,111,133
Crafts, R.H. Sgt, 107
Craig, J.W. Sgt, 106
Craven, F. Sgt, 110
Crean, Capt., 9
Crisford, A.A. Cpl, 28
Crisp, Alex, (74p),77,78,82
Crofts, D.A. Sgt, 110
Crook, AC1, 113
Crooks, W.W. Sgt, 106
Cross, M.M. Sgt, 117
Cross, N.J. AC1, 107
Cross, W. Sgt, 117
Crosson, A.J. Sgt, 110
Crow, E.F.L. F/Sgt, 117
Crowe, H.R. P/O, 108
Crowe, J.W. Sgt, 117
Crowther, A.R. Sgt, 111
Cuffe, Lt, 12,14,113
Culling, M.F. F/O, 112
Culpan, W.J.R. Sgt, 115
Cumming, J.W. Sgt, 65,111,133
Currie, J. Sgt, 108
Curtis, L.W. P/O, 111
Cuthbert, J.E.A. Sgt, 113
Cutts, H.V. F/Sgt, 117,133
Cymbalist, Sgt, 43
Dabbs, J. Sgt, 111
Dabinett, S/Ldr, 21
Daines, G.B. Sgt, 108
Dane, G.A. F/Sgt, 91,113
Dane, S.W. P/O, 42,108,130
Dangerfield, P.E.H. Sgt, 107
Danver, C. F/Lt, 68
Darling, T.A. F/O, 19
Dauncey, W.G.H. Sgt, 107
Davey, W.E. F/O, 63,110,132

Davidson, K.McN. Sgt, 106
Davidson, D. Sgt, 73,113
Davies, A. Flg.Off., (73p)
Davies, A.C.A. Sgt, 108
Davies, D.G. Sgt, 112
Davies, E.E.C. F/O, 112
Davies, Glyn, F/Sgt, (97p)
Davies, I.G., Sgt, 56,116,131
Davies, T. P/O, (73p)
Davis, H.L., F/Sgt, 55,108,131
Dawson, F.L. Sgt, 112
Dawson, M.B. P/O, 106
Day, F.W.R. Sgt, 111
Day, W. (Aircraftman), 85
Deacock, V.A. Sgt, 111
Dellow, C.W. F/O, 108
Dempster, Peter, (84p)
Denier D.E.G. Sgt, 107
Dennis, 'Denny' LAC, 28
Denny, J. Sgt, 109
Derbyshire, A. Sgt, 111
Detley, F.C. Sgt, 111
Deviney, H.A. Lt, 111
Dickinson, S. Sgt, 112
Ditchburn, P.W. Sgt, 110
Dixon, J.M. Sgt, 108,115
Dixon, P.L. P/O, 38,115,130
Dixon, T.D. F/Sgt, 116
Dobson, C.D. F/O, 109
Dobson, G.M.B. 2nd Lt., 10
Doherty, E.B. AC1, 106
Donaldson, D.W. F/O, 29,129
Donaldson, R. Sgt, 106
Dorey, E.H.S. F/O, 87,113,134
Douglas, A.V., W/O, 111
Douglas, J. Sgt, 111
Douglas-Cooper, J.S. F/O, 28,106,129
Dowie, A.W. Sgt, 116
Downing, J.B. Sgt, 115
Drummond, Ian, 98
Drury, D.J. AC2, 106
Duckworth, E.R. Sgt, 112
Duckworth, H.L. Sgt, 108
Duckworth, Leslie, 80
Duguid, A.G. P/O, 15,23,24
Duke of Kent, (38p),47
Dullaghan, S.P. F/Sgt, 112
Duvall, Master Pilot, (104p)
Dyer, J. F/Sgt, 113
Early, F.F. Sgt, 107
Eastin, J. Sgt, 108
Eaton, E.D. Sgt, 112
Edwards, E.D. Sgt, 110
Edwards, F/Lt, 101
Eisenhower, Dwight D. Gen. C in C, 90
Ekelund, J.H. F/Sgt, 57,109,131
Eldridge, J.J. AC2, 113
Elliott, J.N. Sgt, 112
Elliott, M.H. Sgt, 109
Ellis, A.L. P/O, 108
Ellis, F.S. Sgt, 107
Ellis, G.I. F/Lt, 63,110,132
Ellis, W.J. AC, 106
Emden, H.L., F/O, 22
England, S.D. Sgt, 108
Evans, Michael R. F/O, 40,46,50,51,52, 53,130
Evans, R.D. Sgt, 110
Evans, T.E. F/Sgt, 107
Everson, P.M. F/Sgt, 106
Facey, Colin, F/Lt (97p)
Fairfield, W.R.St.G. Sgt, 109
Falck, Wolfgang, 24,26
Farmer, C.D. F/O, 65,116,133
Farmer, J.T. Sgt, 39,107,130
Farnen, E. Sgt, 110
Feakiss, Leslie, 101,102
Fender, J. Sgt, 114
Felstead, E. Sgt, 51,53
Fenton, G.W. Sgt , 39,108,130
Ferguson, B. Sgt, 108
Ferguson, R.C. F/Sgt, 110

Field, L.R. F/O, 26,106,129
Field, M.L. P/O, 53,108,130
Finch, E.H. F/Sgt, 110
Finch, J. S/Ldr DFC AFC, 135
Fisher, F/Lt, 114
Fisher, J.H. P/O, 37,114,130
Fisher, L.R. Sgt, 111
Flack, A.W. P/O, 64,111,132
Flack, B, 60
Fleming, G.B. Sgt, 106
Fletcher, P.O. Sgt, 111
Flint, R.B.L. Sgt, 109
Flockhart, J.S. F/Sgt, 108
Fogarty, Joseph, Gp Capt., 46
Foran, T.W. F/Sgt, 110
Ford, G.R.M. P/O, 106,114
Forsyth G.E. Sgt, 113
Forsyth, H.E. P/O, 64,110,132
Forward, J.M.P. P/O, 55,56,79,80,115,131
Fossleitner, L.V. Sgt, 56,105,109,131
Foster, A.G. AC2, 106
Foster, B.H. S/Ldr, 101
Foster, D.C. Sgt, 116
Foster, F.R. S/Ldr, 135
Foster, L.F. AC2, 106
Fowler, F.D. Sgt, 39,107,130
Fowler, G.H. F/O, 112
Fox, Douglas P/O, 39,41,42
Fox, H.W.G. P/O, 112
Fox, 'Sam' F/O, 90
Frank, N.H. Sgt, 110
Franklin, L. Sgt, 111
Franks, John P/O, 36,37
Fraser, Hugh, 98
Freeman, A.F. Sgt, 19
Freeman, John, 50
Freeman, R.A. Sgt, 111
Freeman, R.J. F/Lt, 69,112,133
Freeman, 'Yorky', (74p)
French, H.J. F/Sgt, 111
French, L.P.J. Sgt, 110
Frost, A.J. P/O, 54,108,131
Fruen, F/O, 101,102,103
Fruin, F. F/Lt, 135
Fudge, D.C.H. Sgt, 111
Fudge, H.P. F/Sgt, 111
Fulton, I.T.S. P/O, 63,110,132
Furness, R.G. P/O, 29,106,129
Futcher, J.V. Sgt, 106
Gaffee, L. Sgt, 111
Gallagher, R. Sgt, 108
Galland, Adolph, Genlt, 87
Garretts, F/O, 101
Geddes, A.McR. Sgt, 112
'Gee', Tony Sgt, 38,45
Gent, R.P. P/O, 108
George, T.A. Sgt, 108
Giacomelli, David, 59,62
Giacomelli, Jake "Fritz' F/Sgt, 59,60,62,116
Gibbins, P.G. Sgt, 107
Gibson, Guy, W/Cdr, 64
Gilberd, M.S. F/O, 109
Gillam, L.G. Sgt, 107
Gillingham, H.J. Sgt, 116
Gillott, H. AC2, 106
Ginn, E.R. Sgt, 110
Gledhill, H.G. Sgt, 106
Goad, G.E. Sgt, 106,129
Goebbels, Josef, 60
Goering, Hermann, 60
Golden, J.G. Sgt, 111
Goldie, A.B. S/Ldr, 135
Goldsmith, B.F. Sgt, 109,115
Golsmith, Sgt, 55,131
Good, G.E. Sgt, 27
Good, M.H. F/O, 58,110,132
Goodwin, Jack, F/Sgt, (97p)
Goodwing, G.H. Sgt, 114
Gosling, G.N. W/O, 112
Gough, H.W. Sgt, 116

Gow, J.G. F/Sgt, 57,60,62,(62p),110, 131,132
Gowans, J.G. Sgt, 112
Grace, J.M. Sgt, 115
Graham, D.A. Sgt, 108
Graham, I.P. F/Sgt, 108
Graham, J.A. Sgt, 107
Graham, R.R. F/Lt, 109
Grant, Gerry Sgt, 81,115
Grant, Peter, F/Lt, 24,26
Grant, S.C. Sgt, 106
Grant-Crawford, I.D. F/Lt, 28,106,129
Graves, Bob, (74p)
Gray, Air Comm., 78
Gray, Arthur, (84p)
Gray, D.J. Sgt, 107
Gray, George, 43,45
Gray, J.W. Sgt, 109
Greaves, W.J. Sgt, 107
Green, N.A.L. F/Sgt, 113
Green, W. Sgt, 109
Greenslade, W.R. S/Ldr, 57,109,131
Greenwood, V.P. Maj., 12,13,135,140
Gregory 'Greg' P/O, (32p),36,37,38,46
Gregson, N.P. Sgt, 109
Greig W. LAC, DFM, 106
Griffith-Jones, J.M. F/Lt, 27,37,129
Grimston, Bruce Rt Hon., 29,33,47
Grove, D.H. AC2, 106
Guepin, Y.J.B. WO2, 110
Guest, D.A.P. Sgt, 111
Gunning, K.S. F/Sgt, 109
Gwyther, J.F. Sgt, 108
Hadden, L.D. Sgt, 111
Haines, S.S.J. Sgt, 112
Haldiman, Lt., 14
Hale, H. Sgt, 107
Hale, R.H. Sgt, 116
Halford, 'Ches', (84p)
Hall, A.D. Sgt, 111
Hall, E.W. Sgt, 111
Hall, G.J.C. Sgt, 110
Hall, W. Sgt, 36,107,130
Hallam, K. Sgt, 114
Hallam, W.T. Sgt, 106
Hamer, H. RAF Regt, 85
Hammond, R.R. Sgt, 106
Hampson, A.N. Sgt, 108
Hampton, Trevor A. F/O, 43
Hanna, C.M. Sgt, 113
Hannaford, W.A. W/O, 112
Hanson, 'Happy', 40,45,53
Harding, E.E. Sgt, 114
Hardman, T. Sgt, 112
Hargreaves, J.D. P/O, 106
Harland, I.W. P/O, 112
Harper, K.A. Sgt, 112
Harris, Arthur, 'Bomber', A.M., 26,50,52, 56,62,90
Harris, D.H. Sgt, 109
Harris, Paul. S/Ldr, 19,21,23,24,26
Harris, R.B. S/Ldr, 55,108,131
Harris, Sgt, 115
Harris, T.H. F/Sgt, 110
Harrison, A.R.J. Sgt, 107
Harrison, G, Sgt, 113
Harrison, G.M. W/Cdr, 135
Harrison, H.H. Sgt, 106,114
Harrison, R. AVM, 75,90,135
Harrison, W Sgt, 37,114,130
Hart, H.J. F/Sgt, 57,109,131
Hart, R.H.S. F/Sgt, 112
Hartley, A. Sgt, 112
Harvie, Ian, 68
Hathaway, R.F. Sgt, 111
Hatherly, L.W. Sgt, 114
Hatton, E.C. Sgt, 108
Havercroft, W.C. Sgt, 111
Hawkins, R.A. Sgt, 108
Hawley, L.R. Sgt, 36,107,130
Haynes, George, F/Lt, (97p)
Hazel, C.W. Sgt, 115

Hazelden-French, E. Sgt, 111
Heal, F.C. Sgt, 117
Heal, R.W. F/O, 112
Heathcote, 'Ginger', 25,26
Hedges, Charles, LAC, 15
Henderson, Brig. Gnl., 9
Henderson, I.S. F/O, 34,107,130
Henderson, J.I. AC2, 107
Henderson, R.R. P/O, 115
Henry, J. AC2, 106
Herbert, B.J. Sgt, 111
Herring, G.W. Sgt, 116
Hewitt, E.S. AC2, 106
Hewitt, J.P.M. F/O, 106
Hickley, P.F. Sgt, 108
Hickman, T. Sgt, 109
Hide, K.J. P/O, 30,107,114,129
Higgins, C.W. P/O, 110
Higgins, T.C. Maj., 13
Higgs, D.R. Sgt, 110
Hill, C. Sgt, 109
Hill, J.E. P/O, 64,116,132
Hills, G.E. F/Sgt, 110
Hinchcliffe, A. AC2, 106
Hinken, Leslie, 29,30,36,42
Hird, E.G. Sgt, 111
Hird, K. F/Sgt, 113
Hislop, B. P/O, (73p)
Hitchman, H.W. Sgt, 117
Hitchmough, R.J.H. Sgt, 111
Hitler, Adolf, 18,29,45,93
Hobbs, J.A. Sgt, 111
Hockley, R. F/Sgt, 55,56,131
Hodge, R.A. F/Sgt, 116
Hodges, A.C.L. P/O, 42,108,130
Hodgkins, J. F/Sgt, 112
Hodgkinson, P. Sgt, 111
Hodgson, R.A. Sgt, 33,114,129
Hoey, AC2, 22
Hogan, W. 2/Lt, 106
Holden, K. Sgt, 114
Holdsworth, F/O, 113
Holland, E.J. Sgt, 107
Holloway, I.A.M. P/O, 110
Holman, F. F/O, 15
Holmes, C.W. DFC, P/O, 134
Holmes, E.C.C. Sgt, 109
Holmes, G.C.C. W/O, 112
Holms, A.H. F/Sgt, 111
Homan, A.J.V. Sgt, 108
Hood, J.F.S. P/O, 116
Hopkinson, S.H. F/Sgt, 110
Hornby, J.B. F/O, 112
Horrocks, J.W. Sgt, 108
Horsefield, J.E. P/O, 37,107,130
Horswell, K.A. Sgt, 113
Hoskins, Capt., 9
Hotchkis, G.S. F/Sgt, 66,111,133
Houlgrave, J.W. Sgt, 110
Houseman, R.E. P/O, 106
Howarth, Harold, 59,60
Howden, C.V. Sgt, 111
Howe, M.J. Sgt, 109
Howell, E.H. F/Sgt, 109
Howell, T.L. S/Ldr, 63,116,132
Howie, C.W. P/O, 106
Hoyland, F. Sgt, 115
Hughes, D. P/O, 112
Hughes, F. Sgt, 109
Hughes, F.L. Sgt, 109
Hughes, W.M. Sgt, 116
Hughes, W.S. Sgt, 110
Hughson, L.B. AC2, 106
Hulse, T.M.F. P/O, 56,79,109,131
Humbles, R.J. Sgt, 111
Humphries, A.G. Sgt, 107
Hunt, E. Sgt, 110
Hunt, E.A.R. F/O, 58,109,132
Hunt, L.A.V. Sgt, 113
Hunt, R.W. Sgt, 108
Hutchings, W.C., DFC, S/Ldr, 57,109,131
Hutchins, C.J.K. S/Ldr, 72,112,133

145

Hutchinson, R. Sgt, 107
Hutson, N.C. Sgt, 108
Hyder, L.A. F/Sgt, 58,116
Immelman, Max. Lt, 10
Inglesby, C. Sgt, 114
Ingram, J.W. 2/Lt, 113
Ising, Geoffrey, Sgt, 46,(46p),78
Isted, E.C. Sgt, 109
Izzard, L.T. F/O, 58,109,132
Jack, Tom, F/Sgt (97p)
Jago, F.D. F/Sgt, 108
Jago, J.B.C. Sgt, 37,107,130
James, A. Sgt, 111
Jamieson, V.R. P/O, 85
Jarret, F.M. Sgt, 107
Jarvis, Jack, 47
Jeal, E. F/Sgt, 68,112,133
Jeffcoate, F.R. Sgt, 112
Jeffrey, J.E. Sgt, 110
Jenkins, P.E.J. Sgt, 109
Jenkins, T.J. Sgt, 116
Jenkinson, F Sgt, 42,115
Jerman, J.A. Sgt, 54,115,131
Jerritt, R.A. Sgt, 106
Jillings, David. Sgt Major, 9
Jinks, W.P. Sgt, 107
Johns, Dennis, 98
Johnson, Amy, 30
Johnson, C.H. Sgt, 108
Johnson, Frank, Sgt, 59,60,62,63
Johnson, H.P. Sgt, 108
Johnson, P.H. Sgt, 111
Johnson, W.F. Sgt, 116
Johnston, J.St G. Sgt, 108
Johnstone, G.A. Sgt, 114
Johnstone, R.N. P/O, 66,67,112,133
Jones, C.G. Sgt, 115
Jones, D.E.W. Sgt, 113
Jones, D.M.P. P/O, 108
Jones, G. Sgt, 111
Jones, G.D.K. Sgt, 114
Jones, L. Sgt, 110,116
Jones, L. F/Sgt, 113
Jones, 'Oak', (84p)
Jones, Sgt, 73
Jones, R.V. Dr, 39
Jones, 2nd Lt., 14
Jordan, H.F. F/Sgt, 108
Jordan, Sgt, 115
Jordan, T.E. Sgt, 108
Kay, L.H. W/Cdr, 88,113,134,135
Kearney, F.T. Sgt, 107
Kearns, Lawrence, 71,82
Keates, J.A. Sgt, 107
Keay, D.G. Sgt, 117
Keeting, M. P/O, 116
Kelleher M.J. Sgt, 108
Kellett, R. W/Cdr, 23,24,26,135
Kelly, F/Sgt, 24
Kelly, P.L.C. Sgt, 110
Kemp, 26
Kemp, C.R. Sgt, 112
Kennedy, B.D.J. Sgt, 107
Kennedy, Ian, 69,(70p)
Kennedy, J. W/Cdr, 135
Kenny, M.T. F/Sgt, 115
Kenvin, P.M. Sgt, 108
Kerr, D.A. P/O, 15
Kerr, Flt Lt, 23
Kerr, H.J.F. Sgt, 114
Keswick, M.McL Sgt, 108
Keymer, J.G. Sgt, 37,107,130
Kidd, W.H.C. Sgt, 106
Kilcoyne, T. Sgt, 113
King, A.J.G. Lt, 106
King, E.G. Sgt, 110
King, F.H. Sgt, 56,109,116,131
King, J.E. Sgt, 108
King George VI, 23,(33p),34,55
Kingham, R.F. F/O, 110
Kirk, E.A. Sgt, 108
Kirkness, D.J. Sgt, 106

Kitchener, Lord, 9
Knight, F.T. F/O, 27,113
Knowles, G.N. P/O, 66,133
Kortwright, N.H. Sgt, 108
Kowalski, L F/Sgt, 108
Kynaston, M.J. F/Sgt, 56,109,131
Lacey, F.A. Cpl, 107
Lampard, Desmond, 18,22,23
Landau, Ron. P/O, 23
Langlais, Georges, Sgt, 45,79
Langlois, Leo, Sgt, 45,46,79
Langridge, J.H. Cpl, 27,106
Langsdorff, Hans. Capt, 26
Latham, Chief Mech., 12
Lauriston, Sgt, 54,115
Lawrence, Roy, 77,78
Lawson, A. Sgt, 115
Leach, C.W.E. Sgt, 110
Leach, J.C. Sgt, 109
Lear, K.F. Sgt, 117
Learner, Arthur, (84p)
Le Blanc, E.J. F/Sgt, 109
Lee, George, Cpl, 23
Leedham, W.J. W/O, 66,111,133
Leeds, J.L. P/O, 29,106,129
Leeman P.I. Sgt, 108
Leighton, I.D. AC1, 106
Lemons, 'Cheese' F/O, 25,26
Lenehan, D. Sgt, 110
Lewis, A.T. Sgt, 115
Lewis, E. Sgt, 110
Lewis, Lou, (70p)
Lickley, G. Sgt, 107
Lilley, J.R. Sgt, 116
Lincoln, E.J. P/O, 73,112,134
Lindhard, S. F/Sgt, 112
Lindsey, F.D. Sgt, 108
Lines, F.N. P/O, 106
Linkley, A. Sgt, 19
Little, H.W. AC1, 107
Littlefield, J.R. Sgt, 107
Lloyd, H. Sgt, 111
Lloyd, R.S. Sgt, 108
Lloyd, R.S.W. Sgt, 30,107,129
Lock, G.J.V. Sgt, 108
Locke, Gordon, 81
Locke, J.B. Sgt, 115
Locke, John Sgt, 80
Lofthouse, Charles P/O, 42,45,78,79,130
London, A.E. F/Sgt, 113
Long, A.J. WO2, 112
Long, C.R. Sgt, 110
Long, W.A. Sgt, 116
Longley, G.E. F/Sgt, 112
Lonsdale, R. P/O, 57,(57p),109,131
Loughlin, Cecil F/Sgt, 62,116
Lovett, 'Al', (84p)
Lowe, G.T. P/O, 66,112,133
Lower, R.W. F/Sgt, 111
Lown, E.A. Sgt, 107
Lowrie, J. P/O, 64,111,132
Lowther, E.W. P/O, 112
Lucas, S.E. P/O, 73,134
Lucy, T.J. Sgt, 111
Ludlow-Hewitt, Sir Arthur,
  Air Chief Marshal, 15
Lukey, Luke, (74p),82
Lumsden, J.F. Sgt, 109
Lunn, S.J. Sgt, 112
Lutzow, 87
Luzmoor, D.A. F/O, 116
Lyne, D.H. F/O, 111
Lynn, J.C. P/O, 39,108,130
Lyons, P. Sgt, 117
Mabey, L.F. Sgt, 114
Macaulay, R. Sgt, 110
Mace, Aubrey, F/Sgt, 53
Mace, A.W. P/O, 115
Mace, F/Lt, 80
MacFarlane, J. F/Sgt, 112
Mackie, J.W. Sgt, 110
MacLeod, N. Sgt, 110

MacLeod, N.A. Sgt, 110
Macnaughton, I.N.J. Sgt, 110
MacNeill, J.B. Sgt, 116
MacPherson, G.J. Sgt, 112
Maddocks, Don P/O, 62
Magson, E. Sgt, 111
Mahoney, J.J. S/Ldr, 65,116,133
Main, Sgt, 115
Malkemus W.R. Sgt, 108
Mandy, V. Sgt, 112
Mann, Frank, 96
Mansell, V.W.J. F/O, 108
Mansfield, Rt.Hon. Terence 'Sandy', P/O,
  40,41,45,47
Manthorpe, A.J. Sgt, 112
Mantle, A.J. LAC, 106
Marett, W.G. Sgt, 107
Marquis of Londonderry, Air Comm., 23
Marr, J.S. Sgt, 30,129
Marsh, Frank H. Lt, 12,113
Martin, A. Sgt, 109
Martin, A.C. Sgt, 106
Martin, D. P/O, 107
Martin, Felix, 82
Martin, G.E. Sgt, 109
Martin, J.R. F/Sgt, 112
Martin, L.C. F/O, 64,110,132
Martin, S. F/Sgt, 109
Martins, Sgt, 78,79
Martins, G. Sgt, 109
Mason, A.L. Sgt, 111
Mathenson, N.E. Sgt, 117
Mather, H.J. Sgt, 112
Matthews, G.G. Sgt, 107
Maverick, Colin LAC, 53
May, A.E. F/Sgt, 65,111,133
May, F. Sgt, 107
Mayo, W.H. P/O, 112,133
McAdie, W. Sgt, 112
McAleese D.P. Sgt, 110
McAllister, N.A. F/Sgt, 112
McAnnally, J. Sgt, 114
McBulloch, H.L. F/O, 106
McCall, W. Sgt, 110
McCallum, L.B. Sgt, 111
McCoy, W.C. P/O, 112
McDiarmid, I.R. F/O, 45
McDonald, D.F. F/Sgt, 108
McDonald, F.G.R. Sgt, 106
McDonald, W.G. Sgt, 113
McDougall, W.A. Sgt, 112
McFarlane, D.A. P/O, 114
McGregor, D. P/O, 112
McHugh, G.F. F/Sgt, 109
McInnes, J.G. F/Sgt, 66,112,133
McIntyre, R.F. F/Sgt, 109
McKee, A. Air Comm, 90,91
McKee, J.J. F/O, 76
McKenzie, K.G. Sgt, 109
McKirdy, A.J. F/O, 116
McKlaird, C. Sgt, 114
McLean, C.K. F/O, 117
McLeod, Sgt, 23
McLeod, W.H. Sgt, 107
McMullen, C.R. F/Sgt, 109
McNamee, D. Sgt, 109
McNarey, D.I. F/O, 110
McQuade, J.E. Sgt, 112
McQuitty, R.J. F/Sgt, 112
McStirling, A. Sgt, 111
McWade, J.R. P/O, 112
Mears, I.A. Sgt, 116
Megran, W.J. Sgt, 107
Menage, T.N. Sgt, 107
Mendoza, P.I.A. P/O, 108
Mercer, L.H. Sgt, 113
Merritt, E.M. P/O, 110
Mertens, P.E.M. Sgt, 107
Meynell, P.R.B. Sgt, 37,107,130
Middleton, Rawdon Hume, F/Sgt,
  29,53,58,(58p),94,105,110,116,124,132
Middleton, R. Sgt, 113

Milch, Erhard. Gen., 15
Miller, F/Sgt, 68
Miller, G.W. WO2, 110
Miller, J.G. P/O, 29,106,129
Miller, K.A.W. F/O, 87,113,134
Millichip, J. Sgt, 108
Mills, D.H. F/O, 112
Mills, P.B. Sgt, 110
Mills, Sir George. A.M., 103
Milstead, Mr, 34
Misseldine, J. Sgt, 110
Mitchell, A.J. Sgt, 107,114
Mitchell, David P/O, 68
Moffatt, W. Pvte, 54
Mollison, Jim, 30
Montgomery, Bernard, Fld Mar., 91
Moodie, K.W.B. F/O, 108
Moore, Alex, 36
More, H.A Sgt, 65,133
More, E.L. Sgt, 109
More, H.A. P/O, 111
Morehen, G.J.P. Sgt, 37,130
Mores, E. Sgt, 108
Moreshead, V.D.E. S/Ldr, 15
Morgan, C. Sgt, 115
Morrice, J. Sgt, 26,106,129
Morris, D. Sgt, 109
Morris, G. Sgt, 108
Morris, S. Sgt, 107
Morris, T.B. Sgt, 111
Morrison, R.R. Sgt, 37,107,130
Morse, W.E.L. F/O, 111
Morton, N. AC2, 107
Moseley, J.K. Sgt, 107
Moss, A.F. AC2, 106
Moss, J.K. Sgt, 108
Mouat, J.H. Sgt, 108
Moynes, C. Sgt, 108
Mulligan, D.H. F/O, 112
Munday, H.F. F/Sgt, 112
Mundell, Sgt, 113
Munro, D.H. Sgt, 115
Munro, D.J. P/O, 112,133
Munson, D.D. Sgt, 113
Murdoch, J.C. Sgt, 106
Murphy, M. Sgt, 106
Murray, H.R. F/O, 112
Murray, P.H. F/Sgt, 110
Mussolini, Benito, 28
Nason, N.J. Sgt, 115
Naylor, E.J. LAC, 106
Neary, L.E. Sgt, 110
Neate, F.G. F/Lt, 56,109,131
Needham, J.J. F/O, 116
Nelson, H. Gp Capt, 85
Nelson, R.M. Sgt, 106
Ness, W. WO2, 111
Newall, J.G. Sgt, 110
Newman, Reg, (74p), (84p)
Newman, Jim, 69,(70p)
Nichol, J.N. Sgt, 109
Nichols, J. Sgt, 112
Nicholls, J. Sgt, 112
Nicholls, R.A. Sgt, 112
Nicholson, L.H. Sgt, 109
Nicholson, T Sgt, 64,132
Niell, J.J.O. Sgt, 110
Nind, J.A.W. Sgt, 117,133
Noakes, S.L. Sgt, 111
Norman, W.E. Sgt, 110
Northcott, C. Sgt, 108
Northover, D.L. P/O, 112
Nunn, R.A. Sgt, 110
O'Brien, J.A. Sgt, 117
Ockenden F.C. Sgt, 107
Ogle, T.G. P/O, 63,110,132
Oldham, Paul Sgt, 62,110
Oliver, C.W.S. F/Sgt, 56,109,131
Orange, W. F/Sgt, 109
Osborn, W. Sgt, 110
Osborne, Lt, 118
Ottaway, A.J. Sgt, 109

Owen, L.E. F/O, 112
Page, V. Sgt, 110
Paige, E. F/Sgt, 113
Pallett, F.C. Sgt, 112
Palmer, J. Sgt, 110
Parish, C.W. P/O, 114
Parish, F/O, 29
Parker, F.L. Sgt, 116
Parker, R. F/Sgt, 112
Parker, W.C. Sgt, 106
Parris, J. Sgt, 108
Parton, A.B. F/Sgt, 111
Pates, Sgt, 114
Paton, E.H. F/Sgt, 112
Patrick, J.W. P/O, 112
Patten, H.W. Sgt, 107
Pay, J.S. P/O, 106,114,129
Payne, A. LAC, 85
Payne, D.M. Sgt, 106,114
Payne, K.S.A. Sgt, 110
Payne, R.C. Sgt, 107
Pay, J.S. P/O, 29
Peacock, A.R. Sgt, 114
Peake, N. Sgt, 108
Pearson, F.A. F/Sgt, 60,63,110,132
Peattie, R.J. F/O, 111
Pebworth, Dennis. F/Lt, 78,79,(79p),109
Peel, J Sgt, 37,107,130
Pengelly, J.C. Sgt, 108
Pennicott, F.J. Sgt, 114
Penning, F/Lt, 101
Pepper, A. Sgt, 107
Percival, C.J. Sgt, 111
Peters, J.P.E., S/Ldr, 135
Petersen, H.R. P/O, 114
Petter, R.A. Sgt, 107
Petts, Sgt, 24,25
Pfieffer, Rolf, Lt, 36,45
Phillips, C.V. Sgt, 108
Phillips, E.A. P/O, 108
Phillips, E.H.C. Sgt, 109
Philp, John. P/O, 56,58,105,110,131,132
Philpot, J.F. P/O, 107
Pickard, Percy. C. W/Cdr, 30,36,46,120
Pickering, W.V. F/Sgt, 109
Pickford, M.E. DFC, W/Cdr, 71,72,135
Pickup, J.D. Sgt, 109
Pierse, Richard A.M., 50
Pike, M.J. Sgt, 109
Pilbeam, A.B. Sgt, 112
Pilgrim, N.C.H. F/Sgt, 117,133
Pilkington, C.L. F/O, 52,108,130
Pitt, Sgt, 19
Platt, K.E. P/O, 107
Plummery, C.F. Sgt, 114
Pole, L.E. Sgt, 109
Pomeroy, P.B. Sgt, 108
Poole, R.W. Sgt, 111
Pope, A. Sgt, 108
Pope, W.R. Sgt, 106,114
Portal, Sir Charles, 54
Porter, A.R. F/O, 64,111,132
Potts, A.F. F/Sgt, 56,109,131
Powell, E.C. Sgt, 117
Powell, W/Cdr, 33,34,36,135
Power, W.M. Sgt, 112
Poynter, D.J. Sgt, 115
Prettyman, E.G. Sgt, 107
Price, F.W. Sgt, 115
Priestley, R.B. Sgt, 112
Prior, E.H. LAC, 106
Prior, J.A. Sgt, 113
Pugh, T.C. Sgt, 107
Queen Elizabeth, (33p),34,55
Quinlan, V.B. Sgt, 107
Quinn, W. AC2, 113
Raffaelli, P/O, 115
Randell, R.B. Sgt, 109
Randell, R.K. F/O, 109
Raphael R.F. Sgt, 109
Rault, A.C. Sgt, 109
Raymond, G.T. F/O, 112

Rearden, G.K. Sgt, 56,105,131
Redfearn, A.R. Sgt, 112
Redman, E.G. F/O, 111
Redman, Reginald, 73
Redmond, J.P. Sgt, 107
Reed, Harold, 38,47
Reed, Sgt, 115
Rees, V. P/O, (73p)
Reid, A.McL. Sgt, 112
Reidmuller, C.C. Sgt, 107
Reynolds, M.P. Sgt, 106
Reynolds, G.S.S. Sgt, 116
Richamn, H.L. Sgt, 113
Richards, L.R. F/Sgt, 112
Richardson, B.A.J. Sgt, 107
Richardson, E.H. S/Ldr, 15,18,135
Richardson, H.R.J. Sgt, 111
Richardson, K.C. Sgt, 66,117,133
Richardson, V.H.G. Sgt, 106
Richman, R.E. F/Lt, 62,110,132
Riddlesworth, F/Lt, 24
Riley, G.H. Sgt, 111
Robbins, R.C.B. AC1, 19
Roberts. Cpl, 15,106
Roberts, D.S. Sgt, 107
Roberts, F. Sgt, 109
Robertson, G.E. Sgt, 56,109,131
Robertson, J.C. Sgt, 107
Robertson, 25,26
Robey, P.H. Brig, 103
Robinson, A. Sgt, 112
Robinson, J.W. Sgt, 113
Robinson, LAC, 28
Robinson, S.E. Sgt, 116
Roderick, K. Sgt, 108
Rogers, W.F.D. Sgt, 110
Rodgerst, C.B. Sgt, 107
Roe, J.R.B. F/Lt, 73,112,134
Rogers, A.D. S/Ldr, 15
Rogers, S.W. Sgt, 64,133
Ronahan, J.M. P/O, 112
Rooney, A.J. Sgt, 117
Roosevelt, Franklin D., 21
Rootes, John Sgt, 33
Roots, K.G. Sgt, 110
Rose, A.W. Sgt, 107
Rose, J.A. P/O, 106
Rosebery, Lady, 47
Rosebery, Lord, 47
Ross. Sgt, 15,106
Rowland, Peter, 63, (74p),77,81
Royde, G.R. F/O, 110
Rugen, J. Flg/Off, (73p)
Runstedt, Gen, 86,87
Rusher, Sydney, 34
Ruskell, K. DFC S/Ldr, 135
Russell, C.E.S. Capt, 12
Russell, G.H. W/Cdr, 23,135
Russell, Peter, 28,42,50
Russell, R.A. Sgt, 109
Rutherford, M.G. 59,60
Ryall, K.J. F/Lt, 135
Ryan, J.J. Sgt, 110
Sach, D.B. Sgt, 110
Sadler, J.W. AC1, 19
Salmond, J.M. Maj-Gen, 140
Salter, F.G. Sgt, 110
Sampson, H.W. Sgt, 109
Sanders, R.V. F/Lt, 68,112,133
Saunders, H.A. Sgt, 111
Saunders, R.P.T. Sgt, 110
Saywood, R.W. Sgt, 114
Scantlebury L.E. Sgt, 108
Scarlett, W.C. Sgt, 108
Schofield, T.E. W/O, 115
Scholey, V. Sgt, 107
Schollum, B.J. F/Sgt, 111
Scotney, C.C.D. Sgt, 111
Scott, F.W.J. P/O, 107
Scott, H.S. Sgt, 111
Scott, J.D. Sgt, 112
Scott, J.J. Sgt, 106

Scott, R.K. Sgt, 64,111,132
Scott, Scottie, (74p)
Scott, W. F/Sgt, 85,113
Searby, John W/Cdr, 65
Searles, E.R. Sgt, 112
Searles, W.G. P/O, 106,114
Seigne, J.D. P/O, 109
Sellers, G.W. F/O, 110
'Sgt Catt', 35,36,47,48
Shankster, S.R. Sgt, 116
Sharpe-Bullen, Frederick, 60
Sharpe, D.E. P/O, 110
Sharrock, A.A. P/O, 117
Shaw, J.A. Sgt, 108
Shea, R.A. Sgt, 108
Shearer, L. Sgt, 108
Shelvington, W.H.A. Sgt, 111
Sheppard, F. Sgt, 110
Shepherd, C.T. Sgt, 108
Shepherd, J. P/O, 111
Shepherd, Richard, 80
Sherriff, T.J. Sgt, 108
Shimmells, K. Sgt, 106
Short, T.H. F/Sgt, 109
Shuster, F/Lt, 101
Sillence, LAC, 15,106
Simmons, C.W. P/O, 56,109,131
Simpson, D.R. Sgt, 109
Sims, L.R. Sgt, 109
Sinton, J.H. LAC, 106
Siwak, A.A. Sgt, 57,109,131
Skelton, A.R. Sgt, 112
Skelton, H. Sgt, 108
Skinner, N.E. P/O, 116
Skinner, R.H. F/Sgt, 110
Sloane, J.E. Sgt, 115
Smallbone, D.C. Sgt, 114
Smart, S/Ldr, (73p)
Smart, S.N.N.O.L.B. Sgt, 108
Smith, A.H. Sgt, 108
Smith, B.E. Sgt, 108
Smith, C. Sgt, 110
Smith, F/Lt, 101
Smith, Gordon, 24
Smith, G.F. F/Sgt, 109
Smith, G.M.R. P/O, 114
Smith, I.J.T. LAC, 106
Smith, L.H. Sgt, 110
Smith, Lt, 113
Smith, M.K. Sgt, 109
Smith, R.L.L. F/Sgt, 66,117,133
Smith, 'Sandy', (84p)
Smith, 'Smudgy', (74p)
Smith, T. Sgt, 111
Smith, T.E. AC2, 106
Smith, W.L. Sgt, 111
Smithers, E. LAC, 85
Somers, L.J. Sgt, 112
Souter, E.G. Sgt, 109
Southall, G.T.P. P/O, 63,132
Sowerby, Sgt, 102
Spark, W. LAC, 113
Speare, S/Ldr, 50
Speer, Albert, 87
Spence, G.J. W/Cdr, 42,135
Spencer, R. Sgt, 109
Spiers, J.H.C. F/Lt, 26,106
Sponsler, H. WO2, 111
Spratt, C.R. F/Sgt, 109
Squires, F. Sgt, 108
Stanley, R.W. WO2, 111
Stean, J.L. Sgt, 112
Steel, C. Sgt, 116
Steels, A.D. F/Sgt, 112
Steer, G.S. F/Sgt, 65,111,133
Steinhoff, Macky, 24,87
Stephen, W. F/Sgt, 110
Sterling, R.C. P/O, 106
Sterrett, K.K. Sgt, 115
Stewart, D.C. Sgt, 38,115,130
Stewart, J. Sgt, 107
Stewart, J.B. P/O, 15,23

Storey, J.H. Sgt, 109
Stover, R.R. WO2, 110
Stracham, J.L. Sgt, 110
Streater, W.B. Sgt, 109
Strutt, Michael, Hon. P/O, (38p),45,46,47,79
Sturgies, Lt., 14
Suggett, C. Sgt, 106
Sullivan, F.W.O. Sgt, 109
Summerson, Bill Sgt, 62,110
Sunderland, Nanton F/Sgt, 63,116
Sutherland, G.K. Sgt, 109
Sutherland, L.G. Sgt, 107
Sutton, W.C. P/O, 109
Swainston, B.S. Sgt, 111
Swindlehurst, R.F. Sgt, 109
Swift, J.H. Sgt, 106
Swift, J.R. P/O, 106
Sykes, Frederick, Capt., 7
Symmons, W.M. Sgt, 107
Tait, G.E. F/Sgt, 109
Taylor, H.S. Sgt, 110
Taylor, R. F/Sgt, (73p)
Taylor, Reg, (74p), (84p)
Taylor, R.J. P/O, 116
Taylor, S.F. Sgt, 109
Taylor 'Spud', 65,95
Taylor, W.L. Sgt, 113
Taylor, W.T. Sgt, 110
Templeman, 'Tosh', (84p)
Tendius, Gerald, (74p),77,78
Thew, W.J. AC1, 113
Third, H.W. Sgt, 107,114
Thomas Peter, 98
Thomas, 'Taffy', 68
Thomas, 'Taffy' (ground crew), (84p)
Thomas, W.E. Sgt, 108
Thomlinson, I. Sgt, 111
Thompson, AC2, 22,106
Thompson, A.A.B. Air Comm., 18
Thompson, J.H. P/O, 53,108,130
Thompson, Geoffrey, 82
Thomson, E.A.R. Sgt, 107
Thomson, J.W. Lt, 113
Thornley, N. Sgt, 116
Thurman, Deryck, 96
Thwaites, E.H.T. S/Ldr, 29,106,129
Tibbits, W.G. F/O, 112
Tighe, L.J. WO2, 109
Tilley, R.E. Sgt, 113
Timney, T.C. P/O, 110
Titmarsh, Mr, 36,45
Todd, Robert F/Lt, 69,(70p)
Tomlin, C.E. Sgt, 64,111,132
Tomoana, T.R-A-H. F/Sgt, 111
Tootell, R.E. Sgt, 88,113
Tootle, F. AC2, 106
Torgalson, J.S. P/O, 29,106,129
Torrance, M.A. Sgt, 109
Tottle, P. F/O, 113
Town, 'China', 68
Trenchard, Hugh, Viscount, 7,9,10,23
Trooter, J.A. P/O, 109
Tulley, V.W. Sgt, 116
Tully, Val, 62
Tunnicliffe V.G. F/Sgt, 112
Tuppen, D.R. P/O, 106,114
Turner, F.W. F/O, 15
Turner, Sgt, 34
Turner, Clifford, Sgt, 80
Turner, J. F/Sgt, 112
Turner, Les, F/Sgt, (97p)
Turtle, R.W.A. F/Lt, 51,130
Tweedie, F.D. Sgt, 117
Uden, J.H. Sgt, 64,111,132
Uhrig, R.J. Sgt, 107
Upson, V.J. Sgt, 110
Uzzell, E.H. Sgt, 109
Vaillant, P.F.R. F/Lt, 114,129
Vallance, L.G. F/O, 110
Vallant, P.F.K. F/Lt, 29
Van-Aardt, L. P/O, 116

Veasey, Sgt, 50
Versey, S/Ldr, 135
Vesey, Cpl, 79
Vickery, R.F. Sgt, 106
Vince, N.E. Sgt, 107,114
Vincent-Welch, S.L. P/O, 37,107,130
Von Richthofen, Manfred, 10
Vosper, Lt, 113
Wait, E.C. Sgt, 111
Waite, R.H.P. Sgt, 115
Wakefield, P.M. Sgt, 108
Wakeling, L.C. Sgt, 106
Wales, P.H. P/O, 113
Walker 'Gus', Gp Capt, 101
Walker, R.T. F/Sgt, 112
Walker, W. Sgt, 109
Wall, R. Sgt, 117
Wallace, J.McR. Sgt, 109
Waller, R.J.S. Sgt, 112
Walsh, Chris, (84p)
Walters, H. Sgt, 110
Walters, H.S. Sgt, 107
Walton, T.P. F/Sgt, 112
Warburton, J.S. Sgt, 111
Ward, C.G.H. Sgt, 107
Ward, D. Sgt, 113
Ward, E. Sgt, 108
Warden, T. Sgt, 112
Wardle, W.H. LAC, 113
Wareham, H.R.B. Sgt, 106
Warner, 'Plum', 47
Warren, L.G. Sgt, 109
Warren, P.J. AC1, 106
Warren, R Sgt, 34,36,45,107,129,130
Wasse, K.M.M. S/Ldr, 36,56,60,135
Waterman, J.A. Sgt, 109
Waters, R.H. LAC, 107
Watson, G. F/O, 112
Watt, F.H.K. Sgt, 110
Watt, G.A., S/Ldr, 55
Watts, Al, Flg.Off, RCAF, (51p)
Way, K.A. Sgt, 63,110,132
Webster, F.R. Sgt, 112
Webster, G.O. Sgt, 107,114
Wells, S.D. F/Sgt, 57,109,131
West, T.A. Sgt, 58,109,131
Westley, J.L.G. Sgt, 107
Westmacott, D. Sgt, 114
Wey, Sgt, 23
Wham, D. F/Sgt, 113
Wheeler, Des, (70p)
Whelans, Sgt, 30
Wheller, H.J. Sgt, 27,106,129
Whitaker, R.F. F/Sgt, 110
White, A.J. Sgt, 110
White, A.T.H. Flt Lt, 15
White, D.B. P/O, 63,110,132
White, E. Sgt, 107
White, F.L.A. F/Sgt, 73,113
White, K. F/O, 108
Whitelock, T. Sgt, 59,60,110
Whitley, J.R. W/Cdr, 135
Whitney, E.W. F/Sgt, 55,131
Whittle, T. Sgt, 108
Whitwell, H.C. Sgt, 109
Whitworth, H. Sgt, 107,114
Wiffen, M. Sgt, 106
Wigfall, C.B.E. W/Cdr, 135
Wigham, W. Sgt, 112
Wilk, J. P/O, 106
Wilkinson, Jack, (84p)
Wilkinson, W.H. Sgt, 107
Williams, B.M. F/Lt, 113
Williams, F.A. Sgt, 111
Williams, G.R. Sgt, 108
Williams, G.W. Sgt, 110
Williams, H. Sgt, 116
Williams, H.T. Sgt, 110
Williams, R.H. Sgt, 110
Williams, S.A. Sgt, 27,129
Williams, T.G. F/Sgt, 110
Williams, T.H. Sgt, 112

Williams, 'Tosh', (84p)
Williams, T.S.M. F/O, 90,134
Williams, W.J. Sgt, 111
Willis, D.G. Sgt, 108
Wilshire, L. F/Sgt, 108
Wilson, Frank Edward, 13
Wilson, L.K.S. P/O, 114
Winchester, H.S. F/O, 111
Wincott, A.R. Sgt, 112
Winston, M.S. P/O, 116
Witton, A.B. Sgt, 114
Wood, A.A. Sgt, 107
Wood, E. P/O, 112,133
Wood, J. Sgt, 107
Wood, V.S. F/Sgt, 116
Woodcock, F.A. Sgt, 106
Woodfield, R.G. Sgt, 110
Woodhouse, G.H.R. F/Sgt, 53,54,115,131
Woods, F.J. Sgt, 115
Wootten, Mike, 81
Wootton, J.M. F/Sgt, 108
Wootton, K.B. F/Sgt, 117
Wragg, H. Gunner, 28
Wright, W.M. F/Sgt, 110
Wunsche, V.F. F/O, 73,112,134
Wyatt, D.J. Sgt, 108
Wyatt, P.C. F/Sgt, 113
Wynn, E.P. P/O, 55,56,79,109,131
Wynne-Cole, B. Sgt, 117
Yarde, B.C. Gp Capt, 91,93,98
Yates, A. Sgt, 116
York, George, F/Sgt, (97p)
Young, C.F. Sgt, 107
Yoxall, A. Sgt, 107
Zambra, Ronald Sgt, 59,60,63,116

**UNITS / ORGANISATIONS**

**British**
No.1 Group, 54,66,87,88,89,90,93
No.1 Air Gunners School, 66,126,133
No.1 Bombing and Gunnery School, 47
No.2 Group, 19,56
No.2 Aircraft Storage Unit, 119
No.2 Lancaster Servicing Unit, 100
No.3 Lancaster Finishing School, 88
No.3 Elementary Flying Training
 School, 47
No.3 Group, Bomber Command,
 15,18,19,21,23,24,26,27,36,37,39,50,
 52,54,56,59,66,67,75,78,79,85,86,87,
 88,89,90,91,93,99,100,101,135,138
No.3 Group Gunnery Flight, 38,120
No.3 Group Training Flight, 119
No.4 Group, 54,66,89
No.4 Maintenance Unit, 119
No.5 Group, 21,51,52,54,66,88,89,99
No.5 Maintenance Unit, 18,120,128
No.6 Group, Bomber Command,
 66,87, 88,89,90,93
No.6 Group, Training Command, 19,23
No.8 Group, 66,87,88,89,90,93,138
No.8 Armament Training Camp, 15
No.8 Maintenance Unit, 119,120,121
No.9 Maintenance Unit, 119,120,121
No.10 Maintenance Unit,
 119,121,123, 125,126,127
No.11 Operational Training Unit, 19
No.12 Maintenance Unit, 121
No.15 Maintenance Unit, 127,128
No.18 Maintenance Unit, 119,120
No.19 Maintenance Unit, 118,119,123,125
No.20 Operational Training Unit, 26,45
No.20 Maintenance Unit, 120,127,128
No.22 Maintenance Unit, 119,120,121
No.23 Maintenance Unit, 119,120
No.23 Operational Training Unit, 121
No.24 Maintenance Unit,
 119,120,121,127
No.27 Operational Training Unit, 121
No.30 Maintenance Unit, 119,120,121

No.32 Base, Mildenhall, 90
No.32 Maintenance Unit, 125,128
No.33 Maintenance Unit, 120,121,128
No.37 Maintenance Unit, 120
No.38 Group, 49
No.38 Maintenance Unit, 121,127,128
No.44 Maintenance Unit, 120,121,123
No.45 Maintenance Unit, 121
No.46 Maintenance Unit, 88,121,128
No.48 Maintenance Unit, 120
No.54 Maintenance Unit, 28,127
No.90 (Signals) Group, 103
No.100 Group, 66
No.149 Squadron Conversion Flight,
 47,49, 55,56,122,123
No.214 Squadron Conversion Flight, 79
No.551 Wing, 103
No.1401 Meteorology Flight, 37,120,130
No.1483 Flight, 38
No.1657 Operational Training Unit,
 55,59, 121,123,124,125,126,127,141
Aeroplane and Armament Experimental
 Establishment, 118
Air Battalion, Royal Engineers, 7
Air Transport Auxiliary, 18,75,119
Auxiliary Air Force, 19
Balloon Squadron, 7
British Ambassador to Peru, 75
British Expeditionary Force, 7,9,11
Central Flying School, 7,10,47
Central Gunnery School, 119
Code and Cypher School, 72
Committee of Imperial Defence, 7
First Army, 10
G-H Training Flight, Feltwell, 88,89
Heavy Conversion Unit, 69
Ministry of Information, 23
Photographic Reconnaissance
 Headquarters, 99
Photographic Reconnaissance Unit, 52
Royal Aircraft Establishment,
 10,118,119,120
Royal Air Force Film Unit, 75
Royal Air Force Staff College, Cranwell,
 85,90,102
Royal Flying Corps, 7
Second Army, 11
Second Tactical Air Force, 103
Training Command, 18
Washington Conversion Unit, 101,103
XXX Corps, 93

**American**
1st Army, 85
3rd Air Division, 89
8th Air Force, 56,65,83,85,89,93,138
9th Army, 85
452nd Group, 45th Combat Wing, 89
728th Squadron, 89
729th Squadron, 89
730th Squadron, 89
731st Squadron, 89

**German**
352nd Infantry Division, 72
915th Infantry Regiment, 72
Belaria, 81
Dulag Luft, 80
Gestapo, 80
Jagdgeschwader 300, 64
Jagdverband 44, 87
Luftstreitkrafte, 9
Imperial German Army Air Service, 9
Luckenwald, 81
Luftwaffe,
 15,18,19,23,24,25,26,27,28,29,
 30,34,37,52,54,62,64,66,87,90
Nazi Party, 15
Stalag Luft 3, 80
Stalag Luft 8B, 80

**PLACES**

**Australia**
Darwin, 23

**Austria**
Austria, 18

**Belgium**
Aarschot, 111
Antwerp, 65,83
Ardennes, 86,87
Brabant, 55,123,131
Brussels, 81
Fort de Cognelée, 12,140,141
Geetbetz, 64,111,124,133
Hondesschoote, 27
Houwaart, 64,125,132
Kasterlee, 110
Knocke, 112,126,133
Liège, 39,118,130
Louvain, 88
Namur, 12,14
Ostend, 72,73
Steene, 53,108,122,130
St. Martens Voeren, near Liège,
 39,107,120,130
Thieulain, 123,131
Tienen, 108
Tilburg, 55
Thorembais St Trond, 107
Tongrinne, 56,109,122,131
Wavre, 39,121,130
Ypres, 9,12,14,140
Zeebrugge, 71,112,126,133

**British Isles**
Abingdon, Berkshire, 136
Acklington, Northumberland, 95
Ascot, Berkshire, 58,116,121,132
Ayr, Ayrshire, 52,123,130
Barton Mills, Suffolk, 28,45,106,120,129
Bassingbourn, Cambridge, 19,102
Beck Row, Suffolk,
 28,30,31,34,36,44,57,78,
 105,106,107,120,129,130
Benson, Oxfordshire, 87,99,136
Berners Heath Range, 23
Binbrook, Lincolnshire, 102
Blackheath Studios, London, 36
Boscombe Down, Wiltshire, 18,50,136
Bottesford, Leicestershire, 89
Boxworth, Cambridgeshire, 42,123,130
Bramcote, Warwickshire, 19
Brandon, Suffolk, 19,110
Broadstairs, Kent, (55p)
Brooklands, Surrey, 9,25,26,121
Brooklands Museum, Surrey, 119
Buckminster, Leicestershire, 13
Bury St Edmunds, Suffolk, 42
Burnt Fen, Norfolk, 26,106,119,129
Cambridge, 62
Carew Cheriton, South Wales, 23
Catterick, Yorkshire, 13
Cavenham, Suffolk, 34
Chedburgh, Suffolk, 85,86
Chelmsford, Essex, 46
Chipping Warden, Oxfordshire, 136
Chivenor, Devon, 67,75
Clacton, Essex, 106,120,129
Cliffe, Kent, 57,109,123,131
Cockfield, Suffolk, 38,115,119,130
Colerne, Wiltshire, 46,75
Coltishall, Norfolk, 26,65,126,136
Coningsby, Lincolnshire, 101,102,103
Congresbury, Somerset, 34
Copmanthorpe, Yorkshire, 13
Cornwood, Devon, 56,109,123.131
Cottesmore, Leicestershire, 103
Coventry, Warwickshire, 43
Cranwell, Lincolnshire, 15
Cromer Knoll, Norfolk, 26,119,129

Deopham Green, Norfolk, 89
Digby, Lincolnshire, 34,107,120,129
Dishforth, Yorkshire, 87
Doncaster, Yorkshire, 51
Dover, Kent, 2
Downham Market, Norfolk, 136
Dunsfold, Surrey, 139
Dymchurch, Kent, 58,116,124,132
Eastling, Kent, 57,109,122,131
Ely, Cambridgeshire,
  28,30,37,70,107,120,130
Evanton, Ross & Cromarty, 15,18,118,129
Elvedon, Suffolk, 39,108,115,121,130
Eriswell, Suffolk, 109
Farnborough, Hampshire, 7,9
Feltwell, Norfolk,
  18,19,23,24,26,37,76,85,87,88,136,138
Ford Junction, Sussex, 11,14,141
Gransden, Bedfordshire, 58,110,122,132
Great Cressingham, Norfolk, 109
Halton, Buckinghamshire, 15
Harraton House, Exning, nr Newmarket,
  27
Hartford Bridge, Hampshire, 73,126,134
Harwell, Berkshire, 136
Harwich, Essex, 34
Havant, Hampshire, 63,124,132
Hednesford, Staffordshire, 23,34
Helperby, Yorkshire, 13
Hockwold, Norfolk, 58,123,132
Hollywell Row, Mildenhall,
  53,108,115,122
Holmsey Green, Suffolk,
  37,107,114,120,130
Honington, Suffolk, 19,22,24,41,48
Hullavington, Wiltshire, 46
Kemble, Gloucestershire, 18
Kinloss, Elgin, 102
Kings Lynn, Norfolk, 23
Lakenheath, Suffolk,
  29,42,47,(49p),50,51,52,53,56,57,(57p),
  59,60,63,(64p),65,69,70,(70p),71,(76p),
  77,79,81,110,111,112,115,116,122,123,
  124,131,133,141
Leadenham, Lincolnshire, 13
Locking, Somerset, 22
Loch Ness, Scotland, 119
London, 13,29,63,65,73
Lossiemouth, Moray,
  26,45,46,47,51,123,130
Lympne, Kent, 14
Manston, Kent, 46,87,93,102
Margate, Kent, 123
Marham, Norfolk,
  18,19,23,24,27,39,46,60, 101,103,141
Market Harborough, Leicestershire, 136
Martlesham Heath, Suffolk, 40
Melton Mowbray, Leicestershire, 13
Methwold, Norfolk,
  19,69,70,71,72,(72p),73,(74p),75,76,
  (77p),82,(84p),85,86,87,88,89,(89p),
  90,91,94,95,98,100,105,113,125,
  127,133,134,136,139,141
Mildenhall, Suffolk,
  15,(17p),18,19,21,22,(22p),23,24,27,
  28,29,30,31,(31p),33,34,35,36,37,38,
  (38p),39,40,(40p),41,42,43,44,(44p),
  45,46,47,51,52,53,57,63,75,90,100,
  101,106,107,108,109,118,120,122,
  123,125,128,129,130,131,132,
  134,136,140,141
Netheravon, Wiltshire, 9,13,23,141
Newcastle, Northumberland, 95
Newmarket, Suffolk,
  19,22,23,24,30,31, 34,39,85,87
North Creake, Norfolk, 71
Oakington, Cambridgeshire, 52
Oakley, Buckinghamshire, 85,139
Orfordness, Suffolk, 35
Peaseland Green, Suffolk, 36,120,130
Pembrey, West Glamorgan, 66,126,133
Pershore, Worcestershire, 136

Peterborough, Cambridgeshire, 70
Predannack, Cornwall, 78
Pulborough, Sussex, 118,129
Ramsgate, Kent, 55,56,116,122,131
Ripon, Yorkshire, 13
Rowley Mile, Newmarket, 19,23
Rushford, bombing range, Cambs, 59
Salisbury Plain, Wiltshire, 7
Scilly Isles, 67
Sedgefield, Co. Durham, 118
Selsey Bill, Sussex, 77,78
Shakespeare Cliff, Dover, 105
Shoeburyness, Essex, 103
Shepherd's Grove, Suffolk, 100,127,134
Shotton Farm, Durham, (17p),18,118,129
Skegness, Lincolnshire, 102
Sothery, Norfolk, 56,123,131
St. Athan, Glamorgan, 77
St. Eval, Cornwall, 88
St. George's Church, Methwold, 6
St. Mawgan, Cornwall, 88
St. Osyth, Essex, 29,121,129
Stamford, Cambridgeshire, 13
Stopham, Sussex, 15,106,118,129
Stradishall, Suffolk,
  19,24,59,77,79,136,141
Sudbury, Suffolk, 63,107,124,132
Swaffam Bulbeck, Cambridgeshire,
  56,108, 122,131
Tallaght, S.Ireland, 12,14,141
Tangmere, Sussex, 18,46,139
Tempsford, Bedfordshire,
  67,76,89,136,141
Thames Estuary, 34
Thetford Forest, 25
The Wash, 26,52,87
Thorney Island, Hampshire,
  73,113,126,134
Toderick Bar, Yorkshire, 51,123,130
Tuddenham, Suffolk, 83,87,99,141
Turnberry, Ayrshire, 13
Upavon, Wiltshire, 7
Upper Heyford, Oxfordshire, 136
Waddington, Lincolnshire, 42
Waterbeach, Cambridgeshire, 87,136
Watton, Norfolk, 37,57,123,131
Wendling, Norfolk, 87
West Bromwich, Staffordshire, 75
Westcott, Buckinghamshire, 136,139
West Malling, Kent, 63
Western Zoyland, Somerset, 50
Wethersfield, Essex, 76
White Waltham, Berkshire, 18
Wing, Buckinghamshire, 136,137
Wisbeach, Lancashire, 96
Woodbridge, Suffolk,
  69,73,82,85,87,88, 90,93,141
Woolfox Lodge, Leicestershire, 75,79
Wyton, Huntingdonshire, 136
Yapton, Sussex, 11,13,140
Yarmouth, Suffolk, 48

**Czechoslovakia**
Plsen, 129
Silesia, 87
Sudetenland, 18

**Denmark**
Aabenraa, 54
Aalborg, 27,(27p),113
Asnaes Peninsula, 54,122,131
Avnø, 81
Broendum, 63,125,132
Copenhagen, 54,108,122,131
Esbjerg, 22,110
Fehmarn Channel,
  69,110,124,126,132,133
Ferne Belt, 54,122,131
Gedser, 81
Great Belt, 54,108,131
Lolland, 122,131
Naestve, 81

Obbekaer, 63,110,123,132
Oster Skerninge, 69,112,126
Risegard, 131
Rødby, 81
Skerninge, 133
Vaerlose, 79

**Egypt**
Ismailia, 23
Shallufa, 100,141

**France**
Abbeville, 66
Abile, 11
Agiulcourt, 54,108,122,130
Aisne R, 9
Alquines, 11,(11p),118,140,141
Amiens, 9,12,36,46,67,68,69,112,126,133
Armentières, 14,113,118,129
Arras, 99,113,128,134
Aulnoye, 68
Bac St. Maire, 14,118
Bailleul, 14
Baudre, 72,112,126,133
Bay of Biscay, 64,77,111,124,132
Bellac, 73
Belval, 110
Bordeaux, 29,37,60,75
Boulogne, 29,73,76,83,106,112,114,120,
  124,125,129,132,134
Bouresse, 72
Boves, 112,126,133
Brest,34,36,37,45,47,50,51,52,67,72,
  73,75,77,79,107,112,113,120,
  125,126,130,134
Caen, 72,75,126,134
Calais, 34,76,83
Carentan, 72
Chavigny, 72
Cherbourg, 69,139
Clairmaris, 11,12,14,106,118,140,141
Clamecy, 73
Compiègne, 9
Corbigny, 73
Courtrai, 14,68,69,118
Coutances/Isigny, 72
Cuissy-et-Gény, 68,112,126,133
Culan, 73
Cussy les Forges, 67,112,125,133
Dieppe, 75,81
Dijon, 46,112,133
Dives R., 72
Dunkerque, 27,28,53,119,129
Esmery-Hallon, 68,112,126,133
Forêt de Nieppe, 75
Fromentel, 75
Gironde R,
  57,64,66,69,109,123,124,125,131,133
Groix, 53
Gueuteville, 62,110,124,132
Haute Savoie, 68
Ile de Groux, 78
Ile de Ré, 75
Ile d'Yeu, 57,109,131
Jilly, 9
Josselin, 72
Juvincourt, (91p),(92p),96,98,139
La Fère, 9
Laon, 68,69,112,127,133
La Rochelle, 64,72,75,77,111,125,132
La Pallice, 64
Le Cateau, 9
Le Havre,
  29,53,72,76,106,114,120,122, 129,130
Le Mans, 73
Le Touquet, 51
Lens, 72
Les Landes, 75
Lille, 14
Lisbourg, 73,112,126,134
Loire Estuary, 111,125,132
Loos, 10

Lorient, 59,60,73,78
Lyon, 69
Marcelet, 72,112,126,133
Marigny, 72
Marle, 73
Marne, 9
Marquise, 11,14,140,141
Maubeuge, 9
Melun, 9
Ménin, 14,106
Merignac, 37,107,121,130
Merville, 14
Mont-Candon, 73,75,81
Mont de Cras, 67,125,133
Mouterre, 71
Neuve Chapelle, 9
Nevers, 73
Paris, 52,69
Prémery, 73
Peret, 71
Péronne, 71,73
Pezarches, 9
Plougonvelin, 73,112,125,134
Plouzane, 37,107,120,130
Pressigny, 72
Quelmes, 11,140,141
Quesnoy, 140,141
Regniowiez, 56,109,122,131
Renaix, 12,113,118
Revigny, 75
Rheims, 96,98
Rhône R, 68
Rouen, 73
Rouen/Sotteville, 56
Roulers, 14
Ruisseauville, 112,125,134
Salon, 28,141
Senlis, 9
Serris, 9
Soissons, 28,106,119,129
Sorbon, 65,111,124,133
St. Amand-les-Eaux, 71
St. Amand Montroud, 71
St. Etienne-de-Montluc, 66,125,133
St. Jean le Vieux, 68,112,126,133
St. Malo, 73
St. Marguerite, 11,12
St. Nazaire, 73
St. Omer, (8p),11,14
St. Quentin, 9,71
St. Sever-Calvados, 37,107,121,130
St. Viatre, 71
Tours, 73
Tournes, 63,124,132
Valenciennes, 10,73
Verdun, 10
Versailles, 18
Vielle St. Girons, 58,109,123,131
Villacoublay, 18
Villefranche, 73
Yvetôt, 72

**Germany**
Aachen, 28,57,109,122,131
Ahlhorn, 103
Arlenbach, 56,109,122,131
Augsburg, 53,126
Berlin, 29,30,37,39,40,42,47,49,54,60,62,
  63,65,66,81,87,88,91,93,95,108,110,
  111,114,115,116,119,121,124,125,129,
  130,132,133
Bichenbach airfield, 12
Bickendorf, 12,140,141
Bocholt, 91,95
Bochum, 28,64,88,91,110,124,125,132
Bonn, 87
Bottrop, 85
Bremen, 26,29,33,34,36,37,38,42,45,48,
  56,93,96,106,107,108,114,115,119,
  120,121,122,123,129,130,131
Bremerhaven, 24,42
Brückhausen, 88

Brunsbuttel, 22
Buer, 95
Chemnitz, 88,89
Cologne,
    14,30,34,35,36,37,38,43,53,54,55,57,
    60,62,64,83,85,86,87,88,90,95,107,
    109,110,111,113,115,116,119,120,121,
    123,124,125,130,131,132,133,140
Dattelin, 90
Dessau, 90,95
Dobersdorf, 58,110,124,132
Dormagen, 64,111,132
Dortmund, 53,63,83,86,88,89,90,91,95,96,
    108,110,122,124,130,132
Dresden, 65,88,89
Duisburg, 32,38,39,55,56,64,79,83,87,88,
    95,108,109,110,115,121,122,123,124,
    130,131,132
Düren, 85
Düsseldorf, 37,56,64,95,109,111,114,116,
    121,122,125,130,131,132
Eder, 22
Elbe R, 27,46
Emden,
    29,36,42,55,56,79,108,114,120,130
Essen, 46,52,53,55,56,60,62,63,79,85,90,
    95,108,109,110,115,122,123,124,130,
    131,132
Frankfurt, 37,56,62,109,115,122,123,131
Friesian Islands, 23,24,46,52,53,54,57,64,
    66, 69,109,112,125,131,133
Fulda, 86
Gelsenkirchen, 29,30,36,55,89,90,91,95,
    106, 107,113,119,120,127,129,130,134
Gneisenau, 91,95
Gremburg, 87,88
Gutersloh, 103,104,(104p),141
Haelen, 108
Hallendorf, 91
Hamburg, 26,29,37,45,46,47,51,53,65,96,
    107,114,120,123,130
Hamm, 29,30,86,91
Hanau, 29,114,120,129
Hangelar, 87
Hannover, 39,65,66,107,108,111,115,117,
    120,121,125,126,130,132,133
Hassel, 108,122
Heinsburg, 85
Heligoland,
    23,23,26,37,54,93,(94p),96,102,106,
    107,120,130
Herringen, 29,106
Herxheim, 66,111,126,133
Hockenheim, 65,111,125,133
Hohenbudberg, 88,113
Homburg, 85
Immerath, 64,110,125,132
Jade Bay, 24
Julich, 85
Kaiser Wilhelm Canal, 21
Kamen, 89,90,95
Karlsruhe, 46
Kasterlee, 64,124,132
Kiel, 29,30,37,40,47,53,63,67,68,79,93,
    107,108,110,112,114,120,121,123,
    125,126,129,130,132,133
Kiel Canal, 21,22,69
Kleve, 52,83,108,122,130
Koblenz, 85,87
Koleda, 29,106,114,120,129
Krefeld,
    57,64,88,109,111,122,125,131,132
Lamsdorf, 62,80
Langel, 65,125,133
Langendreer, 88
Leuna, 87,93
Leverkusen, 85
Liepzig, 30
Lindenburg, 63,110,125,132
Lübeck, 53,56,79,108,115,123,131
Ludwigshaven, 65,88,125,133
Lutzel, 87

Mainz, 55
Mannheim, 37,39,42,58,65,66,107,108,
    111,112,116,117,120,121,124,125,126,
    129,130,132,133
Mitteland Canal, 27
Mönchen-Gladbach, 55,65,88,111,126,133
Munich, 18,30,31,56,62,63,88,93,
    105,109, 116,123,131
Munster, 91,95
Merseburg, 87,93
Neuss, 76,83,85,86,88
Nuremberg,
    42,56,60,63,65,68,87,109,111,
    116,122,124,125,127,131,133,134
Oberhausen, 86
Osnabrück, 56,123,131
Osterfeld, 86,87,89,95
Peenemünde, 65
Potsdam, 93
Recklinghausen, 90
Regensburg, 93
Rheydt, 65,87
Rhine R., 28,86,91,95
Rodenhof, 109
Rostock,
    53,63,78,108,110,116,125,130,132
Ruhr, 28,29,46,47,53,62,79,95,108
Saarbrücken,
    56,79,83,88,109,115,122, 123,131
Sagan, 80,81
Schillig Roads, 21,24,26
Salzbergen, 90,95
Schonhagen, 53,123,130
Schwarzwald, 29,120
Solingen, 85
Sputendorf, 65,111,125,133
Steinfeld, 56,108,123,131
Studernheim, 63,110,125,132
Stuttgart, 54,63,85,108,110,122,124,125,
    130,132
Swinemünde, 68
Sylt,
    24,26,27,28,39,81,93,107,119,129,130
Tonning, 22
Torgau, 93
Trier, 87
Vohwinkel, 87
Wangerooge, 24
Wanheimerort, 108
Wanne Eickel, 88,90,95
Warnemünde, 58,81,110,122,132
Wiesbaden, 113,134
Weiss, 65,125,133
Wesel, 89,90,91,113,127,134
Weser R, 27,96
Wesseling, 85
Westermarsche, 58,110,122,132
Wiesbaden, 88,127
Wilhelmshaven, 21,23,24,26,30,34,60,
    83, 93,96,107,119,120,129,130
Witten, 87,113,127,134
Wittenburg, 81
Wuppertal, 64,111,124,132
Wurm Lake, 88

**Italy**
Foggia, 60
Genoa, 28,30,33,41,46,57,58,109,131
Irasco Finerola, 58,110,122,132
Milan, 28,30,58
Padua, 34
Pomigliano, 141
Turin, 30,33,58,60,105,110,
    111,116,122, 124,132
Venice, 33,34

**Japan**
Hiroshima, 99
Nagasaki, 99

**Netherlands**
Arnhem, 95

Beek, 110
Bergh, 60,63,124,132
Bergharen, 37,121,130
Boxmeer, 62,110,123,132
Delft, 94,139
Delfzijl, 29
Geffen, 56,109,123,131
Gouda, 93,139
Hague, 93,94,96,98,139
IJmuiden, 73
IJpecolsga, 110
IJselmeer, 56,64,108,111,123,125,131,132
Kronenburg, 57,109,122,131
Netersel, 64,111,125,132
Oud Beyerland, 56,109,122,131
Overflakee, 96
Roermond, 39,121,130
Rotterdam,
    43,64,93,96,98,110,124, 132,139
Schelde R., 42,108,121,130
Sevunum, 36,107
Smallebrugge, 64,124,132
Tiel, 57,109,123,131
Venlo, 115
Walcheren, 83,85,86
Waalhaven airfield, 28
West Kapelle, 83,(86p)
Wons, 108,122,131

**Norway**
Aas Fjord, 51
Kattegat,
    109,112,122,125,126,131,133
Lister, 52
Stavanger, 27,120,129
Trondheim, 51,99,128,134
Vaernes, 99,128,134

**Poland**
Poznan, 37
Warsaw, 54,60

**Uruguay**
Montevideo, 26

**INDUSTRIAL TARGETS**

Alma Pluto Benzol Plant-Gelsenkirchen,
    36,89
Castrop Rauxel Synthetic Oil Refinery-
    Dortmund, 85,88
Consolidated I/VI Benzol Plant-
    Gelsenkirchen, 36,90,91,127,134
DeutscheWerke U-boat Yard-Kiel, 93
Emscher Lippe Benzol Plant-Dattelin, 90
Fiat Factory-Turin, 30,105
Hansa Coking Plant-Dortmund, 86,88
Heinkel Aircraft Factory-Rostock, 53
Hermann Goering Coke Works-
    Hallendorf, 91
Krupps Armament Works-Essen, 56
Lübecker Fklundewerke' AG (U-boats)-
    Herrenwyk, 56
Meerbeck Synthetic Oil Plant-
    Homberg, 85
Nordstern Oil Plant-Gelsenkirchen,
    36,85, 89,90
Osterfeldt Benzol Coking Plant-
    Oberhausen, 86
Porto Marghera Oil Refinery-Venice,
    33,34
Renault Truck Works-
    Boulogne/Billancourt, 46,52,78
Rhurstahl Steel Works-Witten, 87,134
Robert Muser Benzol Plant-
    Langendreer, 88
Scholven/Buer Synthetic Oil Plant-
    Gelsenkirchen, 36,90
Skoda Works-Plsen, 30,129
Thyssen Steel Works-Duisburg, 88

**AIRCRAFT**

Airspeed Horsa, 100
Armstrong Whitworth Whitley,
    19,28, 34,54
Avro, 127
Avro 504, 9
Avro Anson, 75,100
Avro Lancaster,
    36,40,42,49,53,54,64,66,71,75,76,81,
    83,(83p),(84p),85,86,87,88,89,(89p),
    90,(90p),91,(91p),(92p),93,94,95,(95p),
    (97p),98,99,(99p),100,101,113,127,
    128,134,138,141
Avro Lincoln,
    100,101,(101p),102,128, 134,138
Avro Manchester, 30,34,42,52,54
B.E.2, 9
B.E.8, 9
Boeing Washington,
    (100p),101,102,128,141
Boeing B-17 Flying Fortress,
    37,65,70, 72,89
Boeing B-29 Superfortress, 70,101
Bristol Blenheim, 19,21,22
De Havilland Mosquito, 36,52,56,
    60,64,65, 66,87,88,89,90,93,100,138
De Havilland Dominie, 100
De Havilland Vampire, 102
Dornier Do 17, 23,30,65
Dornier Do 17Z, 34
Dornier Do 215, 34
Douglas Boston, 56
Douglas Dakota, 100
English Electric Canberra,
    102,103,(103p),(104p),128,141
Farman Shorthorn, 13
Focke-Wulf FW 190, 63,64
Fokker, 10
Gotha, 13
Handley Page, 118
Handley Page Hampden,
    19,26,28,34, 49,54
Handley Page Harrow, 51
Handley Page Heyford, 15,(15p),(16p),
    (17p),18,106,118,119,129,141
Handley Page Halifax, 30,40,49,51,52,66,
    67,68,81,82,89,90,93,100
Hawker Hurricane, 18,37,45,120,130
Heinkel He 111, 30
Heinkel He 115, 28
Junkers Ju 52, 105
Junkers Ju
    88, 32,36,38,40,44,48,63,69, 120,130
Maurice Farman, 9,13
Messerschmitt Bf 109,
    22,23,24,25,69,86,87,88
Messerschmitt Bf 110,
    24,25,26,27,35,53,55,56,62,88,122,130
Messerschmitt Me 262, 87
North American Harvard, 100
North American P-51D Mustang, 87,100
Percival Proctor, 100
Royal Air Factory F.E.2b,
    (7p),(8p),10,(10p),11,(11p),12,(12p),
    13,14,(14p),106,118,129,140
Shorts, 66
Short Stirling, 30,31,40,42,46,49,(49p),
    50,51,52,53,54,(54p),55,(55p),56,57,
    (57p),58,59,59,(59p),60,(61p),62,
    (62p),63,64,65,66,67,68,69,70,(70p),
    71,72,73,(73p),75,76,(76p),77,(77p),
    78,79,(80p),81,82,100,101,105,108,
    109,110,111,112,113,121,122,123,
    124,125,126,127,130,131,132,133,
    134,141
Sopwith Tabloid, 9
Supermarine Spitfire, 18,34,51,100
Vickers Warwick, 100
Vickers Wellington, 18,19,(19p),(20p),21,
    (21p),22,23,24,25,(25p),26,27,(27p),
    28,29,30,(30p),31,(31p),(32p),33,34,
    (35p),36,37,38,39,(39p),40,(40p),41,
    (41p),42,43,(43p),45,46,47,48,52,53,
    54,79,100,106,107,108,119,120,121,
    129,130,134,141
Zeppelin, 13

## MISCELLANEOUS

Abigail Rachel, 42
Administrative Instruction No.44, 85
Administrative Instruction No.49, 85
Advanced Striking Force, 87
Aerial mapping, 99
Air Estimates 1949-1950, 101
Airmens' Mess Staff (1943), (82p)
Air-sea rescue, 55,56,75,82,101,122,131
Alps, 34,41
Annual Reunion Dinner, First, (102p)
Ardent, 102
Atlantic, 66
Atom bomb, 99
Battle of the Atlantic, 36,53
Battle of Berlin, 66
Battle of Britain, 29
Battle of Britain celebrations, 100,101
Battle of Hamburg, 65
Battle of the Ruhr, 62
Beardmore engine, 10,11,12,140
Benina, Western Desert, 105
Bird in Hand, 28,30,31,78
Blitzkrieg, 19,27
Blockbuster, 36,76
Bofors gun, 28
Bomb loading trolley, (16p)
Bomb racks, 9,11,12,(13p),36
Bomb-sight, 10,68
Bristol Aircraft Company, 103
Browning machine guns, 21,30,35
Butlin's Holiday Camp, 102
'Buzz bomb' sites, 69
Camera, 99
Canal Zone, 100
Casualties, 113
Cavalry, W.W. I, 12,15
Central Fire Controller, 101
'Ceylon III', 121
Combat Report Pro-Forma, (48p)
Combined Chief of Staff, 67
Combined Operations Exercise, 76,83
Cookie, 36
Cooper bombs, 14
Court of Inquiry, 85
Daily Express, 37
Daily Herald, 91
Daily Routine Orders, 42
Dams raid, 64
Darkie, 36,46
De-briefing, (71p)
Demobilisation, 99
Devil's Dyke,
D-Day, 71,117
D-Day drop zones
  'Titanic I', 72
  'Titanic II', 72
  'Titanic III', 72
  'Titanic IV', 72
Disbanded, 104
Dummy paratroops, 72,137
Eagle Day, 29
'East India' aircraft,
  41,42,52,55,108,122, 123,130,131
E-boat, 72
Electronic countermeasures, 66
'Elsan Closet', 34,50
Empire Air Day, 18
'FIDO', 42,69
Firestorm, 65
Flak ship, 67,79,81,132
Flame reducers, 12
Flying Piano, 10
Form 540, 46
Form 541, 46
Form 700, 34,54
Frazer Nash turret, 19,23
'Free Hand', 83
Friendly fire, 9,27,29
Gardening, 52,55,60,67,77,79,139
Gas, 9,10,18,19,66,133
Gas detection patch, (73p)

German Condor Legion, Spanish Civil War, 54
Gold beach, 72
'Gondolier', 73,126,134
Great Escape, 80
Ground Control Approach (GCA), 102
Haddock Force, 28
Happydrome, 28
Happy Valley, 79,95
High Heel, 71
Himmelbett, 60,62
Indian Army, 93
Invasion Aircraft, 29
'Journey Together', 76,141
'Kilfrost' de-icing paste, 53
Korean War, 101
La Fete de l'Aire, 18
Lake Geneva, 33
Land Girl, 69
Leaflets, 68,86
Leica Camera, 23
Lewis gun,(8p),11,12
'Lighthouse', 11
Loch Ness Wellington, 26
London air defences, 13
London Gazette, 105
Lone Ranger flights, 104
Lorenz Beam, 39,41
Mae West life vest, 62
Maquis, 66,69,70,133
Master Bomber, 76,83,93,136
Mildenhall Register, 45
Military Defence Aid Program, 101
Mine laying, 52,53,54,55,56,57,59,63,
  64,66,67,68,69,71,72,73,75,77,79,
  81,110,111,112,113,122,123,124,
  125,130,131,132,133,134,135,137,139
Mine laying codes, 139
Mons Wood, 9
Mont Blanc, 33
'Moonlight' runs, 70
Motor Transport Workshops, 85
Munich Crisis, 18
NAAFI, 88
National Air Communications, 19
National Service Air Gunners, 101
NATO exercises, 102
Nickel raids, 26
North Foreland light, 34
Omaha beach, 72
Ombrelle, 102
Open Day, 100,101
Operations
  Bullseye, 64,76,102,124,132
  Cerberus, 51
  Dodge, 100
  Duisburg, 46
  Dynamo, 28
  Exodus, (91p),(92p),93,98,139
  Fuller, 50
  Gomorrah, 65
  Hurricane, 83
  Hydra, 65
  Manna, 93,(95p),98,139
  Millennium, 54,55
  Oiled, 51
  Overlord, 71
  Pandemonium, 56,80
  Ramrod, 73,75
  Sea Lion, 29
  Thunderclap, 88,89
  Titanic, 71
  Whitebait, 65
PAC (Parachute Attached Cables), 28
'Parachutages', 68
Pathfinder Force,
  56,65,66,70,73,85,90,138
Pathfinder Mosquitoes,
  62,64,87,88,89,93
Pinnacle, 102
Prisoner-of-war (POW), (92p),93,99,
  113,114,115,116,117,118,120,121,
  122,123,124,125,126,127,129,
  130,131,132,133,134

Radar
  ABC, 66
  Eureka, 66
  Freya, 24,66
  'Gee',
    39,52,54,68,72,78,83,85,95,138
  G-H, 83,85,86,87,88,89,
    90,91,93,95,98,103,104,138
  "H2S", 65,66,95,99,138
  IFF (Identification, Friend or Foe), 52
  Lichtenstein, 60,66
  Mandrel, 66
  'Oboe', 62,65,66,85,88,90,93,138
  Rebecca, 66
  Serrate, 66
  SN2, 66
Radar School, Feltwell, 83
Radar section, No.149 Sqn.
  (Methwold), (72p)
Radio Counter Measures training, 103
Radios, 21
Ramrod 1152,
'Razzles', 29,120,129
River Plate, 26
Roll of Honour, 6,94,105
Royal Review, (76p), (103p)
Royal Warrant, 7
Runnymede Memorial, 113
Russians, 93,98
San Sebastian, Spain, 77
S.A.S., 72
Scarecrow, 88
Scatter Plan, 19
Schragemusik, 66
Searchlights, 13,64,65,67,78,88,
  130,132
Signal pistol, 11
Soviet Army, rapid advance of, 89
Spanish Civil War, 19
Special Operations Executive (SOE),
  66,67,68,69,71,73,112,113,117,
  125,126,133,134
Squadron aircraft code,
  18,19,(19p), 21,(25p),85,(100p),141
Squadron crest, 12,15,103,(104p)
Squadron disbanded, 104
'Squadron flit', 102
Stalag Luft VIIIB, 62
Stirling 'song', 63
'Sunray' flights,
Swiss Alps, 63
Tail turret (Lincoln), (101p)
'Target for Tonight',
  30,(30p),36,46, 119,120,141
The George, 42
'The Lion Has Wings', 23,141
'The Nuthouse', 125
'The Ozard of Whiz', 41
'The Plumbers', 31
Tiger Force, 99,(99p)
U-boat, 66,68,72,79
Underground resistance
  movement, 66
United Services Review,
  October 21, 1937, 138
Very Pistol/flares, 9,31,72,89,94
Vickers machine guns, 27
Von Richthofen's Flying Circus, 11
V-1 Flying Bomb, 65,73,75
V-2 rocket, 65,76
V-bombers, 103
V-E Day, 94,96
Warsaw Uprising, 60
Warships
  Admiral Graf Spee, 26
  Admiral Hipper, 93
  Admiral Scheer, 21,93
  Centurion, 18
  Emden, 22,93
  Gneisenau, 21,24,36,37,50,51,52
  Prinz Eugen, 37,51,52
  Scharnhorst, 21,24,36,37,50,51,52

  Tirpitz, 51,123,130
  Trident, 52
  Victorious, 52
Western Front, 10
Weygand Line, 28
Wild Boar (Wild Sau), 64
'Window', 65,98
'Window light', 88
Wizard of Oz, 36,37,114,121,130
Zeppelin hangar, 14

## RAF/RFC SQUADRONS

1 Sqn, 9
2 Sqn, 9,10
3 Sqn, 9
4 Sqn, 9
5 Sqn, 9
6 Sqn, 9
7 Sqn,
  9,13,52,69,118,119,121,122, 123,128
8 Sqn, 9
9 Sqn, 21,24,26,36,118,119,120,121
10 Sqn, 15,118
15 Sqn, 45,51,52,101,103,121,122,123,
  124,125,126,127,128
18 Sqn, 10,119
20 Sqn, 10
35 Sqn, 100,128
37 Sqn, 21,24,25,26,119,120
38 Sqn, 13,23,27
40 Sqn, 121,124,128
44 Sqn, 99,101,103,128
49 Sqn, 128
57 Sqn, 101,103,119,121
58 Sqn, 11
59 Sqn, 128
69 Sqn, 128
75 Sqn, 19,99,119,120,121,123,124
76 Sqn, 13
78 Sqn, 118
83 Sqn, 11,128
88 Sqn, 128
90 Sqn,
  37,68,71,79,122,124,125,126, 127,128
99 Sqn, 15,19,23,27,28,34,36,
  118,119, 120,121,138
100 Sqn, 10,11
101 Sqn, 11,66
102 Sqn, 11,103,118,119
103 Sqn, 103
104 Sqn, 103
105 Sqn, 62,138
107 Sqn, 22
109 Sqn, 62,138
115 Sqn, 23,39,75,100,101,
  119,120,121,124,127,128
138 Sqn, 67,71,127,128
139 Sqn, 65
148 Sqn, 11,19,118,119,120,128,141
161 Sqn, 67,71
186 Sqn, 99,127,128
195 Sqn, 93,99
199 Sqn, 66,68,71,125,126
207 Sqn, 100,127,128
214 Sqn, 67,119,121,122,123,124,
  125 ,126,127,128
215 Sqn, 19,119
218 Sqn, 52,68,75,83,85,99,120,121,
  122,123,124,125,126,127,128
300 Sqn, 119
301 Sqn, 121
305 Sqn, 121
311 Sqn, 36,119,120
419 Sqn, 121
460 Sqn, 99
467 Sqn, 99
514 Sqn, 99,127,128
617 Sqn, 64
620 Sqn, 124,125
622 Sqn, 45,99,127
626 Sqn, 128

# AIR-BRITAIN - THE INTERNATIONAL ASSOCIATION OF AVIATION HISTORIANS - FOUNDED 1948

Since 1948, Air-Britain has recorded aviation events as they have happened, because today's events are tomorrow's history. In addition, considerable research into the past has been undertaken to provide historians with the background to aviation history. Over 18,000 members have contributed to our aims and efforts in that time and many have become accepted authorities in their own fields.

Every month, *AIR-BRITAIN NEWS* covers the current civil and military scene. Quarterly, each member receives *AIR-BRITAIN DIGEST* which is a fully-illustrated journal containing articles on various subjects, both past and present.

For those interested in military aviation history, there is the quarterly *AEROMILITARIA* which is designed to delve more deeply into the background of, mainly, British and Commonwealth military aviation than is possible in commercial publications and whose format permits it to be used as components of a filing system which suits the readers' requirements. This publication is responsible for the production of the present volume and other monographs on military subjects. Also published quarterly is *ARCHIVE*, produced in a similar format but covering civil aviation history in depth on a world-wide basis. Both magazines are well-illustrated by photographs and drawings.

In addition to these regular publications, there are monographs covering type histories, both military and civil, airline fleets, Royal Air Force registers, squadron histories and the civil registers of a large number of countries. Although our publications are available to non-members, prices are considerably lower for Air-Britain members, who have priority over non-members when availability is limited. Normally, the accumulated price discounts for which members qualify when buying Air-Britain books can far exceed the annual subscription rates.

A large team of aviation experts is available to answer members' queries on most aspects of aviation. If you have made a study of any particular subject, you may be able to expand your knowledge by joining those with similar interests. Also available to members are libraries of colour slides and photographs which supply slides and prints at prices considerably lower than those charged by commercial firms.

There are local branches of the Association in Blackpool, Bournemouth, Chilterns, Heston/Heathrow, London, Luton, Manchester, Merseyside, North-East England, Rugby, Scotland, Severnside, Solent, South-West Essex, Stansted, West Cornwall and West Midlands. Overseas in France and the Netherlands.

If you would like to receive samples of Air-Britain magazines, please write to the following address enclosing 50p and stating your particular interests. If you would like only a brochure, please send a stamped self-addressed envelope to the same address (preferably 230mm by 160mm or over) - **Air-Britain Membership Enquiries (Mil), 1 Rose Cottages, 179 Penn Road, Hazlemere, High Wycombe, Bucks., HP15 7NE.**

Our website may be found at **www.air-britain.com**

## MILITARY AVIATION PUBLICATIONS IN PRINT
(prices are for members/non-members and are post-free)

### Royal Air Force Aircraft series

| | | | | | |
|---|---|---|---|---|---|
| J1-J9999 | (£8.00/£10.00) | K1000-K9999 | (see The K-File) | L1000-N9999 | (£12.00/£15.00) |
| P1000-R9999 | (£11.00/£14.00) | T1000-V9999 | (£12.00/£15.00) | W1000-Z9999 | (£13.00/£16.50) |
| AA100-AZ999 | (£13.00/£16.50) | BA100-BZ999 | (New edition in preparation) | DA100-DZ999 | (£5.00/£6.00) |
| EA100-EZ999 | (£5.00/£6.00) | FA100-FZ999 | (£5.00/£6.00) | HA100-HZ999 | (£6.00/£7.50) |
| JA100-JZ999 | (£6.00/£7.50) | KA100-KZ999 | (£6.00/£7.50) | LA100-LZ999 | (£7.00/£8.50) |
| MA100-MZ999 | (£8.00/£10.00) | NA100-NZ999 | (£8.00/£10.00) | PA100-RZ999 | (£10.00/£12.50) |
| | WA100-WZ999 | (New edition in preparation) | XA100-XZ999 | (£9.00/£11.00) | |

### Type Histories

| | | | | | |
|---|---|---|---|---|---|
| The Battle File | (£20.00/£25.00) | The Beaufort File | (£11.00/£13.50) | The Camel File | (£13.00/£16.00) |
| The Defiant File | (£12.50/£16.00) | The DH4/DH9 File | (£24.00/£30.00) | The Harvard File | (£8.00/£9.50) |
| The Hoverfly File | (£16.50/£19.50) | The Martinsyde File | (£24.00/£30.00) | The Norman Thompson File | (£13.50/£17.00) |
| The Oxford, Consul & Envoy File | (£25.00/£32.00) | The Scimitar File | (£26.00/£32.00) | The S.E.5 File | (£16.00/£20.00) |
| The Sopwith Pup | (£24.00/£30.00) | The Halifax File | (New edition in preparation) | The Whitley File | (New edition in preparation) |

### Individual R.A.F. Squadron Histories

Hawks Rising – The History of No.25 Squadron (£25.00/£32.00)  
United in Effort – The Story of No.53 Squadron (£15.00/£19.00)  
Always Prepared – The History of No.207 Squadron (£22.00/£27.50)  
Flat Out – The History of No.30 Squadron (£27.00/£34.00)  
Scorpions Sting – The Story of No.84 Squadron (£12.00/£16.50)  
The Hornet Strikes – The Story of No.213 Squadron (£20.00/£25.00)  
Rise from the East - The History of No.247 Squadron (£13.00/£16.50)

### Naval Aviation titles

The Squadrons of the Fleet Air Arm (£24.00/£30.00)  
Royal Navy Aircraft Serials and Units 1911 - 1919 (£12.00)  
Fleet Air Arm Aircraft 1939 - 1945 (New edition in preparation)  
Royal Navy Shipboard Aircraft Developments 1912 - 1931 (£12.00)  
Fleet Air Arm Aircraft, Units and Ships 1920 - 1939 (£26.00/£32.50)  
Fleet Air Arm Fixed Wing Aircraft since 1946 (In preparation)  
Royal Navy Instructional Airframes (£14.00/£17.50)

### Other titles

The K-File (the RAF of the 1930s) (£23.00/£30.00)  
Aviation in Cornwall (£14.00/£17.50)  
Aerial Refuelling at Farnborough 1924 - 1937 (£11.00/£14.00)  
World Military Transport Fleets 2002 (£15.00/£19.00)  
The British Aircraft Specifications File (£20.00/£25.00)  
British Air Commission and Lend-Lease (£23.00/£29.00)  
Broken Wings – Post-War RAF accidents (£21.00/£26.00)  
U.K. Flight Testing Accidents 1940 - 1971 (£16.50/£20.50)  
Spitfire International (£32.50/£39.50)

The above are available from Air-Britain (Historians) Ltd, 41 Penshurst Rd, Leigh, Tonbridge, Kent TN11 8HL or by e-mail to mike@sales.demon.co.uk. Payment in Sterling only. Overseas carriage 15% of the book price, minimum £1.50. Visa, Mastercard, Delta/Visa accepted with card number and expiry date, also Switch (with Issue number).